RECEIVED

DEC 29 2016

P9-ECX-207

TEA IN CHINA

NO LONGER PROPERTY OF
THE SEATTLE PUBLIC LIBRARY

TEA IN CHINA

A Religious and Cultural History

James A. Benn

University of Hawai'i Press

HONOLULU

© 2015 University of Hawai'i Press
All rights reserved
Printed in the United States of America
20 19 18 17 16 15   6 5 4 3 2 1

Library of Congress Cataloging-in-Publication Data

Benn, James A., author.
   Tea in China : a religious and cultural history / James A. Benn.
      pages cm
   Includes bibliographical references and index.
   ISBN 978-0-8248-3963-5 (cloth) — ISBN 978-0-8248-3964-2 (alk. paper)
   1. Tea—China—Religious aspects—Buddhism.   2. Tea—Social aspects—
China.   3. Tea in literature.   I. Title.
   GT2907.C6B46 2015
   394.1'50951—dc23

                                                                2014023171

University of Hawai'i Press books are printed on acid-free
paper and meet the guidelines for permanence and
durability of the Council on Library Resources.

Designed by Erika Arroyo

Printed by Sheridan Books, Inc.

For Emi

Contents

Acknowledgments

*T*his book took a lot longer to write than I expected, but I learned a lot along the way and I would like to thank all those who helped. It all began with Tim Barrett, who suggested for my MA thesis at SOAS that it might be worth investigating ways in which medieval Chinese Buddhists might have promoted tea as a new "sanctioned drug" in place of alcohol. That thesis was completed a long time ago, but as you can see the idea of looking at the religious aspects of tea in traditional Chinese culture has stayed with me. Readers who are puzzled by my sudden switch of interest from self-immolation to tea should understand that this project has deeper roots, although it may have taken longer to come to fruition.

It would have been impossible to write this book without the help of funding agencies that continue to sponsor basic curiosity-driven research, even in difficult times. In particular, I appreciate support from the Social Sciences and Humanities Research Council of Canada, which awarded me a Standard Research Grant. Earlier, the Mellon Foundation supported my stay at the Needham Research Institute (NRI) in Cambridge. I want to thank the Mellon Foundation for allowing me the wonderful opportunity to work at the NRI, one of my favorite places to do research. I am grateful to my many friends and colleagues at the NRI, especially the librarian John Moffett; Chris Cullen, then the director of the NRI; Mei Jianjun, the current director; and the administrator Sue Bennett.

The readers for University of Hawai'i Press were exceptionally helpful. I had many beneficial comments and suggestions from Barend ter Haar and another, anonymous, reader. My editor, the legendary Pat Crosby, was consistently supportive and enthusiastic as always. It was a joy to work again with her and with Stephanie Chun, who copyedited my previous book for the press.

Lots of people offered helpful advice and comments on the writing as it progressed. Unlike me, Steve Owyoung is an actual expert on the history of tea in China and was exceptionally helpful to me in patiently correcting many errors of fact and interpretation. Marco Ceresa is another expert on tea who has been very supportive of this project.

Raoul Birnbaum, a kind and patient reader of my work for many years now, offered invaluable constructive advice. My good friend Chen Jinhua's comments were, as always, multiple, erudite, and practical. My colleagues in Buddhist Studies at McMaster, Shayne Clarke and Mark Rowe, read a full draft carefully and critically. Stuart Young set aside his own work to comment on mine. My thanks to all of these patient readers, who share no blame for the many errors of fact and interpretation that I am sure still remain.

Graduate students at McMaster helped in many ways with amassing information and resources. My thanks to He Yongshan, Randy Celie, Adrian Chih-mien Tseng, and Stephanie Balkwill. Stephanie has had particular success in efficiently locating rare and out-of-print works of secondary scholarship in Chinese. My thanks to her and others who procured books on my behalf in China, Taiwan, Japan, and Korea. Robban Toleno at the University of British Columbia is not my student, but he has research interests that overlap with mine and has been a wonderful conversation partner on the subject of tea and religion in China.

Libraries were essential to the successful completion of this book. I appreciate the efforts of the interlibrary loan team at Mills Library, McMaster University, in tracking down some rare but essential items. The Sinological library staff members at the University of Toronto, the University of Michigan, Yale, Princeton, Harvard, Cambridge, and the University of California, Los Angeles, were also consistently cheerful and efficient.

It has been a real privilege to have opportunities to discuss this project as I was working on it. My thanks to people who invited me to give talks on the subject of tea at Cambridge, Princeton, Columbia, the University of Toronto, the University of British Columbia, and Mount Alison University. It was a great surprise and a special honor to be asked in 2009 to give the twenty-second Sammy Yukuan Lee Lecture on Chinese Archaeology and Art at UCLA on "The Buddhist Arts of Tea in Medieval China." My thanks to the Lee family and the Center for Chinese Studies at UCLA for organizing that event.

For their general assistance and support in answering my random queries, sharing their unpublished work, and the like, I want to thank the following: Bruce Rusk, Carla Nappi, James Robson, Livio Zanini, Ben Brose, Juhn Ahn, Micah Auerbach, and my former colleagues at Arizona State University, especially Steve West and Hoyt Tillman. My thanks to Philip Bloom and Greg

Levine for their help and advice in securing permissions to reproduce some important images held in Japanese collections. George Keyworth and Rick McBride have been comrades in arms for many years now. Although we no longer meet at "Vinaya table," I believe the spirit of that select gathering lives on.

Thanks to the many friends and supporters who gave gifts of fine tea over the years. I hope the book is some kind of repayment for your kindness.

Although many people have contributed time and energy to this book, my wife Emi really did the most. She read the manuscript closely, covering every page with notes, and generally questioned, provoked, and cajoled the manuscript into much better shape. I really appreciate her interest in the book and am grateful to her for creating an environment in which it was fun to write. Pema's help was less tangible than that of others mentioned here, but she was always present to share her wisdom and compassion.

A Note on Editions and Conventions

*I*n this book, I have tried to cite sources from standard modern editions that are readily available so that readers can find the relevant original Chinese with minimal difficulty. I have not hesitated to consult better editions where available, but I have not always cited them.

Works of tea literature such as *Chajing* and *Xu Chajing* are all cited as they appear in a standard modern critical annotated edition: Zheng Peikai 鄭培凱 and Zhu Zizhen 朱自振 2007.

For *Kissa yōjōki,* I follow a modern Japanese critical edition with a modern Japanese translation and introduction: Furuta Shōkin 古田紹欽 2000. For convenience and consistency I have cited Tang poetry from *Quan Tang shi* (*Complete Tang Poetry*), even though it is not the best edition. For individual poets who have separate collections of their work, I have cited poems from modern editions. Dynastic histories follow the *Zhonghua shuju* editions.

Full citations from the *Taishō* canon are given in the following fashion: title and fascicle number (where relevant); *T;* Taishō volume number; text number, page, register (a, b, or c), line number(s). E.g. *Pusa dichi jing* 菩薩地持經 (**Bodhisattvabhūmisūtra*) *T* 30.1581.916b1–11.

Citations from the *Xuzang jing* give references to volume, page, and register.

Citations from the *Daozang* provide references to fascicle, page, and register and follow the sequential numbers given in K. M. Schipper, *Concordance du Tao-Tsang: titres des ouvrages,* Publications de l'École française d'Extrême-Orient; v. 102. Paris: École Française d'Extrême-Orient, 1975.

1

Tea as a Religious and Cultural Commodity in Traditional China

This book is about tea as a religious and cultural commodity in traditional China. That is, it considers the life of tea in China before the nineteenth century, when tea became a global commodity. There are many excellent works about developments in the tea trade during the 1800s and afterward, so I do not wish to duplicate those studies, and in any case I am interested more in the Chinese cultural sphere than in the global marketplace.[1] In this book, we will consider tea as a product (the processed leaves of the cultivated tea plant) and an object of commercial transactions, and we will learn about the history of tea as a drink. But there are some other important preliminary considerations before we can begin. First, what do I mean by saying that tea was a "religious and cultural commodity"? And second, why is this approach to the history of tea useful?

An episode drawn from the famous eighteenth-century novel *A Dream of Red Chambers* (*Honglou meng*) can help us appreciate why it might be worthwhile to think about tea as a commodity with (often intertwined) religious and cultural characteristics. In the forty-first chapter of this sprawling multivolume work, we discover the male protagonist, Jia Baoyu, along with other members of his retinue, appreciating tea in a Buddhist nunnery.[2] The young nun, Miaoyu ("Adamantia"), first serves Baoyu's grandmother, the matriarch of the Jia clan, fetching tea in an exquisite covered porcelain teacup on a lacquered tray. Grandmother Jia brusquely refuses it, saying,

> "I don't drink Lu-an tea."
>
> "I know you don't," said Adamantia with a smile. "This is Old Man's Eyebrows."
>
> Grandmother Jia took the tea and enquired what sort of water it had been made with.
>
> "Last year's rain-water," said Adamantia.

1

While the remainder of the party is served tea in covered cups of thin white porcelain, Adamantia takes Baoyu's female cousins Lin Daiyu and Xue Bao-chai into her private room, where she serves them her own tea in valuable antique vessels. Baoyu follows them in and is allowed to sample Adamantia's finest brew:

> Savoring it carefully in little sips, Baoyu found it of incomparable fresh-ness and lightness and praised it enthusiastically.

Daiyu innocently inquires whether the tea she is drinking is also made with last year's rainwater, only to be sharply corrected by Adamantia:

> "Oh! Can you *really* not tell the difference? I am quite disappointed in you. This is melted snow that I collected from the branches of winter-flowering plum-trees five years ago, when I was living at the Coiled Incense temple on Mount Xuanmu. I managed to fill the whole of that demon-green glaze water jar with it. For years I could not bring myself to start it; then this summer I opened it for the first time. Today is only the second time that I have ever used any. I am *most* surprised that you cannot tell the difference. When did stored rain-water have such a buoyant lightness? How could one possibly use it for tea like this?"

This brief vignette of refined consumption from *A Dream of Red Cham-bers* is, of course, knowingly exaggerated for comic effect, but nevertheless it offers a pertinent example of the heights that tea connoisseurship could reach and of the fact that rare teas, choice springwater, and fine teaware were some-times appreciated in Buddhist monastic settings. The passage shows that tea in traditional China was not just a commodity for everyday ingestion; it came entwined with a host of complex social and cultural associations and assump-tions. In this book, we will explore how such linkages between commodities, materials, and cultural systems were made by looking at a series of key mo-ments in the history of tea in traditional China.

What kind of knowledge or insight could this kind of investigation into tea give us? I believe that it will provide a different perspective on religious thought and practice in China by causing us to appreciate the effects of tea not just on a single person but on a whole society. A study such as this can offer a way to gain access to long-term cultural processes that are not ordinarily vis-ible, and it will require us to consider side-by-side materials from different genres that are normally studied separately by specialists in poetry, travel literature, or religion. Even as we read these materials, however, we should realize that our extant textual and material primary sources are incomplete and uneven, and so inevitably, we will end up focusing on certain types of writing instead of others and examining those artifacts and images that have survived more or less by chance. Also, much of the evidence for the history of tea comes from the elite strata of Chinese society and necessarily reflects the interests of the privileged few. But if we are attentive, we may also be able to catch occasional glimpses of the religious and cultural values of tea in the greater society.

This is a historical study, but not a comprehensive history of tea. It focuses mostly on the dynasties of Tang and Song (roughly the seventh through thirteenth century) as the most innovative and exciting period in tea culture. Most of the major developments in tea cultivation and drinking occurred during this time, although there were certainly significant changes in tea practice during late imperial times. Nowadays, tea is a universal comestible, but this was not always the case, and we can learn much about the rise of new tastes in human societies by studying its growth and development. According to our sources, the habit of drinking tea on a regular basis seems to have begun in medieval China with Buddhist monastics, later spreading to the literati and then, probably quite rapidly, to the wider population. By choosing to concentrate on this formative period, I do not mean to deny that there was a good deal of activity in tea culture later, but only to suggest that later developments—such as the use of loose-leaf tea in the Ming dynasty and the consequent development of the teapot, or the massive expansion of literary works on tea during the Ming and Qing dynasties—were refinements of earlier practices rather than startling new developments. These considerations aside, it is not possible to give an all-inclusive survey of Chinese tea culture in a single volume, so I make no apologies for choosing to concentrate on aspects of the developmental stage. Rather than providing a complete history of tea in China, this work offers a series of vignettes that illustrate the innovative religious and cultural aspects of tea in certain specific times and places.[3]

As we shall see, the story of tea is not one of "timeless unchanging China" but rather the China of dramatic, large-scale, and often rapid changes in the economy (the appearance of paper money and banking systems), agriculture (the development of large and small tea estates on otherwise unproductive land), society (the employment of female tea pickers), and culture (the invention of a corpus of poetry devoted to tea). The growth of tea drinking and tea culture was also dependent on the infrastructure of the Chinese empire that stitched China's macroregions together: for example, the spread of tea from a local tonic to a national beverage would never have been possible without the canal system instituted by the Sui emperor Yangdi (r. 604–618).[4] This imperial infrastructure lurks below the surface of much of what we will be looking at, often unacknowledged and almost invisible in our sources yet nonetheless essential to the success of tea. At the same time, tea acted as a cultural marker—drinking tea was part of being a Southerner in early medieval China, and later it became part of a larger Chinese or Sinitic identity.

Very soon after its appearance on the national stage in the mid-eighth century, tea was being drunk by people at all levels of society, but the cultural practice of tea connoisseurship (in Chinese *pincha,* meaning something like "assessing tea critically") became a marker of wealth, status, leisure, and good taste.[5] Thus, when we contemplate the tea culture of imperial China, perhaps we can find there the first glimmerings of a modern consumer society.

In addition to ideas of consumption, it may also be useful for us to think about the rise of Chinese tea culture by comparing it with the development of "taste" in eighteenth-century England. Taste, a concept that first came to prominence in the late seventeenth century, was employed as an important sign of cultural differentiation in which the value of goods was determined not by their cost alone but by means of the most subtle discrimination between things that most people would find indistinguishable. In an interesting parallel to the Chinese case, the English essayist Joseph Addison (1672–1719) compared a person who had true taste in literary matters with the man who could identify each of ten different kinds of tea or any combination of them.[6] It is worth considering that, while in pre-revolutionary France rules of good taste were dictated by court, in England such rules were disseminated through aristocratic networks, in a way that was similar to the manner in which the rules of tea connoisseurship were spread in medieval China—through specialized treatises on tea and in poetry circulated among literati. Chinese tea connoisseurship, then, was not something that was dictated by the imperial court, even if some emperors (notably Song Huizong, r. 1101–1126) did play an important role in this cultural arena.

Although I have chosen to take a particular approach toward the history of tea in traditional China, one that emphasizes its religious aspects, this book would not have been possible without the work of many Chinese and Japanese scholars of tea who have diligently assembled the necessary historical sources and subjected them to sustained and detailed analysis. In the individual chapters that follow, I will indicate where I have drawn on previous scholarship in Asian languages, but here let me single out some important studies that have informed my understanding of the history of tea in China. An essential resource for the study of tea in China is the collection of tea literature in an annotated critical edition produced by the Chinese historians of tea Zheng Peikai and Zhu Zizhen in 2007. Their work, and mine, is indebted to the many pioneering works of tea scholarship that were produced by scholars in mainland China in the 1980s and 1990s. Chen Chuan's comprehensive history of tea, for example, was produced in 1984 but remains very useful, and the compendium of a vast range of historical texts on tea complied by Chen Zugui and Zhu Zizhen in 1981 is still an indispensable resource. In addition to these books, several long articles on historical aspects of tea culture by scholars such as Cheng Guangyu, Fang Hao, and Liao Baoxiu provide essential data and analysis. More recently, Liu Shufen has contributed some ground-breaking studies of the consumption of tea in Tang and Song dynasty monasteries. For tea poetry, I have learned a great deal from the annotated collection of Tang verse on tea by Lü Weixin and Cai Jiade. In Japanese, Nunome Chōfū has written with authority on many aspects of Tang tea culture. Mori Shikazō's work is very helpful for understanding tea in the context of *materia medica*. Takahashi Tadahiko has offered important insights into Tang poetry on tea and the significance of Eisai's (1141–1215) *Kissa yōjōki*. In short, I have benefited immensely from the expertise of these and other East Asian scholars of tea.

Throughout this book, our assumption will be that tea in China is a historically contingent topic and that it has changed over time. In the following chapters we will observe the complex interplay among different methods of making the beverage itself, advances in the technology used to process tea leaves, and cultural shifts in attitudes toward the drink. The process of making tea, for example, has evolved (or perhaps it has just changed) from simmering fresh leaves in water, as seems to have been done in earliest times, to simmering processed loose tea (Han dynasty through Tang times). During the Tang dynasty (618–907 CE), dried tea in the form of cakes was roasted and ground before being infused with very hot (but not boiling) water. Sometimes the tea was simmered with other ingredients such as citrus peel. In Song times, cake tea was ground up and the powder whisked to a froth in very hot water, resulting in a milky-looking liquid with a head of foam much prized by connoisseurs. It was only from the Ming dynasty (1368–1644) onward that loose tea was steeped in boiling water in a way that is familiar to us today.[7] A cup of tea, then, looked, smelled, and tasted different depending on when and where it was made. It is reasonable to suppose that cultural attitudes to tea changed along with the beverage itself.

SOME BASIC FACTS ABOUT TEA

The botanical name of the tea plant is *Camellia sinensis;* the beverage "tea" is made from its young leaves.[8] The tea plant grows best in mild warm climates. Most Chinese tea comes now from plants grown in hill country in the South. Tea plants probably grew earliest in what are now the southwestern provinces of Yunnan and Sichuan, lands that were on the semi-civilized periphery of China in premodern times. Despite some controversy on the subject, there seems little doubt that China is the original home of tea.[9] Although wild tea may have been growing in Assam from early times, the tea plant was not cultivated there until the British started growing and processing tea on a commercial scale in the 1830s and 1840s.[10] Words for tea used throughout the world ultimately all derive from Chinese. The Sinitic *chá* is the linguistic root for Turkish çay and Russian чай (chai), for example. The English word "tea" (French thé, Italian te, etc.) comes from the Hokkien (Southern Fujian) pronunciation *te*.[11]

One of the benefits of the tea plant as a cash crop is that it can be productively grown on hills and mountains, thus preserving level ground for essential rice cultivation. The association of the tea plant with elevated ground helps explain why Buddhist and Taoist institutions were able to benefit from growing tea, because monasteries were often located on mountain sites with access to fresh running water from springs.[12] Cultivated tea plants (as opposed to wild ones) are normally pruned to a manageable height—not more than six feet tall and usually only waist-high. Pruning to this degree ensures that a steady supply of soft young leaves and buds that are most often used for processing can be easily picked.

Tea contains caffeine: this is the active ingredient that accounts for many of the stimulating effects on the body and mind that were praised by poets and writers in traditional China. Caffeine is a naturally occurring alkaloid, and before the fourteenth century most cultures outside of Europe knew of some plants that contained caffeine or theobromine (an alkaloid similar to caffeine and found in cocoa beans, kola nuts, and tea). Interestingly, Europe's first encounter with caffeine did not come until as late as the seventeenth century.[13] In addition to acting as a mild stimulant, caffeine also has analgesic and diuretic properties. The substance affects the central nervous system, increases mental alertness, facilitates movement of the muscles (including cardiac muscles), and improves kidney function. Benefits commonly attributed to tea in Chinese sources, both pharmacological and anecdotal, include its ability to quench thirst, inhibit sleep, counteract the effects of alcohol, and stimulate the mind.

The taste of tea is bitter and astringent—and these qualities may partly explain its initial popularity in Tang times when a larger number of sweet foodstuffs became available to elite consumers.[14] Chinese authors praised tea for its power to cool the body, reduce fever, and relieve aches in the head and eyes. Also, tea was known to induce urination, promote bowel movement, and slow down diarrhea. There were some other common claims for tea: it facilitates digestion, counteracts fatty foods, and reduces flatulence; it dissolves phlegm, alleviates boils and sores, and lessens pains in the joints; it strengthens teeth; it endows one with a general sense of well-being; and it promotes good health and longevity.[15]

TEA CULTIVATION AND PROCESSING

The ubiquitous green tea bought and consumed today everywhere from Beijing to Baltimore—that is to say, a loose tea, the leaves of which have been pan-fired to wilt them, and then rolled and dried—dates back no further than about the twelfth century in China. Accustomed as we are to this kind of Chinese green tea, we might not immediately recognize the taste or appearance of the beverage that people were drinking in Tang or Song China. Probably in the earliest times (the Warring States period [ca. 475–221 BCE] or perhaps even earlier), the beverage was made from freshly picked tea leaves that were not processed in any way (possibly they may have been dried in the sun). It could not have been a particularly stable product—it had to be consumed locally, more or less on the spot where tea was grown. Developments in tea processing reflected the need to produce a substance that could be transported, stored, and prepared as a beverage wherever and whenever required. At some point before the Tang dynasty, although exactly when remains unclear, we find the development of tea cakes: unfermented tea leaves were steamed, mixed with some binding substance, and then molded into cakes that could be packed and transported over long distances.

Tea processing developed over time, as did methods for the preparation of the beverage. Probably the earliest explanation of how tea was made ready to drink can be found in *Materia Medica of Curative Foodstuff* (*Shiliao bencao*), a compilation of the late seventh century and the most comprehensive surviving Tang work on dietetics (the use of food as medicine):[16]

> *Cha* (tea)—reduces flatulence. It reduces the urge to sleep, relieves boils and itches and dissipates hard stool. It can be kept overnight. The best tea is made from fresh leaves. However, they can be steamed and pounded and kept for later use. When it is too old it may promote flatulence. Traders then adulterate it with freshly sprouted leaves of locust or willow.[17]

This laconic entry tells us that fresh tea was not a stable substance and that unscrupulous merchants were not above trying to improve the look of old tea leaves with fresh sprouts from other plants. Processing tea made it more stable and longer lasting. Tea processes changed along with tastes in consumption and the development of technology. In Tang times, cakes of tea were formed from unfermented leaves that were steamed, pounded, and then molded into shape.[18] During the Song, tea cakes were molded from leaves that had been steamed, pressed, and rolled. As noted, loose green tea—the most common form of tea today, which consists of unfermented leaves that are first pan-fired and then rolled and dried—first makes its appearance during the Yuan and Ming dynasties. If leaves were allowed to ferment, then the tissue of the leaves would be broken down by bacteria, yeasts, or other microorganisms. The application of heat to tea leaves, either by firing or pan-firing them, "fixes" them—arresting the oxidation process (which breaks down chlorophyll and releases tannins, progressively turning the leaves darker)—and allows the tea leaves to remain green in color.

The next major development in tea processing came in the fifteenth century with Wuyi (Oolong) tea, the leaves of which are oxidized after picking and then wilted, pan-fired, rolled, and dried. The final firing halts the oxidization process. This is the variety of tea that became so popular in the West. Fully oxidized black (or red) tea did not appear in China until the mid-nineteenth century and so is not really touched on in this book. Today, tea leaves are prepared by being plucked by hand from tea bushes, dried (either in the sun or in a drying pan or ovens), then rolled, and finally fired in a kiln. In addition to these basic types of tea, distinguished according to production methods, various kinds of scented tea have been made since about 1000 CE.[19]

As we will see, the innovations in the technology of tea processing I outlined earlier were by no means divorced from the story of tea as a religious and cultural commodity. In fact, religious institutions played an important role in some of these developments. Many famous and sought-after types of tea, for example, were first grown on mountain lands belonging to the numerous Buddhist and Taoist monasteries of South China and then processed by the resident monks. Itinerant monks brought techniques of tea production to new areas when they traveled.

Based on the oxidation of the leaves, we can distinguish three main types of tea drunk today: unoxidized (green tea), oxidized (black tea), and semi-oxidized (Oolong tea). Most tea consumed in China now, as in the past, is unoxidized green tea (*qingcha; lücha*). I already noted that tea production methods in medieval China differed from those employed in later periods, and there was also considerable variety in the way in which the beverage was prepared—boiled, briefly simmered, steeped, whipped to a froth, and so on—not to mention the condiments (salt, spices, dried fruit, etc.) that were sometimes added to the tea. Some beverages consumed as tea in Tang times would be almost unrecognizable as such to us now and probably looked more like a kind of soup. A work that I will mention frequently in this study is the widely circulating and well-known *Classic of Tea* (*Chajing*) by Lu Yu (733–804). In chapter six of his work, Lu Yu notes that sometimes such items as onion, ginger, jujube fruit, citrus peel, dogwood berries or peppermint are boiled along with the tea. Such ingredients may be merely scattered across the top for a glossy effect, or they can be boiled together and the froth drawn off.[20]

Lu Yu looked down on this method of preparation, writing that "drinks like this are no more than the swill of gutters and ditches; still, alas, it is a common practice to make tea that way."[21] This distinctive Tang custom of tea preparation is commented on in the poet Pi Rixiu's (838–883) preface to the *Classic of Tea,* in which he states, "Before Jici's [Lu Yu's] time, tea was called *ming* and to drink it one mixed it up [with other ingredients] and boiled it—it was no different from slurping vegetable soup."[22]

The fact that people commonly consumed tea in this soup-like form points to a conception of tea that was primarily dietetic or medicinal. As we will discover, in addition to *Shiliao bencao,* whose entry on tea we read earlier, other *materia medica* from the sixth and seventh centuries also advised their readers to mix tea with scallions, dogwood, and ginger or to make tea congee (rice porridge). Despite the criticisms of Lu Yu, Pi Rixiu, and others, as well as the popularizing of more refined methods of making tea, such medicinal tea broths did not disappear with the Tang. As late as the Southern Song, Lin Hong (twelfth century) was still complaining about such broths in his recipe book, *Pure Offerings for Mountain Dwellers (Shanjia qinggong),* and recipes for various tea congees can be found in Yuan-dynasty nutritional works.[23] In fact, some similar styles of consuming tea are still around today—for example, "ginger-salt tea" (*jiangyan cha*).[24] We will need to bear in mind then that tea was consumed in different forms, in different contexts, and for different reasons.

If, on the one hand, tea connoisseurs despised these popular soup-like concoctions, on the other, they promoted some extremely sophisticated and rare varieties of tea for consumption in the approved manner. By the early Song there already existed a bewildering array of names for various specialty types of tea, most notably the expensive and refined "wax tea" (*lacha*) that usually sold for about twice the price of any other tea. Some types of tea commanded extraordinary prices from lovers of the brew. Handbooks such as *Essentials of Tea Connoisseurship (Pincha yaolu)* were written for connoisseurs, telling them how to avoid being taken in by fake teas or by inferior commodities disguised as more expensive brands.[25]

The tea market extended from common types of tea intended for mass consumption to very high-end "brands" of tea marketed to a discerning clientele on the basis of luxury and rarity. Teas might be distinguished on the basis of their specific origins or the times when they were picked—three days before the early spring festival of Qingming (Pure Brightness), for example, was a highly regarded harvest.[26] In Song times, cakes of tea were often impressed with evocative names and their places of origin; these were local specialties aimed at the well-informed expert sampler of tea. Of course, there was always loose tea available as well, but tea cakes were much better suited for long-distance transportation, enabling products from sometimes peripheral locations to find the best market elsewhere in the empire. This fact gives us an important clue as to the translocal nature of the tea trade: these products were consumed far from their point of origin. People drank tea from places they might never visit, and the religious and cultural aspects of tea were also entwined with the marketing of the commodity.

TEA AND OTHER BEVERAGES

One of the ways in which this book examines the historical trajectories of tea is through its competition with other beverages, particularly alcohol and various popular medicinal decoctions. For example, we might see in the rise of tea in Tang times a victory of a Southern drink over what was popular with pastoral peoples of the Northern plains: milky drinks such as koumiss (alcoholic fermented mare's milk) or yogurt (*lao*).[27] I can illustrate this contrast in beverage cultures rather nicely with an anecdote taken from a Buddhist source, *Record of Buddhist Monasteries in Luoyang* (*Luoyang qielan ji*) of 530 CE. It tells of a man called Wang Su (464–501) who was exiled from his home state of Southern Qi (479–502) and was serving at the court of the Northern Wei (386–534). At first, he could not tolerate the native beverage of fermented milk (*laojiang*). He preferred tea—here called "a beverage of *ming*" (*mingzhi*; we shall discuss the term *ming* for tea in the next chapter)—and so our source claims, he was able to drink a whole bucketful of tea at a time. Years later, he had become so accustomed to life in the North that he could consume milky drinks with ease. The emperor asked him, "How would you compare tea to fermented milk?" To which Wang replied in jest, "Tea does not quite hit the mark; it is but a slave compared to fermented milk."[28] Interestingly, the pious emperor Liang Wudi's (465–549) famous text against consuming alcohol or meat (*Duan jiu-rou wen*) also prohibits consuming milk, honey, cheese, and cream.[29] So there may be a Buddhist aspect to attitudes toward various sorts of animal products just as there was also a later Buddhist endorsement of tea.[30]

Although tea and milk may have briefly been in competition, a more enduring tension existed between tea and alcohol (*jiu*). Tea in China may be considered as alcohol's "other" or perhaps as *yin* to alcohol's *yang*. In terms of their medicinal properties, for example, alcohol is considered heating, whereas tea is cooling. As we have seen, tea was portrayed as a drink that could comfort, relieving humans from various kinds of distress (thirst, fatigue, sickness, or mental anguish), whereas alcohol, despite its many benefits, could be depicted as the agent that induced those same kinds of misfortune. And, as we shall discover, alcohol was prohibited by Buddhism, whereas tea was looked on with favor by the religion.

Both tea and alcohol in traditional China were similarly aestheticized, and both influenced the language of literature and art. Alcohol—*jiu* is commonly translated as "wine" but was usually encountered in the form of a weak ale or similar beverage—was imbued with all kinds of moral qualities in medieval literature.[31] People exchanged alcohol as a gift in a way that they later would with tea. There was a similar culture of connoisseurship around intoxicating liquor as there was around invigorating tea. Both alcohol and tea were compared, for example, with the dew supped by immortals. Were such claims mere rhetoric, or did they reflect a sense that these beverages somehow functioned as portals to other worlds?

The cultural shift from alcohol to tea is certainly a significant one, but in medieval times tea had to compete not only with alcohol but also with a host of other medicinal tonics and decoctions (*tang*): some of these tonics, like ginseng and astragalus, are still commonly drunk today. Probably every scholar of medieval China is familiar with the famous "cold food powder," the popular mineral drug of the time, but the wider range of popular plant-based health tonics and decoctions are not so well known.[32] We need to understand, then, that the rise of tea was by no means an obvious or uncomplicated process. It had to find its place in a marketplace that was sometimes quite crowded with other products.

TEA AND HEALTH

We should consider the effects of tea as the first widespread medicinal substance in China, its blanket coverage perhaps replacing (or overlaying) local knowledge and substances. Note, for example, the term *chayao* (tea medicine, or tea and medicine), which appears frequently in the literature of Chan Buddhism during the Song dynasty and later.[33] Certainly, tea was regarded as a "drink for nourishing life" (*yangsheng yinliao*) in the Buddhist monastery and elsewhere from the mid-Tang. This claim for the properties of tea needs to be understood in the larger context of the ideals and practices of "nourishing life" (*yangsheng*)—that is, promoting health rather than counteracting illness.[34] To offer a mundane example of the medicinal uses of tea, it was employed as a mouthwash—a custom already noted by the poet Su Shi (1037–1101).[35] A thousand years after Su's time, Chairman Mao was rinsing his mouth with tea every morning (and, according to his doctor, he suffered appalling dental health).[36] This practice is not entirely specious, however, because tea actually contains fluoride.[37]

Nowadays, claims about the health benefits of drinking green tea come at us from all sides, and it may be hard to believe that any traditional Chinese sources could have claimed that tea may not actually be that good for one.[38] But in his Southern Song food canon *Pure Offerings for Mountain Dwellers* (quoted earlier), Lin Hong warns about the dangers to health from improperly prepared tea.[39] Later in this book we will consider earlier warnings that excessive consumption of tea might cause "abdominal dropsy" or make one swell up like a frog. Such statements about the dangers of tea drinking were explicitly countered by Fei Wen, who was appointed governor of Huzhou (a major tea-growing area) in 813, in his *Commentary on Tea* (*Cha shu*): "Some say that drinking an excess of tea causes illness. I say it is not so!"[40]

What One Should Know About Diet (*Yinshi xu zhi*), a work on dietetics by Jia Ming (dates unknown) from the end of the Yuan dynasty, tells us the following:

> Tea tastes bitter and sweet. Its nature is cold, but the tea from Jie is only mildly cold. Continuous drinking of tea will make one thin, induce loss of fat and diminish one's ability to fall asleep. Massive amounts of tea, or drinking it after consumption of wine, will allow its coldness to penetrate the kidney and cause pain in the hips and bladder as well as swelling and rheumatism in the joints. It is particularly pernicious to add salt to tea or accompany it with salty food. This is like inviting a thief into one's home. One must not drink tea on an empty stomach. Taking tea while eating chives is likely to give one a bloated feeling. Tea should be drunk when hot. Cold tea will aid the accumulation of phlegm. It is better to drink less of it, rather than more. Better yet, don't drink it at all![41]

In the realm of health and wellness, then, the values of tea drinking were certainly open to question, and we should not assume that tea was always considered the healthy choice in traditional China. The positive values placed on tea by the various authors we will consider in later chapters need to be considered against the background of these critiques of excessive consumption and the dangers of combining tea with other substances.

WHAT IS A "RELIGIOUS AND CULTURAL COMMODITY"?

Why should we and how can we discuss tea as a commodity that had religious and cultural meaning? Or, to put the question another way, how did men and women in premodern China understand the nature of the commodities that they cultivated and consumed? Let us begin by imagining how tea, as commodity or beverage, could exist or act in a religious and cultural context. For example, tea could be used to represent a doctrine or idea. It could embody the sacred. It could be utilized by religious practitioners in order to make merit. For instance, tea could be offered to buddhas, it could be employed in rituals or given as a funeral offering, it could nourish the dead, or it could be offered to quench the thirst of pilgrims. The beverage could mediate between our world and others, between humans and deities or ghosts. Drinking tea could cause altered states of consciousness, heightened sensitivity, or prolonged states of wakefulness, all of which could be interpreted as having religious meaning or significance. Processed tea, loose or pressed into cakes, could be used as a pure gift suitable for exchange between literati and monks. As we will see, tea functioned in traditional China in all these ways.

In this book, then, we will be considering tea as an everyday comestible that points in various ways—via poetic allusions, evocative names, associations with holy figures and sacred places, and the like—beyond the everyday. On the more quotidian level, what expectations did premodern Chinese people have when they consumed tea? They drank to quench their thirst, to elevate their mood, to sharpen thinking, to relax, and to feel better. But where did all these ideas about tea come from? How were they expressed?

Many of the cultural and religious aspects of tea that I mentioned so far are still discernible in China (and beyond) today, but they first appeared in medieval times—a particularly innovative period in China's religious history. We can say with some certainty, then, that people did not simply and without reflection begin to consume a new beverage called "tea" in Tang-dynasty China. From the first, they invested the drink and the commodity (the tea plant and its processed leaves) with meaning. Because, in traditional China, it was difficult to present a new cultural development as an innovation, tea was obliged to be ancient. Thus enthusiasts for the newly discovered drink needed to supply the commodity with a venerable history and a suitably impressive genealogy, even though the origins of tea were in reality probably quite obscure and undistinguished.

Alongside assertions of the antiquity of the beverage, authors drew on the institutions and ideologies of Buddhism to argue the case for tea. They could do so because Chinese Buddhists made an early claim, by rhetoric and by other means, to tea drinking as their own particular cultural practice, one that was defined in opposition to the consumption of intoxicants. This claim proved difficult to dislodge even though later writers on tea may not themselves always have been sympathetic to the religion. Even when tea's associations with Buddhism are not overtly stated, the religion is never far in the background of the literature. We find Buddhist ideas, institutions, and individuals throughout the personal history of the Tang "god of tea" and author of the *Classic of Tea*, Lu Yu, for example. Many Chinese poems about tea have explicitly Buddhist settings, and other tea literature is often embedded in a Buddhist world, frequently mentioning Buddhist monastic sites or personalities as significant in accounts of the finest teas. Interestingly, then, Buddhism seems to have been crucial in what the art historian Craig Clunas calls the "invention of taste" in China. He explains the role of taste thus:

> For if the unequal distribution of cultural resources is necessary to the stratification of society . . . and if those cultural resources are full commodities, available to all who possess the relevant economic resources, what is to prevent the cultural and economic hierarchies collapsing into each other, till the rich are the cultured, and the cultured are the rich? Here, taste comes into play, as an essential legitimator of consumption and an ordering principle which prevents the otherwise inevitable-seeming triumph of market forces.[42]

But although Buddhist ideas, institutions, and individuals were often closely associated with creating a taste for tea, Taoist concepts were by no means absent. Many medieval writers on tea deliberately evoked images of Taoist immortality in their tea poetry and prose. One of the best known tea poems of medieval China is that composed by Lu Tong (795–835) toward the end of his life, commonly known as "Seven Cups of Tea," but actually titled "Written in Haste to Thank Censor Meng for his Gift of New Tea" (*Congbi xie Meng jianyi ji xin cha*).[43] It is replete with Taoist imagery, especially in its most famous lines:

The first bowl moistens my lips and throat.
The second bowl banishes my loneliness and melancholy.
The third bowl penetrates my withered entrails,
Finding nothing there except five thousand scrolls of writing.
The fourth bowl raises a light perspiration,
As all the inequities I have suffered in my life
Are flushed out through my pores.

The fifth bowl purifies my flesh and bones.
The sixth bowl allows me to communicate with immortals.
The seventh bowl I need not drink,
I am only aware of a pure wind rising beneath my two arms.
The mountains of Penglai, what is this place?
I, Master of the Jade Stream, ride this pure wind and wish to return
    home.[44]

Lu's poem—which continues to be popular and much quoted both in the original Chinese and in English translation—presents tea as a kind of powerful elixir that has the ability to transform both the body and the mind. Tea begins by slaking Lu Tong's thirst; then it heals his emotional distress. By the fifth cup, the iniquities of the poet's past lives are dissolved. Ultimately, tea allows the drinker to commune with immortals and journey to the fabled Taoist paradise of Penglai.

What we discover in this poem is something that is common to many cultural productions that were created around tea: the practical/physiological aspects of tea drinking (it relieves thirst, cheers from depression, clears the head, and nurtures the body) are mingled with religious aspirations and imagery (tea eradicates the suffering of the past, it purifies the flesh, and allows the drinker to ascend with the immortals into paradise).[45] This dual aspect of the conception of tea—both this worldly and otherworldly—is a characteristic that we will see repeatedly as we explore our materials. Perhaps then, "drinking tea" in the context of Chinese religion and culture plays a role similar to "breaking bread together" as a religious term in the Western tradition. We may find some instructive parallels with the religious significance of bread in Christian traditions.[46]

Tea in the Tang dynasty was not only a commodity of ordinary daily life but was also used by emperors to give to ministers to show grace and favor, or bestowed by superiors to inferiors as a ritual mark of respect, or set as an official gift between bureaucrats, or passed between friends and relatives greeting each other to demonstrate their bonds of affection.[47] Appreciating the symbolic power of tea as gift will help us to understand some of the contexts in which cultural productions (poems, paintings, texts, and artifacts) were created—for example, Lu Tong's poem, some lines of which were quoted earlier, was written to thank his superior, Censor Meng, for some especially fine tea that he had sent the poet. Because this poem was written in appreciation of a present, how seriously should we take the elevated language that Lu uses to describe the sublime beverage? Perhaps he merely intended to flatter the sender by praising the gift so lavishly; yet even then it is significant that the value that he assigns to tea is primarily expressed in religious terms.

Portrait of the Poet Lu Tong, attributed to Qian Xuan (ca. 1235–1307), hanging scroll, ink and colors on paper, 128.7 × 37.3 cm. Courtesy of National Palace Museum, Taiwan.

No matter how we read the individual literary works, there is no doubt that the shift to drinking tea brought with it a total reorientation of Chinese culture. The preparation and consumption of the new beverage restructured social life, as drinking tea in groups outside of the home soon became a "socially normative" custom. Like coffee (a similarly social beverage), tea drinking went hand in hand with the development of urbanity in early modern China.[48] Although the consumption of tea could be quite informal, it could on occasion be highly ritualized. The serving of tea in nondomestic settings in which men of differing social status came together obviously required some form of etiquette to ensure that no awkwardness arose. It was texts produced within Buddhist monasteries, texts aimed at prescribing monastic behavior, that were among the first to encode (or ritualize?) that etiquette. As we shall see, however, the tea ceremonies (*chali*) described in Buddhist monastic codes of the Song dynasty were not entirely new inventions, but rather adaptations of earlier rules that prescribed correct etiquette between civil servants at state-run dining establishments.[49]

The development of a monastic tea ceremony offers an interesting example of the creation of Buddhist ritual for social/cultural/material reasons, and not so much for doctrinal purposes. For Chinese Buddhist monastics of late medieval and early modern times, tea was a new substance, one not found in Buddhist canonical sources; its use as both an otherworldly offering to buddhas and deities as well as its this-worldly function as social lubricant therefore needed to be carefully codified and controlled.[50]

As the compilers and redactors of Buddhist monastic codes in China knew well, the social consumption of tea created community, reinforcing bonds of affinity and obligation within the monastery and beyond. By drinking tea together, monks and their literati patrons reaffirmed their identity as companions in a common act of connoisseurship, and the exchange of gifts of rare teas established and strengthened social networks between monks and officials. Tea drinking from Tang and Song times onward may be understood as an aspect of a kind of Buddhist universalism that we know was important in medieval China and later—a universalism that can also be seen in such phenomena as mass ordinations, the monthly feasts of lay communities, and festivals, as well as in the religious propaganda of rulers such as Liang Wudi and Empress Wu (Wu Zetian, r. 690–705).[51] Although formal tea ceremonies within the monasteries asserted hierarchy, in writing about less formal gatherings both literati and monks drew attention to the temporary dissolution of worldly status and the possibility of life outside hierarchical structures that could accompany the imbibing of steaming bowls of tea. Lay Buddhist societies formed new communities around the charitable practice of offering tea and tonic decoctions to pilgrims and others.

This brief consideration of tea rituals and ceremonies should alert the reader to the fact that this book is concerned not only with the knowledge of how to grow and process tea but also with the awareness of how to consume it appropriately. Related to the rituals for the consumption and offering of tea is the sacrosanct nature of teaware and tea utensils. These items (according to Lu Yu's *Classic of Tea*) are not to be used for purposes other than the making and drinking of tea.[52] The healthy development and the sophistication of medieval tea culture may be gauged from the fact that there were already large numbers of different tea utensils and wares with specific purposes as early as the eighth century.[53] We know about these objects and their functions from both archaeological finds and from references in literature. Because teaware is a specialized subject with a scholarship all of its own I will not attempt to provide a comprehensive discussion of developments in this area, but only mention relevant examples in passing.

When people think about the religious and cultural aspects of tea in East Asia, they may think of Japan first rather than China, because of the fame of the Japanese tea ceremony. *Cha-no-yu* is a product of fifteenth-century Japan, although its procedures for making tea are derived ultimately from Song practice, and the term *Cha-no-yu* itself is not attested before 1523.[54] In comparison with Chinese tea culture, we may say that *Cha-no-yu* is a relatively late phenomenon. In this book I will concentrate on tea in China, so I will only mention in passing the history of tea in Japan. In any case, it is probably prudent to avoid the teleological approach and instead to consider the Japanese tea ceremony as a cultural artifact of a particular time and place, not as the logical outcome of what went before in China. Nevertheless, given the prominence of the Japanese tea ceremony in the global imagination, it is worth briefly noting some of the roots of *Cha-no-yu* (the term as well as the practice) in Buddhist China.[55] The term itself comes from Zen literature; before the sixteenth century, tea ceremonies were referred to as "tea meeting" (*cha-no-e* or *cha-no-yoriai*). The term is obviously based on the expression *chatō* (Ch. *chatang*) found in Buddhist literature, but in the latter term the words "tea" and "hot water" or "decoction" (*tang*) form a coordinating compound rather than a subordinate one. The term *chatō/chatang* was already present in Chinese literature; for example, it is used in a short treatise by the translator Yijing (635–713) on three kinds of water.[56] In the Japanese monk Eisai's *Drinking Tea for Nourishing Life* (*Kissa yōjōki*), a text discussed in detail later in this book, the term *chatō* must refer to "decoction of tea" because of his use of the parallel term *sōtō* (decoction of mulberry leaves).

We may note here some other examples of the Buddhist elements in the Japanese tea ceremony. The tea room (*chashitsu*) reserved for the ceremony, whose size is four and a half tatami mats measuring three by six feet each, thus forming a square with sides each nine feet in length, is designed to mimic the "ten-foot square chamber" occupied by the famous layman of Buddhist literature, Vimalakīrti, who was celebrated in both China and Japan.[57] According to the scripture that bears his name, Vimalakīrti was a rich man who lived in a small room of ten feet square in Vaiśālī, India, and had a profound understanding of Mahāyāna doctrine.[58] Once, when he fell ill, the Buddha dispatched his senior disciples to visit him, and Vimalakīrti revealed the supreme teaching of emptiness to them. Allusions to the Buddhist scriptures such as this one show that the gatherings of tea aficionados were intended to be serious-minded events. But tea parties in later Japanese history often involved not just the competitive sampling of tea in sacred spaces but also riotous, sensuous fun.[59] Thus we are faced with the irony that tea was steeped in Buddhist lore and yet provoked rather un-Buddhist activities of sex and sensuality.

One question that arises when we consider tea consumption from the perspective of East Asian religion and culture is whether it is meaningful to speak of a "way of tea" (chadao). The term chadao is first attested in Record of Things Seen and Heard by Mr. Feng (Fengshi wenjian ji), an important Tang source for the history of tea to which we shall return later. But what, if anything, does the term mean? Could it refer to a specific path of practice related to tea? Let us look at that first occurrence. Referring to Lu Yu's Chajing, Feng tells us that "thereupon, the way of tea spread greatly."[60] There is no information in this source that tells us what elements or attitudes constituted this way of tea, so it is quite likely that Feng was just using evocative language to describe the popularity of a custom in a way that alluded to other "ways" in Chinese thought and religion.

If there was a way of tea in the Tang it was a way that was far more concerned with material objects, tea utensils, the right kind of water, methods for making tea, and so on, than with any spiritual movement. At least that characterization holds true if we look at the tea literature (chashu) of Tang times in conjunction with surviving artifacts. It is perhaps possible that a more spiritual or etherealized approach toward tea is discernible in Tang dynasty poetry, and this is an issue that will be explored in later chapters.[61]

SUMMARY OF CHAPTERS

Let us look ahead now to the remainder of the book and how the topics I introduced so far will be developed. Chapter Two provides an examination of the surviving sources for the early (pre-Tang) history of tea and an unraveling of the later rhetorical claims for the origins of tea in Chinese antiquity. In

Chapter Three, I discuss the role played by Buddhist ideas, individuals, and institutions in the development of tea during the Tang dynasty. In particular, I argue that Buddhist monks and laypeople were to the fore in attempts to change people's attitudes toward intoxicating substances, and some were seen by their contemporaries as missionaries for the spread of tea drinking throughout the empire. Throughout the book I will draw on sources written in verse to provide evidence for the cultural and religious dimensions of tea in China. There was virtually no tea poetry composed before the Tang dynasty, a time that saw a veritable explosion in the composition of verse dedicated to the subject of tea. In Chapter Four, I focus on the tea poetry of the Tang both to explain this sudden development and to explore the evidence from these sources.

We have already met the "god of tea" and compiler of the world's first book on tea, Lu Yu. I give an account of his life and work in Chapter Five, with special reference to his background and interest in religion. Chapter Six moves the story of tea forward into the Song dynasty and explores tea consumption against the background of the larger beverage culture of the time. I consider both the Buddhist monastic world and developments in secular urban culture. As I already noted, some aspects of Song tea culture were exported to Japan. Although the story of Japanese tea is beyond the scope of this book, the study and translation of Eisai's *Kissa yōjōki* (*Drinking Tea for Nourishing Life*) in Chapter Seven provide some useful material for the history of tea in China. In Chapter Eight, I touch on continuing developments in the religious and cultural history of tea in the late imperial period, and in Chapter Nine I offer some concluding perspectives on this study.

2

The Early History of Tea

Myth and Reality

As I noted in the first chapter, the history of tea in China begins with the publication of Lu Yu's *Classic of Tea* around 780. I will discuss Lu Yu's life and how he came to compose this work in a later chapter, but here we will consider the significance of some of the work's claims. Because of the unreliability of our sources and the lack of a single term for tea (as we will see, the character *cha* is a Tang-dynasty innovation), anything before the date of the *Classic of Tea,* for the purposes of this study, belongs to the prehistory of tea. Nevertheless, tea plants indeed grew and their leaves were consumed before 780, and when Tang authors wrote about tea they could not present the beverage as something novel: it had to be supplied with a venerable past. This chapter provides an examination of the surviving sources for the early (pre-Tang) history of tea and an unraveling of later-created rhetorical claims for the origins of tea in Chinese antiquity.

Today, popular materials on the history of tea frequently attribute the discovery of the plant to the mythical ruler/culture hero Shennong, the Divine Husbandman (traditional reign dates 2737–2697 BCE). But in fact, as far as we can establish from the scattered early textual references, it appears that tea was probably first drunk habitually, for pleasure or for medicinal reasons, in Sichuan (Southwest China) some time before the Han dynasty (202 BCE–220 CE). Although its use spread gradually eastward and to the north, tea was for centuries considered primarily a Southerner's drink—recall the comparison between tea and the Northerner's fermented milk that we read in the previous chapter. By no means was the drink part of mainstream Chinese dietary culture; instead, it was a local specialty that was often quite unknown in other places.

Much of the evidence we will examine in this chapter is necessarily textual, because we do not have a great deal of relevant material data or artistic representations of tea for the pre-Tang period. One has to admit that textual evidence is not necessarily an accurate indicator of what people in premodern times actually consumed or how they did so. Let us remember, for example, the case of the history of noodles in China. Although scholars of culture and foodways pored over the surviving texts, they could not discover any trace of noodles earlier than sources from the Eastern Han (25–220 CE). However, a recent archaeological discovery of a bowl with noodles still contained within it has obliged us to push back the date of noodle consumption to Neolithic times (about 4,000 years ago).[1] It is, then, entirely likely that textual evidence for tea may be trumped by the archaeological record at some point in the future.

In addition to reviewing the sources, we should also consider why Lu Yu and others put so much effort into establishing the antiquity of tea, despite the relative thinness of suitably ancient and canonical material at their disposal. Necessarily, most of the historical sources collected by Lu Yu in his *Classic of Tea* are drawn not from the orthodox mainstream of Chinese literary heritage—the Classics, official dynastic histories, and the like—but rather from more peripheral archives such as anecdotal collections, miracle stories, local gazetteers, and *materia medica* or *bencao* (that is, pharmacopeia or collections of recipes employing animal, vegetable, and mineral products for health care). Lu Yu was not the last author to attempt to establish a venerable lineage for tea; in fact, Chinese historians have still not given up claims for the great antiquity of the practice of tea drinking.[2] No doubt issues of national pride and the pressures of the modern heritage industry sometimes make it difficult for Chinese scholars to report the actual, uncertain state of our knowledge about the pre-history of tea.

THE PRE-TANG TERMINOLOGY OF TEA

Before we consider the sources, we need to review briefly the reasons why our pre-Tang materials are so ambiguous and hard to rely on. The chief problem is that the glyph *cha*, the standard character for tea nowadays and used as such for hundreds of years, did not exist before the Tang. Texts written before that time employed a range of other glyphs to indicate the plant or beverage we know as tea, but those terms were not exclusive to tea and may also have applied to things that are not tea at all. The logograph *cha* is derived from that of another glyph, *tu*, by omitting a single stroke. The character *tu* is found in such early texts as the *Poetry Classic* (*Shijing*) and *Songs of Chu* (*Chuci*). Although it is just possible that *tu* could refer to tea in passages from these classical texts, it is more likely that *tu* indicated a "bitter vegetable" (*kucai*), such as sowthistle, chicory, or smartweed.[3]

Another early Chinese text, *Rites of Zhou* (*Zhouli*), probably dating to the late Western Han, describes the official position of "Keeper of Thistles" (*zhangtu*) in the Ministry of Education, the duties of which were to ensure the supply of *tu* for royal funerals.[4] The *Materia Medica Classic of the Divine Husbandman* (*Shennong bencao jing*), the earliest surviving complete pharmacopeia, dating from probably the first century CE, also identifies *tu* as a bitter vegetable.[5] But the glyph *tu* was also applied to a woody plant such as the tea plant. A similar ambiguity of referent for the term is found in other sources too. In the early lexicon for the Classics, *Approach to the Proper* (*Erya*), for example, *tu* is defined as a bitter vegetable, but the entry on *jia* (another early term used for tea) says that "*jia* is bitter *tu*." As H. T. Huang has noted, the use in sixth- and seventh-century sources of a variant character for *tu* that incorporated the tree radical may have been an attempt by medieval writers to differentiate "woody" *tu* (i.e., tea) from the bitter vegetable *tu*.[6] Clearly, then, even if tea was being consumed in early times it still lacked a name of its own.

As for the use of the character *cha* for tea, early sources that appear to refer to *cha* may in fact have originally read *tu* because it was relatively easy for the single stroke that differentiated the two glyphs to have dropped out during transmission of the texts. Furthermore, early texts that now seem to employ *cha* but that were subsequently complied in large official post-Tang collecteana such as *Imperial Readings of the Taiping Era* (*Taiping yulan*, 983 CE) have to be treated with caution because by the tenth century *cha* was the standard term for tea and copyists in those times may well have replaced *tu* with *cha*.[7] Although it may be potentially confusing, in my references to early sources I have followed the received editions even where the glyph *cha* has probably been substituted for another term by a later copyist.

Apart from *tu*, the other term commonly used for tea in the texts is *ming*.[8] We saw in the previous chapter that the Southerner Wang Su was credited with drinking something called "*ming* beverage" (*mingzhi*) in the passage from *A Record of the Monasteries of Luoyang* comparing tea and fermented milk. That same record goes on to state that a "tea drink" (*mingyin*) was served at the Northern Wei court, although it was only really popular with recent émigrés from the South. Possibly the term *ming* may have applied originally only to late-harvested tea leaves, but in time it became another synonym for tea, especially in pharmacological sources. The commentary by Guo Pu (276–324 CE) on the lexicon *Erya*'s entry on *jia* (the early term for tea we already saw) explains,

The plant is a small tree like the *zhizi* (*Gardenia jasminoides Ellis*). The leaves grown in winter may be boiled to make a soup for drinking. Nowadays, those that are gathered early are called *tu*. Those that are gathered late are called *ming*. Another name for them is *chuan*. The people of Shu (present-day Sichuan) call them *kutu* (bitter *tu*).[9]

This passage provides the earliest description of the tea plant and how its leaves were used. It also locates the custom of tea drinking in Sichuan, a claim that seems to be confirmed in other sources.

The *Newly Revised Materia Medica* (*Xinxiu bencao*) by Su Jing, published by imperial edict in 659 CE and as such the first state-sponsored pharmacopeia in China, gives us some further information on the term *ming*:[10]

Ming is also called bitter *tu*. Its taste is sweet and bitter. It is slightly cold but non-toxic. It alleviates boils and sores; promotes urination; dispels phlegm and relieves thirst. It keeps one awake. It is harvested in the spring. . . . To make a drink from it add dogwood, scallion, and ginger.[11]

From the qualities of the substance (diuretic, thirst quenching, stimulating, etc.) we can deduce that tea is being described here. Tea is presented as a medicinal substance to be consumed in a soup with other ingredients. Another *materia medica* of roughly the same date, *Materia Medica of Curative Foodstuff* (*Shiliao bencao*, ca. 670), has the following entry on *ming* that notes some of the same benefits:

Ming leaves—promote bowel function, dispel heat, dissolve phlegm. Boil to obtain a decoction, which makes a good medium for cooking congee.[12]

This entry in the *Shiliao bencao* is followed by one on *cha* (tea) that I cited in the first chapter. Although *cha* became the standard term for the beverage, *ming* continued to be used to refer to tea in *materia medica* of the post-Tang period, all the way up to the most famous and widely read Chinese pharmacopeia, *Compendium of Materia Medica* (*Bencao gangmu*) of 1596.[13] We may note in passing here the way in which *materia medica* recommended consuming tea: as a soup with other medicinal foodstuffs like scallions and ginger or as the base for a congee (a porridge made of grains, most often rice nowadays). As discussed in Chapter One and as we will see again, Lu Yu consciously set his preferred method of preparing tea against these medicinal recipes, which he labeled "disgusting."

FIRST DESCRIPTION OF THE USE OF TEA

Earlier in the chapter, I reproduced Guo Pu's commentary on the *Erya* entry on the term *jia*. This is the earliest surviving description of the tea plant and its use. But the first record of the glyph *tu* as a possible reference to tea is said to occur in the *Slave's Contract* (*Tong yue*), a famous piece of early Chinese humor. The work, by Wang Bao (fl. 58 BCE), enumerates in ludicrous fashion all the duties of a recalcitrant slave whom the author wishes to purchase.[14] These duties include "brewing tea" (*pengtu*) for guests and "buying tea from Wuyang." Wuyang was a Han-dynasty county located east of present-day Pengshan County and south of Chengdu. Although, of course, we cannot be certain, and some scholars have argued against the identification, it is possible that *tu* refers to tea here, because it is described as being fetched from about thirty kilometers away—a fact that suggests a processed commodity (and perhaps a commercial one) rather than a "bitter vegetable."[15] The Japanese tea historian Nunome Chōfū reports that it takes about four days to walk from Wuyang to Chengdu; presumably any fresh vegetable would have wilted during this time, so it is more likely to have been something dried and easy to carry (such as tea).[16]

But are these two early references from the *Slave's Contract* authentic or are they later interpolations or amendments to the original text? This question was first asked by C. M. Wilbur in 1942.[17] Although H. T. Huang and many Chinese historians have treated the references as rather unproblematic, the Italian tea scholar Marco Ceresa has tried to establish definitively whether they can be considered truly early or not. He points out that there are many problems with the textual transmission of the *Slave's Contract* and that these affect what character (*tu* or *cha*) is used for tea or indeed whether there is any reference at all to tea in the text.[18] For example, the earliest surviving version of the text, found in the Tang encyclopedia *Collection of Literature Arranged by Categories* (*Yiwen leiju*, ca. 640 CE), contains no reference to tea. The *Yiwen leiju* version of the text is also very short, however, and it does not include many crucial parts of the contract (such as the bill of sale) that are known to other sources. The earliest extant version of the text is thus not the best or most complete one.[19] The version found in *Imperial Readings of the Taiping Era* (983 CE) contains only the second reference to "buying tea," omits any mention of "making tea," and anachronistically employs the glyph *cha*. There is, in short, such variance in the two crucial phrases (in some texts Wuyang appears as Wudu, for example) that it is problematic to consider the *Slave's Contract* as a reliable witness to the early use of tea in Sichuan.

Another item of circumstantial evidence that points to the unreliability of the *Slave's Contract* as an early witness of tea is the fact that it is not quoted by Lu Yu in his *Classic of Tea*. Because Lu Yu seems to have been extremely diligent in trying to bring together as many early mentions of tea as possible, no matter how insubstantial, it is hard to believe that he would have omitted references to tea in the *Slave's Contract,* had he known of them. As Ceresa points out, most of the titles of known sources that do mention tea and were omitted by Lu Yu date to the third and fourth centuries CE—much later than the date of the *Slave's Contract*.[20]

Even if authentic, the references in this text do not prove that tea was being drunk, merely that it was being made (actually "cooked" [*peng*]) or purchased. The first reference could well be to "cooking sowthistle" rather than "making tea." Neither *pengtu* nor *pengcha* is a common term for "making tea" in later sources. The reference to "buying tea" is, as we have already noted, less problematic and may well be an authentic witness, even if we do not know what that tea may have been used for.

Yet we do know from other sources that tea was cultivated in Sichuan (especially around Wuyang), so early references to making and consuming tea are not entirely implausible. *Record of the Land of Huayang* (*Huayang guozhi*, 347 CE), which is a history of the Shu region (roughly equivalent to modern Sichuan) up to 138 CE, mentions *cha* as a tribute product, as well as tea-producing locales such as Wuyang and Fuling.[21] The *Slave's Contract* remains an interesting, but potentially unreliable witness to early tea drinking in the southwest of China.

THE EARLIEST RELIABLE TEXTUAL REFERENCE TO TEA

Setting aside the indeterminate evidence of the *Slave's Contract*, the next datable reference to tea is found in *History of the Three Kingdoms* (*Sanguo zhi*, ca. 290 CE). Wei Zhao (204–273) was a historian at the court of the last Wu (222–280) emperor, Sun Hao (r. 264–280).[22] Sun was a hearty drinker, and Wei was often invited to join him in daylong drinking bouts. He had a hard job keeping pace with his ruler at banquets, and so to help him out, Sun discreetly slipped him some tea in place of alcohol.[23] Another late third-century reference (not included among Lu Yu's sources) comes from the miscellany of marvels *An Extensive Record of Things* (*Bowu zhi*) compiled by Zhang Hua of the Western Jin (265–316): "drinking true tea causes a person to reduce [the need for] sleep."[24] This laconic statement is found in the section on "foods to be avoided" (*shiji*).

By the middle of the sixth century CE, it was evident that there was some general understanding of the tea plant and the properties of tea as a beverage, even if the terminology remained unstable. For example, chapter ten of the agronomical treatise *Important Methods for Regulating the People* (*Qimin yaoshu*, 544 CE) contains two separate entries of interest to us: no. 53 *tu* (bitter vegetable) and no. 95 *tu,* with the wood radical, or *cha,* with the wood radical.[25] The quotations under entry no. 95 are from (1) *Erya* on *jia;* (2) *Bowu zhi* on tea and sleep; and (3) *Record of the Land of Jingzhou* (*Jingzhou tudi ji*), which says, "tea from Fuling is the best." Although tea was still associated primarily with Sichuan, it is clear from references such as this that by the mid-sixth century there was a growing awareness of its benefits and properties beyond the Southwest.

Despite the scattered references to tea in specialist literature such as *materia medica* and local histories, it is undoubtedly significant that there is no mention of tea to be found in *Selected Literature* (*Wen xuan*), the greatest comprehensive literary compendium of the period of disunion between Han and Tang. It is hard to imagine that any significant or widespread use of tea could have escaped the notice of this important work, compiled by the Liang dynasty (502–557) prince Xiao Tong (501–531).[26] From the paucity of references in the larger literary arena, we must conclude therefore that tea remained a rare and marginal comestible before the mid-Tang.

As we have noted, much of the uncertainty regarding the earlier textual materials for the study of tea derives from the lack of a stable terminology before the Tang. But what is the evidence for the change of glyph from *tu* to *cha* in Tang times? Gu Yanwu (1613–1682), author of *Tang Rhymes Corrected* (*Tang yunzheng,* 1667), used inscriptional evidence to report on this question:

> During my visit to Mount Tai (Taishan) I had a chance to examine a number of Tang stone tablets with inscriptions of *tu* and *cha.* Those written in 779 (in connection with tea as medication) and 798 (in connection with the use of tea in banquets) contained the word *tu* . . . there was no change in the character. But those inscribed in 841 and 855 had the word *cha,* obtained by removing one stroke from *tu.* Thus, the change must have taken place after the middle years of the Tang dynasty.[27]

Gu's observations on this limited range of epigraphical material found at a single site would appear to hold true also for the larger range of Tang materials: *cha* is a character for tea invented and adopted in the mid-Tang. Because of the earlier uncertainty of referents for characters like *tu, ming,* and *jia,* we can say that in some senses tea (both the beverage and the term for it) was an invention of the Tang dynasty. But that was not the way that Lu Yu and other Tang writers about tea understood the origin of their favorite drink. As we will see, they preferred to locate the discovery of tea not in recent times but rather in highest antiquity. Lu Yu, in a style that was typical of medieval Chinese authors, did not narrate this discovery in his own words, but instead compiled references to tea from earlier sources.

THE DIVINE HUSBANDMAN DISCOVERS TEA

Let us begin by noting some of the authorities cited by Lu Yu for his history of tea as found in section seven of the *Classic of Tea*. We will pay particular attention in our discussion to religious figures and sources. Lu Yu opens this section, "Records" ("Shi"), with a chronological list of personalities associated with tea.[28] The first of these is the mythical ruler of antiquity Yandi (the Flaming Thearch), also known as Shennong (the Divine Husbandman). In section six, "Drinking" ("Yin"), of his work, Lu Yu again states that the practice of drinking tea began with Shennong.[29] Although this assertion has no historical merit, it has proved remarkably tenacious. Shennong is still regularly hailed as the inventor of tea not just in popular works or on internet sites but even in otherwise quite serious works of scholarship.[30]

Who was the Divine Husbandman, and why should this particular figure have been credited with the discovery of tea? In Tang times, Shennong was considered one of the Three August Sovereigns (*sanhuang*), the enlightened rulers who were said to have ruled China in high antiquity. The other constant member of the three was Fu Xi. Lists of the Three August Sovereigns differed as to the identity of the third ruler: the various candidates were Fu Xi's sister Nüwa, Suiren, Zhurong, or Gonggong. Robert Henricks has explained how the tradition of Shennong became entwined with that of an originally distinct figure known as Yandi, so that Tang authors such as Lu Yu conflated them into a single personage known as Yandi-Shennong (Flaming Thearch-Divine Husbandman).[31]

What did it mean to attribute the discovery of tea to this venerable culture hero? As Henricks has pointed out, in medieval times texts circulated that were attributed to Yandi/Shennong but that may not have accorded with prevailing ritual orthodoxy of the day. *Shennong's Documents on Praying for Rain* (*Shennong qiuyu shu*), preserved in the Tang compendium *Collection of Literature Arranged by Categories* (*Yiwen leiju*), for example, advocates the exposure and burning of shamans in order to bring rain at times of severe drought.[32] There was in Shennong, then, an echo of a past in which ritual action was more brutal and direct than many Tang intellectuals might have preferred to contemplate. But, although by Tang times Shennong may have been regarded as a figure who was suitably ancient and wise to have been the first to discover tea, he had in fact rather recently emerged from some obscurity. Like tea itself, Shennong's name is not to be found in the *Classics;* it is also absent from such venerable works as *Mr. Zuo's Commentary on the Spring and Autumn Annals (Zuozhuan), Conversations of the States (Guoyu), Songs of Chu (Chuci), Analects (Lunyu),* and *Classic of Mountains and Seas (Shanhai jing).* His presence is perhaps hinted at in *Mozi,* but Shennong only really becomes visible in the literature of the late Warring States and early Han—in works such as *Mencius, Spring and Autumn Annals of Mr. Lü (Lüshi chunqiu), Book of Zhou (Zhou shu), Book of Rites (Liji),* and *Huainanzi.* A. C. Graham discerned in these materials a philosophical school, which he called the "School of the Tillers" (*nongjia*), for which Shennong was the hero, an emperor "who reigns in perfect peace over an empire of farmers."[33] But it is clearly not the philosophical aspect of Shennong that concerns us here. Rather, we must consider Shennong as the patron saint of farming and inventor of agriculture, the culture hero of antiquity who first taught others the essential skills of plowing the soil, sowing seeds, and harvesting grains and who determined which plants were safe for humans to consume. Here is a typical portrayal of the Divine Farmer from the "Cultivating Effort" (*Xiuwu*) chapter of the important collection of early Han thought, *Book of the Master of Huainan (Huainanzi,* ca. 139 BCE):

> In ancient times,
>> the people fed on herbaceous plants and drank [only] water,
>> picked fruit from shrubs and trees,
>> and ate the meat of oysters and clams.
> They frequently suffered tribulations from feverish maladies and injurious poisons. Consequently, the Divine Farmer first taught the people to plant and cultivate the five grains.
>> He evaluated the suitability of the land,
>> [noting] whether it was dry or moist, fertile or barren, high or
>>> low.
>> He tried the taste and flavor of the one hundred plants
>> and the sweetness or bitterness of the streams and
>>> springs,
> issuing directives so the people would know what to avoid and what to accept. At the time [he was doing this], he suffered poisoning [as many as] seventy times a day.[34]

This version of Shennong, the heroic pioneer who personally tastes and tests the various herbs on behalf of humanity, is the figure that Lu Yu would cast as the discoverer of tea. As Henricks explains, in this passage from *Huainanzi* we see the beginnings of a trend in which Shennong's "selection and classification

of herbs and drugs (*caoyao*) overshadows his earlier image of a farmer working with the 'five grains.'"[35] Also, tea is often associated with healing in the *Classic of Tea* and other sources. In Tang times, Shennong's ability to heal was
thought to have been bestowed on him by the deity Taiyi (Great One), as may
be witnessed in this quotation found in the *materia medica*:

> The Master Taiyi said, "As for all the medicines, the superior category
> nurtures destiny (*ming*), the middle category nurtures [human] na-
> ture (*xing*), the lower category nurtures disease." Shennong thereupon
> requested and received the ability to control and cure.[36]

The logical connection between Shennong and tea is likely to be the fact
that tea was a kind of medicine that had a beneficial long-term effect on the
body and mind. We can see this in the first literary source cited by Lu Yu in
the "Records" section of his *Classic of Tea*, the *Divine Husbandman's Food
Canon* (*Shennong shi jing*), which says: "Tea (*chaming*), when taken over a long
period of time, gives humans strength, contentment, and determination."[37]
What exactly was this food canon, and how was it related to Shennong? A
work called *Food Prohibitions of the Divine Husbandman and Yellow Emperor*
(*Shennong Huangdi shijin*) in seven fascicles is listed in the bibliographic section (*yiwen zhi*) of the dynastic history *Book of the Han* (*Han shu*), although
the text itself no longer survives.[38] This title apparently marks the first identification of the Divine Husbandman with the dietetic branch of Chinese medicine.[39] Later texts mention a *Classic of the Divine Husbandman* (*Shennong jing*),
which may have been the forerunner of the famous *Materia Medica Classic of
the Divine Husbandman* that first appears in the official bibliographies of the
Sui and Tang dynasties and is the first known Chinese *materia medica*.[40]

The *Divine Husbandman's Food Canon* is presumably related to the *Materia
Medica Classic of the Divine Husbandman*, although Lu Yu appears to distinguish between the two titles. It no longer survives, and the only quotations
from it are found in works that postdate the *Classic of Tea* and that reproduce
its quotation about tea. The quotation attributed to the *Divine Husbandman's
Food Canon* in the *Classic of Tea* is not found elsewhere in earlier sources.
There is no evidence to suggest, then, that the *Divine Husbandman's Food
Canon* is a genuinely early source, if it ever existed at all as an independent
work. But as we can see, Lu Yu's *Classic* convincingly linked tea with a culture
hero who was an important figure in the mythology of both agriculture and
medicine. Interestingly, Lu Yu seems to have been the first to make the association between Shennong and tea, but he was by no means the last.

Notwithstanding the strong case made by Lu Yu for the extreme antiquity
of tea, we can find in other Tang sources dissenting voices that present alterna-

tive genealogies of tea, even if these claims are less familiar to today's readers. According to the account of tea found in the handbook of culinary raw materials, *Classic of the Official in Charge of Palace Meals, Manuscript Edition* (*Shanfu jing shoulu*) composed by Yang Ye in the mid-ninth century, the custom of drinking tea first appeared as late as the Six Dynasties (third to sixth centuries CE), nowhere near as early as the age of the Divine Husbandman, as claimed by Lu Yu. Moreover, Yang Ye did not place the popularization of tea in the Tang until the 780s, slightly later than Lu Yu, who dated it to the first half of the eighth century.

> Tea: its consumption was unheard of in antiquity. In recent times, it was only by Jin and after the Song that people from Wu [southeast China] picked its leaves to be brewed, and made tea congee. By the reign-periods of Kaiyuan (713–741) and Tianbao (742–755), tea gradually appeared. But it was only by the Zhide (756–757) and Dali (766–779) periods that it became abundant, and it became popular only after the Jianzhong period (780–783).[41]

Even scholars of later times did not always accept without question the mythical story of the origin of tea promoted by Lu Yu. The seventeenth-century erudite Gu Yanwu, whose interest in the history of tea I noted earlier, writes in his *Record of Daily Knowledge* (*Rizhi lu*) that the use of tea began when "Qin captured Shu" (that is, after 316 BCE), thus making tea a discovery of the Warring States period and not one of high antiquity.[42] However, although there were accounts of the rise of tea drinking that were grounded in the socioeconomic realities of the medieval period, they were no match for the more romantic origin myths found in Lu Yu's *Classic of Tea* and similar sources, which continue to be read as the authoritative history of the beginnings of tea in China.

TEA IN MEDIEVAL ANOMALY ACCOUNTS

Nothing resembling tea appears in the venerable *Poetry Classic* (*Shijing*), a work that has the reputation for mentioning just about every plant grown and used in early China.[43] The lack of suitably impressive quotations featuring tea that could be drawn from classical sources like the *Poetry Classic* probably left Lu Yu with little choice other than to roam further afield into nonclassical materials in search of historical precedents for tea cultivation and consumption. As we have learned, we cannot always determine with precision what plant or beverage is referred to in the pre-Tang sources collected by him. We can be sure, however, that he intended these materials to be understood as referring to tea. If we consider the history of tea that he constructed by presenting these primary sources in chronological order, then an interesting and unexpected picture emerges. We have already seen how Lu Yu co-opted for his chronicle of tea the Divine Husbandman, culture hero and patron saint of both agriculture and medicine. But he also collected and presented a good deal of anecdotal material—some from rather obscure sources—that is of great interest to those of us who study medieval Chinese religions. In the *Classic of Tea* we discover that tea is not just a beverage that is old and esteemed for its pharmacological properties, but it is also a drink that has powerful, often frightening, associations with deities, demons, ghosts, and witches. Lu Yu's contemporaries were being introduced to a substance that was by no means neutral or benign, but was possessed of mysterious and compelling connections to other worlds.

One genre of extra-official and anecdotal materials is particularly visible in Lu Yu's collection of historical precedents: the literature of anomaly accounts (*zhiguai*). Many collections of anomalies (that is, descriptions of encounters with nonhuman beings, miracles performed by manipulators of esoteric arts, strange places, unusual objects, etc.) were composed in early medieval China.[44] Lu Yu evidently had access to a range of such sources and was able to abstract from them a variety of references to tea in unusual, and sometimes quite uncanny, situations. His choice of anecdotes reveals that the discursive realm of tea extended far beyond the mundane world.

The sources cited in the *Classic of Tea* show that the thirst for tea was not confined to living humans. For example, Lu Yu quotes from *Record of Inquiries into Spirits* (*Soushen ji*), an early medieval collection of anomaly accounts, a story about a ghost whose taste for tea continues even after death.[45]

> Xiahou Kai died on account of an illness. A member of his clan, named Gounu, had some experience seeing ghosts and spirits. He saw Kai come to fetch his horse, and also to cause his wife distress. He wore a flat-topped headdress and a single-lined robe. He would sit, as when he was alive, on the great bed by the western wall, and accost people to ask for tea to drink.[46]

An abbreviated version of this same tale can be found in the entry for tea (*ming*) in the early Song encyclopedia *Imperial Readings of the Taiping Era*, although it does not appear in the source (a dynastic history) claimed for it there:

> The *Book of Jin* (*Jin shu*) says, "Xiahou Kai died. Later, his form appeared to members of his family, searching for tea."[47]

There is perhaps some logic to the idea that the dead—especially those who were apparently unaware of their own death—should continue the habits and desires they had while alive. Indeed, the everyday life of ghosts is a common theme in Chinese anomaly literature.[48] But connections between tea plants and the demons who were believed to inhabit mountain wilderness might not be so immediately apparent. On this topic, Lu Yu quotes a revealing account from a later work called *Continued Record of Inquiries into Spirits* (*Xu soushen ji*)—a sequel to the *Soushen ji* collection we encountered earlier. The following events are said to have occurred during the time of Emperor Wudi of the Jin (r. 265–290):[49]

> Qin Jing, a man of Xuancheng, often entered Mount Wuchang to pick tea (*ming*).[50] Once, he encountered a hairy person more than ten feet tall, who led Jing to the base of the mountain. He pointed out a clump of tea plants and then departed. Suddenly, he reappeared, pulled out a tangerine from his bosom and left it for Jing. Jing was alarmed; he returned home carrying the tea on his back.[51]

The version of this tale quoted by Lu Yu is not quite the same as we find it in the received version of the anomaly collection *Continued Record of Inquiries into Spirits* (better known as *Further Records of Inquiries into Spirits*), where it appears in the seventh fascicle of that work. In the received version, the story is set about a hundred years later. Because the collection is topically arranged, this tale appears with others concerned with encounters with demons.[52] Here, for comparison, is that more detailed version of the tale from *Further Records of Inquiries into Spirits*:

> In the time of Emperor Xiaowu of the Jin (r. 372–396), Qin Jing, a man of Xuancheng, often entered Mount Wuchang to pick tea. Suddenly, from the north side of the mountain, there appeared a man, his body more than ten feet tall, completely covered in hair. Jing saw him and was greatly alarmed. He told himself that he would surely die. The hairy man pulled him by the arm and led him to a mountainous path, took him into a place where there were clumps of tea plants, then released him and departed. Jing thereupon picked the tea. In an instant the hairy man returned. He plucked from his bosom twenty tangerines which he gave to Jing. Their sweetness and beauty were extraordinary. Jing thought this really strange. He took his tea and left.[53]

Although the two tales are told slightly differently, they both highlight the role of the anomalous creature—apparently human in form yet freakishly tall, hairy, and incapable of speech—as the demonic guardian of the secret sources of tea. Robert Campany has briefly noted the presence in medieval anomaly literature of "hairy people . . . encountered in the wilds outside cities and cultivated lands—the Chinese 'wild man' sometimes noble in his behavior which only increases his oddity."[54] This particular wild man of the mountains perhaps may also be related to tales about mountain-dwelling apes with a penchant for human females that first circulated in Han-dynasty Sichuan.[55] In considering Qin Jing's discovery of an alternate reality situated directly alongside our own, we should remember that *Further Records of Inquiries into Spirits* also contains a version of the story of Peach Blossom Spring later made famous by Tao Yuanming (365–427).[56] The haunting atmosphere of the strange and of other worlds populated by not-quite-human beings surrounds the wild tea plant and was carried over even into the days of commercial cultivation and harvesting.

Another story to be considered here is taken by Lu Yu from a collection called *A Garden of Marvels* (*Yiyuan*) by Liu Jingshu (fl. early fifth century), although the received version in that collection is different.[57] Again, it shows that tea was not always easily obtained, but was associated with, or protected by, powerful forces. In this case, it is the ghost of a dead human who is placated by offerings of fine tea:

> When the widow of Chen Wu of Yan county was young, she lived alone with only her two sons, all of whom liked to consume tea (*chaming*). In their home was an ancient burial mound, and every time they drank, they would first have to make offerings [to the occupant]. Her two sons resented this and said, "Who knows whose ancient burial mound this is? Why should we vainly go to so much trouble?" They wished to dig it up and remove [the body]. Their mother forbade it and stopped them.
>
> That evening, she dreamed of a man who said, "I have stayed in this mound for over three hundred years, but now your two sons perversely want to see it destroyed. Thanks to your kindness, I have been protected and also you present me with fine tea. Although I am only withered bones, I will not forget to repay you." Come the morning, through the courtyard were scattered hundreds of thousands of cash. They looked as if they had been long buried, but strung together anew. The mother reported this and the two sons were ashamed. From this time on they made offerings even more humbly.[58]

Let us reflect for a moment on the logic of this story. The ghost—who is not related to Widow Chen or her sons and therefore should not expect to receive sacrifices from them—repays the kindness of the widow in cash. What form does the widow's kindness take? She includes the ghost in the family by offering him the tea that she and her sons enjoy. Thus, the dead feast with the living in a single community. As the ghost remarks, the widow protects him. He acts as the male head of household, and she prevents her sons from exhuming his corpse. The ritual/sacrificial use of tea instigated by the young widow, although it later became important in Buddhist settings, may, as this tale seems to indicate, have appeared first at the more informal and domestic level of family religion and not at the more refined institutional level.

Aside from this tale, what else do we know about the ritual/sacrificial use of tea in pre-Tang China? Lu Yu provides an interesting example from the upper reaches of the medieval social scale:

> When Emperor Shizu Wu (r. 483–494) of the Southern Qi, passed away, he commanded: "On my altar, take care not to use an animal in sacrifice. Just set out cakes and fruit, tea for drinking, dry foodstuffs, wine and dried meat and that is all."[59]

The source of this brief record is not cited in *Chajing*, but it seems to be drawn from an edict recorded in the "basic annals" of Wudi's reign found in the official history of the Southern Qi (*Nan Qi shu*).[60] It is difficult to extrapolate much from this information, other than to note that tea could be a suitable offering even to imperial ancestors.

But it was not just the wild or cultivated tea plant that was protected by ghosts, deities, and spirits as was the Widow Chen's. Lu Yu's sources reveal that tea as a commercial product also had otherworldly associations. He includes a tale of a mysterious old woman who sold tea in the marketplace. The source is an obscure collection called *Traditions of the Elders from Guangling* (*Guangling qilao zhuan*) that no longer survives and is not much cited in other sources.[61]

> In the time of Emperor Yuandi of the Jin (r. 317–323) there was an old woman. Every day, alone, she took a container of tea and sat in the marketplace to sell it. People in the market competed to buy it, but from dusk to dawn her container never became exhausted. The cash that she took for the tea, she scattered on the road for orphans, poor people, and beggars. Some people thought this strange, so the provincial officials had her bound and put in prison. Come nightfall, the old woman took the container from which she sold her tea, and employed it in order to fly out of the window of the jail.[62]

This tale seems to offer an interesting twist on a common theme found in anomaly literature: that of the advanced adept who keeps his or her special abilities carefully hidden, often taking on the role of an ordinary commoner or, as in this case, a market trader.[63] The passage may be taken to suggest that selling tea in the marketplace was a very common and unremarkable thing to do, but at the same time, the old woman's use of the tea container (likely a gourd rather than anything made of metal or earthenware) as a means of airborne escape may point toward some deeper and more mysterious connections between tea and flight. Similar such associations were indicated by Tang dynasty poets such as Lu Tong who wrote about the power of tea to transform its drinkers into feathered immortals.

TEA AND THE TAOIST IMMORTAL

Yet another collection of anomaly accounts, *Record of Divine Marvels (Shenyi ji)* by the Taoist priest Wang Fu (fl. ca. 300 CE), provides the first documented association of Taoism and tea.[64] Unfortunately, this collection no longer survives in toto and is known only through a few short, scattered quotations in other sources (such as this one).[65]

> Yu Hong, a man of Yuyao, went into the mountains to pick tea (*ming*).[66] He encountered a Taoist leading three green oxen. He took Hong up to Cascade Peak, and said, "I am Danqiuzi (Master of Cinnabar Mound). I have heard that you, O Master, are skilled in cooking and I have long wished to be favored [by your company]. In these mountains are great tea plants that may be presented to supply you. I beg you that when some day you have leftovers in your dipper, please present them to me." On account of this, Yu Hong made a libation. Afterwards he always commanded his servants to enter the mountains and get the great *ming* from there.[67]

As we shall see in later chapters of this book, Lu Yu and his circle purposefully constructed a powerful new ideology of tea that mingled Buddhist and Taoist ideas and personalities, weaving ancient archetypes into a new cultural model. This brief account offers an opportunity for us to consider some aspects of that process. The "Master of Cinnabar Mound," despite his evocative name and the fact that the *Classic of Tea* labels him as a Han-dynasty transcendent (*xianren*), is in fact scarcely known from other pre-Tang sources. Lu Yu's contemporaries, however, were evidently much taken both with the name of this Taoist tea master and with its associations. Lu Yu's friend, the poet-monk Jiaoran (730–799), in his "Song of drinking tea while seeing off Zheng Rong," writes, "The feathered man Danqiu [Cinnabar Mound] disdained precious foods; he picked tea, drank it and grew feathers."[68] In another poem, "Song of drinking tea, making fun of the Envoy Cui Shi," he writes, "Simply to know the way of tea and the truth: only Danqiu attained such a state."[69] Moreover, Jiaoran clearly associated the master Danqiu with a specific site; in a short preface to this poem he writes, "The *Records of [Mount] Tiantai* (*Tiantai ji*) says, 'Cinnabar Mound produces great *ming* (tea), which when ingested causes humans to undergo a feathery transformation.'" The *Records of [Mount] Tiantai* that we have today does not preserve any such statement.

References to "Master of Cinnabar Mound" in Tang poetry were not always connected to tea. The famous poet Li Bai (701–762) wrote a poem, "Song of the cloudy terrace on the Western Marchmount—seeing off Danqiuzi" (*Xi yue yuntai ge song Danqiuzi*), in which he uses the sobriquet "Master of Cinnabar Mound" to refer to his friend Yuan Danqiu. This work assumes no particular connection between the "Master of Cinnabar Mound" and tea.

How should we understand the name "Master of Cinnabar Mound?" Standard reference works often explain Cinnabar Mound as one of the peaks of Mount Tiantai, but the name probably has more than one referent. The earliest reference to Cinnabar Mound is in the poem "Far Roaming" (*Yuanyou*) from the *Songs of Chu*: "I continued on to the Feathered Persons at the Hill of Cinnabar—Loitered in the long-standing land where death is not."[70] Sun Chuo's (314–371) later "Rhapsody on Roaming Mount Tiantai" deliberately echoes those famous lines: "I continued on to Feathered Persons at Cinnabar Hill, tarried in the Blessed Courts of those who do not die."[71] A second-century commentator on the *Songs of Chu*, Wang Yi, explains that the Cinnabar Mound is a place that is "eternally luminous, both day and night."[72]

The important Taoist writer Tao Hongjing (456–536) also ties together tea and the Master of Cinnabar Mound. In his *Separate Account of Famous Medicines* (*Mingyi bielu*), he writes, "Tea (*mingcha*) makes the body light and changes the bones. In the past, Danqiuzi, Lord of Yellow Mountain, ingested it." A variant of this brief statement is also quoted in the *Classic of Tea*.[73] In short, then, Jiaoran's poetic allusions to "Danqiu the feathered person" no doubt consciously hearken back to these earlier references to Cinnabar Mound, the Master of that name, and to tea itself. Likewise, when Lu Tong wrote his famous poem about seven cups of tea he was drawing on earlier traditions about tea being a kind of elixir that had the ability to transform the body into that of a transcendent—making the body light and changing the bones.

Shan Daokai (mid-fourth century) is hard to characterize as either Buddhist or Taoist in orientation—although his biography appears in the Buddhist collection *Biographies of Eminent Monks* (*Gaoseng zhuan*), it contains elements that mark him as someone with an interest in dietetics and longevity. It perhaps makes most sense, therefore, to discuss him here alongside Taoists with similar interests. In any case, Lu Yu's account of this figure and his relation to tea is not taken from a source that belongs to a particular religious tradition, but rather is adapted from the *Biographies of Those Skilled in Arts* (*Yishu zhuan*) in the official history *Book of Jin* (*Jin shu*):

> Shan Daokai of Dunhuang did not fear heat or cold. He regularly con-
> sumed small stones. The drugs he consumed included the *qi* of pine,
> cassia and honey; as for the rest he took tea or thyme and nothing else.[74]

Who was Shan Daokai and why should anyone have been interested in his diet? The earliest complete account of Shan Daokai's life that we have comes from *Record of Signs from the Unseen Realm* (*Mingxiang ji*), a collection of pro-Buddhist miracle tales compiled in the late fifth century by Wang Yan (b. ca. 454, fl. late fifth–early sixth century).[75] This source discusses Shan's dietary habits in several places, but does not confirm his use of tea. Shan, we are told,

> sought to be poor and lived in rugged mountain valleys, where he ab-
> stained from grain and food (*gushi*). He had previously subsisted on
> flour (*mian*), but after three years, he ingested only refined pine resin.
> After thirty years, he just occasionally swallowed small pebbles. By
> swallowing these small stones, he constantly abstained from alcohol,
> meats, and various fruits. If he suffered from wind or cold, he just
> chewed on pepper or ginger. His *qi* was faint and his strength was weak,
> but his complexion was fresh and glossy.[76]

Later in the biography (which probably drew on multiple sources), we read,

> Abstaining from grains for seven years, he often used various medi-
> cines. The medicines included the *qi* of pine resin and *fuling*.

Shan Daokai was reputed to have lived more than one hundred years and his body was said to have naturally mummified after he died. These achievements account for the interest shown in his diet by his biographies. This person was associated with special foodstuffs (notably the ingestion of minerals), and the biographies are careful to identify the substances he consumed (pepper, ginger, pine resin, etc.). But, as we can see, the sources do not always include tea among the named elements of his diet. The inclusion of Shan Daokai in Lu Yu's materials therefore suggests an interest in making connections between tea drinking and a famous practitioner of longevity, even though the references were scarcely sufficient to support such a claim.

As we can see then, evidence for connections between transcendents and tea is somewhat scattered, but we may certainly detect a conscious trend on the part of writers such as Lu Yu and Jiaoran to put the two elements together. This trend is a significant part of the manner in which Lu Yu and other cultural engineers of the eighth century, such as the poets we will examine in Chapter Four, consciously brought religious and cultural value into their presentation of tea. It was not just a beverage that had a short-term effect on a single drinker, but was potentially transformative for an entire society.

TEA AS A MONKS' BEVERAGE

We know that the sources indicate a relationship between Buddhism and tea that existed by the eighth century, but to what extent were Chinese Buddhist monks "early adopters" of tea? There is, in fact, no evidence for tea drinking by Buddhist monastics in the canonical materials to which we normally turn for information on the social and cultural history of Buddhism. Collections of documents concerned with the propagation of the religion such as *Hongming ji* and *Guang Hongming ji,* encyclopedias like *Fayuan zhulin,* and even catalogs of scripture like *Kaiyuan shijiao lu* (*Record of Teachings* of the Kaiyuan reign period) do not mention tea. In fact, such early anecdotal material as there is may be found only outside the Buddhist canon in sources such as the *Classic of Tea.*

Although the cases we have considered so far in this chapter have mostly been concerned with extraordinary functions of tea—as an elixir or a semimagical substance—some of Lu Yu's historical examples merely show the quotidian uses of tea by religious figures. Such is the case of the Liu-Song dynasty monk Fayao whose biography is cited in the *Classic of Tea* from a collection of monastic biographies. We learn from it little more than the fact that he drank tea in his old age.[77]

In another anecdote relating to the Liu-Song dynasty we may discern the earliest glimmerings of aesthetic judgments about tea made in the context of gatherings that featured members of both the saṃgha and the ruling elite. In this account, aristocrats are depicted paying a visit to an eminent monk (the sobriquet *daoren,* or "Man of the Way," was commonly applied to Buddhist monks) and then exclaiming over the otherworldly taste of the tea they are served. Such scenes were to become commonplace in the later anecdotal literature of tea, so it is worth quoting this early example in full:

Records of the Song (*Song lu*) says,[78] "The Prince of Xin'an, Ziluan,[79] and the Prince of Yuzhang, Zishang[80] paid a visit to the Man of the

Way Xuanji at Bagong shan (Eight Worthies Mountain).[81] When the Man of the Way offered tea (*chaming*), Zishang tasted it and said, "This is sweet dew! How can you say it is just tea?"[82]

Some important aspects to the history of tea are worth noting in these few lines. The aristocrats journey far to visit the monk, rather than the other way around, and the site of their interaction is a mountain. The aesthetic concept of consuming tea in a mountain setting with an eminent monk is one that came to the fore in Tang literature, but appears already to have been taking shape in earlier times. In this brief account we also see the use of religious language to talk about tea. It is worth pausing to reflect on the range of meanings possessed by "sweet dew" (*ganlu*) in medieval times. Sweet dew was a highly symbolic substance in traditional China.[83] An early reference may be found in the *Laozi*: "Heaven and Earth were in harmony, therefore sweet dew descended."[84] The descent of this substance was taken as an auspicious sign that the cosmos was responding to virtuous rule, but the dew was also an elixir that if consumed could bring immortality. These two aspects of sweet dew are nicely conveyed in the sixth-century *Illustrations of Auspicious Omens* (*Ruiying tuji* by Sun Rouzhi):

> When dew is dense, it is sweet dew; if the sovereign displays virtue and benevolence, sweet dew will descend on the grass and on the vegetation. If sweet dew is fresh and scented and descends sweet, grass and trees will flourish. If you consume it, it will confer longevity on you.[85]

In medieval Chinese iconography, sweet dew was depicted as being received by immortals, either in a vessel or in their bare hands.[86] The appearance of sweet dew was a standard omen of true government and thus diligently recorded in medieval literature, but the term *ganlu* was also employed as the standard translation in Buddhist texts for *amṛta,* the nectar of the gods that prevents aging and death and, by extension, a common metaphor for the Buddha's teachings. Perhaps sweet dew was merely employed as a poetic term for tea, but the associations behind the term do point to a tendency to attribute to tea the highest cultural and religious values available.

These passing notices of Buddhist monks consuming tea found in the *Classic of Tea* offer little in the way of hard data for the widespread use of tea in Buddhist communities. They may, however, signal some important directions in the later trajectory of the aesthetic and cultural construction of tea as a rare comestible that needed to be appreciated in the company of learned connoisseurs whether lay or monastic.

Given the presence of tea in these pre-Tang sources, how are we to understand the delay between the discovery of tea in early times and its later diffusion in the eighth century? In fact, a similar lag probably also occurred later with, for example, coffee in Europe.[87] But, as with the rapid boom in Europe of coffee drinking, urban taste in medieval China seems to have changed remarkably quickly.[88]

CONCLUSION

We have confirmed that the pre-Tang terminology for tea is quite unstable and that it is not possible to do any better than Lu Yu in constructing a comprehensive narrative for the early development of tea. What we have instead is a series of unconnected episodes, most of them compiled by Lu Yu in his *Classic of Tea.* The authenticity and reliability of sources that were not compiled by Lu Yu, such as the *Slave's Contract,* remain open to question. Moreover, any early textual evidence is always subject to interpretation because we cannot be certain exactly what plant, foodstuff, or beverage it refers to. The various *materia medica* may be the most reliable sources of information, but in the end but they do not tell us much about the social reality of tea in early times. Overall, it is most sensible to understand tea as a Tang-dynasty invention and to accept that the prehistory of tea is a tale that is impossible to recover.

Given the lack of references to tea in classical sources, Lu Yu had to piece together a history of tea using materials that were not particularly venerable, but came from the margins of unofficial literature and historiography. He made a bold and ultimately successful move in claiming the ancient culture hero Shennong as the inventor of tea, but a close reading of the available sources shows that there was little to support that claim.

Examining the sources pulled together in Lu Yu's *Classic,* we find a surprising amount of anomaly accounts being deployed to substantiate the history of tea. From these accounts we can see that early associations of tea with religious figures are suggestive, but remain diverse and inconsistent. As we shall see in later chapters, however, these were some of the raw materials that were woven into the fabric of tea culture by Lu Yu and his successors. But clearly, the alchemy of culture that provided tea with its religious dimensions was a process that did not really begin until the time of Lu Yu himself. We must move on, then, to look at the specific role played by Buddhism in that process.

3

*Buddhism and Tea during the
Tang Dynasty*

During the eighth and ninth centuries, the drinking habits of Chinese people changed markedly and irrevocably: tea moved into the place previously occupied solely by alcohol. Although this cultural shift is clearly the result of many forces, Buddhist monks and laypeople were at the forefront of attempts to change people's attitudes toward intoxicating substances and were seen by their contemporaries as missionaries for the spread of tea drinking throughout the empire. Alcohol, which was drunk not only for personal pleasure but also to strengthen social bonds as well as for ritual purposes, was faced with a serious rival for the first time in Chinese history.

As we have seen in the previous chapters, up until the middle of the eighth century tea was known only as a minor regional specialty of South China. By the end of the ninth century, however, it had become a vital component in the economy and in everyday life throughout the empire. Buddhists and Taoists had enjoyed a long association with tea in the South, but it was only after Lu Yu's compilation of the *Classic of Tea* and the dissemination of tea drinking by itinerant Buddhist monks that tea culture became widely known and appreciated. The growing popularity of the beverage led eventually to economic developments such as specialist traders in tea, tea monopolies, a tax on tea, and the growth of tea plantations. Medieval writers, stimulated by the new beverage, extolled tea for its ability to fuel long periods of meditation, but they also discovered that, like alcohol, it could provide inspiration for poets and possessed medicinal qualities. As a fashionable and sought-after commodity, tea not only brought with it a certain sobriety and clear-headedness but also profoundly affected networks of knowledge and the very ways in which ideas were exchanged.

The literature of late medieval China reflects both the new enthusiasm for tea and an anxiety about the dangers of alcohol and intoxication. In this chapter we shall sample a variety of texts of different genres to see how Buddhist ideas both drove and were affected by this cultural shift.

In some ways it is possible to see attitudes to alcohol in Tang society as a line that strictly demarcated Buddhism from native traditions: Buddhists—laypeople as well as monks—vowed not to consume alcohol, and this vow formed an important and consistent part of their identity, even if individuals sometimes failed to maintain it.[1] Buddhist attitudes toward tea were much more positive, and although they did not erase the Buddhist distinction of abstention from alcohol, they decisively moved the cultural discourse away from negative characterizations of alcoholic intoxication toward eulogies on the multiple benefits of tea. The broad adoption of tea drinking seems to have spread remarkably rapidly from the composition of the *Classic of Tea* in about 760 to the first tax on tea in 780; within a couple of decades tea had grown from the drink of Southerners and Buddhists into a daily necessity and a major commodity throughout the empire.

The role of religion in this rapid change is apparent even in the life of the *Classic of Tea*'s author, as we shall see in a later chapter. Lu Yu was an orphan and was brought up by a Buddhist monk.[2] In his youth he was a member of a troupe of entertainers, and his first literary production was a joke book that he compiled. As he devoted himself to his more sober work on tea, he became part of a literary circle that included the monk-poet Jiaoran. So influential was the *Classic of Tea* in spreading tea drinking throughout the empire that, as already noted, Lu Yu was later celebrated as the God of Tea (*chashen*) and tea dealers made clay effigies of him.[3] In the Song dynasty, Buddhist historiographers claimed him as a devout layman, and his biography was included in a major comprehensive history of Buddhism in China.[4]

From a variety of surviving poetry and prose of the middle to late Tang period, we know that tea could be invested with great religious and cultural significance. But to appreciate the multifarious ways in which tea was understood in the medieval world we must cut across a broad range of literary materials: elite and popular poetry, plays, treatises, official and private histories, liturgical texts, and monastic regulations. In the realms of knowledge exchange and aesthetics, the new commodity had a particularly noticeable effect. The aristocratic drinking party, the primary locus for intellectual and cultural exchange among the elite, had previously effectively excluded monks and devout laypeople from participating because of the precept against alcohol. Although complete abstinence from alcohol by lay Buddhists was rare, there was widespread acknowledgment that the precept was intended to be observed.[5] Tea drinking, however, allowed monks and literati to meet on the same field and to share in the same aesthetic values, unthreatened by the dangers of intoxication. Their collaboration was driven less perhaps by desire for the physiological effects of tea than by a self-consciously new and sophisticated aesthetic. Monks and scholars thus discovered and promoted a mutually acceptable common ground in their new drug of choice—a popular and effective stimulant with few side effects. Although tea could be (and was) cultivated in sufficient volume for relatively large-scale, low-cost consumption, it was presented in literature as a rare commodity with special appeal to connoisseurs. Tang writings about tea credited the drink with providing the inspiration and energy necessary both for composing poetry and for meditation. Because the rise of tea was paralleled by the emergence of new and distinctive modes of Buddhist practice and rhetoric that featured poetry and meditation, the two eventually became intertwined in the cultural imagination, and tea drinking was later understood to be almost synonymous with Chan Buddhism.

The documents we shall consider in this chapter all touch on aspects of the transformation of Chinese society from one centered almost exclusively on alcohol to one that was also based on tea. Yet no single one of these documents describes this "alchemy of culture" as it occurs; rather, we must patiently put together the story from the mosaic-like pieces. Although Buddhists might not have consciously pledged themselves to transform the drinking habits of the empire, they were closely involved in this process every step of the way. Buddhism was the shared belief of many writers of Tang-dynasty temperance tracts, and so close was the connection between tea and Chan Buddhism that they became, for some at least, almost indistinguishable. By the twelfth century at the latest, Chan monastic codes contained lengthy rules that specified exactly how to conduct tea ceremonies for distinguished visitors.

Although one could certainly approach the topic of the Buddhist influence on beverage culture from the perspective of the *longue durée,* it might be worthwhile to begin with a close look at a single medieval document. By doing so, we may see how some medieval people regarded the two beverages of alcohol and tea and what cultural and religious values, both positive and negative, were associated with each.

A DEBATE BETWEEN MR. TEA AND MR. ALCOHOL

Chajiu lun—the title might also be translated as "a discussion of tea and alcohol"—takes the form of a verbal battle between the two characters of Mr. Tea and Mr. Alcohol. Each competes to show why he is the superior beverage, until a third party unexpectedly enters the arena and wins the debate. The text was evidently a popular work and was not transmitted as part of the higher literary canon, but it shares many characteristics with a now somewhat obscure genre of medieval writing known as "hypothetical discourse" (*shelun*). Hypothetical discourses, about which Dominik Declercq has written so eloquently, are serious dialogically structured texts in which authors defend themselves against interlocutors who accuse them of lack of engagement in public life.[6] *Chajiu lun*, as we shall see, is rather less earnest, but certainly draws on conventions established by more formal types of essay like the *shelun*.

A Debate Between Mr. Tea and Mr. Alcohol survives only by chance, among a small number of manuscripts recovered from the Buddhist monastic library preserved in the Dunhuang caves.[7] We know nothing about the author, Wang Fu, save that according to the preface he was nominated by the local government as a candidate for the advanced scholar degree (*xianggong jinshi*). He was, then, a person of some status in Dunhuang society and was probably conversant with the fundamental texts of the medieval literary tradition. This short text seems to be Wang's only extant work, and although it is not dated, evidence concerning the types of tea mentioned in *Chajiu lun* makes it likely that it was composed some time between 780 and 824.[8] Interestingly, *Chajiu lun* has a later and much longer Tibetan counterpart, "Tea and Chang [Tibetan Beer]," the author of which apparently lived around 1726.[9]

After a brief preamble in which the author sets the scene for the verbal joust, Mr. Tea begins the debate by throwing down the gauntlet:

> All of you, don't make a row and listen to me a little! I am the chief of the hundred herbs and the heart of the ten thousand plants. I am called Mingcao and named Cha (Tea). People send me as tribute to the houses of the five marquises, and present me as a gift to the families of emperors and kings. From time to time I am offered to [the court] and all my life I enjoy prosperity and splendor. Naturally, I am the superior and honorable, and what need is there to say anything else in praise of my merits?[10]

Let us ponder Mr. Tea's opening salvo. His claim to supremacy rests first and foremost on his exalted position in the herbal kingdom. He is the chief herb, the master of plants. Perhaps because of his status, tea is a costly gift that is suitable not merely for the nobility but also for the imperial court itself. Mr. Tea's claim is no idle boast, but accords with what other contemporary authors said about the value of tea in late Tang times. The contemporary miscellany *Mr. Bai's Six Tablets* (*Bai shi liutie*), for example, says of tea that it is not for common people, but is suitable tribute for an emperor.[11] Indeed, although the real age of imperial tea connoisseurship did not begin until the early eleventh century, even nomadic rulers were apparently knowledgeable devotees of

Chinese tea by the early ninth century, and certainly Tang emperors were receiving tea sent to the court as tribute.[12]

> Mr. Changlu was sent as emissary to Tibet, and was brewing tea in his tent.
>   Btsan-po (Tibetan king) asked, "What is this?" Mr. Chang replied, "This clears away one's worries and slakes one's thirst: it is called 'tea.'"
>   Btsan-po said, "I also have this," and he ordered his own to be brought out.
>   Pointing at [each variety] he said, "This is from Shouzhou, this is from Shuzhou, this is from Guzhou, this is from Qimen, this is from Changming and this is from Yonghu."[13]

This event was said to have taken place in the year 781 under Emperor Dezong (742–805), and a corresponding entry from the *Record of Things Seen and Heard by Mr. Feng,* written between 785 to 805, states,

> [Tea] originated in the central plains but has now been brought beyond the frontier. When the Uighurs came to court in previous years, they would drive herds of precious horses to exchange for tea that they brought back with them.[14]

Both of these accounts, official and private, from around the same period of Tang history affirm that, by the late eighth century, tea was already a much desired commodity among the other ethnic groups that surrounded the Tang, not to mention the people within the empire itself.

Alcohol: History, Ritual, Drinking Games

Mr. Tea argues initially from his position as a luxury comestible. Although he does not mention the fact, we have seen in earlier chapters that this status was one that tea had acquired relatively recently. Mr. Alcohol's response, in contrast, stresses his venerable antiquity, marshaling episodes from Chinese history to parade in his defense:

> What a ridiculous speech! From ancient times till now, tea has been disdained while alcohol has been honored. After a goblet of wine had been sprinkled in the river, soldiers of the three armies [of Chu] could all become drunk.[15] When lords and princes drink me they shout, "Long live [the Emperor]!" When the various courtiers drink me they address superiors without fear.[16] I pacify the dead and settle the living,

and the deities are illuminated by my pleasing pneumas. When people are entertained with alcohol and food, bad intentions are always absent. [When people drink] alcohol, there are drinking games that reveal benevolence, righteousness, propriety, and wisdom (*ren, yi, li, zhi*)![17]

Mr. Alcohol's spirited response appeals to a set of virtues that any competent medieval essayist should have been able to work into his writing: historical precedent, the principles of true kingly government, and the positive power of ritual in maintaining human harmony. While not delving all the way back in time to the mythical origins of alcohol, he claims that strong drink has been an actor in the great dramas of the past.[18] The medieval logic that forms the deep structure of Mr. Alcohol's argument would hold that anything (positive) belonging to antiquity ought to be, by that very fact, worthy of veneration.

We can infer that, although tea may be a suitable tribute product, it is alcohol that actually allows imperial government to function. Mr. Alcohol suggests, on the one hand, that rulers are more amenable to advice and remonstrance from their officials if they have had a drink. Those same officials, on the other hand, need alcohol with which to toast their emperor's health and so make a public show of their loyalty. The claim concerning the receptiveness of the emperor to criticism may have just been a generalized hope, but there were certainly well-known instances of large-scale drinking to the health of emperors. For example, when Han emperor Gaozu (r. 206–195 BCE) restored order in the empire, all his subjects toasted his health for a day.[19]

Significantly, Mr. Alcohol makes a strong claim for the vital importance of alcohol in rituals for the dead. The use of alcohol in a ritual context is attested in the oldest written sources that we have for China, and the practice continued to be maintained in the medieval period. In the oracle bone inscriptions, alcohol appears to be the only liquid that was offered—in conjunction with a variety of animal sacrifices—to deities and ancestors.[20] As he points out, deities were thought to delight in the vapors or pneuma arising from the offerings of meat and alcohol placed on the sacrificial altar. For medieval families, alcohol was a necessity for the correct performance of rituals to their departed members.[21] It is telling that Mr. Alcohol explicitly links the power to pacify the dead and the ability to settle the living. If we reflect on how alcohol was used in traditional China (and indeed elsewhere) to reinforce social bonds and create a sense of community, it is clear that these two aspects are intimately related not only theoretically but also in practice.

As for the "drinking games" that Mr. Alcohol mentions at the end of this passage, they were well known in Tang China, although whether they did indeed reveal four of the five cardinal Confucian virtues (benevolence, righteousness, propriety, and wisdom), as he claims, is perhaps open to question. Yet this claim is not completely groundless; in addition to texts on drinking, we know from Tang artifacts that alcohol, literature, and elegant conversation were often combined. The popular, yet refined, game of *Analects* Jade Candle (*Lunyu yuzhu*)—in which participants determined their drinking quota by the selection of lots containing passages from the sayings of Confucius—offers a case in point.[22] Perhaps the *Chajiu lun* is referring to this very game, because it speaks of drinking games that reveal four virtues particularly associated with Confucius. Many of the features of aristocratic drinking parties in medieval times were adopted and adapted from the customs of earlier ages, and displays of literary erudition and spontaneous poetry composition were the order of the day.[23] As Donald Harper notes in his study of *Analects* Jade Candle, many of the rules of Tang drinking games were lost by the Song dynasty, so perhaps the pleasures of refined social drinking were indeed accorded less weight in post-Tang elite society as tea connoisseurship became a more significant mode of social interaction.[24]

The sole surviving Tang work on drinking customs is a treatise by the ninth-century writer Huangfu Song, *Days and Months in the Realm of Drunkenness* (*Zuixiang riyue*).[25] Huangfu's work contains such useful practical advice as how to build an Inebriation Tower (*zui lou*). The need to make a tall wooden structure up which one might clamber to enjoy the view and escape the mundane world without the inconvenience of climbing a mountain perhaps indicates the persistence of some ancient tropes of shamanic flight in the more sophisticated aristocratic environment of the Tang.[26] In any case, as Mr. Alcohol shows us, in medieval times the ritual functions of alcohol were not sharply distinguished from its social pleasures.

Tea as a Luxury Product

The next stage of Mr. Tea's argument is based on the rarity and price of tea as a luxury product: he says that people cross mountain ranges to obtain it, and tea merchants are so rich that they can purchase slaves and concubines, while others store the precious tea powder in gold and silk containers. The transports of the tea merchants are so heavily laden with tea that they cause a tremendous din.[27] Again, Mr. Tea seems to be insisting that he is superior for purely economic reasons. In other words, tea should be regarded as a precious commodity because it is one. It is the inherent value of tea that drives people to obtain it, cultivate it, and move it across the empire.

Famous Brands of Liquor

Mr. Alcohol responds to this depiction of the hustle and bustle of the medieval tea trade with the names of famous medicinal tonics (Zhou, Ganhe ["Continuous Harmony"], Boxing ["Extensive Happiness"], Boluo, Putao, and Jiuyun); brews that are drunk exclusively by immortals ("Jade" [Yu] and "Amber Sap" [Qiongjiang]) or emperors ("Chrysanthemum Flowers" [Juhua] and "Bamboo Leaves" [Zhuye]); and the liquor that made the Lord of Zhao drunk for three years. He reiterates the claim about the social role of alcohol, saying that it is offered to neighbors to show courtesy and is served at the headquarters of an army to resolve differences. Moreover, he claims that these uses have been attested since antiquity.

Buddhism and Tea

To this speech, Mr Tea replies,

> I, Mingcao, am the heart of the ten thousand plants. I am either as white as jade or as yellow as gold. Famous monks, "great worthies" (*dade, bhadantas* or elder monks) and recluses in groves of meditation (*chanlin,* monasteries) all take me while making discourses, for I can clear away their dullness and weariness. I am offered to [the future Buddha] Maitreya and dedicated to [the Bodhisattva] Guanyin. Over the course of a thousand or even ten thousand *kalpas* the various buddhas are pleased with me. Alcohol can destroy families and break up homes and generally cause lascivious and depraved behavior.[28]

In this passage, Buddhism is explicitly associated with tea in a number of ways. First, Mr. Tea reiterates his claims about tea being the chief among plants and its inherent value as reflected in its visual similarity to precious substances such as gold and jade. Next, he attributes some special functions to tea—it keeps monks awake, and it is a particularly appropriate liquid offering to buddhas and bodhisattvas (he names Maitreya and Guanyin, both of whom had significant cults of devotion in medieval times). Firm textual evidence for the latter practice in the Tang has proved surprisingly scarce, although it is certainly true for later times, and the material proof that we have is perhaps not as convincing as some have claimed.[29] We can find one roughly contemporary example of offerings of tea on Buddhist altars in the travel diary of the Japanese monk Ennin (794–864), who was in China from 838 to 847. He makes quite a few references to drinking tea in monasteries and elsewhere and frequently mentions tea as a gift given by or to monks or as a commodity for barter (for example, Ennin complains at one point that he paid a pound of tea for some soy sauce and vegetables "but they were not fit to eat").[30] On the one hand, Ennin tells us nothing about methods of drinking tea or about any monastic tea ceremonies he may have witnessed. On the other hand, he offers important evidence about the ritual offering of tea when he describes a Buddhist ceremony held at the monastery Zhulin si on Mount Wutai in 840:

> In response to the invitation we went to the ritual place and saw the religious arrangements for worship. Along the walls inside the hall were placed in order the portraits of the seventy-two sages and saints. Valuable banners and jewels in all the beautiful colors of the world were spread out and displayed, and carpets of varied colors covered the whole floor. Flowers, lamps, fine incense, tea, medicines, and food had been placed in offering to the saints.[31]

We can see then that, at this major monastic site, tea had taken its place among standard appropriate offerings (flowers, lamps, incense) to buddhas, bodhisattvas, and deities. Mr. Tea's claims about the Buddhist roles for tea seem to reflect reality and are not just idle boasts.

As for Mr. Tea's assertion of the ability of tea to stave off sleep and its utility in doing so for Buddhist monks in particular, these qualities had already been noted by the earliest observer of tea as a national drink rather than a regional specialty. It was during the Kaiyuan period (713–742) that this significant association between Chan monks and tea was first made. In *Record of Things Seen and Heard by Mr. Feng* (a source from which I have quoted before) we read,

> Southerners like to drink [tea], but at first few northerners drank it. In the Kaiyuan reign period there was Master Demon-Queller (Xiangmo) of Lingyan si on Mount Tai (in present-day Shandong).[32] He strongly propagated the teaching of Chan. In the study of meditation he emphasized not sleeping, and also not eating in the evening. So he allowed all [his followers] to drink tea. People adopted it from them, and everywhere they boiled and drank [tea].[33]

According to this contemporary witness, then, tea was definitely a novelty in the North until one Chan monk started the craze for the drink as part of the austere religious training that he imposed on his disciples. It is possible that Xiangmo Zang inherited his interest in tea from Chan masters who were originally from the South where tea had long been popular, such as his own master Shenxiu (ca. 606–706) who had resided on Mount Dangyang in Jiangling (near modern Jiangling City in Hubei Province).[34] The famous tea of the time called "Southern wood" (nanmu) was a product of that same area.[35]

Thus, Mr. Tea links together the benefits of tea—which he conceives of in Buddhist terms—with the beginnings of his argument against alcohol (alcohol is detrimental to family life), which we shall see him develop.

Tea as an Unhealthy Drink

Mr. Alcohol counters—perhaps in response to Mr. Tea's earlier claim about the intrinsic value of the drink—that tea is in fact a cheap commodity when compared to wine. He says that a big jar of tea is worth only three cash. He continues to stress the venerable antiquity of alcohol and its use in great banquets and entertainments of the past. No one, he says, would be willing to sing and dance for just a cup of tea. Then, perhaps rather surprisingly, he switches his attack on tea to the realm of health. He warns of the dire consequences of overdosing on tea:

> To drink tea is only to get backache. [If one] drinks too much, one will be sick in the stomach. If one drinks ten cups in a single day one's intestines will be like a drum. If one were to drink it for three years one would certainly be repaid with the appearance of a frog with abdominal dropsy.[36]

Although green tea is almost universally regarded as healthy these days, it seems that in Tang times Mr. Alcohol was not the only one to denounce the new substance as an inherently dangerous drug liable to cause bloating and other health problems when taken to excess. An anecdotal collection, *New Tales of the Great Tang* (*Da Tang xinyu*), informs us that the Right Rectifier of Omissions Wu Jiong (fl. ca. 726) wrote a "Preface Against the Drinking of Tea" (*Dai yincha xu*), some time during the Kaiyuan period.[37] Although the work sadly no longer exists, an abstract survives, which begins thus:

> [Tea] cleans out what is stagnant or blocked up, but the benefit lasts only for a single day and is only temporary. It weakens the *qi* and violates the essence (*jing*) so that the accumulation of harm to the body is indeed great. If [people] obtain any improvement [in their health] they attribute it to the power of tea, but if there is some misfortune, they don't say it is the fault of the tea. Isn't it rather that when good

fortune is close at hand it is easy to realize it, but when ill-fortune comes
who [dares] see it or speak of it?[38]

Although Wu Jiong and Mr. Alcohol attribute slightly different symptoms
to tea drinking (weakening of *qi* and damage to the essence as opposed to abdominal bloating), they are equally vehement in their characterization of tea
as a dangerous substance.

The Dangers of Intoxication

As the debate continues, Mr. Tea again boasts of his fame and fortune and then
takes the argument to Mr. Alcohol with accusations about the intoxicating
effects of strong drink:

> You, Mr. Alcohol, make people intoxicated and muddled. Having
> drunk alcohol, people become garrulous. In front of commoners on
> the street at least seven out of ten drinkers ride home on the backs of
> [their friends].[39]

But Mr. Alcohol, in his reply to these charges, keeps the discussion away
from intoxication and places it squarely in the realm of culture, returning again
to his themes of history and ritual. He claims that the sayings passed down
from antiquity credit alcohol with the ability to nourish life, drive away worry,
and cultivate wisdom. He repeats his assertion that tea costs less than alcohol
(three cash for five bowls as opposed to seven cash for half a glass). Alcohol is
necessary for courteous treatment of one's guests. He adds that alcohol is vital
for the correct performance of music at state functions, saying "if [the musi-
cians] drank tea all morning, they [would not] dare to touch their instruments
even a little."[40]

Mr. Tea concludes his argument by pointing out some types of human behavior associated with drunkenness. He says that men do not go to drinking
establishments until they are fourteen or fifteen (presumably implying that alcohol is an acquired taste). He alludes to contemporary stories about the gibbon (*xingxing* or *shengsheng*) that lost its life because of its weakness for alcohol.[41] He disputes the charge that tea causes illness and says rather that alcohol
causes drinking diseases. Citing another Buddhist example, he refers to King
Ajātaśatru, crown prince of Magadha at the time of the Buddha and son of King
Bimbisāra, who killed his parents because of alcohol.[42]

On account of alcohol, Mr. Tea says disapprovingly, Liu Ling (d. after 265)
became drunk for three years. Liu was one of the Seven Sages of the Bamboo

Grove and author of the famous poem "Eulogy on the Virtues of Wine" (*Jiu de song*).[43] Finally, Mr. Tea concludes with more everyday examples. Ultimately, he says, the drunkard ends up under arrest:

> The magistrate will ask him to pay some fines. The big cangue is put round his neck and the timbers on his back. Then he will burn incense [promising] to give up alcohol. He will repeat the name of the Buddha and beg Heaven for mercy.[44]

Mr. Tea appears to strike hard with a message that combines tea drinking with temperance. But in the end the argument is won by neither Mr. Tea nor Mr. Alcohol. The conflict is resolved by the appearance of Mr. Water, who proclaims his superiority both as one of the Four Elements (interestingly, he refers to the Buddhist concept of the four gross elements [*sida*] rather than the native tradition of five agents [*wuxing*]) and also as the source of both tea and alcohol. Mighty though he is, however, he says,

> I do not call myself capable and sainted, so what need is there for both of you to argue about your merits? From now on, you must be friendly and cooperative, so that wine shops will be prosperous, while tea houses will not be poor . . . and if people read this text they would never suffer from being mad with alcohol or tea![45]

So, Mr. Water offers a viable "third way" between alcohol and tea, one in which the commercial health of the empire is assured, while people avoid the dangers of overindulgence in either beverage.

In the *Chajiu lun*, Buddhist doctrines and practices underlie many of the arguments that Mr. Tea makes against drinking alcohol. Although statements that condemn drinking to excess can be found in the Confucian Classics, any larger concept of "temperance" in medieval China is most likely to have been of Buddhist inspiration.[46] Before we can assess the Buddhist impact on Chinese drinking culture we need to get some sense of the roles of alcohol in medieval society.

THE CULTURE OF ALCOHOL IN MEDIEVAL CHINA

Although alcohol has certainly contributed to European cultural history, there is probably no equivalent in the Western canon of a group of esteemed culture heroes such as the Seven Sages of the Bamboo Grove, for whom the pursuit of intoxication was almost a holy mission.[47] Nor is there a text that equates with what one might call the "alcoholic utopianism" of a work such as Wang Ji's (585–644) *Record of Drunk-Land* (*Zuixiang ji*).[48] In the literature of early medieval China there seems to have been a common association between intoxication and spiritual freedom—exemplified in the "free and easy wandering" extolled by Zhuangzi. As we already noted in our discussion of *Chajiu lun*, alcohol was used in communication with the extra-human world; it was a necessary component of state ritual; and it was also required at rituals for weddings, births, and funerals.[49] Alcohol was offered explicitly so that the spirits should become drunk.[50] Even in the relatively refined language of Tang poetry we catch the occasional echo of the kind of shamanic intoxication that belonged to much earlier manifestations of Chinese religious life. Major poets such as Wang Wei (701–761) and Bai Juyi (772–846), who presented themselves as sincere believers in Buddhism, also wrote numerous poems about the joys of drinking.[51] Bai, in particular, frequently lauded both alcohol and intoxication, although, as we shall see, he also wrote a good deal about tea.[52]

In medieval China, the state occasionally attempted to regulate alcohol manufacture or consumption, although it is impossible to gauge the effects of these measures. Except for a couple of edicts promulgated by the emperors Gaozu in 619 and Suzong (r. 756–762) in 758, regulations concerning alcohol during the Tang were mainly concerned with taxation on alcohol and maintaining the state's alcohol monopoly.[53] In fact, Tang emperors seem to have done more to encourage drinking than to restrict it. Great public drinking festivals called *pu* (bacchanals) that originated in the Han were revived under the Tang to celebrate military victories or the birth of an imperial heir.[54]

If literati-poets, such as the Seven Sages of the Bamboo Grove and their later imitators, distinguished themselves from those who were politically powerful by indulging in heavy drinking and drug taking, then Buddhists in general distinguished themselves by the disciplined control of what they ate and drank. In the aristocratic milieu of the Six Dynasties and the Tang, alcohol not only acted as social lubricant and muse but also provided a common field of interaction for educated men (and, more rarely, for educated women).[55] It was from this arena that Buddhists found themselves excluded by virtue of their precept against alcohol. Buddhists' attitudes to alcohol probably brought them up against non-Buddhist cultural values more than, say, their attitudes toward meat, music, and dancing—all of which were also constrained by their precepts.

Although any assault on alcohol during the Tang came primarily from the Buddhist quarter, one should not entirely rule out other intellectual and religious positions—that of Taoism, for example. It is true that Sima Chengzhen (647–753), Shangqing patriarch and advisor to Emperor Xuanzong (r. 712–55), did caution against alcohol in his *Discourse on Sitting in Oblivion* (*Zuowang lun*), but many other Taoist texts recommend consumption of alcohol in moderation.[56] A search of a representative collection such as *Seven Slips from a Cloudy Satchel* (*Yunji qiqian*)—a Song dynasty compilation of earlier materials—provides no evidence of any coherent and widely attested condemnation of drinking in Taoist sources equal to that found in Buddhist materials. Medieval Taoist prohibitions of alcohol, where they can be found, often seem to be imitations of Buddhist models.[57]

Buddhist Precepts Against Alcohol

The proscription of drinking intoxicating substances is basic to the practice of Buddhism throughout the world. The precept against consuming alcohol is one of the five precepts observed by laypeople (*youpose wujie,* Skt. *upāsaka pañca śīla*): not to kill, not to steal, not to partake in illicit sex, not to lie, and not to drink intoxicating beverages. Rules against drinking also appear in the ten precepts taken by novice monks and nuns, the forty-eight bodhisattva precepts, and the various *vinaya*s intended for monks and nuns. According to the *prātimokṣa* (the rules recited by monks and nuns every fortnight), the consumption of intoxicating liquor by a *bhikṣu* (*biqiu,* ordained monk) was classified as *pātayantika* (*boyeti*; i.e., an offense that requires confession).[58] However, there is evidence that suggests that in fifth-century China there was a certain amount of anxiety concerning both the handling and consumption of alcohol, which meant that this rule was interpreted more harshly than perhaps originally intended. It was the fact that the laity also vowed not to drink that seems to be the cause of problems concerning the classification of the transgression of drinking alcohol for monastics. But, given that the notion of abstinence from alcohol had no native antecedents, it is perhaps not surprising that precepts-scriptures aimed primarily at the laity and produced in China made such a great issue of this particular precept.[59]

What seems to have particularly influenced Chinese Buddhist attitudes toward strong drink were the numerous lists given in scriptures of the karmic consequences that were said to ensue from consuming alcohol. The scriptures place particularly heavy emphasis on the misery to be endured by the drunkard and his or her family in the present life, rather than on punishment in hells and suffering in lives to come. For example, one influential (apocryphal) scripture concerned with precepts for laymen, the *Upāsakaśīla sūtra* (*Youpose jie jing*), lists five losses: loss of wealth, ill health, bad reputation, stupidity and, after death, descent into hell where one suffers "the bitter grief of hunger and thirst without limit."[60] The authoritative compendium of Mahāyāna lore and doctrine in medieval China, *Treatise on the Great Perfection of Wisdom (Dazhidu* lun), lists no less than thirty-five losses, and the apocryphal scripture on precepts for novices *Śramanerikaśīla sūtra* (*Shamini jie jing*) thirty-six, including losing the way (both metaphorically and literally); broken homes; danger to the body; failure to venerate Buddha, dharma, and saṃgha; the inability to chant the scriptures; and being ignorant for successive rebirths.[61]

Legally minded Buddhist authors had to consider every possibility connected with strong drink, even the case of making or accepting a gift of alcohol. The *Daśabhūmikavibhāṣā* (*Shizhu piposha lun*), an important commentary of the ten stages (or *bhūmi*s) of the bodhisattva's career, explains that a bodhisattva may give a drink to someone who needs it, out of charity, but that later he or she should teach the recipient to give up alcohol and to concentrate on developing wisdom instead.[62] But the *Upāsakaśīla sūtra* is less tolerant: "The bodhisattva . . . never gives alcohol, poisons, swords, spears and so on to people no matter whether they have attained self-mastery or not."[63]

The *Scripture of Brahmā's Net* (*Fanwang jing*) is a fifth-century Chinese apocryphon that had wide-reaching influence throughout East Asia.[64] Although the bodhisattva precepts contained therein are generally considered to be more lenient than the precepts of the monastic *Vinaya*, the precept concerning alcohol carries an extremely harsh karmic penalty:

> If, with your own hand, you pass a beaker of alcohol to someone who drinks it, then for the next 500 rebirths you will be born without a hand. So how much worse would it be if you had a drink yourself?[65]

This dire karmic punishment appears in the second of the forty-eight minor precepts of the *Scripture of Brahmā's Net*. The fifth of the ten major precepts (which in imitation of the *Vinaya* are termed "*pārājikas*" [offenses entailing defeat]) is as follows:

> If a disciple of the Buddha trades in alcohol himself or teaches someone else to do so, or is cause, condition, dharma, or karma, of trade in alcohol [he is *pārājika*]. He may not deal in any alcohol whatsoever. This is because alcohol gives rise to the causes and conditions of wrongdoing. A bodhisattva is supposed to induce wisdom in living beings; if on the contrary he produces in living beings a mind which backslides, then this bodhisattva is *pārājika*.[66]

Thus, we can see that in the Chinese version of the bodhisattva precepts, which applied to the laity as much as to the saṃgha, the precept against alcohol carried much more weight than in the Indian *Vinaya* texts, which do not generally discuss karmic penalties. We may suppose that, as with the promotion of vegetarianism in Chinese Buddhism, the laity were actually the impetus for change regarding attitudes to alcohol rather than the monastic community.[67]

This brief survey of the proof texts available to learned medieval Buddhists shows that there was no shortage of material at hand for a campaign against intoxication. Although there were obviously a few loopholes in the regulations, overall the karmic consequences of drinking alcohol were paraded at length and in fairly stark terms. Materials produced in China (as opposed to translated texts) were among the least tolerant in this regard.

Attitudes Toward Alcohol in the Dunhuang Manuscripts

One particular indigenous Buddhist manuscript from Dunhuang, *Great Extended Flower-Ornament Scripture of the Ten Evil Categories* (*Dafangguang huayan shi-e pin jing*) is unequivocal in defining abstention from alcohol as a cardinal virtue of the Buddha's true disciples.[68] Despite the ten categories mentioned in its title, the scripture in fact concentrates on only three evil acts—drinking alcohol, eating meat, and not respecting fast days. It begins by enumerating five means of cultivating virtue: not killing, not behaving licentiously, not drinking alcohol, not eating meat, and always practicing compassion. Then the Bodhisattva Kāśyapa asks the Buddha,

> "Has the world-honored one preached that those who have accepted the Buddha's teaching should not drink alcohol?"
>
> The Buddha replies,
>
> "All those beings who do not drink alcohol, these are my true sons and are not ordinary people but good sons. . . . Those who have received the precepts, whether they received the five precepts, or the two hundred and fifty precepts, or the complete precepts of dignified deportment, none of them are allowed to drink. . . . If a monk or a nun breaks this *prātimokṣa* [rule], then they will go to hell. If a lay person breaks [this rule] and does a wrongdoing which is *duṣkṛta* [a minor misdeed], then they will be in hell for 80,000 kalpas. . . . Those who have received my precepts may not pour drinks for other people, may not enter wine shops, encourage other people to drink, or ferment liquor with others. . . . They may not pour drinks for monks. If they do, then for 500 lifetimes [they will be born] with no arms. They may not ferment liquor with monks. If they do then for 500 lifetimes they will be deaf; their hearing will be cut off; they will never hear sound or speech. If they force a monk to drink they will fall into *raurava* hell."[69]

We can see then, that some members of the medieval Buddhist community were keen to construct the true disciple of the Buddha as someone who
not only did not drink but who also did not participate in the wider culture of
alcohol (they "may not pour drinks for other people, may not enter wine shops,"
etc.). The consequences of doing so were karmically dire and spelled out with
considerable relish—disfigurement, deafness, rebirth in hell.

But were Buddhist monks and laypeople in fact as assiduous in avoiding
alcohol as the prescriptive texts would have us believe, particularly when alcohol was easier to preserve than water and probably often tasted better? The
household accounts of Buddhist monasteries and the statutes of lay societies
preserved among the manuscripts from the oasis town of Dunhuang indicate
that drinking alcohol was not just a vice that was occasionally indulged in by
monks and laypeople. On the contrary, alcohol consumption seems to have
been a significant, even defining feature of the religious practice of lay Buddhist societies and a part of the everyday consumption of a Buddhist monastery, at least at Dunhuang where fresh-tasting springwater might have been
hard to come by.[70]

Communal eating at vegetarian banquets seems to have been the most significant feature of the normative practice of lay Buddhists at Dunhuang. According to ancient custom, participants in these banquets were required to contribute to them. Each member was obliged to attend and to provide specific
quantities of flour, oil, and alcohol. Failure to attend meant that the person would
be fined, usually a measure of alcohol.[71] These societies often included members of the saṃgha, who were apparently subject to the same statutes. The evidence from stele inscriptions, Dunhuang materials, and biographies of monks
shows that these lay associations were a feature of popular religious life from
the fifth century into the Song dynasty.[72]

A number of institutional accounts from four Buddhist monasteries at
Dunhuang have been preserved, and it is possible to reconstruct the monthly
consumption of alcohol for one of them at least.[73] The amount of the annual
budget for alcohol could be as much as 9 percent of the total expenditure.[74] Monasteries at Dunhuang both purchased alcohol and made it themselves. The monastic accounts also record occasions for which alcohol had to be purchased
specially, usually to greet the arrival of senior monks from elsewhere or to receive government officials. Alcohol was consumed on festival days, such as the
Buddha's birthday and the ghost festival. It was also used in religious ceremonies and given to monks in exchange for their labor (physical or spiritual).[75]
These fascinating historical documents reveal that for the monks in some Dunhuang monasteries alcohol was both a daily necessity and appropriate for
special occasions.

In addition to its recreational or social uses, we know that alcohol was employed medicinally in Buddhist monasteries of medieval China.[76] There is plenty of evidence that monks were drinking nonmedicinal alcohol as well.[77] Jōjin, the Japanese monk who visited Northern Song China, records in his diary many occasions on which he drank alcohol in monasteries along with his Chinese colleagues.[78] Alcohol was used in monastic rituals during the Tang and Song, especially the rites of esoteric Buddhism.[79] The alcohol was not only to be used as an offering but also to be consumed by the ritual officiant.[80]

We have seen, then, that the relationship between Buddhism and alcohol was complex. On the one hand, prescriptive and normative texts marked clear boundaries for Buddhist practitioners around the consumption and manufacture of alcohol. But on the other hand, Buddhist institutions and their inhabitants were too closely entwined with the larger society in which alcohol was the social and ritual lubricant to be able to avoid it completely. The tension between these two realities was impossible to resolve without the introduction of a substance that could substitute satisfactorily for alcohol—tea.

BUDDHISM, TEA, AND MATERIAL CULTURE

Evidence from an Early Seventh-Century Painting?

This study has mostly depended on textual sources, but it is possible that the earliest representation of the consumption of tea in a Buddhist monastery is found not in literature, but in a specific painting: *Xiao Yi Trying to Swipe the Lanting Scroll*, attributed to Yan Liben (?–673).[81] It is worth taking some time to examine this painting to see if it can be used as evidence in our exploration of the Buddhist uses of tea.

To understand the scene that this famous painting depicts, we need to know something of the back story. The Tang emperor Taizong (r. 626–649) was a connoisseur of calligraphy. He was keen to acquire Wang Xizhi's (ca. 321–379) famous masterpiece *Lanting ji xu* (*Orchid Pavilion Preface*)—certainly the most renowned piece of calligraphy in China at the time. On three occasions he sent emissaries to request it from Biancai, an elderly monk living in a monastery in South China who was reputed to have possession of it. But each time, Biancai said that it had not survived the wars. Finally, Taizong dispatched Xiao Yi, a grandson of one of the last Southern monarchs, to request it from Biancai. Xiao Yi appeared to Biancai dressed as an ordinary scholar not related to the central government. The two of them got along very well. After a series of visits, Xiao Yi brought out a painting to show Biancai and, during their discussion,

Xiao Yi Trying to Swipe the Lanting Scroll, attributed to Yan Liben (d. 673). Handscroll: ink and color on silk 27.4 × 64.7 cm. Courtesy of National Palace Museum, Taiwan.

told him that he possessed calligraphy by Wang Xizhi. Biancai asked him to bring the pieces the next day, and when he did, Biancai commented, "These are authentic but not of the first rank. I happen to have a truly exceptional work, the original of the *Orchid Pavilion* manuscript." Xiao Yi feigned disbelief, so the next day Biancai took his treasure out of hiding and showed him the original *Orchid Pavilion Preface*. Xiao Yi purposely said that it was a fake, and the two of them got into a heated argument. Irritated, Biancai failed to put the priceless document away before he headed off to participate in a monastic ritual. Xiao Yi took the opportunity, snatched *Orchid Pavilion Preface*, and rode off.

It is not quite clear what moment of the story is depicted in Yan Liben's painting: has Xiao Yi cast off his disguise yet, or is he still working to gain the old monk's trust? Colophons on the painting disagree as to what exactly is happening, although one draws attention to the lifelike way in which the two attendants, at the bottom left of the composition, are depicted. These attendants are shown brewing tea on a stove for the monk Biancai and his guest. We can be fairly sure that it is tea they are making, rather than any other decoction, because on the table next to the two figures is a tea roller that would have been used to crush the leaves to powder. Interestingly, the written source describing the recovery of the manuscript, He Yanzhi's (d. after 722) *Record of Lanting from Beginning to End* (*Lanting shimo ji*), says that Biancai and Xiao Yi drank not only tea but also "medicinal alcohol" together before composing verse.[82]

If this painting is genuinely the work of the early Tang artist Yan Liben, it would show tea being brewed in a monastic setting in the seventh century. That would make it earlier solid evidence for a connection between tea and Bud-

Detail of *Xiao Yi Trying to Swipe the Lanting* Scroll. Courtesy of National Palace Museum, Taiwan.

dhism than the literary proof texts that we have discussed so far. However, Yan probably did not paint it, because the provenance is quite weak—there is no mention of a painting on this subject by Yan until the end of the Northern Song (early twelfth century). Although the painting is old, it probably does not date back further than Song times, and by provenance alone it cannot safely be attributed to the Tang artist. At best it represents a Song painter's idea of a monastic scene in the Tang. It would have been quite plausible to depict a monk and a literatus discoursing together while servants prepared tea for them.

The Imperial Teaware of Dharma-Gate Monastery

Moving away from paintings, let us turn now to material objects and what they might reveal about the religious history of tea. The most famous and historically important selection of early teaware in China is that found in 1987 in the crypt under the pagoda at Dharma-gate monastery (Famen si) about 140 kilometers west of the Tang capital Chang'an, now the city of Xi'an.[83] On August 24, 1981, a portion of the Ming-dynasty brick pagoda at Famen si collapsed. On April 3, 1987, a group of archaeologists examining the foundations of the pagoda discovered an underground crypt.[84] The crypt consists of a steep ramp, leading to an antechamber and three inner chambers, arranged north–south. The crypt, intact since it was sealed in 874, contained more than 400 objects, including more than 120 pieces of metalwork, many of them extremely fine pieces in silver-gilt. Also found there were four finger-bone relics of the Buddha, each encased in a set of reliquaries.

Although there is no real consensus about the purpose of the utensils, some items among the metalwork have been identified as used specifically for the

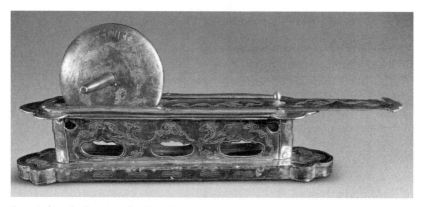

Tea grinder, gilt silver, inscribed 869 CE, 27.5 cm, Famen si, Fufeng, Shaanxi.

Covered basket, ninth century CE, gilt silver, 17.8 cm, Famen si, Fufeng, Shaanxi.

Tea sieve, gilt silver, inscribed 869 CE, 9.8 cm × 14.9 cm; weight
1.47 kg. Famen si, Fufeng, Shaanxi.

making and consuming of tea. Many of these tea utensils are inscribed, so we
know they were made in the imperial workshops in 869. The question is, what
are they doing buried under a Buddhist pagoda, in proximity to a famous finger-
bone relic of the Buddha? The objects identified as items of teaware include
two lidded metalware baskets, one with a design of flying geese on an inter-
locking coin background. These have been described as baskets for drying tea
leaves, although there is no evidence that they were employed for this purpose.[85] There is a metalware stove that has been described as a tea brazier, even
though the original inventory of items in the crypt and the archeological report both describe the object as an incense burner, which seems more likely.[86]
Perhaps related to this brazier (if that is what it is) is a pair of fire tongs.[87] More
likely to have actually been used in preparing tea are a silver-gilt spoon decorated with clouds and lotuses and a silver measure with gold-plated flying geese.[88]
One item that is indubitably connected to tea is the magnificent silver-gilt tea
roller with flying geese and floating clouds.[89] Similar tea rollers may be seen
being used to crush tea leaves to powder in paintings such as the one attributed to Yan Liben.

These truly extraordinary silver-gilt items were among those originally donated by the Tang Emperor Yizong in 873 as part of a particularly intense relic-
enshrinement project.[90] This significant archeological find from 1987 has been
called on as ninth-century evidence for the use of tea in a Buddhist setting
and by some scholars as evidence for the use of tea in specifically esoteric (or
tantric) Buddhist rites. Such a claim is made, for example, in an article on the

Canister, gilt silver, decorated with
dancing figures. 24.7 cm high. Famen si,
Fufeng, Shaanxi.

Famen si teaware by Patricia Karetzky, who writes that "as the many tea-service
objects with Buddhist décor found at Famen suggest, tea drinking was also part
of esoteric Buddhist ritual."[91] In this case, however, the evidence is not sufficient to support claims for an intimate connection between tea and Buddhist
ritual at Famen si. Although the excavated items of teaware are significant for
the history of tea consumption in Tang China, their proximity to Buddha relics alongside so many other items from the imperial household requires that
we consider not their function, but their value. We know from archeological
and textual evidence that people donated all manner of things to relics of the
Buddha because they were precious and personal to the donor, not because of
any ritual function they may have had. Elite Tang women are often described as
making offerings of their silver hairpins, but that fact does not lead us to speak
of "esoteric Buddhist hairpins." Also, it is quite hard to find much "Buddhist
décor" on the objects in question. On Buddhist ritual objects we might expect
to find images of buddhas, bodhisattvas, deities, and vajras. But the Buddhist

Anterior chamber of Famen si crypt, as discovered in 1987.

décor on the teaware seems to amount to no more than a couple of apsarases on the tea sifter.[92] These finely made pieces certainly attest to something—but it is not anything we could identify as an "esoteric Buddhist tea ritual."

Part of the identification of the teaware rests on the assumption, made early on by scholars with regard to this site and uncritically repeated ever since, that the underground chambers at Famen si were laid out like esoteric Buddhist maṇḍala and that the relic crypt should be understood as an esoteric ritual space. Although we can forgive these scholars' enthusiasm for being the first to identify material data for Tang-period Chinese esoteric Buddhism, the evidence for this claim about maṇḍala at Famen monastery is slight.[93]

If the articles of teaware are not ritual items, then what are they? First, let us establish where these pieces were found in the relic-enshrinement crypt. Photographs taken at the excavation in 1987 show that the teaware was part of an unstructured pile of items in the anterior chamber—just what we would expect of a heap of precious donations left close to the relic chamber.[94] The original inventory tablet for the crypt records two sets of offerings by the throne: a first set of 122 items donated in 873 following the arrival of the relic in the capital city, and a second set of 754 items "newly endowed" to mark the return of the relic to the Famen monastery. The first set consists mostly of ritual and ceremonial paraphernalia. The second set, by contrast, consists of caps, shoes, clothing, bedding, games, and other everyday objects, including our tea utensils. The inventory notes how much the items weigh. Obviously weight is not a highly relevant factor when considering ritual function, but it is quite significant when considering the power of donations to relics—one needs to know their worth. In the first instance, these objects are worth their weight in gold and silver, but they were also personal objects for the imperial family—and as such they were given to a relic to make karmic connections, not to be used in ritual. Although we cannot speak of a special esoteric tea offering, we know that, by the late ninth century, the imperial court was using high-quality luxury items of teaware that were so valuable they were offered to relics of the Buddha in the hopes of generating massive amounts of merit for the Tang imperial family.

TEA IN THE TANG BUDDHIST MONASTERY

Because the artistic and archeological evidence for consumption of tea in Tang monasteries has turned out to be somewhat of a red herring, we must turn again to literary sources. A work by the Vinaya master Yijing (635–713), *Essential Methods for Receiving and Using the Three Kinds of Water* (*Shouyong sanshui yaoxing fa*), insists that Buddhist monks use pure water when making medicinal decoctions, sweetened drinks, or tea.[95] We will discuss the consumption of medicinal and tonic decoctions in the monastery in a later chapter. Elsewhere in the same work, Yijing, who spent much time in other parts of Buddhist Asia, noted that monks in India did not drink tea.[96] If that was so, then perhaps he took his own tea with him on his peregrinations, because in his travel diary Yijing writes:

> Tea (*ming*) is also good [in addition to ginseng]. During the more than twenty years since I left my native country, this alone was medicine for my body and I hardly had any serious disease.[97]

Yijing's medicinal use of tea matches well with the presentation of tea in the *materia medica* of around the same period that I noted in the last chapter. One wonders if Yijing introduced any of his Indian colleagues to the beverage or whether he conserved supplies for his own use. Another well-known Tang Vinaya master, Daoxuan (596–667), criticizes wasteful monks who do not finish their tea.[98]

As the historian Liu Shufen has pointed out in a series of important articles, we probably need to understand monastic tea culture not in isolation but rather within the larger context of medicinal decoctions (*tang*) and other tonics consumed in the medieval monastery.[99] We can see this fairly easily if we consider how frequently the term "tea" appears in our monastic sources as part of a compound such as *chayao* (tea and medicine) and the related term *chatang* (tea and decoction).

Biographies of Tang- and Song-dynasty monks and other historical sources reveal quite an array of medicinal beverages consumed in the monastery: lotus leaf decoction (*heye tang*), Chinese yam (or cinnamon vine) decoction (*shuyu tang*), and tangerine-peel decoction (*jupi tang*).[100] Tangerine-peel broth might have honey added to it, so it would have been similar to the kumquat tea (*jinjie cha*) available today that is made from kumquats and honey or rock sugar. During the Tang, in secular society, tangerine-peel decoction was considered beneficial for digestion, and so it is not surprising to find it in the monastery as well. We will learn more about this culture of tea and decoctions in Chapter Six.

BUDDHIST TEA MASTERS

In this book we have encountered some famous personalities associated with the growth of tea culture in Tang times. Some, like Lu Yu and Xiangmo Zang, had Chan connections, and the association of Chan masters with tea is also noticeable for some more obscure figures in the history of tea. For example, the section on tea (*chuanming men*) of *A Record of Things Pure and Strange* (*Qingyi lu*) attributed to Tao Gu (903–970) notes two men with particular tea-related skills.[101] The first was a Chan master called Fujin (or Fuquan, d.u.) of Jinxiang in Shandong who was able to make images appear on the surface of the hot tea, a talent that drew large crowds of onlookers.[102] The second is Wenliao, a monk from the southern kingdom of Wu, who was so good at "cooking tea" (*pengcha*) that he won the admiration and patronage of the southern prince Gao Jixing (fl. 907–924).[103] What is the nature of the skills that were involved here? Another passage in *A Record of Things Pure and Strange* may be of assistance in understanding the context:

> "One Hundred Entertainments of Tea (*cha baixi*):" Tea prospered beginning in the Tang, but in recent times, inferior brews flow and circulate. Aside from that, some have distributed miraculous instructions that can cause currents of liquid in the decoction to form the shapes of creatures, such as birds, beasts, insects and fish, different kinds of flowers and herbs, patterned cleverly like a painting. But after just a moment the images are dispersed. This is tea magic, which contemporary people call "the one hundred entertainments of tea."[104]

What is described here is the art of rapidly drawing images or even writing lines of poetry on the surface of the tea with a brush. The natural oils of the tea and its fine powdered form in hot water allowed for the creation of quite detailed but fleeting images in the tea. This practice has recently been revived, and many examples of the evocative images so produced may be found online.[105] Given the involvement of named Buddhist monks in mastering such techniques, it is interesting to reflect on the ways in which this practice seems to emphasize a Buddhist view of the illusory, temporary, and conditioned nature of reality.

TAOISM AND TEA

It was not only Buddhist monks and monasteries that had a connection with tea. We can also find mentions of tea in the Taoist institutional record. For example, the *Minor Record of the Southern Marchmount* (*Nanyue xiaolu*) by Li Chongzhao records the history of the Southern Marchmount up to the late ninth/early tenth century.[106] There we read an account of a Taoist monastery ("abbey") located on the Marchmount and the use of tea in its fundraising efforts:

> Abbey of the Nine Perfected (Jiuzhen guan): During the Kaiyuan reign period of the Tang, there lived Celestial Master Wang Xianqiao (d. 759).[107] At first, when the Celestial Master was a practitioner-novice, his dao-nature was empty and bright and he possessed an extraordinary determination. Hence, he took from the Marchmount more than two hundred bricks of tea to the capital; he carried a tea container into the city walls to make charity through tea. Suddenly, one day he encountered strongman Gao (684–762).[108] When Gao saw him he realized he was special and inquired whence he had come. Wang replied, "I am a practitioner-novice from Nanyue, and now the roof of the Abbey of Nine Perfected, where I live, has collapsed. So I have brought tea to sell and recruit donors for it."[109]

Gao arranged for Wang to have an audience with Emperor Xuanzong who sent him back to Nanyue with lavish gifts. The roof of the abbey was repaired as Wang had intended.[110] This brief anecdote from a Taoist collection offers a nice example of the practical benefits of tea for religious institutions. By the mid-eighth century, Buddhists and Taoists alike had learned that there was money to be made for their institutions by selling tea. Over time, it tended to be Buddhist monasteries that benefited most consistently from the tea trade.

Aside from this example, there is not a great deal of specific evidence to show that Taoists were quite as closely associated with tea as their Buddhist counterparts. However, we do know, for example, that the court made gifts of tea to Taoist monastics, as it did to Buddhists.[111]

As we shall see in the next chapter, Tang tea culture had a marked effect on the literary arts, especially poetry, but it also influenced the visual arts. Here is a fascinating description (from a work by one of Lu Yu's associates) of the psychotropic effects of tea intoxication and the religious vision (or hallucinations?) that it affords one Taoist artist. This comes from a work found in the Taoist canon, *Master of Mysterious Truth*, (*Xuanzhen zi*) compiled by the poet and landscape artist Zhang Zhihe (730–810).[112] Zhang describes an encounter he had with the artist Wu Sheng:

> Wu Sheng was skilled at the art of painting demons. While drunk with laughing he bowed to the Master of Mysterious Truth and poured alcohol in his goblet; while drunk on alcohol, he bowed to the Master of Mysterious Truth and poured tea in his cup. He spoke of his method of painting demons, saying "What is my method? I have the *dao,* that's all. Once when drunk on tea, in the middle of the night I could not sleep, I had a pure spirit and pure thoughts/concerns, I let go of the existence of the ten thousand things, and forgot about even a single thought."[113]

As with some poetic representations of the creative power of tea, we see that the beverage is credited with a power similar to that of alcohol. It makes the artist "drunk" while simultaneously allowing him to become one with the *dao,* move beyond discursive thought, and access the true wellspring of creativity. This was a powerful claim for a relatively new substance.

CONCLUSION

In many ways then, it seems as if Mr. Alcohol was right when he claimed that he was integral to traditional Chinese culture. At least in Dunhuang, it seems that monks and devout laypeople still needed alcohol no matter how much they might have condemned it. Nevertheless, from the mid-eighth century, tea did offer a stimulating alternative that could be (and often was) unambiguously identified with Buddhism. The promotion of tea was indeed coupled with arguments against alcohol that drew on a large and varied body of Buddhist materials. The influence of Buddhist temperance tracts on the habits of the empire is one possible explanation for the cultural shift, but perhaps the change in Tang drinking habits reflects a larger change in the *zeitgeist*. I suspect that the An Lushan rebellion of 755 may have played a part in the decline of the drunk poet as a cultural role model and the consequent rise of the positive image of the nonworldly, tea-drinking Chan master. Certainly the literati of the late Tang seem less carefree than their earlier counterparts. The terrible bloodshed and dislocation caused by the rebellion and the comparatively brutal life of the ninth century may have sobered up Tang China even more effectively than any Buddhist temperance movement.

Can we know anything about how contemporary literati viewed the shift from alcohol to tea? I believe we can learn a lot from the following brief passage, likely a preface to a collection of poetry composed during the festival of the third day of the third month, by an intellectual of the late eighth and early ninth century, Lü Wen (772–811):[114]

Preface for a tea banquet on the third day of the third month.[115]

The third day of the third month, is the *shangsi* day when drinking is ritually purified. All the scholars debated substituting tea for alcoholic drinks. Then we plucked flowers, and relaxed in garden seclusion. Pure winds drove away people, but to the day's end we remained joyful. Lying down, we pointed out the green haze; seated, we held onto the fragrant branches. Idle orioles approached our mats and did not fly away. Red stamens shook onto our clothing but did not scatter. We then ordered poured out the fragrant froth. We let it float in plain wine-cups, with its lushly congealed amber color. [Tea] does not cause men to get drunk, but subtly awaken to pure thoughts. Even the broth of the five cloudy transcendents cannot exceed this. Seated to my right are the talented masters Zou from Nanyang and Duke Xu of Gaoyang. With these two or three fellows we momentarily enjoyed being beyond the dusty world [of saṃsāra]. How could we not voice lyrics?

Here we have a contemporary witness to the power of tea to act as a suitable substitute for alcohol at gatherings of scholars and as a stimulant for their composition of verse.

Let me close with a Tang poem, which I think may serve as an appropriate bookend to Mr. Alcohol and Mr Tea's argument.

Tea
fragrant leaves, tender buds.
The desire of poetic guests, the love of the saṃgha.
Cut and ground white jade, red silk woven on a loom.
Boiled in a pan—the color of yellow pistils,
swirled around in a bowl—blossoms of yeast mold.
At the end of the night it invites you to accompany the bright moon,
before dawn it makes you face the morning mist.
Washing it down, people of the past and present never tire.
Who can make such a claim after getting drunk?[116]

As we have seen in this chapter, Buddhist monks were involved both in encouraging temperance by highlighting the social problems associated with alcohol and in promoting the spread of tea. Buddhism can therefore be identified as a major factor in the transition from one "sanctioned drug" to another. In the next chapter we will look at more examples of how this transition was reflected in poetic culture.

4

Tea Poetry in Tang China

*W*hy choose to devote so much attention to poems written about or featuring tea that were written during the Tang dynasty? First, the writing of verse was perhaps the most important expression of culture during the period when tea drinking emerged, so reading poetry can tell us a great deal about the trajectories of the practice that we may not be able to discern from other literary sources. Second, as the most highly regarded and prestigious form of cultural expression in medieval times, verse not only expressed ideas but actually shaped attitudes. To some extent, then, poets told people what and how to think about tea. The values associated with tea today—that it is natural, health-giving, detoxifying, spiritual, stimulating, refreshing, and so on—are not new ideas, but ones shaped in Tang times, by poets. Third, although it is true that there exists plenty of tea poetry from later periods, much of this work alludes to these earlier expressions, so it makes sense to explore the poems of the Tang in some detail and to leave the study of later materials to another time and place.

In tea poetry we can catch a glimpse of the cultural synergy created by literati, poets, and monastics gathering to share and construct new standards of connoisseurship and creativity, as well as to develop new themes and imagery.[1] Questions about how tea was to be drunk, how it was to be appreciated, and its range of symbolic meanings were often worked out or elaborated on in verse. Thus, we can extract much valuable data about tea culture from poems that remain available to us. Also of interest to this project is the fact that, as we shall see, a sizable amount of tea's value was expressed in verse using religious terminology or imagery. As for the quantity of poems about tea, what started as a trickle in the mid-Tang became, by the end of the dynasty, a full flood of tea-related verse. Tang poets addressed a range of topics in their verses on tea. Surviving poems describe the color, aroma, and taste of the beverage; methods for preparing tea; the shape of teaware; settings for drinking tea; appreciation of the various aesthetic, medicinal, and psychoactive qualities of the beverage; as well as—to a lesser extent—the world of tea growing, picking, and preparation. Poets, as the cultural engineers of Tang times, had to invent a new world for tea to inhabit. Rather than create just a single cultural space, they made many, all of them interconnected to some degree. These multiple cultural spaces also intersected geographically and ideologically with religious systems. Thus, we need to read Tang tea verse carefully and contextually to appreciate its multiple implications. There are a large number of extant Tang poems concerned with tea, and a full study of them would far exceed the confines of this chapter. Instead, I have chosen to focus on a few of the more significant poets and a selection of representative works.

A NEW SUBJECT FOR VERSE

The High Tang (713–765) period was seen by later critics as a golden age of poetry, and it featured prominently the work of the two poets who were to become most often identified with Tang verse in China and beyond—Li Bai (701–762) and Du Fu (712–770).[2] Writing about tea was by no means a minor literary phenomenon during this period: some of the most famous figures in the history of Chinese verse, including Li Bai and Du Fu themselves, wrote poems connected with tea. But the choice of this new topic was in fact an unprecedented development in the history of Chinese verse. There are very few references to tea in pre-Tang verse. The examples of early medieval poetry selected in the *Classic of Tea*—Zuo Si's (250?–305?) "Spoiled Daughters" (*Jiaonü shi*) and Zhang Mengyang's (*zi,* Mengcai, late third century) "Climbing the tower in Chengdu" (*Deng Chengdu lou shi*)—are the only examples to be found in poetry of the Jin dynasty (265–420) onward. As I have already noted, in the Six Dynasties period tea was a Southerners' commodity, but it seems that poets from the South had little to say about the drink other than in passing. Perhaps we can infer from this scant evidence that, before the Tang, tea was consumed simply to quench the thirst or for medicinal reasons, and there was nothing in the commonplace beverage to attract the attention of the poet. Further, if we examine the corpus of Chinese poetry from the Six Dynasties period into the Sui and even the early Tang, we find no poems composed about tea. Tea, as a major topic or ancillary subject of Chinese verse, is entirely absent until the beginning of the eighth century.

Zuo Si's third-century poem "Spoiled Daughters" contains lines that depict two young women eager to consume a peddler's tea: "So impatient for tea/ They huff and puff at his brazier."[3] But the emphasis in the poem is on the antics of the daughters of the title, not the tea itself, and this focus is quite different from what we find in Tang-dynasty verse—poems exclusively devoted to the subject of the beverage.

Zhang Mengyang's poem about the White Rabbit tower (*baitu lou*) in Chengdu in present-day Sichuan claims that "the taste of tea is superior to that of the six pure liquids, its aroma penetrates the nine regions."[4] To place the taste of tea above those of the canonical liquids found in the *Rites of Zhou* is a strong claim for what was at the time more of a local specialty than a well-known product. The line immediately preceding that—"There is food in the tripods, we go in at leisure, the amenities are supreme perfection"—however, hymns the abundance of Chengdu's foodstuffs in general. Such emotions, associated with drinking tea in a fertile place surrounded by a profusion of comestibles, are rarely evoked in Tang verse. Elite Tang poets tended rather to situate tea drinking in solitary, mysterious, sometimes even desolate places. In brief then, the two early verses cited by the *Classic of Tea*, although of historical interest, have little in common with Tang verse on tea and supply scant information on tea that cannot be gleaned elsewhere.

Later, we shall discuss at length Li Bai's sole work devoted to tea, so we ought also to mention Du Fu's tea poetry, such as it is. There are two examples illustrative of connections with Buddhist monks and two associated with the life of rustic leisure.[5] The most cogent are the lines from "Poling a skiff" (*Jin ting*):

> here come some tea and sugarcane juice, brought down from the
>   house
> our earthen pots are just as good as any made of jade![6]

In Du Fu's presentation of the joys of bucolic life, tea is an unpretentious refreshment to be poured into an earthenware pot like sugarcane juice, so it is not the same as the brewed or whisked tea usually extolled in Tang poetry. In the third of five pieces titled "Back at General He's" (*Chongguo He shi wu shou*), the poet remarks laconically, "Good to drink tea in this spring breeze."[7] Certainly, then, we can see that Du Fu does not invest tea with the kind of religious and cultural significance that we see in the verse of some other Tang poets. For him, it was evidently more of an everyday comestible that the poet might mention in passing but would not dwell on at length.

BUDDHIST IDEAS IN TEA POETRY

As I already noted, according to contemporary writers, the popular habit of drinking tea originated in the Kaiyuan reign period (713–742) with the Chan

Master "Demon-queller" Zang on Mount Tai, and then it spread throughout the Tang empire. The sudden appearance of tea in poetry at around the same point in time should not surprise us, because it only confirms other evidence for an explosion in the popularity of tea consumption in the mid-eighth century. Furthermore, we should not be surprised to discover a close association of tea with Buddhist sites and personalities in Tang poetry. To offer a relatively unremarkable example of this association, Cai Xiji, a poet who was active early in the Kaiyuan period, mentions "tea and fruit" (*chaguo*) as a typical monk's evening meal in the last line of his "Ascending to Master Ran's meditation chamber at Fuxian Monastery."[8] This is the earliest extant Tang poem in which tea is mentioned, and yet it is clear that Cai did not intend to highlight "tea and fruit" as anything particularly out of the ordinary. It is interesting to note that, like Master Demon-queller, the monk mentioned in Cai's poem, Zhanran, was also affiliated with Northern School Chan.[9] Whether intentionally or not, the rise of Chan Buddhism and the development of tea drinking were often linked in Tang sources. But the offhand mention of tea in a Buddhist setting by a minor Tang poet is by no means representative of the full range of interplay between tea and Buddhism that we can discover in other verse by more prominent and prolific writers.

One particularly well-known eighth-century poet with Buddhist sympathies who left us some poems concerned with tea is Wang Wei (701–761).[10] In addition, some of Wang's notable High Tang contemporaries such as Cen Shen (715–770), Li Jiayou (fl. eighth century), and Wei Yingwu (737–792) also composed some tea-related verse.[11] From the references to tea that survive in the major eighteenth-century collection *Complete Tang Poetry* (*Quan Tang shi*), the Tang poet who mentioned tea most frequently was Bai Juyi (772–846). But to put this fact in perspective, no more than thirty of Bai's poems refer to tea, and that is a relatively small number compared with the size of his corpus (more than 2,800 poems). This statistical data show that, although tea poetry may have been culturally significant in content and influence, it remained very much a minor genre in terms of the overall amount of verse produced during the High Tang.

Wang Wei's connections with Buddhism are well known, but his poems on tea do not appear to contain any obvious Buddhist connotations. Wang mentions tea in three of his surviving poems. A line in "For Censor Wu" (*Zeng Wu guan*) says, "This guesthouse in Chang'an is scorching hot/ without tea gruel (*mingmi*) it's hard to resist the summer."[12] "Mr. Xu, Vice-Governor of Chouyan, came to seek me but did not find me in" (*Chouyan shaoyin Xu sheren jianguo buyu*) contains the lines, "I wish you had simply poured out a bowl of tea with me/ then taken my horse to ride home."[13] In the context of the poem as a whole, this line speaks to the power of tea to ward off sleep: on being revived with a cup of tea, the drinker feels no fatigue from the excesses of the night before. In another poem, "Farewell to the younger brother of Yan, Governor of Henan, who came to lodge at my broken-down hut" (*Henan Yan yin di jian su pilu fang bieren fu shiyun*), Wang Wei describes how "flower liquor harmonizes with the pine chips/ the fragrance of tea permeates the bamboo and silk."[14] We may infer from this image that tea would have been served alongside alcoholic beverages like flower-infused liquor in the poet's household. From these three passing references, it is obvious that in Wang Wei's time tea was already in widespread use as a common beverage, appreciated for its thirst-quenching and cooling properties and known as a reviving stimulant. Wang Wei's poems also show that there was no conventional expectation that tea should be invested with profound religious or aesthetic meaning, and that to do so was a choice that poets themselves made.

If Wang Wei's poems feature tea only in a background or incidental role, some of his contemporaries, in contrast, placed the new commodity center stage in their works. Wei Yingwu was one poet who was not afraid to make tea the star of one of his poems, "Joy at seeing tea growing in the garden":

> Its pure nature cannot be sullied,
> When drunk it cleanses dust and worries.
> This plant has a truly divine taste,
> And originates in the mountains.
> After I have taken care of my responsibilities,
> I plant a tea bush in my uncultivated garden.
> It is happy to grow with the other vegetation
> And to speak with a person in solitude.[15]

This is a short poem, but it contains a few interesting and novel ideas that deserve analysis. First, the tea plant is attributed with specific extra-mundane properties: it has a pure nature that cannot be stained or tarnished. This idea is most likely indebted (perhaps indirectly) to medieval Chinese Buddhist ideas about the pure buddha nature (*foxing*) that all beings were thought to possess. As we know, this doctrine originally applied only to sentient beings, but was in Tang times extended even to plants and trees.[16] This interpretation of Wei's understanding of tea is strengthened when we read in the next line that tea has the ability to "cleanse dust and worries." "Dust" (*chen*) in Buddhist texts commonly stands for the delusions and impurities that obscure our true awakened nature. The term *fan* can mean "worry" or "anxiety," but is also part of the compound *fannao*, a common Buddhist term meaning "afflictions" (Sanskrit: *kleśa*). Thus, these lines present tea with a strong Buddhist inflection at the same time as they echo statements found in the *Classic of Tea* about the ability of tea to dispel angst. Furthermore, the tea plant is depicted growing alongside other vegetation in the same way that a sage, or bodhisattva, dwells among ordinary people despite his or her awakened mind or pure unsullied nature. As if to reinforce this religious reading, the poet tells us that tea has a "divine" or "numinous" (*ling*) taste. Thus, in these few lines, we can see how Tang poets might consciously link Buddhist doctrine with their praise of a new beverage. Thus was a highly influential nonworldly aesthetic around tea constructed in a few subtle lines.

THEMES OF LONGEVITY AND TRANSCENDENCE

Certainly, there are some interesting notions in Wei's short poem about the pleasures of growing tea, but they are underdeveloped when compared with the work of some later poets. In the poetry of the High Tang, probably the most significant poetic representation of tea for our understanding of the range of religious meanings brought to the commodity is that found in Li Bai's famous "Responding to a gift of Transcendent's Palm tea from Yuquan sent by my nephew the monk Zhongfu, with preface." The preface and the poem itself relate how in 752 CE the poet received from his nephew a rare tea known as "Transcendent's Palm" (*xianrenzhang cha*) from Yuquan (Jade Spring) monastery in Jingzhou.[17] In the preface, Li Bai explains how this tea got its name: after the picked tea leaves are dried in the sun, they form a solid mass in the shape of a hand. Clearly, the tea being described here was understood to be a precious and symbolic gift from a monk to a literatus and was appreciated not just for its commercial value. Significantly, this is the first poem to feature the name of a particular variety or brand of tea in its title. The evocative, almost devotional, language used by Li Bai to write about tea in both the preface and the poem merit our close attention:

Preface

I have heard tell of Yuquan monastery in Jingzhou and the nearby pure creeks and mountains.[18] The mountain caves contain many stalactite caverns, and in these caverns many jade springs intertwine and flow. Within, there are white bats the size of ravens. According to the scriptures of the transcendents, one name for such a bat is "transcendent rat."[19] After they have reached the age of one thousand years, their bodies become as white as snow. They hang upside down from their perches, and probably it is because they drink the water from the stalactites that they live so long. By the banks of the water, tea plants grow, their stems and leaves like jade. Only Master Zhen of Yuquan si is able to always pick and drink this tea.[20] He is more than eighty years old, but his complexion is as rosy as peach or plum. This tea, pure of fragrance, smooth and mature, is different from other kinds, because it allows one to return to youthfulness, banish decrepitude, and attain human longevity. When I traveled to Jinling, my kinsman, the monk Zhongfu, presented me with several tens of pieces of tea leaves; they were curled like fists and multilayered, their shape resembled a hand. Hence, this is called "Transcendent's Palm tea."[21] He was newly arrived from the mountains of Yuquan, and we had not seen each other for a long time; thus he sent me this present gift accompanied by verses which obliged me to respond. So I wrote this in order that eminent monks and great hermits of later times will know that transcendent's palm tea came from the son of Chan, Zhongfu, and the Layman of the Blue Lotus, Li Bai.[22]

I once heard of the Jade Spring Mountain,
Many of its mountain caves are stalactite caverns.
There, transcendent bats as big as white ravens,
Hang upside down, reflected like the moon in the clear streams.
Tea plants grow from rocks in the midst of this,
While the Jade Spring flows, never ending.
The roots and branches are doused with fragrant juice.
Once picked and consumed, the tea will nourish the muscles
     and bones.
Old bushes, their green leaves curled up,
Their branches intertwined.
When the tea is dried, it makes the shape of a transcendent's palm
With which one might pat [the transcendent] Hongya on the
     shoulder.[23]
Such a thing has never been seen in this world,
Indeed, who has ever even passed on its name?
You, Nephew Ying, the dhyāna master,
Have sent me this along with fine verses.
Your clear mirror reflects Wu Yan,[24]
I look at myself, put to shame by Xi Shi's beauty.[25]
In the morning I sit with ample delight,
Sending up a long chant to all the various deities.[26]

In this poem, addressed to a Buddhist monk in response to a gift of tea from a major Buddhist monastery, Li Bai writes about tea primarily in the language of Taoist immortality. He also points to the way in which this previously unknown "transcendent's palm" tea might be brought to the attention of the world—through verse. In the preface, he spends considerable time and attention establishing the numinous and otherworldly setting in which this tea is grown and, by extension, makes claims for the supernatural properties of the tea itself. According to him, then, the tea plants grow by the banks of some mountain springs that flow through mysterious caverns populated by large, long-lived white bats. The bats owe their astonishing longevity (more than a thousand years) and their unusual color to the fact that they drink the mineral-rich milky water that drips from the stalactites in the caverns.[27] The tea plants evidently benefit in a similar fashion from this water too, although they remain jade-green rather than white like the bats. But we know that the leaves of these plants are possessed of life-extending properties because they are harvested by the Buddhist recluse known as Master Zhen of the Jade Spring. Thanks to his tea-drinking habit, this monk (most likely the Buddhist Vinaya master Huizhen of Yuquan monastery) retains a peachy, youthful complexion despite being more than eighty years old. Li is explicit about the life-extending qualities this particular tea possesses: "this tea . . . is different from other kinds, because it allows one to return to youthfulness, banish decrepitude, and attain human longevity."

Li goes on to explain why the tea is called Transcendent's Palm. Unlike the highly processed cakes of tea that were commonly consumed by Tang tea connoisseurs, the long leaves from the Yuquan monastery were naturally sun dried, curling up to take the form of a hand. These naturally dried leaves would have produced a tea that was quite different from that made from cakes of tea in which the leaves had previously been rinsed, steamed, pounded, and baked. After Li receives a sample of this tea as a gift from his nephew, a Buddhist monk from Yuquan monastery, he expresses the hope that the verses exchanged between the two (including this very poem, of course) will spread the reputation of this extraordinary substance. Li's preface reveals an awareness that verse, especially that composed by a famous poet, could endorse and enhance the value of a particular variety of tea. This type of high-level celebrity endorsement, advertising, and commodification of tea began in the High Tang and remained a prominent feature of later tea culture.

Li Bai was not the only poet to use the language and imagery of transcendence in association with tea. Li Hua's (d. ca. 769) poem "Monastery of Cloud Mother Springs" (*Yunmuquan si*), for example, makes similar claims about tea as an elixir with the potential to bring longevity and health:[28]

> Glossy medicinal herbs growing in luxuriant meadows,
> Their *qi* soaks into the tea cups and emits a pleasant fragrance;

Drinking this sap makes you live a long time,
Consuming it harmonizes the body.[29]

The preface to this poem tells us more about the mineral-rich water with which this tea was made:

Xuanshi shan (Mount Mystery Stone), west of Dongting Lake, is commonly called Hei shan (Black Mountain). South of the mountain is a Buddhist monastery. The monastery leans up against a pine-covered peak, and below it there is Cloud Mother Spring. The spring emerges from the rock, runs in a stream and divides into branches that flow all around the courtyards and buildings. It comes out like milk and by the end of the stream it is like a pure sap. Boiling tea, soaking and steaming (grains), watering the garden, or rinsing the teeth—all of these things it is used for. It will not overflow when there is a flood, nor become exhausted when there is a drought.

From Black Mountain northwest to Shimen (Stone Gate) and southeast to Dongling (East Mound) to a circumference of twenty five *li,* the entire area produces mica. Walls, steps and paths, all glisten like arrayed stars. The wellspring and the valley stream are both pure white in color. Many of the village people attain long life, and do not suffer from any illnesses of the stomach or from scabies.

Li Hua's preface informs us that in the grounds of this mountain monastery the famous water of Yunmu ("Cloud Mother") spring flowed and the medicine or tea made with that water was able to extend human life. It is worth noting that "Cloud Mother" was a Tang term for the mineral mica, so a similar principle is operating here as we found expressed in Li Bai's poem: the tea plants in question were nourished by mineral-rich springwater containing traces of either mica or limestone from stalactites. Mica, like limestone stalactite, was commonly used in long-life elixir recipes in Tang times.[30] In addition, both "Jade Spring" (*yuquan*) and "Cloud Mother" (*yunmu*) are also names of elixirs. In Taoist physiology, the "Jade Spring" also refers to the base of the tongue, where beneficial saliva is produced and used to irrigate the interior of the human body during breath control exercises.[31] Obviously, the springwater used to make the tea was seen to be endowed with numerous positive qualities. An interest in tea stimulated an interest in the properties of various kinds of springwater with which it might be made.

Despite the association of tea with Buddhist monks and monasteries revealed in these poems of Li Bai and Li Hua, some of the early references are more ambiguous about religious affiliations of consumers of tea, and poets also on occasion invoked other types of recluses than Buddhist. During the early period of the mid–eighth-century "tea craze," Chu Guangxi (707–759), in his "Composed while eating tea congee" (*Chi mingzhou zuo*), writes, "Tarrying long, we cook up the tea congee, together we eat bracken."[32] These lines were probably composed when visiting a recluse on Mount Mao, the site associated with the famous Shangqing revelations, so Chu's companion could well have been a Taoist priest.[33] The term *chazhou* for tea congee (a rice porridge made with the liquor from boiling tea) is attested early and frequently, especially in the *materia medica,* but the word translated here as "bracken," *juewei* ("royal fern," *osmunda regalis*), referred to a foodstuff particularly associated with recluses in Tang times.[34] There are very few specific mentions of tea in Tang poems concerned with Taoism or Taoists. But it appears that tea was of some importance in the eremitic lifestyle during the Tang, and tea congee was in some way more connected with that vocation than were other methods of preparing and consuming the beverage. The range of evidence from medieval times suggests that a tea congee, tea porridge, or tea soup was seen as a medicinal, dietetic, or nutritional comestible that contrasted with the more refined methods of preparing tea advocated by Lu Yu and others.

TEA IN THE BUDDHIST MONASTERY

Sometimes, the poet writes of a particular tea associated with a named Buddhist monastery, as we have seen earlier with Li Bai and Li Hua's verses. Sometimes, he describes sharing tea with a particular eminent monk. But some Tang poems are centered on the experience of simply being in a monastery and drinking tea. This experience and its evocation in literary and artistic works were significant for the development of a tea-centered aesthetic that continued through later periods.

A poet of the High Tang, Cen Shen, writes about staying overnight in a monastery and seeing a tea garden there.[35] In a poem composed in the autumn of 763, "In late autumn, meeting Metropolitan Governor Yan in the bamboo studio of the auspicious rear hall" (*Muqiu hui Yan jingzhao houting zhuzhai*), the poet employs descriptions of the color and aroma of tea to evoke the scene: "a cup of fragrant tea the color of tender shoots/ the window is cold, the bamboo sounds dry."[36] For this poet, the monastery is a place for quiet reflection—and tea the perfect accompaniment for moments of solitary introspection. However, high-ranking officials who used tea to entertain their guests usually made people the subject of their verse rather than the tea itself. The poems of Li Jiayou, for example, mention tea in five different contexts: the tea garden in spring at Yangxian; "sipping tea while studying true verses" (*chuoming fan zhenji*) with the old monk at Jianfu si; sending off people with tea; drinking tea alone; and drinking tea at banquets.[37] From this diversity of settings, we can see that by Li Jiayou's time tea had reached into every aspect of officials' lives. But let us examine one of these pieces that is set in a Buddhist monastery:

> *Composed in the cell of Master Yi of Jianfu monastery*[38]
> I burn incense alone in the empty chamber,
> In the silence of the lonely forest the sound of the stone chime
>   endures.
> I gaze idly at a clump of bamboo,
> Growing old seated on this corded chair.
> Sipping tea, I glance through the true gāthās,
> I light a lamp to aid the twilight.
> A person returns, and from afar I send him off.
> Their footsteps move away on the encircling veranda.

In addition to tea, Li's verse mentions the corded chair, an important innovation in the history of furniture (and human posture) in China with which Buddhists were closely associated, as John Kieschnick has shown.[39] The image of the literatus playing at being a monk, seated in his exotic chair and reading Buddhist verse while sipping tea, was an important element in the construction of an idealized or aestheticized setting for the appropriate enjoyment of tea. As we shall see, this ideal situation for refined and meaningful tea consumption was one that continued to resonate for literati through late imperial times.

Tang poets often gave credit to tea for inspiring their verse. In one of the many verses Tang intellectual Liu Yuxi (772–835) composed in response to Bai Juyi, "Answering Letian's 'Resting at Leisure'" (*Chou Letian xianwo jianji*), he writes,[40]

> Tea aids the liveliness of poetic feelings,
> As ale brings out the effect of medicine.[41]

Liu points to one of the functional aspects of tea—it inspires poetry in the same manner as alcohol enhances the effects of medicinal herbs. He also wrote at more length about the experience of tasting tea with companions. Here is Liu's "Song of sampling tea at the monastery of Western Mountain" (*Xi shan lanruo shicha ge*):[42]

> Behind the dwellings of the mountain monks there are several clumps
>   of tea plants.

When spring comes, among the reflecting bamboo, new buds
    come up.
Spontaneously, for your guest you doff your robe and arise,
Personally approaching the tea plants to select the "eagle tufts."
Then you roast the tea leaves and the fragrance fills the room.
Next, you pour out water from Golden-sands Spring, splashing from
    the stone stairs.
The sound of a downpour in the pines entering the tripod,
A white cloud fills the cup with floating flowers.
The perfume hits the nostrils and disperses last night's drunkenness,
Pure and austere it penetrates the bones and drives out inner worry.
Whether from sunny cliff or shady slope, each tea has its own *qi,*
But none compares to that grown in the moss beneath bamboo.
Although the Fiery Emperor may have tasted tea, he did not yet
    understand how to brew it,
If the "Master of Paulownia" had the recipe, he scarcely knew the taste
    of it.
The new shoots, half unfurled, are like clenched fists.
From being picked to being brewed with only minutes to spare.
The fragrance subtly resembles magnolia impregnated with rose
The color of the jade herbs by the edge of the wave is without
    compare.
The monk says that the divine taste goes well with quiet reclusion,
For his honored guest he personally attends to this rare and
    exceptional tea.
He does not hesitate to package it so I can take it back to my
    provincial office.
But brick wells and bronze stoves would damage its nobility,
What can one say of this spring tea from the summit of Mount
    Guzhu,
Which, enveloped in white and sealed in red, travels dusty roads?
In order to know the pure and simple taste of this flowery milk,
One should be a person who lives on rocks and sleeps in clouds.

    Liu's poem is unusual for the sustained focus he brings to the materiality
of tea—its production, preparation, and distribution. It also provides valuable
anecdotal evidence for the growing of tea around the monks' quarters at one
particular monastery on Mount Guzhu. We will encounter teas from this site
in later chapters, and we know from other sources that rare teas often grew in
small plots in and around monastic buildings on mountain sites. Liu also describes the making of tea for an honored guest: the host personally selects the

finest new buds, roasts them, and boils fresh water from the local spring to make a fragrant cup. The poet notes the appearance and aroma of the tea, casually demonstrating his own connoisseurship as he proclaims the virtues of this particular tea that was grown in moss beneath bamboo. Interestingly, he repeats Lu Yu's claim about Shennong (here called the Fiery Emperor) being the discoverer of tea, but locates the joys of drinking this "rare and valuable" spring tea firmly in the present rather than in high antiquity. The Buddhist monk is presented as a refined guardian and connoisseur of this fine "flowery milk" with its "pure and simple taste." Liu claims that transporting tea, "enveloped in white and sealed in red," will damage its flavor and that one must be a mountain-dwelling recluse to know its true taste. Again, it is the poet who brings together the elements of the tea aesthetic, focusing on an idealized monastic life far from the grim complications of the official's lot.

Another verse by Liu Yuxi, "On an autumn day I pay a visit to Dharma Master Hongju's Monastery, on my way to be sent back to Jiangling" (*Qiuri guo Hongju fashi siyuan, bian song gui Jiangling*), uses tea in a much more oblique manner to evoke the experience of meeting with an eminent monk:[43]

> Looking at paintings, walking through the entire long corridor,
> Seeking the monk, a path of seclusion.
> Small pond, with its crane, is clean,
> Ancient tree along with its cicada are autumnal.
> Guest arrives, tea smoke rises,
> Birds return, lecture mats are taken away.
> Floating cup, take leave the next day,
> Looking at each other, water is vast and boundless.

Here, tea is merely glimpsed in the form of smoke or a cup, but its appearance is clearly intended to arouse in the reader a host of associations with the contemplative life of the Buddhist monk. These verses by Liu give some idea of the range of ways in which poets wrote about tea—whether as the subject of their verse or as an element in a larger lyrical repertoire with which they might inspire emotional responses to human interactions. Many mid-Tang poets wrote about tea and monasteries or hermits, in addition to the examples already given. Meng Jiao (751–814) frequently mentioned drinking tea in monasteries in his poems.[44] Many of Zhang Ji's (767–830) poems are concerned with the concepts of reclusion and solitude and incorporate mentions of tea. It is fair to say that the image of the literatus sharing tea with an eminent monk became an established convention in Tang verse.

TEA AND FRIENDSHIP; FEASTING AND PARTING

For some Tang poets, tea offered an opportunity to allude to possibilities for transcending this world, even when the poem was framed in terms of mundane human emotions. The following poem by Qian Qi (722–780) is titled "Tea Banquet with Zhao Ju." An early tea poem composed in the High Tang, it is one of the first to highlight tea as an essential element in a banquet or feast. In this case, it is, of course, rather a modest banquet: only the poet and his friend are present. In its few lines we see the poet pick up on some themes I have already noted: tea is compared with the drink of the immortals and lauded for its abilities to wash away the dust of the worldly mind:

> Beneath the bamboo, words are forgotten as we face the purple tea.
> It is superior to the flowing vapors upon which feathered
>   transcendents become intoxicated.
> Our minds thoroughly cleansed of dust, our joy is far from being
>   extinguished.
> Slanting shadows of trees full of singing cicadas.[45]

Tang poems that mention the serving of tea at banquets, such as this one, tend to emphasize the pleasant and tranquil atmosphere that prevails as the participants share tea at their leisure, whereas those that describe the use of tea to send off guests are usually intended to evoke feelings of reluctance to be parted. Obviously, Tang literati with active careers in the civil service experienced many such farewell gatherings because they were regularly recalled to the capital to serve there or dispatched to new posts in the provinces. Li Jiayou's poem "An autumn morning's tea banquet at the Eastern Peak by Zhaoyin monastery, sending off my wife's younger brother Yan Bojun on his return to Jiangzhou" (*Qiuxiao Zhaoyin si dongfeng chayan song neidi Yan Bojun gui Jiangzhou*) nicely illustrates how a Tang poet might see off a friend or relative at a Buddhist monastery and provide him with tea for the journey:[46]

> Ten thousand paddy fields of new rice surround this mountain
>   village,
> We traverse several *li* of deep pine forest to arrive at the gates of the
>   monastery.
> Fortunately, we have fragrant tea to leave for the young man,
> I cannot bear to see off the prince's son amidst the autumn grasses.
> Amidst the smoke and dust we regret that we must part and lament
>   the barriers between us,

The township is so desolate, who could bear to speak of it?
Do not find it strange that at the crossroads, I alone am weeping,
Like Wei Shu, I remember in particular the kindness of my wife's
    family.[47]

When Yan Zhenqing (709–784)—a figure we will discuss later in connection with the life of Lu Yu—was the district magistrate (*cishi*) of Huzhou, he collected the verses of local literati who had been his guests. Linked verse had been popular among Six Dynasties poets, but had fallen out of favor in the Tang until revived by Yan and Lu Yu's friend, the monk-poet Jiaoran.[48] Tea even appears in the title of Yan's collection "Linked verses composed while drinking tea on moonlit nights" (*Wuyan yueye chuocha lianju*).[49] There, Yan writes,

"Flowing flowers" purify the muscles and bones,
penetrate and cleanse the source of the mind.

Although Yan's friend Lu Yu did not take part in these particular poetic gatherings, some of his influence remains—the term "flowing flowers" (*liuhua*), which describes the appearance of tea in a bowl, is also found in the *Classic of Tea*. These lines offer a nicely concise example of the qualities often claimed for tea in Tang verse: that it could purify not only the body but also the mind. Yan wrote many linked verses with Lu Yu, of which eight examples survive, although none are concerned with tea.

TEA IN THE POETRY OF THE MONK JIAORAN

Although Lu Yu left little of his own ideas about tea in poetic form, his friend and accomplice, the Buddhist monk Jiaoran, composed many verses on tea. Jiaoran was very famous as a poet in his own day, but is better remembered by later generations as a critic and theorist of verse.[50] Because of changes in literary taste, he is scarcely recognized today as a major Tang poet. As we might expect, most of Jiaoran's tea poems are about the place of tea in the life of a monk. Their language emphasizes interior purity and simplicity, and many of them suggest links between Chan Buddhism and tea. Jiaoran's affiliations with the early Chan tradition of the eighth century are relatively complex, but suggest that he was involved with some of the major trends in doctrine and practice of his day.[51]

A good example of how tea was to be prepared elegantly and the benefits of consuming it may be found in Jiaoran's "Making fun of the Envoy Cui Shi" (*Qiao Cui Shi shijun*):[52]

A man from Yue brought me some tea from the Shan valley stream,
I plucked these golden buds and lit the fire beneath the bronze tripod.
In plain porcelain, white as snow, floats the fragrant froth,
Is it not even better than the transcendents' nectar of jade pistils?

The first drink dissolves torpor and sleepiness,
A radiant feeling fills heaven and earth.
The second drink purifies my spirit,
Like a sudden shower washes away the light dust.
With the third drink I immediately attain the *dao,*
Why labor so hard with the mind to destroy the afflictions?

This substance, so pure and lofty, remains unknown
     to the common world.
People of this world who drink alcohol only beguile themselves.
How sad: Bi Zhuo alone at night among the wine casks.[53]
How laughable: Tao Qian lying beneath the hedge!

When you, Marquis Cui, sip, your appreciation does not stop.
Your ardent singing startles the ears of others.
Who knows the way of tea that is complete and authentic?
Only Cinnabar Mound could attain such a thing.[54]

In these lines, Jiaoran claims that tea can purify the spirit and cause one
to attain the *dao,* and—as we may have expected from our discussion of tea
and alcohol in the previous chapter—he explicitly contrasts the "spiritual" consumption of tea with the worldly and deluded drinking of alcohol to excess,
even by such famous poets as Tao Yuanming (Tao Qian). In addition, the line,
"why [must one] labor so hard with the mind to destroy the afflictions?" relates
specifically to contemporary Chan rhetoric about so-called sudden awakening.[55]
In other words, Jiaoran took tea quite seriously in his poetry.

Let us reflect on why Jiaoran chooses to make such lofty religious claims
for the properties of tea—that it is powerful enough to enable one to do no less
than "attain the *dao.*" Despite his use of the term *dao* (Way), Jiaoran, of course,
does not intend to invoke a specifically Taoist concept; medieval Buddhist texts
in Chinese routinely refer to the attainment of awakening, or *bodhi,* in the same
way. But was such a claim merely part of the Buddhist propaganda against consuming alcohol that I mentioned in the previous chapter, or were the physiological effects of consuming tea actually thought to match the experience of
attaining awakening? How serious was Jiaoran in stating that drinking tea could

lead one to the ultimate goal, given that he was a dedicated and experienced religious practitioner as well as a poet? How should we understand statements about the accomplishment of religious aims when they appear in cultural contexts that we would not immediately understand as religious? These questions are not easily answered, but deserve consideration as we read the works of Jiaoran and his contemporaries.

Jiaoran's "Making fun of the Envoy Cui Shi," is not the only place in which he draws parallels between Chan Buddhism and tea. For example, in another poem he writes, "[C]onsciousness miraculously hears the subtle sound of the spring/ awakening is deep like the purest tea."[56] On a more practical note, he describes how "[o]n a clear night we gather at my monastery/ brewing tea and opening the window of Chan." From this line we get some sense of how tea was employed to ward off sleep for the practice of meditation at night. For Jiaoran, tea was connected to both Chan doctrine and Chan practice.

In "Drinking Mount Tianmu tea with Lu Xun, sent to the Layman Yuan Sheng" (*Dui Lu Xun yin Tianmu shan cha yin ji Yuan zhushi Sheng*), we read this contemplative description of making tea and its purpose:

As I empty the pan, bubbling, it makes foam,
As I hold the bowl it gathers and gives rise to flowers.
Coming together for Chan and scriptures,
Temporarily, we buy a way out from the snares of sleep.[57]

In other words, Jiaoran and his companion are able to pursue their study of Chan and Buddhist sutras because tea liberates them from sleep. But tea is not simply a functional stimulant; it also has aesthetic properties—it produces flowers in the tea bowl as it is poured in. And, as we saw in Yan Zhenqing's verse, the method of making tea to which Jiaoran alludes here is completely in accord with that described by his friend Lu Yu in the *Classic of Tea*.[58] In addition to its overt religious content, then, it appears that Jiaoran provides here the earliest description of Lu Yu's contemporary method of brewing tea to be found in Tang poetry.

Jiaoran not only composed lines about consuming tea but he also wrote about the process of gathering the leaves. In the following poem, which is more about tea than Chan, still Jiaoran cannot resist making reference to transcendents in connection with tea picking:

Song of [Mount] Guzhu sent to Pei Fangzhou[59]
I have a cloudy spring, close to Mount Guzhu;
In the mountains, I am occupied with matters of tea.

When the shrikes are singing, the fragrant herbs die;
Then mountain folk gradually wish to harvest the seeds of tea plants.
On the day the red-backed shrike flies, the fragrant herbs flourish
    again;
It's time for this mountain monk also to pick tea.
For a long time I have been accustomed to go picking without caring
    how far I go:
In the shadow of a lofty peak, or in the sunshine on a low cliff.
At the base of the Great Cold mountain, the leaves are not yet
    growing,
And at the base of Mount Lesser Cold, the leaves have just begun to
    unfold.
The girls of Wu, carrying baskets, ascend the blue-green slopes
Their heady perfume is caught up in their spring clothes.
Lost in the mountains, I am suddenly covered in falling blossom,
As I cross the stream I am startled by the cries of flying birds.
My tea garden is not far and I pick among the dew,
As I return, the glistening dew is still dripping.
At first sight, the buds are better than jade flowers,
A pinch of tea infused is superior to golden liquor.
Last night on the Western Peak, the rain fell,
This morning, seeking fresh tea buds—where were they?
The green shoots flecked with pink were already old.
If there were many people in the market seeking "purple bamboo" tea,
Who really knows green shoots or purple bamboo?
When the day's pickings last only until evening it's a shame.
Like the True Man of Great Purity awaiting Ziyuan,[60]
I put some of this tea aside and think of you.

In this poem, Jiaoran, in reality both an elite monastic of high birth and an influential and well-connected poet of his day, casts himself as a simple "mountain monk" wandering in the hills in search of wild-growing tea. He compares the tea to the kinds of divine products of the heavens—the tea buds are finer than jade flowers, the beverage itself is better than golden liquor. Finally, he likens himself to the Han dynasty transcendent "True Man of Great Purity" who waits for his disciple Ziyuan. Although much of the poem concerns the physical reality of tea growing in the mountains and the experience of picking the finest leaves, the poet still makes constant reference to the extra-mundane qualities of tea, always seeking to place the discourse about tea on a more ethereal level.

As I have already noted, Jiaoran was a friend and collaborator of Lu Yu, and he wrote one famous poem in which he celebrates that relationship and their tea-drinking activities. Jiaoran's poem describes a Buddhist monk (himself, of course) celebrating the festival of the ninth day of the ninth lunar month by drinking tea with Lu Yu, a figure who is primarily claimed for the literati tradition, despite his monastic upbringing and lifelong association with Buddhists. The poem also alludes to the work of the famous Tao Yuanming, the first poet to celebrate the festival of the Double Ninth and to fix its association with drinking chrysanthemum petals in wine.[61] Because *jiu* (nine) is a homonym for *jiu* (long-lasting) the Double Ninth was associated with longevity; hence the custom of ingesting a chrysanthemum elixir. For a Tang audience reading this poem, the allusion to Tao Yuanming would have exemplified the idealized entwining of intoxication and spontaneity that was central to Chinese high culture of the time.[62]

> *Drinking Tea with the Recluse Lu Yu on Double Ninth*
> On the day of Double Ninth, in a mountain monastery,
> By the Eastern fence, chrysanthemums bloom yellow.
> Common folk float them in their wine,
> But who can explain how they would improve the flavor of tea?[63]

In this short piece, Jiaoran quite consciously contrasts alcohol with tea, physical longevity with spiritual immortality, and Lu Yu with Tao Yuanming, and—just to make clear his own perspective—he situates the scene in a Buddhist monastery on a Chinese mountain. The poem can be read as a bold attempt on Jiaoran's part to relocate the entire culture of poetic composition around tea rather than alcohol. Like many of Jiaoran's poems about tea this one has quite a light and playful quality.

We can see from these poems that Jiaoran did much to advance the major elements of a new aesthetic based around the consumption of tea. He described appropriate settings (monasteries, mountains) and participants (literati and monks) and applied the religious language of both Taoism and Chan Buddhism to the preparation and consumption of the beverage. Perhaps these poems themselves are no longer considered masterpieces of Chinese literature, but their effect on Chinese culture was nevertheless far reaching as other poets and authors adapted their ideas and language.

LU TONG'S "SEVEN CUPS OF TEA"

One example of a poet who seems to have responded to Jiaoran's tea poetry is Lu Tong (795–835). His famous lines that I quoted in the first chapter describing the effects of drinking tea appear in "Written in haste to thank Imperial Censor Meng for his gift of freshly picked tea," a poem of thanks from a high official who has received a gift of leftover tribute tea sent to the court from the tea plantations of Yangxian.[64] It would be helpful to consider those lines in the context of the whole poem.

1.
The sun is high as a ten-foot measure and five but I am fast asleep.
The dispatch-rider bangs at the gate, loud enough to rouse the Duke
    of Zhou!
He tells me that the Censor sends a letter;
The white silk envelope is sealed and stamped in triplicate.
As I break the seals, I seem to see the Censor himself,
And I count these three hundred "full-moon" tea cakes.

2.
I heard that since the New Year he had gone into the mountains,
When hibernating insects awaken in the spring breeze.
Before the emperor tastes the tea from Yangxian,
The common plants dare not blossom.
The humane breezes secretly nurture the pearly tea sprouts,
In the early spring they coax out buds of gold.
Picked fresh, roasted until fragrant, then packed and sealed:
To call it perfectly refined and perfectly good is no exaggeration.
After being presented to His Majesty, the remainder should be
    distributed among princes and nobles;
By what chance has it reached the hut of this mountain hermit?
My brushwood gate is closed, keeping out worldly visitors;
I don my gauze cap, and in solitude I brew and taste.
Clouds of emerald that even the wind cannot disperse,
White flowery froth radiantly congeals on the surface of the bowl.

3.
The first bowl moistens my lips and throat.
The second bowl banishes my loneliness and melancholy.
The third bowl penetrates my withered entrails,
Finding nothing there except five thousand scrolls of writing.
The fourth bowl raises a light perspiration,
As all the inequities I have suffered in my life,
Are flushed out through my pores.
The fifth bowl purifies my flesh and bones.

The sixth bowl allows me to communicate with immortals.
The seventh bowl I need not drink,
I am only aware of a pure wind rising beneath my two arms.

4.
The mountains of Penglai, what is this place?
I, Master of the Jade Stream, ride this pure wind and wish to return
    home.
In the mountains, transcendents look down on the land below,
These places are pure and lofty, sheltered from wind and rain.
How could they know the bitter fate of the millions of common
    people
who toil and suffer beneath the towering cliffs!
On behalf of the Censor I will ask them about the common people;
and whether they will be able to rest in the end.[65]

The lines describing the effects of drinking bowl after bowl of tea are now probably the most famous and often-quoted example of Tang tea poetry, although the trope is already present in Jiaoran's description of drinking three cups of tea in "Making fun of the Envoy Cui Shi." According to Lu, repeated drinking of tea has the effect of stopping thirst, raising the spirit, and forgetting worldly cares, and when the fifth and sixth cups reach the belly one is able to enter the world of the immortals—just as we saw in Jiaoran's work. Although it is difficult to determine how sincere the poet was in writing this extravagant hymn to tea, we can certainly say that the work had a profound effect on the cultural reception of the beverage. In many ways, Lu Tong's piece functioned as the poetic counterpart to Lu Yu's prose *Classic of Tea,* and whatever his motivation for writing it, the content seems to have been appreciatively received and taken seriously by later writers. Although it represents only one approach to tea poetry, it clearly inspired many others to reach similar heights of sophistication in their descriptions of the beverage and its effects.

BAI JUYI AND TEA IN THE MUNDANE WORLD

Bai Juyi was the Tang poet who mentioned tea most in his poems, but the descriptions are not as lengthy or refined as in the poems we have looked at so far. The theme found in his poetry is often simply the superiority of tea over alcohol, but he also wrote about tea as a kind of hangover cure. In "Lord Xiao sends me new tea from Shu" (*Xiao yuanwai ji xin Shu cha*), for example, he writes,

The bowl filled with this milky liquid must truly be admired,
How much more so in the depths of spring when alcohol makes one
    thirsty?[66]

Yet, many of his poems are about the power of alcohol being superior to that of tea.[67] As far as Bai was concerned, it seems that the beverage to chase off depression was still alcohol, and of course he claimed to be more interested in drink than he was in either the Buddhist or Taoist way of life.

In Bai Juyi's "After eating" (*Shi hou*) we see a simpler depiction of tea with none of the aesthetic associations with reclusion, meditation, or immortality that we have seen in many of the other examples of Tang verse:

Having done eating I go to sleep,
Waking up, two bowls of tea.
Raise my head to see the sun's shadows,
Already returned to being slanted in the southwest.
A happy person regrets the fast disappearance of daylight,
A sorrowful person feels sick of the slow passage of time.
Those without worries nor delight,
Simply let life be.[68]

Bai's poems about tea avoid much of the lofty language and recondite allusions that we find in other Tang tea poetry. They are mostly set very firmly in the everyday realm and are intended to evoke the worldly emotions of loss, regret, and separation. Again, we see that Tang poets, even those with pronounced religious sympathies and affiliations such as Bai, were able to exercise considerable discretion in how they chose to write about tea. Here is another verse by Bai that deploys tea as a medium to express feelings of friendship over distance, and again the language is very simple and direct:

"Sent to Liu from Tongzhou as I leisurely rest"[69]
Sitting to sip refreshing cold water,
Watching the simmering of jadeite green dust.
There is no way for me to take a bowl
And send it to the one who loves tea.

Some of Bai's poems focus just on the experience of making tea. The poem, "Thinking of someone upon simmering tea with mountain springwater" (*Shan quan jian cha you huai*), gives us some sense of the subjective experience of making the beverage in Tang times.[70] For example, boiling the water for tea in an earthenware bottle (rather than an open pot) meant that one could not see the bubbles forming in the water as it heated: one then could only know what stage the water was at by the sound it made. This technological aspect accounts for the fact that Tang poems refer frequently to the sound of boiling water, rather than what it looked like. Another of Bai's tea poems focuses on the materiality of fresh tea, sent to him by a friend, and on the experience of making it:

> "Thanking Director Li Six for sending new tea from Shu"
> Our old relationship remains close and complete, our former
>   friendship most intimate,
> The share of new tea has reached my sickly body.
> Encased in red paper, with your letter appended,
> Ten cakes of green tips picked in Spring "before the fire"[71]
> To the boiling water I add another ladle, and it simmers with "fish
>   eyes."[72]
> Tea powder drops from the measure, and I mix in the dust.
> You did not send it to others, but first to me,
> This must be because I am a connoisseur of tea.[73]

The poem helps us understand how choice tea was used as a gift, accompanying the letters that kept elite social networks among literati alive in premodern China. Bai Juyi describes himself as a "connoisseur," but he was not dependent on such gifts sent from afar as this one to maintain his tea habit. He had his own tea garden, as he tells us in these lines from "My newly erected thatched hut below Incense Burner Peak" (Xianglu feng xia xinzhi caotang).[74]

> I built my cottage up against the cliff
> And dug out a gully to open up a tea garden.

Bai produced many verses on tea similar in content and emotional texture to those quoted earlier; however, for the most part they remain resolutely fixed on the everyday aspects of tea drinking and its associations with Bai's companions, either present at the poet's side or separated by time and distance.[75] Yuan Zhen (779–831) was a good friend of Bai Juyi's, and he also loved tea. His principal contribution to tea poetry is his verse in the shape of a Buddhist stūpa that I quoted in the previous chapter. Contrasting Yuan and Bai allows us to view the spectrum of poetic uses to which tea was put in the Tang. We can see that there was no real consensus about tea and that poets could combine an interest in both the material and spiritual aspects of the beverage. A close study of Tang tea poetry, including many other examples I do not have space to mention here, shows that the subject of tea was taken up in different ways. Some poets crafted multiple verses around the refined qualities that they found in tea, quickly reaching for the otherworldly language of Buddhism and Taoism to evoke the numinous power of the substance. Others dealt with tea on the level of an everyday necessity, weaving it into their evocations of human emotions. Both kinds of writing had an effect on Chinese tea culture.

CONCLUSION

As we discovered in the previous chapter, tea was essentially a Tang invention. Without a deep reservoir of precedents in the classical literature or in the work of canonized poets such as Tao Yuanming, Tang authors had to find a way to write about tea more or less from a standing start. In this chapter we have seen the range of choices that they made—they wrote about tea as a substitute or complementary antidote for alcohol, they emphasized the material aspects of tea and the process of making the brew, and they eulogized its psychoactive properties in spiritual and sometimes specifically religious terms.

Certainly, Tang poets played a key role in making a new cultural space for the elite appreciation of tea, and they often located tea growing and consumption in religious environments such as monasteries. Their work on this new frontier of poetry was to frame much of the cultural activity around tea for the next ten centuries or so. The poems (especially Lu Tong's lines) would be cited and alluded to by generations of tea connoisseurs and poets to come. As we have seen, Tang poets invented much of the terminology and aesthetics of tea and drew heavily on religious sources to do so. The fact that someone like Bai Juyi could write about tea without recourse to this vocabulary and conceptual framework shows how much this religious framing of tea was a deliberate choice made by other poets.

5

The Patron Saint of Tea

RELIGIOUS ASPECTS OF THE LIFE AND
WORK OF LU YU

*T*his chapter introduces the life and works of Lu Yu (733–804), author of the world's first book devoted to tea, the *Classic of Tea (Chajing)*.[1] As we shall see, both Lu's life and his work were strongly shaped by the religious climate of medieval China. Lu was orphaned at a young age and was brought up by the abbot of a Buddhist monastery. As he grew up, he rejected the monastic life, enjoyed a brief career as an entertainer, and spent most of his adult years mixing in literary and intellectual circles that included the Buddhist monk-poet Jiaoran, whom we met in the previous chapter; the noted Buddhist scholar of Vinaya and famous calligrapher Huaisu (737–799 or 725–785); as well as nonaffiliated intellectuals and authors of important Taoist works. But Lu Yu's connections were not confined to institutional forms of religion; so influential was the *Classic of Tea* in spreading tea drinking throughout the empire that soon after his death Lu Yu was already known as the God of Tea (*chashen*) and tea dealers were making offerings to clay effigies of him.[2]

In terms of the religious dimensions of Lu Yu's life, there is not only the question of his Buddhist upbringing to consider but also his later self-identification and his associations with figures of other religious backgrounds. As for his work on tea, we also have to ask to what extent tea drinking was an element of practices of reclusion known to some Buddhist monks that was then perhaps aestheticized, popularized, and commodified by Lu Yu. From that perspective, we should note the known Buddhist (Jiaoran) and Taoist (Zhang Zhihe and Li Ye [Li Jilan, d. 784]) associates of Lu Yu and their influence on his life and on his writing. Lu Yu worked in a literary and cultural circle that was extremely productive in the realm of ideas; as we shall see, its members not only wrote poetry but were also involved in some of the major religious developments of the eighth century, especially relating to the creation of Chan ideol-

96

Porcelain figure of Lu Yu, God of Tea.
Five Dynasties.

ogy and literature. Understanding the religious roots and ramifications of the aesthetic turn represented by Lu Yu's *Classic of Tea* is one of the purposes of this chapter.

LU YU IN HISTORICAL CONTEXT

Lu Yu was probably quite a prolific author, although most of the works ascribed to him have not survived. In his remarks on Lu Yu's autobiography, the eleventh-century statesman and historian Ouyang Xiu (1007–1072) listed titles attributed to him totaling more than sixty fascicles.[3] Lu Yu wrote on a diversity of topics, including genealogy, historical biography, local history, and dream divination. But, as Ouyang notes, only the *Classic of Tea* continued to be transmitted in his day. It is therefore difficult to assess the *Classic of Tea* against the background of Lu Yu's greater literary oeuvre, but we can say that it was on the development of tea culture that he had the greatest influence.

The social and political background to Lu Yu's life was undoubtedly significant in shaping his attitudes and interests as a writer. The relative peace and
prosperity of the Kaiyuan period (712–756), during which Lu Yu grew up, contrasted sharply with the turmoil of the An Lushan rebellion (755–763) and its
aftermath.[4] This rebellion's destructive effects on the imperial administration
and the massive displacement of the population ripped apart the social fabric
of the Tang elite and had a marked impact on intellectual and religious life as
thinkers sought to come to terms with the radical and unforeseen shift in the
world order. Lu Yu and his contemporaries were profoundly affected by the sudden and shocking failure of the central government and the abrupt sweeping
away of the old certainties of life.[5] Lu Yu himself responded to the crisis in verses
titled "Quadruple Sorrow" and "Rhapsody on the Non-clarity of Heaven."[6]
So, we should remember not only the long-term historical significance of Lu
Yu and his work but also the immediate cultural context in which he operated.

Looked at from the long-term perspective of the history of tea, the appearance of the *Classic of Tea* marks the definitive shift from drinking tea primarily for medicinal/wellness purposes to the much broader consumption of the
beverage in all kinds of private and social situations. To put it another way, Lu
Yu, with his network of contacts with literati and monk-poets, was a foundational figure in the transformation of tea drinking from a minor localized custom into a kind of art form and practice that became a defining feature of the
larger Chinese cultural milieu. This change was effected not only through works
penned by Lu Yu himself but also by the construction of a language and aesthetics of tea appreciation by those around him and those later authors inspired
by his *Classic* to pen their own works.

Lu Yu was by no means an obscure figure while he was alive, and after his
death, his fame only increased. We already noted the ninth-century author Pi
Rixiu's account of Lu Yu's legacy for tea; in the preface to his "Various Poems
on Tea" (*Cha zhong zayong*), which dates to 853–855, Pi again notes the shift
from alcohol to tea and singles out Lu Yu for his work in popularizing the
latter.[7] The Late Tang monk Qiji composed "Passing the former home of Lu
Hongjian [Lu Yu]" (*Guo Lu Hongjian jiuju*), which promoted the status of the
sage of tea. Commemorative works such as these were by no means unusual in
the century or so after Lu Yu's life.[8] Even in much later times, there was considerable interest in Lu Yu the man as well as in his *Classic*—for example, Chen
Jiru (1558–1639), the famous late Ming arbiter of taste, recorded a previously
unknown anecdote about Lu Yu pushing a servant girl into the fire when he
came home to discover she had burnt the tea leaves he had left her to dry.[9]

Let us examine for a moment Pi Rixiu's late ninth-century account of the
rise of tea and Lu Yu's role in it.

According to the *Rites of Zhou,* the department of the Regulator of Alcohol distinguished four beverages, the third of which is called "broth." Also, the responsibilities of the person in charge of broth were to supply the king with the "six beverages" (water, broth, purified rice wine, watered wine [called *liang*], fermented rice spirit, strained rice spirit). These were all to be stored in the Alcohol Department. Zheng, [the] Minister of Agriculture said, "mix water with alcohol," and surely people of that time followed in using alcohol and rice wine as a drink.[10] The so-called six beverages refer to weak alcohol. How could it be that Master Ji has edited the *Erya* to say, "*Jia* is bitter *cha,* but we don't drink it." Could the sages have commended anything more useful? Moreover, herbs and trees for the service of humans should be gathered according to season.

As for matters of tea, from the Zhou down to our present dynasty, the master of Jinling, Lu Jici (Lu Yu) has discussed them in detail. Before Jici's time, tea was called *ming* and to drink it one mixed it up [with other ingredients] and boiled it—it was no different from slurping vegetable soup. Jici composed the first *Classic* [of Tea] in three fascicles, thereupon he distinguished its origins, specified the utensils, instructed on growing it, fixed the vessels for serving it, and made rules for preparing it. Drinking it relieves disease and expels pestilence even better than the physician. How could its benefits for humankind be considered trivial?

When I first obtained Jici's book, I considered it was complete. Later, I treasured his *Record of Mount Guzhu (Guzhu shan ji)* in two chapters. In it are many matters of tea. Later, there was Wen Yun of Taiyuan and Duan Beizhi of Wuwei; each added ten or more stories about tea which survive in regular volumes; so as for matters about tea from the Zhou to today, ultimately no information is lacking. In the Jin, Du You had a *fu* about *chuan;* and Jici wrote the "Tea Song."[11]

Pi's brief synopsis of China's beverage history from the high antiquity of the Zhou dynasty to present times and of the cultural shift from drinking alcohol to drinking tea (not as a medicinal soup, but rather as a refined single-ingredient beverage), composed fifty years after Lu Yu's death, shows how rapidly Lu's work and its message had been assimilated at the elite level. As far as late Tang literati were concerned, the recent turn toward tea was not the accidental or impersonal effect of market forces or changing tastes among the masses; it had a known and sagely instigator—Lu Yu. Although we are not obliged to accept the veracity of this version of events, which privileges the written word above any other means of disseminating tea drinking, we have to recognize that for elite authors this was the dominant narrative about the power of Lu Yu and his writing.

SOURCES FOR THE LIFE OF LU YU

Some of the major contours of Lu Yu's life are not easy to establish; despite our access to multiple sources, including his own writing, considerable confusion and contradiction remain around some of the most basic facts. Even his own account of his life often sheds little light on the matter. In 761, when he was only twenty-nine years old, Lu Yu wrote an autobiography titled *Autobiography of Instructor Lu* (*Lu Wenxue zizhuan*). That work was later anthologized in an important early Song encyclopedia, *Blossoms and Flowers from the Garden of Literature* (*Wenyuan yinghua*).[12] In addition, a note appended to Qiji's poem on "Passing Lu Hongjian's Former Residence" indicates that a copy of the autobiography was carved on the stone well near Lu Yu's old home.[13] Lu also merited an official biography in the "recluses" section (*yinyi zhuan*) of the official dynastic history *New Book of the Tang* (*Xin Tang shu*). Because of his background and connections with eminent monks, the Buddhist chronicle writer Nianchang (1282–1344) included an entry on Lu Yu in his *Comprehensive Record of the History of the Buddhas and Patriarchs* (*Fozu lidai tongzai*).[14] Another important later source is that contained in a collection of the lives of Tang poets, *Biographies of Talented Men of the Tang* (*Tang caizi zhuan*), by the Yuan-dynasty statesman and poet Xin Wenfang (fl. 1300).[15]

Looking beyond these more substantial biographical materials, we also find important information contained in briefer anecdotal accounts. *Supplement to the State History* (*Guoshi bu*), a miscellaneous collection of anecdotes, observations, and lore compiled in the 820s by the court official Li Zhao (died before 836), has a number of entries concerned with tea and one devoted to Lu Yu's life.[16] *Record of Tales of Cause and Effect* (*Yinhua lu*) is a collection of anecdotes from the Tang period written by Zhao Lin (*jinshi* 834) that also contains a brief discussion of Lu Yu.[17] The Song collection *Extensive Records of the Taiping Era* (*Taiping guangji*) preserves an entry on Lu Yu from the early ninth-century *Biographical Records of the Great Tang* (*Da Tang zhuanzai*).[18]

Lu Yu's *Autobiography of Instructor Lu* has been translated in full by Victor Mair and is the subject of an important study by Nishiwaki Tsuneki.[19] It is a remarkable document, one of the earliest autobiographies in Chinese literature, but it does not resolve many of the ambiguities around Lu Yu's life. Composed in a playful, self-conscious, and ironic style, but by no means devoid of pathos and genuine emotion, it presents the young Lu Yu as an eccentric recluse who "would frequently walk alone in the wilderness reciting Buddhist scriptures or chanting ancient poems."[20] In the autobiography, which takes the form of a self-written biography composed in the third person, the author plays self-consciously with the imagery of rustic simplicity—he describes himself as "clad only in a gauze kerchief, vine sandals, a short shirt of coarse wool, and a pair of underpants"—and conceals as much as he reveals about his life and his opinions. His autobiography does seek to make him unusual, and he does indeed seem to have enjoyed an unconventional life. Lu Yu was not just an armchair expert who drew on the works of others; rather, he made on-the-spot investigations of mountain springs and experimented with growing tea in various locations. Although many interesting religious currents can be detected throughout his life, it probably makes most sense to treat the story of Lu Yu in roughly chronological fashion, drawing on the multiple extant sources, as I do next.[21]

THE MYSTERIOUS ORIGINS OF LU YU

Let us begin with Lu Yu's birth and origins. He gives away little substantial information in his autobiography, recording only that "[i]t is not known where he was from," and adding later, "An abandoned waif at the age of three [sui], Lu Yu was taken in and raised in the Jingling meditation chapel by the great master Ji."[22] Later biographies add the picturesque detail, found earliest in the Supplement to the State History, that the monk Zhiji (the "great master Ji" of Lu Yu's own account) discovered the infant by the banks of a river.[23] Much later sources, such as the local gazetteer for Tianmen County, describe how the Chan master Zhiji was passing by a stone bridge one day in late autumn when he heard the faint sound of an infant wailing midst the cries of the wild geese among the riverside reeds. The old monk followed the sound to discover a small child, frozen, trembling, and crying without cease. The wild geese had spread their wings to protect the boy from the bitter wind. The master, filled with compassion, wrapped the boy in his monk's robe and took him back to his monastery where he raised him.[24] The association with wild geese in Lu Yu's infancy seems to be a back-formation derived from his personal name, Hongjian ("wild goose ascending"), which I will discuss later. All the sources agree that the foundling Lu was adopted in the twenty-third year of the Kaiyuan reign period (735) at the age of three sui, which means that Lu Yu was born in 733. It is not clear how the boy's age at the time of his abandonment was determined or known. It is possible that it was known by his parents or other relatives when he was given to the monk Zhiji for adoption.

We can already see what may appear to be mythical elements in the life story of Lu Yu—his strange appearance, his abandonment at birth, his adoption by a Buddhist monk, and signs of his early prodigy. We may question whether these aspects represent veritable records of the man's exceptional nature or merely the conventions of hagiography, and we may profitably place Lu Yu's biography alongside that of contemporary religious figures such as the sixth patriarch of Chan, the monk Huineng (638–713).[25]

We do not know a great deal about Lu Yu's adoptive father. In Lu's autobiography he calls him Master Ji in the normal respectful manner. *Yinhua lu* refers to him as "a monk of Longxing monastery, surnamed Lu," and only *Guoshi bu* provides the two characters of a dharma name: Zhiji.[26] The name of the monastery of which he was the abbot is incorrectly given in *Yinhua lu*: it was not Longxing but Longgai si, later renamed Western Stūpa (Xi ta) after the memorial pagoda for Zhiji that was erected beside it.[27] The monastery was located on the banks of West Lake, Jingling (Tianmen County in modern Hubei), and had been established during the Southern Qi dynasty (479–502) when it was known as Fangle si. It must have been a monastery of some prestige in Sui times because it housed a relic of the Buddha dispatched there during the famous Renshou era (601–604) imperial relic-distribution campaign.[28] The Tianmen County local gazetteer of 1987 claims an earlier connection of the site with the eminent monk Zhi Dun (314–366).[29] It is not known when Longgai monastery ceased to operate, but no trace of it now remains.

Although Lu Yu certainly presents himself as a solitary orphan, there is some evidence to suggest that he may have had siblings. Some of his associates in later life, such as Yan Zhenqing and Dai Shulun (732–789), addressed poems to him as "Lu Number Three" (*Lu San*).[30] This sobriquet may perhaps indicate that Lu had two older brothers. Alternatively, perhaps the number could have indicated his rank among other disciples of Zhiji.

Lu was his surname, Yu his personal name, and Hongjian ("wild goose ascending") his style name. But some playful uncertainty is introduced in the autobiography, where the author claims, "[S]ome say his style was Yu and his name was Hongjian, but it is impossible to know who is right."[31] This statement appears to have confused Ouyang Xiu, who took it to indicate that the "autobiography" of Lu Yu could not have been written by the man himself.[32] Another personal name was Ji, and he also used the style Jici, as we saw earlier in Pi Rixiu's work. But where did he obtain these names if he was a foundling brought up by a monk? In his own account of his life, Lu Yu offers no explanation, and we find a variety of stories in the other sources. *Guoshi bu* reports that his adoptive father chose his name by divination from *Yijing* (*Change Classic*). Hexagram 53 (*jianyu*) of *Yijing* reads, "The wild goose gradually advances to the heights (*lu*). Its feathers (*yu*) may be used as ornaments." Therefore, the monk gave the boy Lu as his surname, [Yu] as his personal name, and Hongjian as his style name. This is the earliest record of the origin of Lu Yu's unusual names. Other accounts, such as the *Xin Tang shu* biography, say that Lu Yu divined the name for himself. The biography in *Tang caizi zhuan,* which is much later than the others, insists that Lu Yu consulted the *Change Classic* in search of a name when he rejected the Buddhist tonsure (probably around the age of eight or nine).[33] If he really only acquired a name this late, we must wonder what he was called as a young child.

According to *Yinhua lu* and *Da Tang zhuanzai* he took his surname Lu from the secular name of his adoptive father. The *Yinhua lu* account may have some reliable information on this point because Liu Zhongyong (d. 775), the maternal grandfather of the author of the work, had a close personal relationship with Lu Yu and may have known some facts of his life firsthand.[34] It would also accord with what the Tang legal code says about adoption: "If the child has been abandoned and is three years of age or less, he can be adopted and he takes their [his adoptive parents'] surname."[35] Certainly, the adoption of a surname would have been a much more common practice in traditional China than determining a surname by divination, for which the case of Lu Yu seems to offer the sole well-known example.[36] We know of Buddhist monks (like Li Bai's nephew, for example) who divined their dharma names from *Yijing,* so this practice may have been the inspiration behind the story of Lu Yu's naming.

CHILDHOOD IN THE MONASTERY

Lu Yu does not comment much on his childhood in the monastery, and other sources such as his official biography are vague on this period of his life and his precise status. They state only that the monk "raised" the child and make no mention of him administering the tonsure or a novice's precepts to his disciple.[37] Only the Yuan-dynasty biography found in *Tang caizi zhuan* explicitly states that Lu was "ashamed to take the tonsure" (*chi cong xuefa*).[38] In the autobiography, Lu Yu claims that he learned to read from the age of nine *sui* and that his master explained the vocation of Buddhist monastic life to him. Lu Yu, however, responded to this approach as follows:

> To be cut off from one's brothers, to have no further descendants, to wear the robe and shave the head, to call oneself a disciple of Śākyamuni—if the Confucians were to hear of this, would they proclaim it to be filial behavior? Would it be all right if I request that you teach me the writings of the Confucian sages?[39]

The monk insisted that his adopted son study Buddhist texts, while Lu Yu remained adamant that he wanted to read the Classics. Frustrated, the monk pretended not to love his ward and charged him with menial tasks around the monastery—sweeping the grounds, cleaning the latrines, mixing plaster for the walls with his feet, carrying tiles for roof repairs on his back, and herding thirty head of cattle. It is interesting to note, as John Jorgensen has done, that this part of the autobiography seems to mirror the early life of the Chan sixth patriarch Huineng, another orphan who was put to work in the monastery threshing room.[40] Because there was no paper on which to practice his writing, Lu Yu reports that he would trace the characters on the back of his cattle with a bamboo stylus. The calligrapher-monk Huaisu, for whom Lu Yu later composed a biography, makes a similar claim about his own youth.[41] There may well have been an element of personal myth-making in the story that Lu Yu's sources tell of his childhood and of his precocious interest in the Classics.

One day, Lu Yu acquired from a local scholar a copy of Zhang Heng's (78–139) famous "Rhapsody on the Southern Capital" (*Nancheng fu*).[42] He could not read it, but imitated the behavior of young students he had seen—sitting upright in the pasture with the scroll unrolled in front of him and mouthing the words. When Zhiji learned of this development, he feared that his charge's mind would be affected by secular texts and so had him confined to the monastery. The boy's task was to cut back weeds under the supervision of the head gateman. But Lu Yu was already in love with literature, and when he recalled certain characters he would go into a trance, causing the supervisor to beat him until his stick broke.

Eventually, in 745 at the age of thirteen, Lu Yu ran away, joining a troupe of performers and composing his first literary work—a joke book in three fascicles.[43] Zhiji found him and brought him back to the monastery, promising to allow him in the future to study non-Buddhist works and to practice his calligraphy. At some point, Lu Yu also acquired the habit of drinking tea from his foster father, and it is said that after Lu Yu left the monastery, for many years Zhiji would not drink tea made by anyone else. Lu Yu likewise remained very fond of his adoptive father. A dozen years or so after Lu's death, his friend Zhou Yuan (fl. 773–816) wrote a text called "Posted to Jingling, on travelling to the Western Stūpa, I wrote these three emotional responses" (*Mushou Jingling yin you sita zhu san huoshuo*) in which he describes the stūpa erected for Zhiji:[44]

> On the eastern side of our prefecture, there is a place that is shaped like an inverted cauldron. It is round like the crown of one's head, and in the middle stands a stūpa. The bamboo there grows as thick as one's arm; their green canopy covers the image of someone who died, [Lu] Hongjian's original teacher. How sad is this crown-shaped place! Bamboo of Chu encircle the stūpa. The monk within the stūpa is the monk

whom Lu Yu served. The bamboo before the stūpa is the bamboo that Lu Yu planted. Gazing at the sky, the monk's image is muddied and the bamboo broken. The branches and leaves are old and Lu Yu is already gone. As the governor of the place, I came therefore to venerate the temple at its heart. In the bright daylight there is no fragrant smoke from Lu Yu. I give a long sigh at this wretched desolation, my robe rustling as the wind blows through the thorns.[45]

As we can see then, although Lu Yu spurned the monk's life, he by no means turned his back on his adoptive father and his religion, and he must have spoken to his companions of his continuing affection for both. Although we cannot tell for sure, it is possible that Lu Yu himself was responsible for the stūpa that commemorated his father the monk. In his own time, Lu was evidently regarded as a thinker with distinctly Buddhist affiliations, but his love for the worldly classics by no means entailed a complete break with his early upbringing.

LU YU'S PRECOCIOUS TALENTS

Lu's literary talents were first spotted by Li Qiwu (d. 762), a former governor of Luoyang. Because of a scandal at court, he had been demoted to the prefect of Jingling in the seventh month of Tianbao 5 (746).[46] He first met Lu Yu at a feast where the young man had been hired to direct the entertainment.[47] Li presented the youth with his own poetry collection. Clearly, to have entered elite literary circles at the young age of fourteen Lu Yu must have shown early signs of ability. His skill in tea connoisseurship was developing at the same pace as his aptitude for literature; as early as 750, when he was eighteen *sui*, Lu Yu was already sampling teas and gathering information about them. In 751 or 752, Li Qiwu returned to the capital, but Lu Yu soon made another important early literary connection with the poet and official Cui Guofu (678–755), who had been demoted to adjutant (*sima*) of Jingling County.[48] This promising start to Lu Yu's career was, however, soon to be abruptly terminated by events on a much greater scale.

RELOCATION TO THE SOUTH

In 755, the general An Lushan rose in rebellion and marched on the Tang city of Luoyang, and Lu Yu's new patron Cui Guofu died. In 756, rebel forces captured the Tang capital, Chang'an. At the age of twenty four, Lu Yu, along with many other refugees from the Central Plain, fled south of the Yangzi River to escape the chaos caused by the rebellion. He arrived first in Wuxing in Hu-zhou and subsequently spent the next forty-eight years wandering around the Jiangnan region devoted to the pursuit of tea and literature. He first met Jiaoran—probably the most famous poet in southeast China at the time—in 757 at his home monastery of Miaoxi si on Mount Zhu in Wucheng County, Wuxing.[49] So began a lifelong friendship that never faded over the next forty years. Around this time he met another notable poet-monk of the same mon-astery, Jiaoran's pupil Lingche (746–816). Lingche taught the famous Tang poet and thinker Liu Yuxi (772–842) to write poetry in his youth, and Liu later wrote a preface for a collection of the monk's poetry.[50] Lingche is also a significant figure in the history of early Chan literature, having written the preface to the important *Chronicle of Baolin monastery* (*Baolin zhuan*).[51] Lu Yu resided at Mi-aoxi monastery for the next three years. Although the An Lushan rebellion and its aftermath were a catastrophe for the Tang, for Lu Yu these events threw him together with significant religious and intellectual figures he might otherwise never have met.

Lu Yu's activities were not restricted to Buddhist institutions and figures. He also visited a site that was very important to the Taoist Shangqing tradi-tion, Mount Mao in Jiangsu, to gather tea in 759. The next year, he was at Lake Tai where he sampled the water from the spring at Wuxi and later composed the *Record of Huishan Monastery* (*Huishan si ji*), which, like most of his works, does not survive. He returned to Wuxing and built a hut on the banks of Tiao stream, to the southwest of Miaoxi monastery. During this period of his life he began to associate with Dai Shulun, the famous female poet Li Ye, and others.[52]

Around this time, Lu Yu traveled throughout Yangzhou and Zhenjiang, sampling water from the various mountain springs for his project on tea. He went to Mount Qixia in present-day Nanjing to try the local tea, and there he began a close friendship with Huangfu Ran (714–767) and his younger brother Huangfu Zeng (d. 785?), both successful "advanced scholar" (*jinshi*) civil ser-vice examination candidates from Danyang. Both the Huangfu brothers wrote poems about him: "Seeing off Lu Hongjian to pick tea at Qixia monastery" (*Song Lu Hongjian Qixia si cai cha*) by Huangfu Ran and Huangfu Zeng's "Seeing off the Man of the Mountains Lu Hongjian to pick tea" (*Song Lu Hongjian shan-ren cai cha hui*).[53] Jiaoran's poem, "Going to Danyang to seek the recluse Lu and not finding him" (*Wang Danyang cun Lu chushi buyu*) also dates from this time.[54] The Huangfu brothers are mentioned in Jiaoran's verse as well as by an-other friend of Lu's, Quan Deyu (759–818), who was one of the most impor-tant statesmen and thinkers of the time. As we can see then, although he was driven from his home by unfortunate events, Lu found significant and presti-gious new connections and opportunities in the South and associated with the most interesting and exciting thinkers of his day.

Here is how Lu Yu describes himself in 761, the year he composed his autobiography:

> At the beginning of the Taiyuan reign period (760–761), Lu Yu built a hut by the bank of Tiaoxi stream. He closed his door and read books, refusing to mix with rogues, though he would spend his whole days chatting and convivializing with eminent monks and lofty scholars. Often, he would travel back and forth between various mountains and monasteries in his little slip of a boat, clad only in a gauze kerchief, vine sandals, a short shirt of coarse wool, and a pair of underpants. He would frequently walk alone in the wilderness reciting Buddhist scriptures or chanting ancient poems. Striking the forest trees with his staff or dabbling in the flowing water with his hand, Lu Yu might dilly-dally hesitantly from morning until evening and on into the darkness of night after the sun had gone completely down, whereupon he would return home wailing and weeping. So the southerners would say to each other, "Master Lu must be today's Madman of Chu."[55]

Lu Yu presents himself here as a hypersensitive wanderer in search of truth and beauty. Living in a simple hut, he still manages to maintain relations of the most elevated and sincere kind with other scholars. As for his religious interests, clearly they still inclined to Buddhism—he mixes with eminent monks and regularly recites Buddhist sutras. Much of what we know about Lu from other sources confirms this image of his life in seclusion.

In the same year that he composed his autobiography, 761, he also completed a first draft of the *Classic of Tea*. In 762, when Lu Yu was thirty, his former mentor Li Qiwu died. For the next two years, as he revised the *Classic of Tea*, Lu based himself in Wuxing, but made extensive trips around Jiangnan to make on-the-spot investigations of tea. He did not confine himself to merely observing, but planted tea himself at various sites. On Mount Guzhu in Changsheng County (present-day Changxing), Mount Tanggong in Yixing County (present-day Yixing), and other mountains, Lu Yu cultivated tea plantations so that he could observe how tea grew in different locales.

LU YU AND FRIENDS

It is not always easy to reconstruct Lu Yu's life. For some periods, we catch only fleeting glimpses of him in the poems written by his friends or by himself. From 763 to 769, between the ages of thirty-one to thirty-seven, Lu Yu was mostly living on a certain Mount Long (Long shan, "Dragon Mountain")—but which particular mountain by that name is not entirely clear. It was either Long shan in Jiangning County in Runzhou or Long shan in Wuxi in Changzhou. Jiaoran has a poem titled "On the topic 'night rains dripping on the steps,' seeing off Lu Yu on his return to Mount Long" (*Fu de yeyu kongdi jie song Lu Yu gui Long shan*).[56] Some time during this period, Huangfu Ran was laid up sick for the spring season in a villa at Lake Tai, and Lu Yu came to visit him. Huangfu wrote a poem that implies that when Lu Yu left him he went on to Yuezhou (present-day Shaoxing).[57] Lu Yu's own poem "A small mountain east of Kuaiji" (*Kuaiji dong xiaoshan*) offers further evidence that Lu Yu was in Yuezhou.[58]

In 764, when he was thirty-two, according to what he tells us in the *Classic of Tea,* the special custom-ordered tea brazier with intricate and symbolic decoration that he had commissioned was completed.[59] From 765 to 767 he went from Wuxing to Mount Jun at Yixing in Changzhou to gather samples of tea. In 768–769, his friend Jiaoran had a grass hut constructed on the banks of Tiao stream, a distance of thirty *li* from Lu Yu's hut that he had built in 760.[60] Jiaoran invited Lu Yu to his grass hut in 770, and Huangfu Ran died around this same year.

In 772, Lu Yu began an important association with another very significant figure of the late eighth century, Yan Zhenqing (709–785). According to Yan's stele inscription for Miaoxi si, in that year the statesman and intellectual Yan entered Wuxing and first met Lu Yu.[61] Also, this was the same year that Yan met the Taoist poet Zhang Zhihe whom I have already mentioned.[62] In 773, Lu Yu, along with Jiaoran, Zhou Yuan, and fifty other literary men, gathered at Yan Zhenqing's residence to compose the 360-fascicle *Sea of Rhymes, Mirror of Sources* (*Yunhai jingyuan,* no longer extant), a major classified dictionary arranged in rhyme order.[63] This was clearly a significant literary project, and again Lu Yu found himself in the most refined company. During this time, Lu often participated in banquets hosted by Yan Zhenqing, and together they completed the "Wuxing collection" (*Wuxing ji*) of their writings in ten fascicles.

Lu Yu's time with Yan produced more than just literature; there were also other significant markers of their companionship. On the twenty-first day of the tenth month of Dali 8 (November 10, 773), the "Three *Gui*" pavilion on Mount Zhu was completed. Lu Yu had designed this structure, Yan Zhenqing put up the capital and wrote the plaque for it, and Jiaoran immortalized the pavilion in verse.[64] Yan relates how it got its name with reference to the characters used to designate days, months, and years in the traditional sexagenary cycle:

> Because it was built on a *guihai* day, the twenty-first, in the tenth month, of which the first day was a *guimao* day, during the winter of a *guichou* year, Retired Scholar Lu [Yu] named it the Three *Gui* Pavilion.[65]

Amy McNair explains the sophistication of Lu's choice of name in her study of Yan Zhenqing: "The name of the Three *Gui* (san gui) Pavilion is a pun twice over, playing on the three types of cassia (*san gui*) on Mount Zhu, a term also used as a metaphor for three high dignitaries."[66] The naming of this pavilion offers a nice example of Lu Yu's sophisticated wit in action. We imagine that Yan must have appreciated finding such convivial and intelligent company so far from the metropolis.

Yan Zhenqing's intellectual circle was a highly eclectic one in terms of religious interests, but its members all shared well-developed literary and artistic tastes and abilities. Yan's own family background was Confucian, but he expended considerable efforts in renovating altars to renowned Taoists of the past, and the stele inscriptions that he composed for Taoist saints such as Wei Huacun (252–334) demonstrate that he was well versed in Taoist lore.[67] Although Yan himself was probably not a practicing Taoist, he had close associations with Taoist figures of his day and was celebrated as a Taoist immortal after his death.[68] An important Taoist member of Yan's literary salon was Zhang Zhihe, author of *Xuanzhen zi* (*Master of Mysterious Truth*).[69] I quoted an anecdote from this work in an earlier chapter. Yan Zhenqing composed Zhang's epitaph, which also mentions Lu Yu. Whatever their backgrounds, all the members of Yan's circle shared a strong interest in language and some background in the study of Laozi and Zhuangzi. In these aspects, they were similar to the Six Dynasties poets whom they emulated in their writing of linked verse—a genre that itself had long fallen from fashion until Yan and Jiaoran revived it.[70] In Lu Yu's personal life, he had strong connections with practicing Buddhists and Taoists as well as literary men with well-developed interests in self-cultivation.

The mid-770s saw significant changes for Lu Yu and the group around Yan Zhenqing. His friend Zhang Zhihe died some time between 774 and 778. In 775, Yan Zhenqing helped Lu Yu build the Qingtang villa, otherwise known as "Lu Yu's new residence." Between 775 and 776, Jiaoran once came to visit him there and wrote a poem to commemorate the occasion.[71] Finally, in 777, Yan Zhenqing returned to the capital, and his association with Lu Yu came to an end. Between 777 and 778, Lu Yu built a temporary hut for reclusion on Mount Jun where Jiaoran once visited him, composing the poem "Joyfully, District Magistrate Quan of Yixing and I came to Mount Jun, gathering at the other residence of Retired Scholar Lu Yu at Qiantang."[72]

LU YU IN LATER LIFE

Around 780 the *Classic of Tea* was published when Lu was forty-eight years old. The work was initially finished in 761, and some corrections and additions were then made, but the last event referred to in the book is from 765—the year after the end of the An Lushan rebellion. In addition to the publication of what was to be his most famous work, 780 was a turning point for Lu Yu in other ways. Having assiduously avoided government service in his early life, in the 780s Lu Yu finally became part of the imperial civil service. Between 780 and 783, Lu Yu was appointed Instructor to the Crown Prince (Taizi wenxue), then resigned, took up an appointment as Great Supplicator in the Court of Imperial Sacrifice (Taichang si taizhu), and then quit that position.[73] It was a short and probably rather ineffective government career. He seems to have exerted little influence on state policy or court politics during his time in office.

The 780s saw the waning of Lu Yu's generation as his friends and collaborators began to pass away. In 784, the poetess Li Ye was executed by the emperor Dezong for having written a poem to the rebel general Zhu Ci (742–784) urging him to seize the throne as emperor, set up a state called Great Qin, and change the reign name to Yingtian ("Responding to Heaven"). Since 760, Li Ye had maintained her connections with both Jiaoran and Lu Yu, and even though Li Ye was much older than him, Lu Yu must have retained some affection for her. In 785, Huangfu Zeng died, and so did Lu's former patron Yan Zhenqing.

After Lu Yu's brief time in office, he returned to his familiar haunts in the South, and in 785 he had a new house built northwest of Fucheng in Shangrao County, Xinzhou. His friend the poet Meng Jiao (751–814) came to congratulate him and wrote a poem to commemorate his new dwelling.[74]

In 786, Li Qiwu's son, Li Fu, became governor of Rongzhou (present-day Rong County in Guangxi).[75] Li Fu was to be Lu's major patron in the 780s and 790s. Zhou Yuan's piece, "Posted to Jingling," that I quoted earlier, shows that in 786, Lu Yu, Zhou Yuan, and Ma Zong had gone on an extended visit to Yan Fu's house and that they were there until 794 when Li Fu was reinstated as governor of Huazhou and Lu Yu departed. In 789, Li Fu was appointed joint governor of Guangzhou and Lingnan military commander. Lu Yu, Zhou Yuan, and Ma Zong all accompanied him to his new post. When Li Fu went to pay obeisance to his ancestors in 792, Lu Yu either went with him or in that year returned to his Qingtang villa in Wuxing. The next year, Li Fu was appointed governor of Huazhou (present-day Hua County in Shaanxi). From 793 onward, Lu Yu resided in Suzhou and for a long period at Huqiu—perhaps up until 798. It was during that time that his old friend Jiaoran came to call and wrote his famous poem, "Calling on the Recluse Lu and not finding him in."[76] In 794, Li Yu was appointed governor of Huazhou (present-day Hua County in Henan), and Zhou Yuan accompanied him there.

During his later life, Lu Yu continued to write books, even after the publication of *Classic of Tea*. In 795, he completed his *Record of Successive Officials in Wuxing* (*Wuxing liguan ji*) in three fascicles and *Record of the Gov-*

ernors of Huzhou (Huzhou cishi ji) in one fascicle. We cannot really be sure where he lived after 794, but it is possible that he remained in Hunan to write the biography of his friend, the calligrapher-monk Huaisu, another former companion who had pre-deceased him.[77]

To the end of his life, Lu Yu maintained an active interest in tea. In 796, he was on Mount Huqiu tasting water and planting tea. Li Fu, his patron in later life, died in office in 797. In 799, Lu Yu returned to Wuxing, likely because he knew that his friend Jiaoran was on the point of death. Jiaoran probably died in 800, and four years later in 804, Lu himself passed away in Wuxing.[78] From a poem written by Meng Jiao we can infer that Lu Yu was buried by Jiaoran's stūpa, on the banks of the Tiao stream in front of Miaoxi monastery on Mount Zhu.[79] Companions for so long in life, it seems fitting that they should have remained together in death.

THE CLASSIC OF TEA

Lu Yu's famous Classic is not particularly substantial for all its influence. It is three fascicles and about 7,000 characters in length—for comparison, this makes it about 2,000 characters longer than the Daode jing. Although not prolix, the work is comprehensive in coverage, including informed discussion of the horticulture and manufacture of tea, as well as its history and the method for the preparation of the beverage. The title of the work may be seen as provocative or grandiose, elevating tea to such heights that only a "scripture" or "classic" was suitable to describe it. But the appropriation of the term jing for his work appears to have garnered no particular censure from Lu Yu's contemporaries or from later scholars. For its structure and contents Lu Yu had no particular precedent, although in dividing up the three fascicles into ten sections it is possible that Lu was drawing, perhaps unconsciously, on models drawn from Buddhist and Taoist rules for monastic life that tended to exhibit similar organizational structures.[80]

The first three parts of the Classic are concerned with the tea plant, instruments used in manufacturing tea, and methods for harvesting and production. The fourth part is devoted to utensils used in preparing and serving the beverage, and the fifth describes how tea is prepared and brewed. Part six prescribes how tea should be drunk. Part seven contains excerpts from primary sources in the history of tea such as those discussed in an earlier chapter. In part eight, Lu Yu lays out the main tea-producing areas of his time—most of which he had visited in person on several occasions over the years. In part nine, he describes some exceptions to the rules found in earlier sections, and the final section explains how the text of the work should be copied and displayed.

The style of the *Classic* is direct, informed, and authoritative. Lu Yu presents information about tea and its manufacture in a concise and unembellished manner. His writing only occasionally slips into a more personal and lyrical mode, as when he describes the design of his personal tea brazier.[81] Instructions on the preparation of tea are given very precisely and in a didactic step-by-step fashion. The *Classic of Tea* seems designed to be kept at hand and consulted frequently by the budding tea connoisseur, rather than read through in a single sitting. It is more of a manual than a theoretical treatise. Overall, it has a markedly practical orientation, and there is nothing in the voice of the work or its language that would seem to make it a "classic." It appears that Lu Yu aimed to be comprehensive and informative rather than particularly profound or philosophical in his treatment.

Although the *Classic of Tea* was a unique document, Lu Yu and the *Chajing* by no means offered the definitive word in medieval tea culture. For example, Lu's method of making tea by boiling it up with a rich froth on top was superseded relatively soon by other ways of preparing the beverage. Also, in its lengthy discussion of the necessary equipment for preparing and serving tea the *Classic of Tea* makes no mention of utensils like the tea stand (*chatuo*) that later became quite important.[82]

There were essentially three ways of making tea in China: steeping tea leaves in hot water and allowing the flavor to flow out, mixing powdered tea with a stream of hot boiled water from a ewer (a method that came to dominate in Song times, as we shall see), and boiling tea, which was what Lu Yu did. To boil tea using his method, one begins by taking a tea cake in bamboo tongs, toasting it by the brazier, then grinding the tea, and sifting it to produce a fine powder.[83] The water for tea is heated in a round cauldron on a brazier, and at the first boil, described as "fish eyes," a pinch of salt is added to it. Given Lu Yu's disdain for additives in tea, the use of salt seems counterintuitive, but adding some minerals to water for tea remains a common practice even today and is widely considered to enhance its flavor by softening the water. At the second boil, known as "strung pearls," one reserves a dipperful of the boiling water. At the third boil, one should introduce the powdered tea into a small whirlpool in the cauldron created by rapidly stirring the water with the tongs. Then, the tea is served by ladling it out into bowls, each topped with a generous amount of froth. It is clear from the *Classic of Tea* that, in Lu Yu's opinion, the right kind of froth was essential to the proper enjoyment of tea.

THE *CLASSIC OF TEA* AND ITS LATER IMITATORS

The *Chajing* inspired the development of a (minor) literary genre known as *chashu* (tea literature): prose works dealing with tea in its various aspects—

cultivation, harvesting, preparation, drinking, taste, literary history, and so on.[84] *Chashu* might focus on a single, specialized aspect of tea—such as the choice of water for making the beverage (for example, *Record of Water for Brewing Tea*)—or, like the *Classic of Tea* itself, aim at more comprehensive coverage of topics related to tea. The number of *chashu* varies depending on how one classifies the various works; scholars have suggested twenty-eight, fifty-eight, or ninety-eight titles as belonging to the genre. But we may get some idea of the immediate influence of the *Classic of Tea* by looking just at the works that were produced in the Tang by literati who were inspired by Lu Yu's foundational work.

A work called *Cha shu* (*Commentary on Tea*) is attributed to Fei Wen who lived in the early ninth century. This title is noted only in the *Xu chajing* (*Continued Classic of Tea*) of 1734 by Lu Tingcan.[85] Marco Ceresa claims that it is not quoted in any premodern work, and *Xu chajing* cites only a fragment of it.[86] But it was in fact quoted in a Southern Song collection.[87] What survives from it is a very concise essay, just a couple of hundred characters in length, on the origin and nature of tea.

Zhang Youxin (*jinshi* 814) composed the *Record of Water for Brewing Tea* (*Jiancha shui ji*).[88] As one of the "eight important figures and sixteen gentlemen" (*baguan shiliuzi*) in the retinue of Li Fengji (758–835), Zhang was involved in the factional strife of the 820s.[89] The original title of the work was *Shui jing* (*Classic of Water*), presumably in imitation of the *Classic of Tea,* but to avoid confusion with the more famous Three Kingdoms geographical work of the same name it was retitled as a "Record."[90] The *Record of Water for Brewing Tea* was directly inspired by Lu Yu's work, because it includes the classification of types of water first made by him in the *Classic of Tea.* The interest of literati in the refined consumption of tea spurred a trend for ranking different water sources and for a connoisseurship of water that ran parallel to the fascination for tea. Three Song dynasty treatises on water were later appended to Zhang's work: *Complete Critical Remarks for Preparing Tea* (*Shu zhucha quan pin*) by Ye Qingchen (fl. 1025); *Record of Water of the Daming Reign Period* (*Daming shui ji*), by Ouyang Xiu; and *Record of Water of Mount Fucha* (*Fucha shan shui ji*) also by Ouyang Xiu. That a major writer and intellectual like Ouyang was willing to pen works on water shows that the topic was by no means trivial for the Tang and Song elite.

Record of Water for Brewing Tea has two parts. The first is a classification of water in seven grades according to Liu Bochu.[91] Part two consists of a narrative in which Zhang Youxin tells of how Lu Yu expounded a classification of water in twenty groups. In the spring of 814, Zhang arrived at Jianfu monastery in Chang'an for a reunion with friends. There, he encountered Li Dechui (d.u.) and went to the cell of the monk Xuanjian located to the west of the monastery. He found there a monk from Chu with a basket containing numerous texts. Zhang picked one up and found it inscribed with the title *Record of Brewing Tea* (*Zhucha ji*). The colophon explained that during the reign of Emperor Daizong (r. 762–779), Li Jiqing was prefect of Huzhou. When he arrived in Weiyang (modern Yangzhou) he met Lu Yu. Li learned how to prepare tea from the famous master of tea and then asked his opinion on the quality of various types of water. Lu responded with the list of twenty types. If we are to believe its compiler, then, the origin of the text was a conversation between Lu Yu and Li Jiqing—we might thus compare it with the putative oral origins of Chan discourse records or of the *Analects* of Confucius. The conversation was supposedly transcribed by Li and then attached as a colophon to another text (unknown to us now). Having casually chanced upon this text, Zhang turns it into an appendix to a classification by quite a different author and thus creates a new text called *Record of Water for Brewing Tea*. This would make Zhang simply the compiler of two already extant ideas—he would have added nothing of his own.

Up to this point (if we believe Zhang) the history of the text is fairly straightforward, if picturesque. However, beginning in the Song dynasty we find the belief that the twenty types of water represent a lost work by Lu Yu called *Water Connoisseurship* (*Shui pin*).[92] Thus, there exist two different theories for the origin of the text. On the one hand, it was the chance discovery of a hitherto unknown transcript of an "oral teaching" by Lu Yu. On the other, it is not clear why Zhang would need to invent the conversation with Li Jiqing, if the text was already authentically in circulation. Ouyang Xiu proposed a third solution: the classification of water in twenty types, he says, was not made by Lu Yu because it contradicts the pattern established in his *Classic of Tea*. He also criticized the classification of Liu Bochu for not following the standards set in the *Classic of Tea*. For example, the twenty-point classification includes water from waterfalls, whereas *Classic of Tea* says that water from pools and waterfalls should not be drunk.[93] In the *Chajing*, Lu Yu had established that the water from mountain springs is the best, that taken from rivers is average quality, whereas water from a well is of the lowest quality. But there are examples in *Record of Water for Brewing Tea* of river water ranked higher than springwater (water from the Nanling tributary of the Yangzi is ranked #7) and water from a well ranked higher than water from a river (waters from the Guanyin monastery in Danyang and the Daming monastery in Yangzhou are #11 and #12). Therefore, Ouyang concluded, the classification is not the work of Lu Yu, but had been improperly added by Zhang. Modern scholars are generally more lenient in judging the veracity of Zhang's work. The disputes and debates around the authenticity of the text show how seriously Lu Yu's work and its legacy were taken by literati in the centuries after his times.

Record of Harvesting Tea (Caicha lu) is a work of around 860 by Wen Ting-yun (ca. 812–870), a famous poet and writer of the late Tang.[94] His numerous biographical sources do not note the date or circumstances of composition of the Record of Harvesting Tea. The surviving fragment of the Caicha lu consists of a mere five characters, each of which is followed by a short story containing (except in one case) the same character.[95] The stories concern tea, and the characters are bian "select," shi "have a passion for something," yi "change" (no anecdote attached), ku "bitter," and zhi "send." From these few indications it could be inferred that the Record of Harvesting Tea was a collection of anecdotes about tea. However, it is not clear why the anecdotes are placed where they are or how to explain those characters that do not relate especially to tea.

Although some works on tea were composed by relatively famous and prominent authors, others had more obscure names attached to them. The various editions of Assessing Sixteen Kinds of Boiling Water (Shiliu tang pin) show the author as Su Yi (zi: Yuanming) of the Tang. In an edition contained in Speeches from the Suburbs (Shuofu), a collection of anecdotal material compiled by the Yuan scholar Tao Zongyi, the name appears as Su Yu. Nothing is known of Su Yi. According to the Monograph on the Authenticity of the Ancient Books of Zheng Hall (Zhengtang dushu ji) by Zhou Zhongfu (1768–1831), the author lived between the Song and Yuan, but the text is mentioned in Tao Gu's Record of Things Pure and Strange, so it must be earlier than that work and has to date to the late Tang. The title does not appear in any ancient bibliographic catalog. This omission is understandable because originally it was not a separate work, but part of the ninth fascicle of a book called Traditions of the Immortal Shoots (Xianya zhuan) by Su Yi. The work Traditions of the Immortal Shoots has been lost, but the portion in question is preserved in Record of Things Pure and Strange. From Record of Things Pure and Strange we also learn that the original title was Sixteen Methods for Boiling Water (Tang shiliu fa). The title sometimes appears as Tang pin (Categories of Boiling Water).

Among the chashu works concerned with the water for making tea, Assessing Sixteen Kinds of Boiling Water is an exception, because it does not address the choice of water based on its origin, but rather describes the behavior of water under the action of heat and in response to different types of fuel, containers, and so on. This was a topic that Lu Yu had already addressed in his Classic of Tea, albeit at shorter length. The work distinguishes four groups of water, depending on the degree of boiling (three types), slowness or speed with which it is poured (three types), type of container (five types), and type of fuel (five types). The circulation of this work shows how eager readers were for texts that elaborated on the aesthetic first outlined by Lu Yu.

Finally, Record of Mount Guzhu is attributed to Lu Yu himself; the title refers to Mount Guzhu in Huzhou, site of some of the most famous tea of Lu's day and later. Of the original text, only five phrases, quoted in later works, survive.[96] Of these five, three refer to anecdotes found in part seven of *Classic of Tea*. This work, if it ever existed, was probably rather slight.

This brief survey of other tea literature in Tang times shows that Lu Yu's *Classic of Tea* had little to challenge it in terms of its sophistication, depth of knowledge, and breadth of interests. Although it may have inspired a good deal of literature on the subject of tea, the *Chajing* remained the undisputed "classic," often imitated but never equaled.

CONCLUSION

Lu Yu was a man with an interesting background and life, but had he not caught the cultural wave of tea drinking with his *Classic of Tea*, his life probably would have been little more than a brief footnote in history. Despite attempts by later authors to play down his Buddhist affiliations, he clearly retained a good deal of affection and respect for his monk-father, and much of his adult life was marked by his close friendship with the monk Jiaoran, who combined a facility in composing verse with serious Buddhist practice. Lu Yu's background in Buddhist practice and doctrine no doubt influenced the content and structure of his classic, but it did so quite subtly. There is no doubt that he was interested in producing a work that was quite nonpartisan in its message—he wanted to share his knowledge of tea as widely as possible. From his association with Yan Zhenqing's literary salon, we know that Lu was celebrated in his own time mostly as a gifted thinker and writer, rather than as an advocate for a particular religious ideology. He seems to have been open to eclectic interests and to have had a strong distaste for the stifling routine of government service. He had the good fortune to meet and collaborate with some of the most interesting and creative figures of his day—Yan, Zhang Zhihe, Huaisu, Li Ye, and Jiaoran—and perhaps he influenced their thinking as much as he influenced their preferences for tea. From this chapter we have learned, again, that the rise of tea was no accident and that it was not determined by purely economic or demographic factors. On the contrary, a great deal of thought and intention went into the promotion of a new beverage for a new age. Although there was other tea literature in the Tang, Lu Yu's work was clearly the most complete and influential text on the subject. Works by other authors, whether on tea or water, remained in the shadow of the *Classic of Tea*.

6

Tea

Invigorating the Body, Mind, and Society in the Song Dynasty

Song dynasty tea culture was considerably different than it had been in the Tang because of some important developments in areas such as horticulture, state policy, urbanism, and changing tastes in elite and popular culture. The most significant change in the production of tea was the opening up of Fujian as the source of the prestigious "tribute tea" (*gongcha*) that was sent directly to the imperial court.[1] Fujian was not much developed in Tang times and had not played a significant role in tea production.[2] As we will see later, Buddhist monks were often in the forefront of developing new areas for cultivation in Fujian and elsewhere. The second major factor in Song tea culture was primarily economic: tea dealers benefited greatly from the new features of the economy that emerged in Song times such as paper money and the availability of credit. Outside of Fujian, tea growing was a major and profitable industry in Sichuan when, under the so-called New Policies of Wang Anshi (1021–1086), a tea market agency was established that bought up the tea in Sichuan and used it to trade with Tibetans for cavalry horses.[3]

Technological advances were also significant along with changes in patterns of tea production. Song ceramics, famous for their aesthetic refinement, were now used as specialized teaware in elite circles. In particular, black or dark-colored utensils were appreciated for their contrast with the pale foam produced from the finely powdered tea that Song connoisseurs preferred. Tea bowls were supplanted by wide, shallow saucers (*jian*). But developments were not restricted to the material world; in the realm of aesthetics connections were made between tea drinking, the *qin* (Chinese zither), and "pure conversation" (*qingtan*). We begin to see tea and the *qin* mentioned in conjunction in Song poetry.[4] As we noted in our discussion of Lu Yu and his circle in the previous chapter, there was a self-conscious reworking of "pure conversation" motifs from the Wei and Jin dynasties, but with tea now substituted for alcohol in gatherings

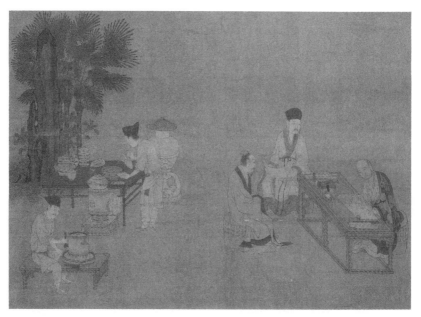

Crushing Tea by Liu Songnian (ca.1155–1224), ink and colors on silk, 44.2 × 61.9 cm. Courtesy of National Palace Museum, Taiwan.

of literati. In other words, trends that had begun in Tang times were taken in even more self-consciously refined directions as tea connoisseurship became an important marker of literati taste. So much was at stake in the world of tea, both in terms of money and prestige, that the counterfeiting of famous brands of tea became common.

Other important features of Song-dynasty tea culture were the competition of tea against medicinal decoctions that enjoyed a strong vogue, especially in the new urban areas of South China, and the role played by Buddhist monasteries in formalizing rituals for the consumption of both tea and decoctions. The Song dynasty was an important creative period in all areas of Chinese tea culture, and new religious factors played an important role in the shaping of that culture.

THE NORTHERN PARK AND IMPERIAL TEA CULTURE

Although tea was a common everyday necessity at all levels of society by the beginning of the dynasty, much of the history of Song tea culture is dominated by developments at the elite end of the scale.[5] The intersection of commerce and elite taste were particularly visible in Fujian. For example, many "state ovens" (*guanbei*) for drying and processing tea in northwest Fujian, particularly in Jian'an and Jianxi districts, were privately owned, despite the name.[6] The emphasis in these enterprises was on the quality of the product over quantity, which always remained quite small. Likewise, picking tea leaves in the tea estates of Fujian was not a question of brute labor, but was a sophisticated operation—the tender leaves were to be picked using the fingernails not the fingers, lest the tiny precious buds be contaminated by human sweat.[7]

The Northern Park (Beiyuan) in Jian'an was the most renowned district in the regional tea industry of the Song. It is well known today not only because there are a number of surviving descriptions of the park but also because this plantation supplied the tea that Song emperors drank. Thus, although the Northern Park was much less significant economically than other tea-producing areas, we know much more about this relatively small imperial plantation than we know about the many other tea enterprises that surrounded it.

How did the single site of the Northern Park rise to such extraordinary prominence? In the 930s, the ruling Wang family of the southern kingdom of Min requisitioned a private tea estate southeast of Jianzhou. In 943, the kingdom of Southern Tang enlarged the site and named it "Northern Park." The story told by Song historians is that the Southern Tang essentially nationalized all the tea-producing areas under their control, forcing people of all six counties to work these plantations as their corvée service to the state. Thus, when the Song took control, they "returned everything but the Northern Park to the people" and only the inhabitants of Jian'an were henceforth liable to corvée service.[8]

By 993, the Northern Park consisted of a strip of hills along the eastern branch of the Jian river, only about twenty *li* in length and containing twenty-five fields and between thirty and forty small "processing stations" that carried out the first stages of tea production. Because picking and processing the tea were such skilled operations, the authorities at the Northern Park soon gave up on using untrained corvée labor and began to hire professional workers. By the Chunxi reign period (1174–1189), the average wage for the several thousand workers, who slept in dormitories on site, was as much as seventy cash a day plus food. After the Mongol Yuan conquest of China the Northern Park was abolished as a state operation, but wax teas (*lacha*) from Jian'an were presented to the court until 1391, when the first Ming emperor, Taizu (r. 1368–1398), ordered that their manufacture be discontinued because it "overtaxed the people's strength." Because the technology and expertise required to produce these teas had never been exported to other tea regions beyond Jian'an, the unique and expensive wax teas effectively disappeared forever.[9]

In Song times, there were basically two types of commercial tea: cake tea (*piancha*)—which came in both regular and waxed forms, and loose tea (*sancha*). The finished product from the Northern Park plantations was molded and pressed into small cakes that were embossed with ornate insignia such as dragons and phoenixes.[10] These tea cakes were notoriously costly and exceptionally time consuming to produce.[11] First, only the very smallest buds were picked—it took hundreds of thousands of these minute leaves to produce a single cake of tea. The leaves were graded by the number of leaves per shoot—only buds with a single leaf (top quality) or at most two leaves (medium quality) were to be used.[12] The leaves were rinsed four times so as to be absolutely clean before they were steamed. Steaming was a delicate and precise process—if the buds were oversteamed the leaves would turn yellow and the taste of the tea would be flat, and understeaming would leave the leaves green and the tea grassy-tasting. The steamed leaves were subsequently cooled and excess water was pressed out. Then the leaves were placed in a heavy press overnight so as to extract as much juice (*gao*) as possible. This pressing stage was designed to ensure that the resulting beverage was not too dark and bitter.[13] The next day, the tea leaves were pounded with a mortar and pestle with some added water to make a paste. This paste was then poured into a mold, impressed with the appropriate insignia, and the molded tea was heated, then roasted, and blanched in boiling water repeatedly. Next, the cakes were allowed to dry slowly over low heat.[14] Then, they were cured and smoked. This stage was quite lengthy, requiring six to ten days for thinner cakes and ten to fifteen days for thicker ones. Once cured, the tea cakes were slightly steamed and then cooled rapidly with fans. This process gave the cakes a glossy sheen that explains why this particular kind of tea was known as "wax tea."

Some tea cakes were given a fragrance, utilizing quite expensive ingredients such as "dragon brain" (Borneo camphor), a practice of adulteration that influential Song writer on tea Cai Xiang (1012–1068) criticizes in his *Record of Tea* (*Cha lu*).[15] Tea cakes came in different sizes (3.5 cm to about 10 cm in diameter) and colors—red, green, yellow, and black. They were known by brand names that alluded to their appearance or costliness such as "Golden Coin," "Inch of Gold," "Peerless Buds of Longevity," "Ten Thousand Spring Silver Leaf," and "Dragon Buds of Ten Thousand Year Longevity."[16] The cakes were packaged as luxury goods, encased in bamboo, bronze, or silver and then wrapped in bamboo leaves and silk. Counterfeiting of these rare and expensive commodities was rife, and one surviving manual aimed at wax tea connoisseurs, *Essentials of Tea Connoisseurship* (*Pincha yaolu*), carefully instructs its readers in how to distinguish the genuine article.[17]

Perhaps a good example of the sophisticated heights of Song-dynasty tea connoisseurship is Emperor Huizong's (r. 1101–1126) famous work of 1107, *Es-*

says on Tea from the Daguan Reign Period (*Daguan chalun*).[18] The extraordinary refinement of Huizong's tea practice, along with his surprisingly detailed knowledge of the practicalities of tea cultivation, as well as the thriving trade in counterfeit cakes of tea, may be seen in the following passages:

How to Judge the Quality

Teas vary as much in appearance as do the faces of men. If the cake of tea is loose, its surface will have a wrinkled pattern; if it is dense, its grain will be tight and solid. If [the cake] is made on the day [the tea was picked] its color will be light purple. If it is left overnight before being processed, its color will be dark black. If there is a fat that congeals like red wax, then the tea powder will be white, but will become yellow once infused. If there is a fine paste like green jade, then the powder will be ashen, becoming white upon infusion. There are teas which are magnificent in their outward appearance and yet inwardly inferior, there are teas which are inwardly illustrious and yet look undistinguished, so as for differences or similarities it is hard to argue about them or seek them; the color may be glorious and subtle, but not mingled; the substance may be mixed but it does not float; holding it up it is congealed and knotted when one grinds it, it rings; it is appropriate to investigate them for their fine qualities. If you obtain what is indicated by the intentions of words, then it is fitting to use the mind to understand; also there are some people who are greedy for profit; in buying they seek externally already dried patterned buds, which they use for manufacture; they grind it and make it into cakes, changing it by means of a mold. They model them after the cakes of famous manufacturers, but the surface is tight and the color is glossy. How can one avoid choosing these?[19]

Huizong was well informed about wax tea and was able to write with authority on the subject, but he himself preferred white tea, as he writes:

White Tea

The powers of white tea are unique, and it is different from ordinary teas; the branches [of the tea plant] are elaborate, and its leaves are shiny and thin. The plants grow wild among cliff forests; there's nothing that anyone can do about this. There are no more than four or five families who grow only one or two shrubs, of which only two or three produce [leaves]. There are not many leaves and it is extremely difficult to steam and dry them; if there is the least failing with hot water or fire, then they change into ordinary-grade tea. The manufacturing process is very subtle, but if one is able to get it just right, then this tea will be really brilliant, like jade among uncut stones, it excels. If its steaming and drying are done right, it has no equal.[20]

We can see then, that tea connoisseurs at all levels of society took a strong interest not only in the finished product but also in the raw materials of tea—where and how the tea plant was grown—as well as the intricacies of the manufacturing process. Rarity was not just an issue for the finished product as it appeared in the capital; connoisseurs were also keenly interested in almost-wild teas that were cultivated in extremely small batches and that were particularly challenging to process. In Huizong's writing about white tea we can see the extreme refinement of taste in action.

In addition to the tea cakes we have discussed so far, loose tea was produced in Sichuan, Jiangsu, Zhejiang, and elsewhere in Fujian. "Twin Wells" (*shuang-jing*), from the garden owned by the family of the calligrapher and poet Huang Tingjian (1045–1105), is a particularly famous example of a Song-dynasty loose tea.[21] Twin Wells was a white tea made from tiny buds that were covered in a furze that was so fine it looked white. These buds were picked, rinsed, and steamed and then gently dried to preserve their distinctive curled shape. Huang Tingjian's friends called the tea "Eagle Talons" or "Eagle's Grasping Claws" because of the hooked shape of the leaves. Leaf teas such as these were considered so precious that Su Shi noted in a poem that he personally supervised the making of the tea, not daring to entrust it to a servant.[22]

By the eleventh century, the arts of tea were very developed. In elite circles, tea was made in the following manner, as described in Huizong's *Essays on Tea from the Daguan Reign Period*.[23] One begins by wrapping the tea cake in clean, good quality paper. Then it is pounded with a mallet; the resulting pieces are ground to powder with a roller and then sifted through a sieve several times to the fine consistency of rice flour. A scoop of the tea powder is placed in a warm shallow bowl (*jian*). Then a fixed amount of hot water is poured in a thin stream with force from a narrow spouted ewer (*ping*); this is referred to as "pointing tea" (*diancha*), and it will produce a creamy tea mixture. Then one adds the remainder of the water and whisks the tea to a froth with a bamboo whisk. Then, the foamy tea is drunk in a few sips, avoiding the sediment. Additional water may be added to the sediment and whisked up to six more times. Leaf tea, no matter how fine the quality, was also ground to a powder and brewed in the same manner as cake tea.[24]

Cai Xiang, a native of Fujian, is now renowned as a great connoisseur of tea.[25] He was the author of *Record of Tea*, a work intended for an imperial

Tea Contest, attributed to Liu Songnian, ink and colors on silk, current whereabouts unknown.

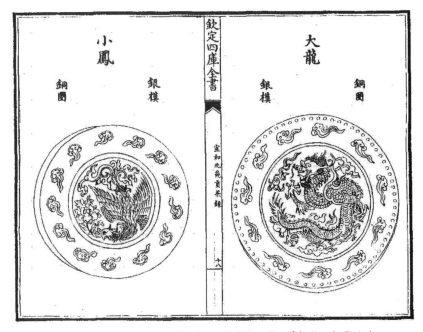

Illustrations of cake tea from *Record of North Garden Tribute Tea of the Xuanhe Period*.

Stoneware ewer for pointing tea,
Northern Song.

audience, and the originator of the term "pointing tea" (*diancha*) to describe the method of pouring a thin stream of hot water into fine tea powder. *Diancha* became the generic term for making tea throughout the Song dynasty.[26] The elite practices of tea contests and "examining tea" were first described by Cai Xiang and required dark *jian*-ware bowls because the tea and the froth being judged were so pale. In addition to fancy frothy teas consumed by the elite, tea continued to be made by boiling tea powder or simmering leaves as it had been in earlier times.

In Song times, tea was consumed in everyday situations, as well as in specialized refined gatherings of the elite that focused on pleasure. For example, tea and courtesans were often mentioned together in poetry, and there is evidence that gatherings of literati featuring tea, "tea lyrics" (*chaci*), and female companionship ("singing girls") occurred even in Buddhist monasteries.[27] We should contrast this type of sensual gathering with more chaste tea parties involving monks discussed later in the chapter. Also, we know that there was a literati practice of sipping tea while viewing pictures.[28] These and other customs such as drinking tea after alcohol have left their traces throughout the literature of Song times. In short, tea and tea drinking characterized and made concrete the bonds of friendship between literati, but inevitably the activities around tea came to be seen as formulaic and cliché. Eventually, disenchantment with the cultural value of tea gatherings gave rise to the kind of satirical view that we see in chapter 64 of the famous Ming novel *Journey to the West*, in which the monk Tripiṭaka is captured by tree demons and lured into a tea-drinking poetry party.[29]

TEA IN THE SONG BUDDHIST MONASTERY

To properly understand tea culture in the Song we need to consider not only elite literati views but also the role of the Buddhist monastery in the cultivation, processing, and consumption of tea. Although the evidence is fairly scattered, it is possible to pay close attention to the sources and build up some picture of the ways in which Buddhist institutions and their inhabitants contributed to the various aspects of tea culture. New types of historical materials available to us for the Song period and later sometimes reveal the identities of specific monastic institutions involved in tea production; it is difficult to have access to this local level of detail when we look at tea in earlier periods. These new sources include local gazetteers and the *gong'an* ("public cases" or kōans) and *denglu* ("flame records" or "transmission of the lamp") literature produced by the Chan school. As we have seen, tea connoisseurship was quite refined in Song times, and some Song-dynasty Chan masters earned distinguished reputations as experts in the preparation of tea.[30] Rulers had long sought to include religious figures in their networks of obligation by using tea as an appropriate mark of esteem. Already during the Five Dynasties period in South China, tea was presented as a gift, along with medicinal drugs, by the court to eminent Buddhist monks (and indeed to ordinary monks, nuns, and Taoists). A typical example is Qian Chu (r. 947–978), the King of Wu-Yue's gift of mineral drugs and tea to the monk Xiji (919–997) of Guoqing monastery.[31] Tea, along with medicinal and herbal decoctions, was routinely presented to officials at court during the Song.[32] In addition, tea was sent as a diplomatic gift in Song international relations.[33]

The growing demand for tea required new land for cultivating tea plants, and Buddhist monks and monasteries played important roles in opening up new tea-producing areas for development.[34] Beyond the immediate confines of the Northern Park, the basis for tea production in upper Fujian as a whole was the "tea household" (*chahu*), a term that in this region designated owners of tea-producing land and associated processing operations. Not only peasants, smallholders, and landlords but also Buddhist and Taoist monasteries

registered as "tea households." Monastic involvement in the Fujian tea industry may be seen in an edict of 1113 that states that monasteries "be treated as
tea households if they pick and process more than 500 catties (about 320 kilograms) annually."[35] Buddhist and Taoist institutions remained major players
in Fujian's tea industry through the nineteenth century.[36]

Religious establishments played key roles in tea-producing areas outside
Fujian too. As an example of specific correspondences between Buddhist institutions and types (or brands) of tea we can look at four famous teas associated with Buddhist monasteries in Song-dynasty Hangzhou: Baoyun (Precious
Cloud), Xianglin (Fragrant Grove), Baiyun (White Cloud), and Chuiyun (Hanging Cloud).[37] An entry from *Gazetteer of Lin'an from the Xianchun Reign Period [1265–74] (Xianchun lin'an zhi)* by Qian Shuoyou provides a revealing
glimpse of how tea was presented in a source devoted to local history and
geography:

> For tea as an annual tribute, consult the older gazetteer. That which
> is produced at Baoyun nunnery in Qiantang is called "Baoyun (Pre-
> cious Cloud) tea." That which is produced at Xianglin cavern at the
> Lower Tianzhu (monastery) is called "Xianglin (Fragrant Grove) tea."
> That which is produced at Baiyun peak at the Upper Tianzhu monas-
> tery is called "Baiyun (White Cloud) tea." A poem by (Su) Dongpo
> [Su Shi] says, "When rain falls from White Cloud peak, the spears [tea
> leaves] are made new."
>
> In addition, Baoyan chapel and Chuiyun pavilion both produce tea.
> Dongpo has these lines, "Joyful on account of a gift of new Chuiyun
> tea, I respond with a [tea] cake [embossed with a] great dragon, and
> playfully compose this little verse: 'The wonderful offering arrives, a
> fragrant gathering, delicately boiling they sustain the Grand Provi-
> sioner.[38] Picking out buds and dividing them up, with my tea-colored
> tongue, I respond to your fresh tea leaves by sending a dragon teacake.'"
> Also (he wrote), "Travelling round all the Buddhist hermitages, in a
> single day I drank seven bowls of tea. I playfully composed this:
> 'What is the use of Emperor Wei's single medicinal pill compared to
> my consuming Lu Tong's 'seven bowls' of tea? Now both northern
> and southern mountains, and the all famous mountains of the outer
> seven towns, all produce tea.[39] In recent days, the monks of Jing shan
> harvested [tea] before the rains came, from which I send you this small
> container-full.'"[40]

This gazetteer contains practical information about where the best teas are
produced and interweaves it with apposite lines from the most famous poet of

Song times, Su Shi (Dongpo). Su in turn makes reference to teas from other Buddhist sites and alludes to earlier poetry on tea—Lu Tong's famous description of the effects of consuming seven bowls of tea that I discussed earlier.

As we can see from this typical gazetteer entry, for Song writers such as Su, the association between Buddhist sites and famous teas was a natural one and did not require additional explanation or apology for the connection between holy sites and commercial activities. The famous tea produced at Baoyun nunnery offers significant evidence that Buddhist institutions housing nuns as well as those that were home to monks were involved in tea growing and processing. Tea could have provided an important source of revenue for some nunneries that otherwise found it hard to compete with monasteries for lay patronage. The monasteries mentioned here and in other similar gazetteers were by no means all small institutions; Xingsheng wanshou monastery on Jing shan was one of the leading Chan establishments of the Song dynasty and was particularly associated with the famous Chan Master Dahui Zonggao (1089–1163). At the height of its prosperity in Song times, it housed more than 1,700 monks.

Famous teas with Buddhist associations such as Twin Wells and Yanzhu were also to be found in Jianzhou and Zhangxing zhou.[41] Another famous tea grown on the grounds of a Buddhist institution is Rizhu tea from Zhaozhou. The *Kuaiji Gazetteer of the Jiatai Reign Period [1201–1204]* (*Jiatai Kuaiji zhi*) describes it thus:[42]

> Rizhu peak is fifty-five *li* southeast of Kuaiji county. Below the peak there is a Buddhist monastery called Zishou. Its southern exposure is called Youche ("oil press"). From dawn to dusk there is often sunshine there, and the tea that grows there is truly extraordinary; thus it is called "forged by the sun."

The gazetteers sometimes give us concrete details that explain how and where some famous teas were grown, but sometimes present only tantalizing glimpses of a world that we cannot quite perceive completely. One example of such a glimpse is the appearance of the intriguing phrase *siseng yuanhu* ("monastic plantation household"), which we find in the gazetteer for Ruizhou.[43] We know that *yuanhu* is an administrative term used to designate a household engaged in tea planting—like the term *chahu* ("tea household") discussed earlier. But what exactly was a "monastic plantation household"? It might perhaps refer to monks who planted and harvested tea together at the same time, or perhaps it meant a plantation household made up of both monks and laypeople. In any case, this phrase is further suggestive evidence of the direct participation of Buddhist monks in the commercial world of tea cultivation and processing. The teas in question were not just basic commodities for local consumption, but high-class luxury comestibles much prized by elite connoisseurs and priced accordingly.

TEA IN CHAN LITERATURE AND LIFE

The literature of Song-dynasty Chan Buddhism is littered with mentions of tea drinking, tea halls, and tea plantations.[44] The ubiquity of such references shows that tea was a basic daily necessity in Chan monasteries when these works were composed. However, some connections between tea and Chan may not be as close or as early as they first appear. The famous phrase from the *kōan/gong'an* literature, "go drink tea!" (*chicha qu*), is attributed to the Chan Master Zhaozhou Congshen (778–897), but cannot be found in sources contemporary with that figure. Certainly it appeared in many later sources. An important collection of "flame records" (accounts of the transmission of the Chan teaching), *Essentials of the Five Records of the Transmission of the Flame (Wudeng huiyuan)* compiled by Puji (1179–1253), for example, records the following series of exchanges:

> The Master (Zhaozhou) asked a monk who has just arrived, "Have you been here before?" [The monk] replied, "Yes, I have." The Master said, "Go drink tea."
>
> He then asked another monk the same question, and the monk replied, "No, I have not." To which the Master said, "Go drink tea."
>
> Afterwards, the abbot asked him, "The monk had been here before, and you said to him, 'Go drink tea.' The second monk had not been here before, and you said to him also, 'Go drink tea.' Why is that?"
>
> The Master beckoned the abbot to come closer, which he did; then the Master said, "Go drink tea."[45]

The expression "go drink tea," which was understood to be Zhaozhou's way of saying that awakening is inseparable from the daily routines of life, became very popular. In time, it became one of the key catch-phrases of Song-dynasty Chan literature, cited hundreds of times, but for our purposes it serves as an important marker of the ubiquity of tea in the Chan monastery. Probably it also specifically reflects a Song-dynasty monastic custom we will discuss later—that a traveling monk on arriving at a new monastery would be served a cup of tea.

The confluence of tea and Buddhist language is by no means confined to Chan texts. As we saw in earlier chapters, literati made use of Buddhist terminology in their writing about tea. A particularly revealing term, "the *samādhi* of pointing tea" (*diancha sanmei*), can be found in Song verse; for example, in Su Shi's preface to "Sent to Master Qian of Nanping":

> Master Qian of Nanping is amazing in matters of tea. He himself said that it is experienced in the mind and expressed with his hand, but cannot be studied by verbal transmission. On the twenty-seventh of the tenth month, having heard that I was visiting Shouxing monastery, he came from afar to serve me tea, and so I wrote this poem to present to him.

The poem itself contains the following lines of interest to us:

> This morning, the Man of the Way has come off Mount Nanping,
> And I have come to examine this hand which has the *samādhi* of
>   pointing tea
> . . .
> The creamy flowers of Mount Tiantai are rarely seen in the world,
> The master of the Jade River, the wind beneath his arms, where is he
>   now?[46]
> The master would like to write a sequel to the *Classic of Tea*,
> To ensure that the name of the Venerable Qian never disappears.[47]

As we have already seen, Su Shi wrote frequently about tea in Buddhist settings.[48] Obviously, he is slightly hyperbolic here in his description of the monk's skill at making tea, but the term he uses, "the *samādhi* of pointing tea," offers a powerful way of linking Buddhist practices with worldly customs—suggesting that the most refined method of making tea might require a deep meditational state that an eminent monk could be expected to access. The poem places the secular official in the position of awe-struck spectator to the monk's skill, and it suggests that Buddhist monks might be appropriately celebrated in literary works on tea.

The same striking phrase, "the *samādhi* of pointing tea," also appears in a work by Su's friend, the monk Huihong (1071–1128), who includes in his collection *Stone Gate's Literary Chan* (*Shimen wenzi Chan*) a poem on "Pointing Tea without study" (*Wuxue diancha*). A note on these uses of the term *samādhi* (meaning something like "absorption," the word is used in Buddhist materials to indicate high levels of meditative concentration) can be found in Wang Rixiu's (1127–1162) commentary on the *Diamond Sutra* where he explains that, although *samādhi* has technical meanings concerned with the practice of meditation, it is also used in the vernacular sense of "a wonderful ability." Thus, he says, "Someone who is good at 'pointing tea' is said to possess the *samādhi* of pointing tea and someone who is good at composing literature is said to have the *samādhi* of composing literature."[49] No doubt for some writers there is nothing especially profound lurking behind this phrase, but it does show the creative intertwining of Buddhist language with Chinese aesthetics that we have noted elsewhere in this study.

TEA AND MEDICINAL DECOCTIONS IN MONASTIC LIFE

The great Japanese scholar-monk Mujaku Dōchū (1653–1745) long ago noted the significant role played by Buddhist monasteries in the development of tea culture. His lexicon of Zen monastic terminology *Notes on the Utensils for Zen Monasteries* (*Zenrin shōkisen*) contains an important entry on *sarei* ("tea ritual" or "tea ceremony"). The cognate term *chali* is not attested in Chinese sources prior to Chan materials dating to the Song, and we may assume that any written evidence for a specific ritual for the consumption of tea in monasteries cannot be found much earlier than the tenth century. The invention of a tea ritual to be employed in Buddhist monasteries offers an interesting example of the creation of a religious ceremony for social/cultural/material reasons rather than doctrinal ones. There was no overwhelming doctrinal need for a tea ritual, but there were many social reasons for its necessity.

To understand the place of tea drinking in the Buddhist monastery and in society more generally, we need to widen our scope from looking at monastic tea rituals so as to understand Song-dynasty beverage culture as a whole. So far, we have considered tea mostly in opposition to alcohol, but in Song times people had a much wider range of drinks from which to choose. There was a particular enthusiasm at all levels of society for beverages that had medicinal qualities—what we might today call "health drinks"—made of aromatic herbal ingredients. We can best understand this interest in medicinal decoctions as part of a larger vogue for medicine as food, or "dietetics," which was current in Song times.[50] To appreciate the cultural and religious significance of tea, we have to consider it in the context of this wider beverage culture and this vogue for consuming herbal preparations for nourishing life. If people wanted an alternative to alcohol, tea was not the only choice.

Tea in fact did not entirely drive out alcohol from monastic culture in any case; the Japanese monk Jōjin (1011–1081) records being offered both tea and "medicinal alcohol" (along with fruit) on a couple of occasions during a visit to Mount Tiantai.[51] Elsewhere, he describes drinking alcohol given to him by laymen.[52] Su Shi famously refers to monks who speak of alcohol as "*prajñā* decoction" (*bore tang*).[53] Even so, tea was a basic necessity for Chan monastics, along with congee, rice, and decoctions, as can be seen from the frequent mention of these comestibles in the "pure rules" of Buddhist monasteries and in the Chan literature of "recorded sayings." For example, the "Head of the Hall for Extending Life" (*yanshou tangzhu*) was responsible for taking care of sick monks. One of his duties was to manage and prepare for daily requirements for the sick, "such as wood, charcoals, rice, noodles, oil, salt, vegetables preserved with salt, tea, soup, medicine, ginger, Chinese jujube, dried plums, and other household goods."[54]

Tea had become a necessity for both monasteries and ordinary households. But alongside tea, Song people also enjoyed a range of decoctions, broths, and juices not just for their taste but also for their medicinal qualities. Let us consider first an example of a health drink that was already known in Tang times. Here is a recipe for a chilled tisane made from *huzhang* (Tiger Stick, polygonum cuspidatum or giant knotweed):

> In the summer months, it is decocted with licorice; the color is a delightful shade of amber, pleasing to the eye, and the taste is sweet and delicious. It is bottled and put to chill in a well until ice-cold. It is then decanted into white porcelain or silver vessels, and drunk as a beverage like tea. People nowadays call this *leng yinzi* (cold beverage), and rate it more highly than tea.[55]

We can tell from the description that this refreshing cordial is not a common person's beverage. The emphasis on the aesthetic quality of the drink, and the pricy utensils with which it was served show that it was more likely consumed by the elite. Giant knotweed, whose tender shoots can be eaten like asparagus, was employed in the Chinese pharmacological repertoire to combat high fevers, agitation and distress; to quench thirst; as a diuretic; and to expel all kinds of toxins associated with heat. But this recipe does not describe the kind of herbal drug that might be prepared and administered in controlled doses by a supervising doctor. Rather, this is a much more dilute preparation that can be drunk at will in the summertime, just like tea. Because of this mode of enjoying pharmacologically active ingredients in relatively small and uncontrolled doses, it may be helpful to compare this and other decoctions to the kinds of health drinks or sports drinks that we consume today.

Tea was noted for its medicinal qualities and particularly favored by Buddhist monks because it aided digestion, increased concentration, and reduced the need for sleep. These qualities were seen as beneficial to practitioners of meditation. In addition to this giant knotweed tisane, other medicinal beverages (*yinzi*) in Tang times were already explicitly described as alternatives to tea, and some were specifically aimed at monastic consumers. The eighth-century *Essential Secrets of the Imperial Library* (*Waitai miyao*) by Wang Tao contains a "new recipe for a tea substitute" (*Daicha xin yin fang*) consisting of fourteen ingredients, ground to powder and prepared as a decoction:

> It is particularly recommended for eminent scholars of Chan; it frees the internal organs and regulates the blood vessels. Just a little brings great benefits, conferring inexhaustible mental vigor. It is especially effective when drunk to satiety.[56]

This recipe, although it was for a medicinal decoction and not a popular drink, shows that tea and other health drinks were recommended to practitioners of meditation ("eminent scholars of Chan") for their ability to sustain an attentive mind in a healthy body. This and other tea substitutes used in Tang times may have had similar physiological effects as tea, but certainly tasted quite different because licorice was usually a prime ingredient and made the drink much sweeter than tea.

Lest we find it strange that medieval monks would be interested in such worldly concerns or presume that they might have been reluctant to use performance-enhancing aids to meditation, there is ample evidence for modern interest in health drinks in the Buddhist monastery. For example, Robert Buswell, in his *Zen Monastic Experience,* reports widespread use by contemporary Korean monks of Chinese herbal medicines designed to increase stamina, along with other health fads such as the consumption of powdered pine needles or a kind of "iron-water" made with scrap metal oxidized in water.[57] As we will see later, in medieval and early modern times the use of medicinal decoctions within the monastery was so common as to become standardized.

Although medicinal beverages and health drinks were known in Tang times, they were consumed rather differently in the Song, where they were obliged to compete with tea in the open urban market. Anecdotal collections abound with examples of the commercialization of tea and other drinks, especially in the city. In the Northern Song capital of Kaifeng, we are told, "The vendors of drugs and beverages call out their wares with all kinds of patter."[58] In the Southern Song capital of Hangzhou (then called Lin'an),

> There are breakfast stalls selling medicinal decoctions (*tangyao*) like *erchen tang,* and pills and concoctions for regulating *qi,* bringing down retrograde *qi,* and settling and nourishing original *qi.*[59]

Erchen tang was a typical medicinal decoction in Song times and is still drunk today. Its ingredients are dried tangerine (*chen*) peel, root of pinellia (one of the most important herbs in Chinese medicine, used to dry up phlegm and prevent coughing, nausea, and vomiting), *fuling* (poria cocos, a kind of fungal parasite that grows on the roots of pine trees widely used to strengthen the spleen and increase vitality), and, of course, licorice to provide the necessary sweetness and flavor to mask the other ingredients.[60]

No fewer than twenty-six prescriptions for various kinds of medicinal decoctions are listed in *Prescriptions of the Taiping Era Pharmacy for the Welfare of the People* (*Taiping huimin heji jufang*), published in 1107.[61] Decoctions included those made of cardamom (*doukou tang*), Banksia rose (*muxiang tang*), Osmanthus fragrans (*guihua tang*), peppermint (*bohe tang*), perilla (*zisu tang*), jujube (*zao tang*), magnolia bark (*houpo tang*), apricot frost (*xingshuang tang*), fresh ginger (*shengjiang tang*), black cardamom (*yizhi tang*), and fennel (*huixiang tang*) as well as decoctions with descriptive names like "breaking qi" (*poqi tang*) or "five flavors" (*wuwei tang*).[62] From other sources we know that decoctions of *fuling*, "red arrow" (*chijian, Gastrodia elata*), astragalus (*huangqi*), ginseng, sweet bean, and even minerals like mica (*yunmu*) were popular.[63] As we have already noted, licorice (*gancao*) was a key ingredient in many of the recipes for these beverages.

Although the recipes were quite different in terms of ingredients, they were all clearly designed to be both strongly aromatic and tasty (hence the liberal use of licorice). If such decoctions were to compete with tea and alcohol, then they also had to be easy to make and to drink. Medicinal decoctions were sold as "instant drinks" consisting of about five grams (1 spoonful, *qian*) of powdered ingredients to which boiling water was to be added and then stirred. The method of preparation for decoctions was thus very similar to that of tea, which in Song times was also finely powdered and whisked up with boiling water poured in a thin stream from a metalware ewer.

If we look at the intended physiological effects of the decoctions, we will see that most of the medicinal ingredients—Banksia rose, cloves, sandalwood, turmeric, etc.—were classified in the *materia medica* as drugs that regulated *qi* and strengthened the spleen, or they were thought to strengthen *qi* in the lungs and aid with digestion (platycodon, *jiegeng*; apricot kernels).[64] Tea, in contrast, was described in the *materia medica* as a substance that was diuretic, aided digestion, increased concentration, and reduced the need for sleep. Physiologically, we can consider tea and decoctions as complementary in effect.

Song-dynasty city dwellers varied the beverages they drank according to the season.[65] In the tea shops in Lin'an, we are told that "powdered tea or yangu decoction (*yangu tang*) were sold in the winter time; while plum blossom liquor was sold during the summer period."[66] In addition to medicinal decoctions, many other kinds of refreshing beverages were sold, including sweet bean soup, coconut wine, pear syrup, stewed plum juice, honey water, papaya juice, and, of course, tea.

Just as contemporary medical writers may inveigh against the dangers of consuming too many "health drinks," Song medics also wrote about the perils of abusing medicinal decoctions. Kou Zongshi, a famous pharmacologist of the eleventh and twelfth century, warns against the abuse of perilla, which many people enjoyed taking almost on a daily basis. Perilla was understood to invigorate both the spleen and the lungs viscera:

It can be used in powder form, and has a fragrant odor. Nowadays, people drink it as a decoction from morning to night which is not salutary. Doctors believe that fragrant herbs are a cause of illness among the rich and powerful. They produce cold in the spleen and stomach, and if taken to excess cause chronic diarrhea, often without the individual realizing.[67]

Eventually, warnings such as this by medical men, along with the cost of certain ingredients, brought an end to the craze for medical decoctions. Although some continued to be drunk, it was tea that was allowed to continue as the Chinese health drink par excellence.

Comestibles in China often played multiple roles, and tea, like alcohol, was used not just for drinking: it could also be employed to make religious offerings. We see a similar modality for medicinal decoctions. According to the *Dream of the Splendors of the Eastern Capital* (*Dongjing menghua lu*),

On the eighth day of the fourth [lunar] month, which is the birthday of the Buddha, the ceremony of washing the Buddha was held at the ten major Chan monasteries. A syrupy decoction of fragrant herbs was boiled up and passed around. This was known as "water for washing the Buddha."[68]

Like alcohol and tea, then, medicinal decoctions could also serve an important ritual function.[69] This aspect of their use demands that we consider them as a significant, culturally meaningful part of the larger world of Tang-Song beverages and comestibles.

Tea culture in the Five Dynasties and Song must be understood against this background of dietetics and health-giving beverages. The need to do so is particularly acute when we look within the Buddhist monastery, where we find regulations for the formal consumption of tea and decoctions side by side. Unfortunately, this dialectic between tea and decoctions has been hard to spot because we have not always understood the meaning of the term *tang* in our texts.[70] *Tang* can mean boiling or very hot water, water that has been used to cook items of food, or a soup or broth. As we saw earlier, *tang* was commonly used in Song sources to designate an herbal decoction. However, in her important English translation of a major Chan monastic code, *Pure Rules for Chan Monasteries* (*Chanyuan qinggui*), Venerable Yifa—a scholar of Chinese Buddhism who is herself a nun—translates *tang* as "sweetened drink."[71] In doing so, she follows the Tang monk Yijing's (635–713) travel diary recording Indian monastic customs of making offerings of honey, ghee, and the "eight syrups." But, as Liu Shufen has pointed out, even on that basis the translation choice is not accurate because not all of these syrups are sweet.[72] In any case, as we have seen, in Song times *tang* frequently referred to medicinal decoctions, and there was monastic ritual for the serving and drinking of those decoctions, just as there was for tea.

As Morten Schlütter has argued, Song monastic institutions were acutely aware of the patronage games that they had to play with state and local elites.[73] The attention devoted to hosting literati by abbots using tea offers a fine example of how that awareness played out, but the insistence on correct etiquette and decorum in the serving of tea and medicinal decoctions permeated even relationships within the monastery among monks.

When a wandering monk (*guada,* "one who hangs up his possessions") arrived at a Chan monastery for a temporary visit, he was required to present himself first at the office of the chief monk (*tangtou*). The chief monk would receive him and serve him tea (*chicha*). This requirement is probably the referent for Zhaozhou's instruction to "go drink tea!" According to the monastic regulations, the traveling monastic should present his official monastic certificate, and the chief monk would respond by apologizing to the traveling monastic for any lack of hospitality. The regulations note explicitly that no decoction was to be served to the wandering monk at this time. Rather, after serving him tea, the chief monk should simply show the visitor to the monk's hall and arrange a space for him based on his level of seniority.[74]

Although at first this regulation may seem inconsequential, in fact it offers an important clue that monastic customs followed secular etiquette in observing a policy of "tea first, decoction later" (*xiancha houtang*). The theory behind this protocol was that when a guest arrives he should be welcomed with tea; before he leaves (because his mouth may be dry from chatting) he should be presented with a bowl of tonic decoction to relieve his weariness.[75]

We discussed earlier the Song method for making tea by "pointing" (*diancha*) a thin stream of hot water into powdered tea. This same method was the one employed in Chan monasteries for making both tea and decoctions.

There are many references to pointing tea in the monastic codes (*qinggui*, "pure rules") of Song-dynasty Chan monasteries because their authors were careful to prescribe exactly how monastic tea ceremonies—which were often held to host visiting officials—should be staged. Although this method of pointing tea was ubiquitous in Buddhist monasteries, one still finds ample references in the literature to "boiling tea" (*jiancha*). But the phrase does not necessarily imply that the tea itself is being boiled; it could just refer to boiling the water for tea.[76] Also, the method of pointing tea in monastic ceremonies was intended to retain an egalitarian aspect in which all monks were to drink the same tea. *Chan Master Cishou's Admonitions for Instructing the Assembly* (*Cishou chanshi shizong zhengui*) specifies that, when there is a monastery tea ceremony, monks may not use their own personal stores of tea powder.[77]

The method of making decoctions was similar to that of tea, as I have already noted. The drugs were crushed to a powder called "decoction powder" (*tangmo*) to which boiling water was added.[78] A story in *Taiping guangji* about the Tang physician Sun Simiao illustrates this fact when he instructs a monastic servant to prepare a medicinal decoction in the same manner as tea.[79]

Confusion about the terminology for beverages, as well as their preparation and serving, in the Song-dynasty monastic codes has obscured our view of the extent to which tea and decoctions were equally important, ritually and socially, in Buddhist monasteries. For example, the term *jiandian* in the monastic codes can indicate pointing tea (*diancha*), pointing decoctions (*diantang*), or both simultaneously.[80] But scholars have interpreted the term differently, some claiming that it refers to tea and snacks (*dianxin*, viz. *dimsum*).[81] Venerable Yifa's rendering of *jiandian* and *chatang* as "formal tea ceremony" and "lesser tea ceremony," respectively, is particularly misleading because, as we have seen, protocol specifies the serving of "tea on arriving and decoction on leaving" in both secular and monastic contexts.[82] The *Chanyuan qinggui* itself specifies that "ritual is required for both tea and decoction."[83] The monastic tea ceremony (*chali*) was essentially no different from its "decoction ceremony" (*tangli*). Just as teas and decoctions were consumed according to the seasons in the secular world, so the *Chanyuan qinggui* instructs the abbot's attendant (*tangtou shizhe*) to "make tea or decoction each in accordance with the season."[84]

DECOCTIONS IN THE MONASTERY

We can piece together evidence from various sources to learn about the consumption of medicinal decoctions in Song monasteries. The *Abbreviated Rules of Purity for Small Monasteries* (*Shōsōrin ryaku shingi*) compiled by Mujaku Dōchū in 1684, based on Chinese models of monastic regulations, contains a line drawing of a "decoction bowl" (*tangjian*) with a saucer and small spoon. A brief passage below the image describes how to grind up the drugs for the decoction and then mix up the decoction in the bowl.[85] That same text also contains an entry for a "decoction ceremony" that was similar in style to a monastic tea ceremony. There is some material evidence too; an excavation from a Liao-dynasty tomb at Chifeng dating to 959 turned up a silver bowl, saucer, and spoon that look very similar to what Dōchū illustrates.[86]

The archeological evidence gives us some clues about the consumption of medicinal decoctions in the monastery, but like tea, decoctions were used not just for drinking. As we have already seen, in lay practice medicinal decoctions could be used as Buddhist offerings in the same manner as tea. According to the *Abbreviated Rules of Purity for Small Monasteries,* on the anniversary of the Buddha's Nirvāṇa (the fifteenth day of the second lunar month), one should offer tea, fruit, and medicinal decoctions to the Buddha.[87] The text gives quite a detailed description of how the offering is to be made.[88] Also, tea and medicinal decoctions were often offered to pilgrims as a form of Buddhist charity, and there were lay associations that formed exclusively to perform this mission.[89] Conceptually, tea and medicinal decoctions seem to have been treated as equally appropriate offerings to buddhas and to recipients of charity.

What particular decoctions were popular in the monastery? According to the *Song Dynasty Biographies of Eminent Monks,* decoctions made with tangerine peel or mountain yam were the choice of many Buddhist monks. Tangerine peel decoction is mentioned frequently in Chan histories and recorded sayings and must have been part of the regular diet in larger institutions. For example, in the early Song dynasty, the monk Wuen (?–986) of the Ciguang chapel in Hangzhou was particularly strict with his disciples. In particular, he held them to the monastic rule that monks were not permitted to eat any food after noon. One of his disciples was caught drinking mountain yam decoction (*shuyu tang*) and was forced to leave the monastery.[90] It seems then, that for some Buddhist monks, these decoctions counted as food and not medicine.

Although tea and medicinal decoctions were often formally balanced within the monastic diet, sometimes the two beverages were combined. The Song-dynasty compendium of Taoist texts, *Seven Slips from a Cloudy Satchel* (*Yunji qiqian*), in an entry devoted to "Consuming pneuma and abstaining from grain" (*fuqi jueli*), says, "If a decoction medicine is required, then apricot, ginger, and honey in good tea from Shu will do no harm; if one's strength is not perfect it is appropriate to use this to balance and strengthen the body."[91] This Taoist recipe shows that tea remained well integrated into the repertoire of herbal tonics.

TEA CEREMONIES AND THE MONASTIC CALENDAR

Tea and medicinal decoctions were ubiquitous in monastery daily life and ritual practice, but they were especially noticeable at particular times that were crucial to the regulation of the monastic calendar. Formal tea and decoction ceremonies described in the monastic rules were of three basic types. First, tea was used in the daily monastic routine: this type of ceremony included the serving of tea for circumambulating the saṃgha hall on the first and fifteenth of the month (*shuowang zuntang cha*), tea for ascending the hall five times (*wucan shangtang cha*), and "bathing tea" (*yucha*)—that is, tea served on monastery bath day. The formal serving of medicinal decoctions was regulated in a similar fashion: the rules stipulated the decoction at the audience [with the abbot] (*fangcan tang*) and the decoction for chanting (*niansong tang*). Second, formal tea ceremonies were held on the four seasonal nodes of the Chinese calendar (*jie*): the fifteenth day of the fourth lunar month (*jiexia*, beginning of summer), the fifteenth of the seventh month (*jiexia*, end of summer), the winter solstice (*dongzhi*), and the new year (*xinnian*). Third, the monastic assembly came together and consumed tea at gatherings to mark appointments to and retirements from certain monastic offices.

The nodal days of the calendar were marked by multiple ceremonies for the consumption of tea and medicinal decoctions by the inhabitants of the monastery. The evening before the nodal day is when the first decoction ceremony would be held, and there followed three further days of tea and decoction ceremonies.[92] These formal nodal day ceremonies were conducted in the saṃgha hall. In *Pure Rules for Chan Monasteries* the ceremonies are referred to as "brewing and pointing within the saṃgha hall" (*sengtang nei jiandian*).[93] The ceremonies described in the text are essentially all based on the same template that can be seen in the nodal day ceremony as laid out next.

The night before the nodal day, all the monks in the monastery gather, chant scriptures, and then partake in the communal ritual consumption of decoctions. The ritual is constructed on a guest-host model, with different monastic officials playing assigned roles. The chief guest is the abbot of the monastery who is invited by the prior (*kusi*). The ceremony is based on long-established imperial court etiquette, which makes a basic distinction between civil and military officials. Like court officials, the monks are divided into an east side and a west side.[94] The "night before" ceremony is held by the "east-side" officers for the "west-side" officers, with the monks of the monastery as the "other guests" (*peike*). This example, which is typical of monastic ceremonies for both tea and decoctions, shows an interesting use of a guest-host structure within the monastery itself, as well as the way in which monastic hierarchies were consciously modeled on time-honored prototypes for ritual conduct found within the imperial court. The formal consumption of tea in the monastery was thus both communal and highly structured.

For the day of the seasonal node itself and two days afterward, according to the *Pure Rules for Chan Monasteries,* senior monastic officials issue a series of invitations to the tea ceremonies. First, the supervisor invites the abbot and assembly for tea; second, the *karmadana* invites the abbot and assembly; and finally, the administrator of the front hall asks the assembly from the rear hall to tea.[95] Tea, initially consumed on a casual basis for practical reasons in the monastery, was thus now being employed to ensure the regulated functioning of a complex human organization in harmony with the changing of the seasons.

Monastic tea and decoction ceremonies were conceived as very solemn rituals with little room for spontaneity or relaxation. *Pure Rules for Chan Monasteries* describes a tea or decoction ceremony in the saṃgha hall that can be divided into two parts. First, before drinking tea or decoction, formal invitations are issued, and there is the first ritual circumambulation of the hall. Second, the tea or decoctions are brought in and served, then they are consumed along with medicinal pills, and finally the assembly is dismissed.

Tea ceremonies were formally announced to the monks by means of "tea (or decoction) posters" (*chabang, tangbang,* or *chazhuang*) that were displayed in the monastery.[96] These documents pay a great deal of attention to the minutiae of protocol and ritual. The posters were written on silk to convey their formality. They had to specify the nature of the ceremony, the time, location, and the invited guests. Sometimes, they were brushed by famous literati and prized for their calligraphy. The most famous *chabang* was written by the monk Puguang in the Yuan dynasty and later permanently inscribed in stone at Jietan Temple on Mount Song. It was engraved on four tablets separately on both sides, giving eight parts in total, and was renowned because of the quality of Puguang's calligraphy.

A seating plan was to be displayed outside the monks' hall on a public noticeboard, and there were also place cards on the individual seats.[97] The monastic code instructs monks to find their names before taking their seats.[98] In addition to arranging the seats, the monastic servants were to set out at each place tea cups or decoction cups as appropriate, saucers, tea powder, and medicinal pills for tea (*cha yaowan*). They were also to provide tea trays, incense, and flowers and have pure fresh boiling water standing by in the ewers.[99] The arrangements were complex, so that the ritual could proceed smoothly.

We can see from *Pure Rules for Chan Monasteries* and from evidence in other monastic codes, as well as Mujaku Dōchū's later encyclopedia, that much of the ritual action in the tea ceremony is oriented toward the niche in the hall containing the image of the "holy monk" that was a common feature of the saṃgha hall in Chan monasteries.[100] The person conducting the ceremony makes ritual obeisance (*wenxun*), bowing before the holy monk with joined palms. After the drinking of tea is over, the host bows again to the holy monk and circumambulates the hall.[101] Thus the key elements in the tea ceremony ritual are obeisance, burning incense, and circumambulating the hall. The celebrant performs obeisance to the assembly, the holy monk, and the incense burner before any tea or decoction is served. Although the models for the tea ceremony derived ultimately from court ritual, the compilers of the "pure rules" ensured that the ceremony was shaped to Buddhist ends through practices that directed merit toward the saṃgha—circumambulation, obeisance to the holy monk, and offerings of incense.

Nothing was taken for granted in the performance of these rituals, and Chan authors often stipulated in detail how and why the various elements were to be executed. There is a nice description of some of the processes involved in the ceremonies in Qingzhuo Zhengcheng's (1274–1339) *Lesser Pure Rules of Chan Master Dajian* (*Dajian chanshi xiao qinggui*):

> Now, in all ceremonies for tea and decoctions, one joins the palms of the two hands (this is called "joining palms") and with joined palms one makes a bow (this is called "salutation") . . . [monks] in the two groups are all standing outside the door, ranked by seniority, as it is not appropriate for people to meet individually (this is called "entering salutation"). The entire assembly enters and stands at their seats, the officiant makes a medium salutation and asks them to sit (this is the "bowing salutation for taking seats"), and when everyone is seated, the officiant makes a minor salutation. Then, the monks burn incense in front of the brazier, and retire with a minor salutation (this is called "bowing for the incense"). After the tea and decoction are finished, the bowls are all removed and then the officiant takes one step and bows (this is called "bowing for the tea"). When the servants have taken away all the bowls and the officiant withdraws and stands to the side, the ceremony is complete.[102]

The practice of circumambulating the hall has many meanings in Chan ritual. In the case of tea or decoction ceremonies, it indicates both an invitation to attend the ceremony and, at its conclusion, a dismissal with thanks. The use of incense during the ceremony also has a ritual function. The first burning of incense is intended to summon the sages and ordinary people of the ten directions. The second burning of incense serves to invite the monks. The offering of incense is clearly very important for the ritual—*Pure Rules for Chan Monasteries* provides detailed instructions as to how the incense is to be burned—and we should also recall that tea and incense are often mentioned together in tea poetry.[103] The formal dismissal at the conclusion of both the tea and decoction ceremonies again shows their ritualized nature and the need to mark clearly both the commencement of the ritual and its successful conclusion.

The term *xingcha* ("processing tea") is used in Chan monastic literature to refer to the ritual process of fetching boiling water in a ewer into the saṃgha hall and pouring it into cups with tea powder placed in them. The term is clearly intended to be analogous to the older Buddhist ritual term *xingxiang* ("processing incense"). When all the participants have a cup of tea in front of them, this stage is called *chabian;* then and only then may the monks drink. Some cold water is dripped into each cup and a tea whisk (*chaxian*) is used to blend or whisk the tea to a froth, just as in the usual manner outside the monastery.[104] Analogous terms, *xingtang* and *tangbian,* were used for decoction ceremonies. The decoctions were apparently not whisked as tea was, but the illustration of the decoction cup in Dōchū's work features a small spoon that presumably was used to stir and blend the decoction. Because there were likely insoluble ingredients in these decoctions that would otherwise form a sediment, it would be imperative to stir the mixture.

After the two circumambulations of the hall, medicinal pills were distributed to monks attending the tea ceremony. There are even instructions about how to eat the medicinal pill in *Pure Rules for Chan Monasteries:* "do not throw it into your mouth or chew loudly."[105] Medicinal pills were commonly served along with tea on less formal occasions in the monastery as well. The Japanese pilgrim Jōjin reports in his *Record of Visiting Mounts Tiantai and Wutai* (*San Tendai Godaisan ki*) that in 1072 Great Master Guangzhi invited him to take tea and two medicinal pills at Chuanfa chapel, in Taiping xingguo monastery in Bianjing (present-day Kaifeng).[106] These medicinal pills were known outside the monastery too. The Tang physician Sun Simiao's *Supplementary Prescriptions Worth a Thousand in Gold* (*Qianjin yifang*) contains a discussion of "tea medicinal pills" (*cha yaowan*).[107] On this evidence we know that the "medicinals for tea" (*chayao*), or sometimes simply *yao* (medicines), referred to in the *Pure Rules for Chan Monasteries* were most likely a kind of pill. The later annotators of *Chanyuan qinggui* claim that these "medicinals" could refer to sweets or dimsum (snacks) and Yifa uses the word "confections" in her translation, but these glosses do not reflect actual practices at the time the code was compiled. The consumption of these medicinal pills was an important part of the tea ceremony, so we should reflect on this interesting confluence of ritual, self-care, and commodity. There is evidence that a specific medicinal, *fengyao* ("medicine taken against wind"), may also have been taken with the tea consumed on bath days.[108] As we noted earlier, by the Yuan dynasty, the fashion for dietetics and health tonics had changed, and monastics appear to have ceased consuming tea medicinals on a regular basis.

These tea and decoction ceremonies were among the most ornate and solemn rituals regularly held in Song monasteries, but they owed much to forms of ritual outside the monastery walls. The scholar-monk Mujaku Dōchū already alluded to the origins of many of the elements of these ceremonies in court ritual, and I noted earlier how the hierarchy of monastic officials mirrored those found in the imperial bureaucracy. Both the ritual of serving tea itself and the seating plans echoed court and official models of etiquette.[109] In particular, tea and decoction rituals drew on regulations for official banquets (*huishi*) held in Tang and Song times.[110] From the early Tang onward, the court and local administrations as part of their regular business held banquets for bureaucrats. These banquets had a specific location, a dining hall (*shitang*), and a fixed etiquette.[111] The protocol for a banquet was written on a wooden board and hung in the dining hall.[112] The construction and décor of the dining hall were definitively prescribed.[113] If officials broke the rules, they were liable to punishment. Chan monasteries also posted details of rituals on the walls. Zhengcheng explains that tea ritual instructions were posted outside the officiant's office and in the guest quarters of the monastery. The intention was that monks should be as well versed in ritual as were Confucian literati.[114]

Monastic seating plans and the physical layout of the saṃgha hall for tea ceremonies matched court models quite closely. The monastic seating plan had a bureaucratic equivalent: the monastic incense burner (*xianglu*) corresponded to the brazier (*xunlu*) and incense table (*xiang'an*) that were required when officials had an audience with the emperor. At imperial audiences, officials stood in two ranks on either side of the chamber with the emperor at the head—just as monks were arranged with the abbot at the head.

Some monasteries even had specific "tea halls" (*chatang*), or "tea rooms" (*chaliao*) as dedicated sites for the provision of tea and decoctions. For example, Chan master Kai of Furong at Tianning monastery wanted to concentrate on his religious practices, and therefore, when visiting monks arrived he did not host them with tea, but had a tea hall where the monk might obtain his own.[115]

In Song-dynasty Chan monasteries, monks were supposed to "ascend the hall" to consult with the abbot about their progress in meditational cultivation every five days: the first, fifth, tenth, fifteenth, twentieth, and twenty-fifth

days of every lunar month. The content of the consultation on the first and fifteenth lunar days was distinct from the other days, being even more serious.
The Dharma seat (*fazuo*) was set up, and when the abbot finished his teaching, a notice would be put up to announce "circumambulation of the hall and
drinking of tea" (*xuntang chicha*). Thus tea was used to mark important stages
in the practice of individual monks as well as of the whole community.

Bathing was not an everyday occurrence in the monastery, but when the
bath was open, the monastic codes required that tea and medicine be served.
Pure Rules for Chan Monasteries prescribes the duties of the "bath master"
(*yuzhu*):

> The day before setting up the bath, the bath master scrubs down the
> bathhouse and begins boiling water. On the day of the bath, before
> mealtime, he posts the announcement for the "opening of the baths,"
> the "rinsing of sweat," or the "cleaning of the hair." In the bathhouse,
> the bath master decorates the area designated for the Holy Ones, sets
> out clean towels, incense, flowers, lamps, and candles, and prepares
> "wind medicine" and tea sets for all the monks.[116]

Tea and medicinals thus had an important role to play in the way that monastics took care of their bodies. As the outside of the monk's body was made
clean by bathing, so the insides were strengthened by tea and medicine.

Tea was served multiple times on formal occasions when monks took up
or retired from administrative positions within the monastery (*zhishi cha*). The
usual term of office for senior positions in the monastery was one year. The *Pure
Rules for Chan Monasteries* specifies, "When a new appointment is needed, the
abbot invites the administrators, the chief officers, the retired staff, and the senior retired staff to have tea."[117] The abbot announces the new candidate for
the position and solicits advice from the monastic officers. When consensus is
reached, the candidate is invited along with guests and tea is served again. Later,
the new senior officer undertakes a formal tour of the various quarters, and a
decoction is served in the abbot's quarters. "On the same day or the next, the
new administrator sponsors a tea ceremony and then withdraws."[118] The next
day the prior holds a special feast, and "[t]he day after the feast, the abbot holds
a special tea ceremony in the saṃgha hall for the new and old administrators."
The protocol for this ceremony is described in detail, including the appropriate wording to be used on the tea posters, where they should be placed, and
how personal invitations should be issued. Finally, "one by one, tea ceremonies are sponsored by the administrator, the chief seat, and the chief officers
for the old and new administrators. If the assistant prior, the cook, or the

superintendent is in the storage hall or if the rector is in the rectory, he also holds a tea ceremony."[119]

As we can see, tea played a vital role in the social life of large Chan monasteries in Song times and was an essential element in some of the most important ritual occasions in the monastic calendar. The serving of tea allowed senior monastics to demonstrate their familiarity with correct protocol, it showed respect to others, and it provided a welcome break from monotonous routine. Rituals around tea also emulated the kind of banquets and drinking parties that contemporary secular officials would be expected to host on taking up new appointments. Tea was a vital social lubricant for monastic communities and essential to the regular functioning of their administration and their calendar.

CONCLUSION

In Song times we see a dramatic increase in tea production, with consequent effects on the economy. At the same time, tea had to compete not only against alcohol but also medicinal and herbal decoctions. Because the market for these tonics was driven by a "craze" for dietetics that peaked during the Song dynasty, it has been hard to appreciate just how much attitudes about tea were affected by this larger arena of "health drinks." Only by looking carefully at our sources in their Song-dynasty context can we appreciate the extent to which tea was consumed in parallel with decoctions of various kinds both in the monastery and without.

We have noted in this chapter the invention of tea rituals in the monastery and their important role in reinforcing hierarchical structures within the monastery and building bridges with patrons and officials outside the monastery. We have also seen how tea became a ubiquitous feature of religious literature, particularly in Chan collections, as well as how Song poets continued to build on the work of their Tang predecessors to make claims for otherworldly powers of tea and tea masters, now presented as possessing the "*samādhi* of tea." Although types of tea and methods of preparation had changed markedly since Lu Yu's time, his work continued to inspire Song authors to make authoritative claims about the best teas and mountain springs. Tea was both commonplace and casually consumed in everyday life and at the same time subject to increasing formalization and ritualization in its preparation and consumption.

7

Tea Comes to Japan

EISAI'S *KISSA YŌJŌKI*

*I*n this chapter, I discuss the religious dimensions of the introduction of tea to Japan from China. In particular, I focus on the complex religious and cultural associations with tea found in *Kissa yōjōki* (*Drinking Tea for Nourishing Life*) by the Japanese monk Eisai (1141–1215).[1] Although it may seem strange to devote so much attention to a text by a Japanese Buddhist monk as part of a book about tea in China, there is much to be gained by approaching this important source from a continental perspective. First, because Eisai spent a considerable period of time in China, his firsthand experience with the consumption of tea and other decoctions there informs his work. He offers a unique perspective on religious and cultural aspects of tea in China, including important eyewitness accounts of methods of tea production and consumption in late Southern Song Zhejiang—a time and place for which we have little other data. Second, his text contains many elements taken from the continent that are rearranged in a new and distinctive configuration. Eisai's creative display of knowledge, techniques, concepts, and language from the mainland offers an excellent opportunity to reflect on the meanings of tea in China.

The monk Myōan Eisai traveled to China twice, first in 1168–1169 and again, for a longer stay, in 1187–1191, although he probably set out with the intention of reaching India on this second journey.[2] He brought back to Japan both tea seeds and an interest in the curative powers of tea, which he demonstrated in 1214 when his shogun fell ill. The title of his work, *Kissa yōjōki,* which we could translate as "an account of drinking tea to preserve life," could lead one reasonably to suppose that the text is primarily about drinking tea as a wellness practice. In fact, tea is but one of the substances and techniques introduced by the piece. Although Eisai's work has rightly been acknowledged by scholars as the first Japanese treatise on tea, it also deals with such diverse topics as the harmony of the five viscera within the body, the use of esoteric mantras and mūdras for healing, the decline of the Buddhadharma, varieties of disease and demonic possession that may be cured by ingesting mulberry in various forms, and the benefits of consuming ginger and various other aromatic substances. At first, this short but dense document may appear to be no more than a haphazard jumble of opinions, citations from other sources, personal observations, and recipes for patent medicines, but if we understand it in its early thirteenth-century context it has much to tell us about how Eisai and his contemporaries understood the role and function of tea in a Buddhist context.

Drinking Tea for Nourishing Life offers a particularly rich example of the interplay between commodity, religion, wellness, and conceptions of the human microcosm. Because Eisai's text does not fit particularly well into narratives about the development of *cha-no-yu* in Japan, it has often been given only cursory examination by historians or treated as little more than a somewhat eccentric curiosity.[3] But now that we have looked at Song tea culture and its close involvement with medicinal decoctions and dietetics, we are much better placed to understand the messages that Eisai was trying to communicate. *Drinking Tea for Nourishing Life* represents a bold attempt to move a commodity (tea), a theory (dietetics), and an esoteric technological system (the complex interplay of flavors, viscera, mantras, and maṇḍalas) across cultures from China to Japan, and for that reason it is worthy of our close attention. Also, it contains some rare direct observations on tea picking and processing in late Southern Song Zhejiang that are of particular interest to historians of Chinese tea.

We will discover that there are multiple logics operating in *Kissa yōjōki*. For example, Eisai's short work specifies a number of different, and perhaps incompatible, vectors for disease. He also provides an inconsistent account of how tea works as a medicine; this oscillating viewpoint is due to the fact that he has drawn models from divergent Chinese sources (including oral information) and presented them in a hybrid form in which competing ideas are not completely synthesized. Perhaps the inconsistencies are due to Eisai's own lack of medical training, but perhaps also these contradictory models actually did coexist side by side in contemporary China. Despite its conceptual challenges, Eisai's text is important not only for the history of tea but also for the history of medicine in East Asia. Historian of Japanese medicine Andrew Goble recently indicated the significance of *Kissa yōjōki* as "the first evidence in nearly three centuries that knowledge of Chinese medicine was being obtained directly from living Chinese."[4]

AN APPROACH TO *KISSA YŌJŌKI*

Later, we will examine a full translation of *Drinking Tea for Nourishing Life*, but first I will offer a synopsis of the text, so that we may consider its structure and content. Next, we shall explore the underlying theoretical assumptions made by Eisai—why and how should tea work on the human body as he claims? Then, we will establish what kinds of disease Eisai has in mind and go on to see how tea is said to cure these specific ailments. Finally, we will reflect on how to understand *Kissa yōjōki* as a hybrid work that incorporates several distinct perspectives on health, medicine, and the body and represents them in a way that appears to privilege a Buddhist perspective.

SYNOPSIS OF *KISSA YŌJŌKI*

Introduction
Part 1
On Techniques for Harmonizing the Five Viscera
  Quotations from Esoteric Buddhist texts
Six sections on tea:
  1. The names for tea.
  2. Shape of the tea plant.
  3. Functions of tea.
  4. Times for picking tea.
  5. Conditions for picking tea.
  6. Investigating the production of tea.

The first part of the text has the most to say about tea, but not all of the information comes from Eisai himself. Much of the data in the six sections on tea are copied more or less verbatim from the extensive unit on tea (s.v. *ming*) found in the Song-dynasty encyclopedia *Imperial Readings of the Taiping Era* (*Taiping yulan*) interspersed with Eisai's own observations.[5] Eisai does not reveal that his quotations are drawn from the collectanea, so the unwary reader could easily suppose that the Japanese monk was a dedicated investigator of the literature of tea who had discovered and carefully collated the twenty-two literary sources himself.

Part 2
On Techniques for Exorcising Demons.
  Quotations from Esoteric Buddhist texts.
Five types of disease:
  1. Drinking water disease.
  2. Struck by wind disease—the hands and feet do not obey the mind.
  3. Not eating disease.
  4. Boil disease.
  5. Lower-leg pneuma disease.

Prescriptions using mulberry:
   1. Mulberry congee.
   2. Ingesting mulberry wood.
   3. Infusion of mulberry.
   4. Chewing mulberry wood.
   5. Mulberry-wood pillow.
   6. Ingestion of mulberry leaves.
   7. Ingestion of mulberries.
Ingestion of Gaoliang Ginger
Drinking Tea
Ingestion of Reduction of Five Aromatics

As we can see from the table of contents, the second part of Eisai's text hardly seems to mention tea at all—in fact tea appears to be presented in this section as considerably less efficacious against disease than various prescriptions involving mulberry wood, leaf, and fruit—substances that were well known to the Chinese *materia medica.* So, it is important to bear in mind the relative weight accorded to tea in the text overall as we continue our investigation.

THE THEORY OF *KISSA YŌJŌKI*: PLACE, TIME, AND THE FIVE AGENTS

Recognizing the limited amount of space that Eisai devotes to tea in his treatise and the range of the other topics that he addresses, let us now try to understand his assumptions about tea and its ability to promote wellness. Part of Eisai's argument about the efficacy of tea rests on his conception of the geography of Asia. He states that both India and China "value and respect" tea and that the drink had been enjoyed in Japan in the past. This is an interesting claim, because there is very little evidence that tea was actually consumed in medieval India. We know that in fact tea was used in China long before it was known in India and that when Chinese Buddhist monks like Yijing went to India they took tea with them. Although Eisai's vision of the transnational reach of tea is not one that matches the extant historical record, it is a revealing one because it places Japan in a familiar geographical position vis-à-vis India and China. Like Buddhism itself, in Eisai's vision, tea comes to Japan from these hallowed places. Eisai appears to assume that this account of the sacred geography of tea is self-evident—although he returns to the idea in a couple of places, he does not argue the case very strongly or cite evidence for the claim.

Eisai's argument for the adoption of tea drinking by his fellow country-men begins in earnest not with place but with time. He adopts a Buddhist cosmological framework to argue that, since the beginning of the *kalpa*, human beings have become weaker and also that traditional forms of medicine—he specifies acupuncture, moxibustion, and the consumption of decoctions—have now been rendered ineffective by the general degeneration of the cosmos over time. Because these former curative methods are no longer in accordance with circumstances, they need to be modified and supplemented. Moreover, he says, it is now thousands of years since the time of the great doctors of antiquity—Jīvaka in India and Shennong (the Divine Husbandman) in China—so that medical methods are wrongly employed and cause death.[6] Eisai thus introduces tea as the latest and most current medical technique from China.

In his introduction, Eisai explains how he thinks tea works systemically in terms of the five viscera, which was a long-established model in Chinese med-icine.[7] He tells us,

> Of these five viscera the heart viscus is the sovereign. As for the meth-ods of fortifying the heart viscus, the drinking of tea is the most mi-raculous technique. When the heart viscus grows feeble, then all the five viscera give rise to disease.[8]

This is a particularly striking vision of the mechanism of tea's influence on the body, because as we have seen, no one in China appears to have made any state-ment about the medicinal efficacy of tea in quite the same manner. Where did Eisai get this idea about "fortifying the heart viscus" with tea? Rather startlingly, the concept is not grounded in any source that we have mentioned so far in this study. Eisai's text proper begins with a quotation from what appears from its title to be an esoteric Buddhist ritual text, *Secret Excerpts from the Proce-dure for Destroying the Hells with the Utmost Excellent Dhāraṇīs* (*Sonshō da-rani hajigoku hō misshō*), which is reported to say,

1. The liver viscus prefers acid flavors.
2. The lung viscus prefers pungent flavors.
3. The heart viscus prefers bitter flavors.
4. The spleen viscus prefers sweet flavors.
5. The kidney viscus prefers salty flavors.

The quotation goes on to makes further correlations with the Five Phases (Wood, Fire, Earth, Metal, Water) and the Five Directions (East, West, South, North, Center) that can be best rendered diagrammatically as:

Liver	East	Spring	Wood	Blue/Green	*hun* (soul)	Eyes
Lungs	West	Autumn	Metal	White	*po* (soul)	Nose
Heart	South	Summer	Fire	Red	*shen* (spirit)	Tongue
Spleen	Center	Between Seasons?	Earth	Yellow	*zhi* (will)	Mouth
Kidneys	North	Winter	Water	Black	*xiang* (imagination)	Marrow/Ears

Eisai then uses these correlations drawn from the esoteric text to make the following argument about the efficacy of tea, which amplifies the point he makes in his introduction to the text:

The five viscera are receptive to different flavors. If one flavor is over-favored and too much of it enters [the body], then that organ grows strong and oppressive and nearby viscera will respond by producing illness. Now as regards four of these flavors—pungent, acid, sweet, and salty—as they have always been present, we have always consumed them. However, since we have always lacked any kind of bitter flavor, we have never consumed this flavor. For this reason four of the viscera have remained strong while the heart viscus has remained weak. Thus, illness has arisen. When the heart is sick, then all flavors become repugnant. What one eats, one vomits out, and so one is unable to eat [at all].

But now, when one drinks tea the heart viscus becomes strong and there is no disease. One should be aware that when the heart viscus is sick a person's skin and flesh have a bad color, as the life upon which they depend is being destroyed.

In Japan we do not consume bitter flavors. Only in China do people drink tea, and as a result the heart viscus does not get sick and thus they live long lives. Our country is teeming with sick and emaciated people—this is simply because they do not drink tea. When people's hearts and spirits are out of sorts, this is exactly the time when they should be drinking tea which will arouse the heart viscus to prevent the myriad illnesses. When the heart viscus is cheerful, then there will be no severe pain felt from the other viscera, even if they are suffering illnesses.[9]

In this passage, Eisai extrapolates from the textual source into the realm of personal experience. His theory is in fact a hybrid—it draws initially on the correlations found in the Buddhist ritual manual and then goes on to insist that the difference between Japan and China is that in China people have access to a crucial flavor that is missing in Japan and that, moreover, tea is the substance that supplies that missing flavor. The authority for that diagnosis is probably no more than the fact that Eisai had been to China, because it is difficult to find any operating theory of dietetics in early thirteenth-century Japan that might have made any similar observations about the lack of bitter flavors in the Japanese diet.

If we think about the correlations between the five viscera and five flavors in terms of Chinese *yin/yang* theory, we can agree that the heart viscus is indeed classified as *yin* and that bitter taste is also *yin*. But even so, Chinese authors of *materia medica* literature do not seem to have linked the bitter taste of tea with its effect on the heart viscus (or any of the other viscera for that matter). We will see, however, that the correlation of flavors with viscera was of interest to Chinese authors of a different kind of literature.

Let us see if we can evaluate the foundation of Eisai's claim. From even a very cursory examination, it is difficult to accept the schema quoted by Eisai as being part of a genuine translation of an Indian esoteric text. It features so prominently a system of five agents and their correspondences with other sets of five—long understood as one of the hallmarks of Chinese thought—that one's initial reaction would be to categorize this *Procedure for Destroying the Hells with the Utmost Excellent Dhāraṇīs* as a Chinese creation and not a translation from an Indic source. So, we first need to establish the identity of the text that Eisai is quoting here and whether it is, in fact, Chinese in origin. Although no text by the name *Secret Excerpts from the Procedure for Destroying the Hells with the Utmost Excellent Dhāraṇīs* survives, Chen Jinhua has demonstrated that the quotations within it bear an uncanny resemblance to another text called *The Esoteric Dhāraṇīs Related to the Three Kinds of Siddhi [attainment] Which Allow One to Destroy the Hells, Transform Karma, and Transcend the Three Realms* (*Sanzhong xidi podiyu zhuanyezhang chusanjie mimi tuoluoni fa*, J. *Sanshu shitchi hajigoku tengosshō shutsusangai himitsu darani hō*), preserved as number 905 in the Taishō edition of the Buddhist canon and there credited as a translation by the Indian esoteric master Śubhakarasiṃha (Shanwuwei, 637–735).[10] However, despite the presence in that text of multiple correspondences among sets of five, typical of the writings of Chinese theorists of the five phases from the Han dynasty onward, the text is in fact a Japanese creation, masquerading as a translation into Chinese of an Indian original and composed in Japan some time between 902 and 1047.[11]

The origins of this particular set of correspondences between viscera, directions, seasons, flavors, and so on, which are found in Eisai's *dhāraṇī* text, do seem to be drawn ultimately from Chinese sources, including Buddhist texts such as Tiantai Zhiyi's (538–597) masterwork, *Mahāyāna Calming and Contemplation (Mohe zhiguan)*. *Mahāyāna Calming and Contemplation* makes some very similar statements about the correlation between flavors and the viscera—to give just one example here, Zhiyi says that "bitter flavors strengthen the heart and damage the liver."[12] We can conclude then that Eisai does not quote Zhiyi directly, but he does draw on an apocryphal text, probably Japanese in origin, that contains a sophisticated set of correspondences based on five agents theory and earlier articulated in part by Zhiyi.

Having determined one of Eisai's proof texts to be a Japanese Buddhist apocryphon, we may be prepared for the identity of another source cited by Eisai: *Excerpts from the Rituals of the Maṇḍala of the Five Viscera (Gozō mandara giki shō)*. This text not only correlates the five viscera with buddhas and bodhisattvas but it also instructs the practitioner how to strengthen the five viscera through forming mūdras and intoning Sanskrit syllables. For example,

> The liver equates with the East and Akṣobhya Buddha, also with Bhaiṣajyagururāja Buddha. It is in the Vajra section of the maṇḍala. Forming the Single-pronged Vajra (*dugu*) mūdra and intoning the *a* syllable mantra, will embrace and support the liver viscera, so it will be forever free of disease.

Excerpts from the Rituals of the Maṇḍala of the Five Viscera, like the other esoteric text quoted by Eisai, appears to be another collection of excerpts taken from *The Esoteric Dhāraṇīs Related to the Three Kinds of Siddhi* that I mentioned earlier.[13]

Having provided the theory behind his text on tea and grounded it solidly in esoteric Buddhist sources, Eisai provides practical applications related to the five flavors and goes on to develop his theory of dietetics based on correlations among the five phases:

> These five flavors are as follows. Acid tastes: these are oranges, mandarin oranges, citrus fruits, etc. Pungent tastes: these are ginger, garlic, Gaoliang ginger, etc. Sweet tastes: these are sugar, etc. Also, all foodstuffs have sweetness as their nature. Bitter tastes: these are tea, *qingmuxiang* (Aristolochia Recurvilabra), etc. Salty tastes: these are salt, etc.

The heart viscus is the gentleman (*junzi*) of the five viscera. Tea is the chief of the bitter tastes. Bitter is the paramount taste of all the tastes. On account of this, the heart viscus loves this taste. The heart viscus prospers, and thus brings peace to all the viscera.

If a person's eye has a disease, one knows that the liver viscus is damaged. By using medicine with an acid nature one can cure it. If the ear has a disease, one knows that the kidney viscus is damaged. By using medicine with a salty nature one can cure it. If the nose has a disease, one knows that the lung viscus is damaged. By using medicine with a pungent nature one can cure it. If the tongue has a disease, one knows that the heart viscus is damaged. By using a medicine with a bitter flavor, one can cure it. If the mouth has a disease, one knows that the spleen is damaged. By using medicine with a sweet nature, one can cure it.

If the body is weak and the thoughts are dissipated, one knows that this is also a case of the heart viscus being damaged. Drink tea frequently and the power of one's pneuma will be strengthened.

In this passage, Eisai combines scriptural citation with personal experience to argue that the Japanese are particularly susceptible to disease because their heart viscus (usually correlated with major-*yin*) is weak and needs to be supplemented by drinking tea—the only source of the missing bitter flavor. As far as we can ascertain, this argument and its theoretical foundations appear to be Eisai's own unique formulation, but his need to advance this new knowledge was stimulated by the range of terrifying diseases currently haunting the elite of Japan, some of which are mentioned by name in his text.

SPECIFIC DISEASES IN *KISSA YŌJŌKI*

We saw in the synopsis of the text that the second part of *Kissa yōjōki* mentions some specific diseases that appear to have plagued Japan in Eisai's day.[14] The signs of "drinking water disease" were dry throat and the need to drink water continuously.[15] These symptoms were reported by many of the Heian aristocracy, and the disease has been identified with diabetes. "Struck by wind disease" refers to a stroke or something similar, in which the patient loses control of the limbs. The disease of "not eating" appears to be no more than a reference to symptoms of loss of appetite, whereas "boil disease" is a catchall term that covers various skin conditions. "Lower-leg pneuma disease" came to be identified with beriberi in nineteenth-century Japan, but the term has a much longer and more complex history.[16] In this disease, pathogenic pneuma gathers in the feet; if it rises to the heart, the sufferer may die. In Song-dynasty China it was associated with women and was thought to threaten generative vitality because it might strike at the womb.[17] However, that does not seem to be quite the disease Eisai has in mind. He says, "This illness comes from eating to repletion in the evening. Going into the night while being full, the alcohol and food are harmful." And the cure, he says, is to consume mulberry congee, mulberry infusion, Gaoliang ginger, and tea. Some of these dietary cures match those prescribed by the Tang-dynasty physician Sun Simiao in his treatise on lower-leg pneuma disease, but tea is not among the substances listed by Sun.[18] It is interesting to note that a disorder that was gendered in Song China is not so marked by Eisai, but it is not clear what conclusions we may draw from that omission.

These five named diseases, which Eisai tells us are ultimately caused by the kinds of demonic infestation that are common in the "final age," can all be cured by mulberry in various forms. But, he says, tea will cure them too. We will discuss his prescription of tea later.

In addition to the specific diseases pertaining to Japan, Eisai discusses the "diseases of warmth" (wenyibing) found in South China.[19] If we came across the term wenyi or wenyibing in a medical text from Song China, we might translate it as "epidemic." However, it is not clear how Eisai understood the term, which is why I have opted for a more literal rendering. We should note that here he appears to offer a different explanation of how tea works against these diseases of warmth. It does so not by strengthening the heart viscus, but by balancing out sweet foods and easing digestion. This is how he explains these diseases and their treatment:

> Tea expels diseases of warmth (wenyibing). "Southerners" (nanren) means people from Guangzhou and so on. This region is a land of pestilential warmth (zhangre) (this region also has insect diseases [chongbing]). When people from the Chinese capital are posted here, nine out of ten do not return. The foodstuffs taste delicious but are hard to digest. Therefore many eat betel nuts and drink tea. If one does not drink it, then there may be harm to the body. Japan is a cold land and therefore we do not have this problem. But the South is wild and mountainous and so China did not reach there. This is because it is a land of pestilential warmth.

In short, what we find in Kissa yōjōki is not so much a panegyric on the virtues of tea, but rather a presentation of a variety of diseases, a variety of cures (not all of which feature tea), and a hybrid—or perhaps unarticulated—concept of how tea works medicinally. Sometimes this concept features tea implicitly as a bitter, *yin* substance that strengthens the heart viscus, but at other times the power of tea is derived not from its flavor, but from other, different properties such as its ability to improve digestion. In addition to his pharmacological theories, Eisai's understanding of five phases theory privileges a Buddhist version of this cosmology—thus, we may see him as promoting a particularly Buddhist view of tea as a medicine.

Here is Eisai's medical prescription for tea:

> Using really hot water (*baitang*), make a decoction and ingest it. Use two or three square-inch spoonfuls [of powdered tea]. Suit yourself as to the amount of water. For a simple decoction a small amount is fine. Again, follow your inclination.
>
> As for timing, you must drink tea to digest food. When you drink, you should only drink tea, or drink mulberry decoction. Do not drink any other decoction. If you do not drink decoctions of mulberry or tea, then all kinds of illness will arise.

It is interesting to note that he seems to describe the making of loose tea, such as Huang Tingjian's Twin Wells variety, and not any kind of wax tea. Eisai's description of how to prepare tea as a beverage, although very abbreviated, matches what we know about "pointing tea" in the Song, although here tea has a distinctly medicalized form. In this presentation, then, tea is a decoction just like mulberry decoction.

We can usefully compare Eisai's prescription for tea with that of a Chinese author who was more or less Eisai's contemporary. Lin Hong (twelfth century) says the following in his *Pure Offerings for Mountain Dwellers* (*Shanjia qinggong*), where he discusses both pointing tea and decocting it:[20]

Offering of Tea

> Tea is medicinal. By brewing it and consuming it, one drives off stagnation and [improves] digestion. But, if one uses hot water to "point" it, then it will do the reverse, causing stagnation in the diaphragm and harming the spleen and stomach. Now, in this generation, those who are found of profit often pick other leaves and mix them in to make the powder; furthermore they are lazy about the frying process, so therefore this [processed tea powder] may cause harm. The proper method now is to pick leaf buds or use the pieces of the plant's calyx, brewing the tea over a fire in water from a flowing source. One should wait a while after eating before drinking it. [Su] Dongpo's verse says, "Water from a flowing source requires cooking with an active

flame." He also says, "The flavor of a cup of tea after a meal is truly profound." This is the method of brewing and consuming tea. The *Classic of Tea* also says, "River water is best, with mountain and well water both next to it." Our present generation not only does not discriminate among waters, but moreover adds salt and even fruit; this truly harms the proper flavor. People do not know that one uses scallions to drive off confusion and only plum to dispel tiredness, but if one is neither confused nor tired, why the need to use them at all? Among tea aficionados of the past, there were none like the Master of the Jade River [Lu Tong], of whom I have only heard of his taking [his tea] brewed. If he had used hot water to "point" it, how could he have drunk as many as seven bowls? A poem of [Huang] Shangu (Huang Tingjian) says, "Boiling water sounds like the breeze in the pines; early vanquishing most of my sickness." If alcohol were like this, then one's mouth cannot speak it, and one's heart fills with happiness, and one realizes a deep understanding of Chan.[21]

So, we can see that in Eisai's time, despite the ubiquity of powdered tea made using the pointing method, there were still those in China who championed the brewing of carefully selected tea leaves as the appropriate and healthy method. Eisai very likely drew on this conception of tea as a healthy beverage in his presentation. Certainly that view of tea predominates in *Kissa yōjōki* in contrast to the more aestheticized view of tea drinking as an elite pastime for connoisseurs that he might otherwise have promoted to his patrons in Japan.

CONCLUSION

Kissa yōjōki is a unique text that presents many challenges to our comprehension. Viewing it in light of contemporary issues in health, tea culture, and Buddhist doctrine in both China and Japan can give us a better understanding of what Eisai was trying to achieve. Placing Eisai's text in conversation with Lin Hong's work on dietetics reminds us that Chinese views of what tea was and how it was to be drunk were as fluid in the late twelfth century as they were in the mid-eighth century. Whatever Eisai was trying to import, it was not tea as a refined drink of poets and scholars, nor was it the monk's aid to meditation. Rather, it was something that had both impeccable Buddhist credentials and direct practical applications for those suffering from the demonic diseases that ran rampant in the final age.

What follows is a full and annotated translation of this fascinating text.

Translation.[22]

A RECORD OF DRINKING TEA AND NOURISHING LIFE

By Eisai, former acting sōjō and holder of the position of the great upādhyāya of the Dharma seal (Hōin dai oshō-i), who went to China in search of the Dharma.

PREFACE

Tea is a transcendent drug for nourishing life and a miraculous technique for extending one's lifespan. The places where it grows in mountains and valleys are spiritual and numinous, and the people who pick it prolong their lives.

India (Tianzhu) and China (Tangtu, the land of Tang) both value and respect it, and in our country of Japan we also used to enjoy it and cherish it. From ancient times until today it has been considered a unique and special transcendent drug. It is indispensable.

It is said that at the beginning of the *kalpa*, humans were equal to *deva*s. But now, humans are gradually declining and getting weaker. It is as if the four great elements (*sida*) and the five viscera (*wuzang*) were rotting.[23] This being so, when we employ acupuncture and moxibustion they both cause harm, and when one uses decoctions (*tang*) as a cure they are also ineffective.[24] So, those who are treated with these cures gradually become weak and die, which is indeed lamentable. If these medical techniques from the past are not modified, but continue to be used in order to cure people of the present, then it will be rare indeed that they are appropriate to circumstances!

In my humble opinion, of the myriad things which were created by Heaven, the creation of humans should be considered honorable. As for humans' preserving the whole of their lifespan, guarding life (*shouming*) should be considered worthy. The source of preserving one's whole lifespan is in nourishing life. To manifest this technique of nourishing life one must keep the five viscera at peace.

Of these five viscera, the heart viscus is the sovereign. As for the methods of fortifying the heart viscus, the drinking of tea is the most miraculous technique. When the heart viscus grows feeble, then all the five viscera give rise to disease.

It is now over 2,000 years since Jīvaka (Ch. Qipo, J. Kiba) passed away in India. In these latter times (*moshi*), who knows how to take the pulse of the blood correctly? Shennong of China (Hanjia) vanished some 3,000 years ago. In current times, what principles are there for drugs and their flavors? So, lacking anyone whom one can consult on the signs of illness, there is pointless suffering and pointless injury. If there is some error in requesting the method of healing, then moxibustion is employed in vain and causes needless harm.

I have heard that the ingestion of drugs according to present medical techniques causes damage to the mind-ground. This is because the drugs are not appropriate to the disease. When moxa is employed it causes premature death. This is because the moxa and the pulse are in conflict. It would be better to investigate customary practice in China (daguo), and to make known recent methods of treatment there. I therefore present two general approaches and make known the signs of illnesses prevalent in these latter times. I hope that they will be of use to later generations, and will benefit all beings.

On the first day of the first month, Spring, Kenpo 2 [kōjutsu] (12th February, 1214), respectfully prefaced.
    I. The Approach of the Harmony of the Five Viscera
    II. The Approach of the Exorcism of Demons

I. THE HARMONY OF THE FIVE VISCERA
Secret Excerpts from the Procedure for Destroying the Hells with the Utmost Excellent Dhāraṇīs (Sonshō darani hajigoku hō misshō) says:
1. The liver viscus prefers acid flavors.
2. The lung viscus prefers pungent flavors.
3. The heart viscus prefers bitter flavors.
4. The spleen viscus prefers sweet flavors.
5. The kidney viscus prefers salty flavors.

It also makes correlations with the Five Agents (Wood, Fire, Earth, Metal, Water) and the Five Directions (East, West, South, North, Center):

Liver	East	Spring	Wood	Blue/Green	*hun* (soul)[i]	Eyes
Lungs	West	Autumn	Metal	White	*po* (soul)	Nose
Heart	South	Summer	Fire	Red	*shen* (spirit)	Tongue
Spleen	Center	Between Seasons?	Earth	Yellow	*zhi* (will)	Mouth
Kidneys	North	Winter	Water	Black	*xiang* (imagination)	Marrow/ Ears

---

[i] Note that *Kissa yōjōki* presents these five pneumas in a different order from that found in traditional sources, or in *Taishō* 905. See Chen 2009, 242n.176.

The five viscera are receptive to different flavors. If one flavor is over-favored and too much of it enters [the body], then that organ grows strong and oppressive and nearby viscera will respond by producing illness. Now as regards four of these flavors—pungent, acid, sweet, and salty—as they have always been present, we have always consumed them. However, since we have always lacked any kind of bitter flavor, we have never consumed this flavor. For this reason, four of the viscera have remained strong while the heart viscus has remained weak. Thus, illness has arisen. When the heart is sick, then all flavors become repugnant. What one eats, one vomits out, and so one is unable to eat [at all].

But now, when one drinks tea the heart viscus becomes strong and there is no disease. One should be aware that when the heart viscus is sick a person's skin and flesh have a bad color, as the life upon which they depend is being destroyed.

In Japan we do not consume bitter flavors. Only in China do people drink tea, and as a result the heart viscus does not get sick and thus they live long lives. Our country is teeming with sick and emaciated people—this is simply because they do not drink tea. When people's hearts and spirits are out of sorts, this is exactly the time when they should be drinking tea which will regulate the heart viscus to prevent the myriad illnesses. When the heart viscus is cheerful, then there will be no severe pain felt from the other viscera, even if they are suffering illnesses.

Also, *Excerpts from the Rituals of the Maṇḍala of the Five Viscera (Gozō mandara giki shō)* says,

> Use the secret mantras to cure.
> The liver equates with the Buddha Akṣobhya in the East, and with Bhaiṣajyagururāja Buddha. It is in the Vajra section [of the maṇḍala]. Forming the single-pronged *vajra* (*dugu/dokko*) mūdra and intoning the *a* syllable mantra will empower (*jiachi*) the liver viscera, so it will be eternally free of disease.[25]
> The heart equates with the Buddha Ratnasambhava in the South and Ākāśagarbha. It is in the Treasure section. Forming the "Precious Form" (*baoxing/hōgyō*) mūdra and intoning the *hrīḥ* syllable mantra will empower the heart viscus, so it will be free of disease.
> The lungs equate with the Buddha Amitābha in the West and with Guanyin/Kannon. They are in the Lotus section. Forming the Eight-petaled [lotus] (*baye*) mūdra and intoning the *trāḥ* syllable mantra will empower the lung viscus, so it will be free of disease.

The kidneys equate with the Buddha Śākyamuni in the North and with Maitreya. They are in the Karma section. Forming the karma mūdra and intoning the *aḥ* syllable mantra will empower the kidney viscus, so it will be free of disease.

The spleen equates with the Buddha Mahāvairocaṇa in the Center and with the Bodhisattva Prajñā. It is in the Buddha section. Forming the Five-pronged *vajra* (*wugu/goko*) mūdra and intoning the *vaṃ* syllable mantra will empower the spleen viscera, so it will be free of disease.

When the five sections [of the maṇḍala] are empowered, then this is the means of curing the interior. When the five flavors nourish life, then these are the cure for external diseases. Interior and exterior mutually aid and protect the body and life.

The five flavors are as follows. Acid flavors: these are oranges, tangerines, citrus fruits etc. Pungent flavors: these are ginger, garlic, Gaoliang ginger, etc. Sweet flavors: these are sugar, etc. Also, all foodstuffs have sweetness as their nature. Bitter flavors: these are tea, *qingmuxiang* (Aristolochia Recurvilabra), etc. Salty flavors: these are salt, etc.

The heart viscus is the lord (*junzi*) of the five viscera. Tea is the chief of the bitter flavors. Bitter is the paramount flavor of all the flavors. On account of this [correspondence], the heart viscus loves this flavor. When the heart viscus prospers, it thus brings peace to all the viscera.

If a person's eye has a disease, one knows that the liver viscus is damaged. By using medicine with an acid nature one can cure it. If the ear has a disease, one knows that the kidney viscus is damaged. By using medicine with a salty nature one can cure it. If the nose has a disease, one knows that the lung viscus is damaged. By using medicine with a pungent nature one can cure it. If the tongue has a disease, one knows that the heart viscus is damaged. By using a medicine with a bitter nature, one can cure it. If the mouth has a disease, one knows that the spleen is damaged. By using medicine with a sweet nature, one can cure it.

If the body is weak and the thoughts are dissipated, one knows that this is also a case of the heart viscus being damaged. Drink tea frequently and the power of one's pneuma will be strengthened. The power and capacity of tea I have selected according to time and category below. There are six items.

1. Understanding the Names for Tea (*Cha*)[26]

The *Erya* (Approach to the Proper) says, "*Jia* is bitter *cha*. One name is *mao*.[27] Another name is *ming*. When it is picked early, it is called *cha*. When it is picked late it is called *ming*. Western Shu people call it *ku cha* (bitter tea).[28] (Western Shu is the name of a state.)[29]

It is also said, "In Chengdu prefecture, 5,000 *li* west of the Chinese capital, everything is delicious (*mei*).[30] The tea there is also delicious."

The *Record of Guangzhou* (*Guangzhou ji*) says, "Gaolu (*cha*): one name for it is *ming*."[31]

Guangzhou is 5000 *li* south of the Song capital. Also, it is close to the Kunlun states.[32] The Kunlun states also border on India (Tianzhu). Now, precious things from India were transmitted to Guangzhou. Deliciousness depends on the location, and the tea is also delicious. This region has no snow or frost but is warm. In the winter, padded clothes are not worn. This is why the tea tastes delicious. Because the tea is delicious, it is called *gaolu*. This region is a place of tropical fevers (*zhangre*). Nine out of ten people from the north suffer harm when they come there. The myriad things taste delicious, and therefore many people desire them. This being so, before eating many people eat betel nuts (*binlangzi*), and after eating many people drink tea. Travelers are strongly urged to drink a lot, in the hope that their body and mind will not be hurt. Therefore, betel nuts and tea are extremely valuable and important.

The *Gazetteer of Southern Yue* (*Nanyue zhi*) says, "Guoluo cha: one name for it is *ming*."[33]

Lu Yu's *Cha jing* says, "There are five kinds of names for tea: 1). it is called *cha*; 2). it is called *jia*; 3). it is called *she*; 4). it is called *ming*; 5). it is called *chuan*.[34] (Adding *mao* makes six.)

The Prince of Wei's *Record of Flowers and Trees* (*Huamu zhi*) says, "Ming."

2. Shape of the Tea Plant

Erya says, "The plant is small and similar to gardenia (*zhizi*) wood."[35]

Record of the Lord of Paulownia (*Tongjun lu*) says, "Tea leaves are shaped like gardenia."[36]

The *Classic of Tea* says, "The leaves are like gardenia leaves. The blossom is white, like wild rose (*qiangwei*)."[37]

3. Functions of Tea

The *Record of Wuxing* (*Wuxing ji*) says "West of Wucheng county there is Mount Wen. There is produced imperial *mao*."[38] ("Imperial" means that it was tribute presented to the emperor.)

Records of the Song (*Song lu*) says, "This is sweet dew. How can you call it tea (*chaming*)?"[39]

The *Expanded [Er]ya* (*Guangya*) says, "This drinking of tea relieves alcoholic intoxication and causes people not to sleep."[40]

An Extensive Record of Things (*Bowu zhi*) says, "Drinking true tea causes people to sleep less."[41] (Sleep causes people to be ignorant and vile [*meilie*]. Also, sleep is an illness.)

The *Divine Husbandman's Food Canon* (*Shennong shi jing*) says, "Tea (*chaming*) ought to be taken for a long period of time as it gives humans strength, contentment, and determination."[42]

The *Materia Medica* (*Bencao*) says, "Tea tastes sweet and bitter, it is cold in nature but nontoxic. If one consumes it then one will be free of ulcers or boils. It is diuretic; it reduces sleep; it eliminates thirst caused by fever; and reduces indigestion (*sushi*). All illnesses arise from indigestion."[43] (When indigestion is reduced, there is no illness.)

Hua Tuo's Essays on Food (*Hua Tuo shilun*) says, "If tea is consumed for a long time, there is an increase in thought."[44] (Mind and body are free of illness; thus there is an increase in thought.)

Retired Scholar Hu's Treatise on Food (*Hu jushi shizhi*) says, "If tea is consumed for a long time, there is a feathery transformation. But if it is consumed in conjunction with *jiu* (Chinese chives), it causes the human body to grow heavy."[45]

Tao Hongjing's *New Record* (*Xin lu*) says, "Drinking tea makes the body light and removes pain in the bones. Pain in the bones is the same as lower-leg pneuma (*jiaoqi*)."[46]

Record of the Lord of Paulownia says, "When tea is boiled and drunk, it causes people not to sleep."[47] (They do not sleep and thus do not get sick.)

Du You's (date unknown) "Rhapsody on Tea" (*Chuan fu*) says, "Tea harmonizes the spirit and harmonizes the interior. Exhaustion and laziness are pacified and expelled."[48] (*Nei* [interior] means the "Five Inner [organs]" *wunei*. This is another name for the Five Viscera [*wuzang*].)

Zhang Mengyang's "Climbing the tower in Chengdu" (*Deng Chengdu lou shi*) says,[49]

> The taste of tea is superior to that of the six pure liquids,
> its aroma penetrates the nine regions.
> Human life is not yet peaceful and happy,
> but this substance temporarily may be enjoyed."[50]
>
> (The "six purities" [*liuqing*] are the six cognitive faculties [*liugen*].[51] Nine Regions [*jiuqu*] means China [Handi], also called *jiuzhou*. *Qu* means *yu* [region].)

The *Supplemented Materia Medica* (*Bencao shiyi*) says,

> *Gaolu* is bitter (*kuping*). It can be made into a drink that slakes thirst. It expels plagues. It prevents sleep. It benefits the waterways [within

the body]. It brightens the eyes. It grows in the mountains of the Southern Seas. Southerners really esteem it."[52]

Tea expels diseases of warmth (*wenyibing*). "Southerners" (*nanren*) means people from Guangzhou and so on. This region is a land of pestilential warmth (*zhangre*) (this region also has insect diseases [*chongbing*]). When people from the Chinese capital are posted here, nine out of ten do not return. The food-stuffs taste delicious but are hard to digest. Therefore many eat betel nuts and drink tea. If one does not drink it, then there may be harm to the body. Japan is a cold land and therefore we do not have this problem. But the South is wild and mountainous and so China did not reach there. This is because it is a land of pestilential warmth.

The *Record of Mount Tiantai* (*Tiantai shan ji*) says, "If tea is consumed for a long time, one will grow feathers."[53] (This is said because the body becomes light.)

The "Section on Tea" (*Chabu*) in *Mr. Bai's Six Tablets* (*Baishi liutie*) says, "Given as tribute to the emperor."[54] ("Given as tribute to the emperor" means that it is not the comestible of lowly people.)

A *shi* poem from *Mr. Bai's Literary Collection* (*Baishi wenji*) says, "Noon tea can drive off sleep." (Noon refers to the time of a meal. The tea, because it is drunk after the meal, is called "noon tea." If the meal is digested, then there will be no sleepiness.)

Mr. Bai's Poem on "Summer" (*Bai shi shouxia shi*) says, "Sometimes, I drink one teacup (*ou*) of tea (*ming*)."(*Ou* is a refined name for a small vessel called "tea cup" [*cha jian*]. Its mouth is wide and its base is narrow. In order to ensure the tea does not go cold for a long time, the base of the vessel is narrow and deep.)

It also says, "By destroying sleep, thus is made manifest the power of tea."(One drinks tea, and to the end of the night one does not sleep, but the next day the body has no pain.)

It also says, "Thirsty from alcohol, in the late Spring I drink one bowl of tea." (When one drinks alcohol, then the throat becomes dry, inducing one to drink. At such times, one should drink only tea. One should not drink other kinds of decoction or water, etc. because that would give rise to all kinds of illness.)

The *Text on Filiality* (*Guan xiao wen*) says, "The filial son only presents this to his parents." (This is said because it causes one's mother and father to be free of illness and to live long lives.)

A song of Song people says, "The spirit of sickness is swiftly driven away by rituals with tea wood."

The *Supplemented Materia Medica* says "Of the decoctions given above for driving out illness, the most valuable is tea."(Above, in all the realms of the *devas*, as well as below, among humans; as for drugs, each can cure one disease, but only tea can cure the myriad diseases.)

4. Times for Picking Tea[55]

The *Classic of Tea* says, "Generally, the time for picking tea is during the
second, third and fourth months."

The *Records of the Song (Songlu)* say, "In the first month of Dahe 7 (833) Wu
and Shu sent tributes of new tea, but it had all been made in mid-winter.
The ruler promulgated an edict about this which said, 'The 'new tea' sent
as tribute is that which is produced after 'Birth of Spring' (*lichun*).' "[56] (The
intention was that if tea were produced in the winter, it would involve hardship for the people. So after
this edict it was all produced after the "Birth of Spring.")

The *Tang History* (*Tang shi*) says, "In the Spring of Chenyuan 9 (793), there
was a tax on tea." (A refined name for tea is "Early Spring" (*zaochun*). It is also called *yaming*.
This is the meaning.)

As for the current Song method of picking tea, in the Emperor's upper
garden there is a tea plantation. During the first three days of the year, he
gathers his subordinates and they enter within. Speaking in loud voices, they
wander about, coming and going. Then the next day, they take one or two
measures of tea buds. Using silver tweezers they pick it, and afterward make
wax tea (*lacha*). A single spoonful [of the tea powder] is worth up to one thousand strings of cash!

5. Conditions for Picking Tea

The *Classic of Tea* says, "If it is raining, then do not pick the tea. Even if it is
not actually raining, but there are clouds, then do not pick it." ([Also, in
these conditions,] do not roast tea or steam it, because the potency will diminish.)

6. Investigating the Condition of Tea

I saw the circumstances of the cultivation of tea in the Song. It is picked in the
morning, then steamed, then roasted. One who is lazy and negligent would
not be able to do such things. They regulate the fire and on the roasting mats
they lay out paper. The paper does not burn but one uses skill to roast [the tea].
They cannot be slack or remiss and they do not sleep the whole night. Within
one night, the roasting is complete. Then, they fill a good jar and using a bamboo leaf they firmly seal the mouth of the jar. As long as one does not allow
any wind to enter, then it will last for years, and not be spoiled.

Above is the method for nourishing life in the final period. Perhaps because people of our country do not know the method for picking tea, therefore
they do not use it. They oppose it and disparage it, saying "it is not medicine."
This is a case of not knowing how the virtues of tea may be attained. When I,
Eisai was in China, I saw people honor and esteem tea as if it were the apple of
their eye. Like a loyal minister giving a donation to an eminent monk, the

meaning in the past and present is the same. They had many kinds of sayings about tea and I cannot record them all. A Chinese doctor told me, "If a person does not drink tea, the effect of the medicine will be lost and they cannot obtain a cure for their illnesses. This is because the heart viscus is weak. Hopefully, good doctors in the end times will thoroughly know this."

End of *Kissa yōjōki,* first fascicle.

Kissa yōjōki second fascicle

II: METHOD FOR EXORCISING DEMONS
The *Secret Manuscript of the Rituals of General Daigensui (Daigensui daishō giki misshō)* says,[57]

> In the end times, humans will live for one hundred years. The four monastic assemblies mostly transgress the monastic decorum. In the time when people do not follow the teaching of the Buddha, nations will be barren and chaotic. All the generations will perish. In these times, there will be ghosts, goblins, and demons (*gui, mei, wangli-ang*). They will cause disorder to states, and afflict the people. They will cause all kinds of illness, but there will be no curative arts. Medical knowledge will not know [of these diseases]. Drugs will not cure them. There will be no means to save people from long illnesses, ema-ciation, and exhaustion. But, at that time, if there is one who grasps this *Daigensui daishō* mind-spell and recites it, the demons will turn tail and scatter. The host of diseases will suddenly be eradicated and cured. One who practices this, deeply abiding in this access and cul-tivating this method, even with only a little power, will definitely erad-icate illness. If one experiences illness again, then pray to the Three Jewels. If this does not have an effect, then this is because the person treats the Buddhadharma lightly, and does not have faith. In such a time, Daigen recalls his original vow, and brings about the efficacious result of the Buddhadharma. He eradicates diseases, and causes the Buddhadharma to flourish again. He empowers spiritual efficacy, and even the attainment of the fruits of the path.

If we reflect on this [passage], then we know that the symptoms of illness in recent years have been just so. These symptoms are not caused by cold, nor by heat, nor by earth and water, nor by fire and wind. Thus, doctors in recent times have made many errors. The symptoms of the diseases are of five kinds, as below.

1. Drinking-water Disease

This disease arises from cold pneuma. If one consumes mulberry congee (*sangzhou*), then in three to five days there will certainly be an effect. Always shun leeks, garlic, and scallions and do not eat them. When symptoms of demonic illness increase, then additional methods for curing will have no effect. It is just that cold pneuma is its origin. If one consumes mulberry gruel then only one in a hundred will not return to normal. (The prohibition on leeks is because they cause the illness to increase.)

2. Struck by Wind Disease—the Hands and Feet Do Not Obey the Mind

Cases of this disease have become numerous in recent years. It also arises from cold pneuma, etc. Using acupuncture and moxibustion to let the blood flow, or hot water cures to cause sweat to flow are harmful. Always avoid fire, and shun baths. Just act as in normal times, do not avoid the wind, do not have dietary restrictions but slowly consume mulberry congee, and mulberry decoctions. Gradually, you will return to normal—only one in a hundred will be in any danger. If you wish, at bathing times, boil a tub of mulberry and you can bathe once every three to five days. But, when bathing, do not make the sweat run. If the pneuma from the hot water enters within, it will cause the sweat to flow, and lack of appetite will necessarily develop. This is the premier method of curing. It is the method of curing for the three kinds of pneuma: cold pneuma, water pneuma, and warm pneuma. Also, one can do likewise for illnesses caused by demons.

3. Not-eating Disease

This disease also arises from cold pneuma. It is good to bathe and make sweat flow, but facing a fire may be dangerous. In both summer and winter, cooling the body is the wonderful method. In addition, consume mulberry congee.

The three types of sickness above all come from cold pneuma, so the method of curing them is the same. In the last period, many diseases are caused by demons. Therefore one uses mulberry to cure them. Beneath the mulberry tree the hordes of demons do not come. Also, this transcendent medicine is paramount. Do not doubt it!

4. Boil Disease

In recent years this disease appeared due to water pneuma, and various forms of heat. It is not a carbuncle (*ding*), nor a tumor (*yong*). Therefore people do not recognize it, and therefore many fail to treat it. It is simply that it arises from cold pneuma and is made manifest. The large and small boils do not sustain fire. Because of this people doubt that they are malignant boils. If one applies moxibustion, then one obtains a fiery poison, and therefore the swelling increases. The fiery poison cannot be cured. Great yellow, water cold, stone cold are dangerous.[58] If one employs moxibustion there is increased swelling; if one employs cold, there is increased enlargement. It can be regarded as extraordinary; it can be taken in one's stride. If the boil comes out, then people do not ask if it is strong or mild; they do not know if it is good or bad.

Ox-knee root (*niuxi gen*)—pound it and bind it.[59] Use sweating to draw out the boil. Dry it and draw it out again; then the side will not swell. It will ripen and burst without any bother, and a thick fluid will come out. Stick on a catalpa leaf. The fluid of the malignant poison will all come out. People of the world use plantain (*cheqiancao*), but this is strongly contraindicated. Consider it and consume mulberry congee, mulberry decoction, and five-flavor decoction. If the condition is severe, then employ moxibustion and also rely upon the prescription. It is said that when you first see the boils, garlic will temporarily eradicate them. Cut a slice as thick as a coin, and apply it to the top of the boil. With the moxa, firmly stamp it, like a small bean in size. Cauterize the top of the garlic. When the garlic is burnt, then you should stop. Do not damage the skin or the flesh. This is the secret method. Then its full power will weaken. The fire *qi* will not manifest, and there will definitely be an effect. After moxibustion, apply ox-knee [root] juice. Also, one may apply catalpa leaf. However, one should not apply plantain.

There is also banana root, which is divinely efficacious.

5. Lower-leg Pneuma Disease

This disease comes from eating to repletion in the evening. Entering the night while being full, the alcohol and food are harmful. The cure is not to eat to repletion in the afternoon. For this, one also consumes mulberry congee, mulberry decoction, Gaoliang ginger, and tea. These are marvelous methods for preserving life.

Shindo isho (medical books newly imported [from China]) says, "People who suffer from lower-leg pneuma, should eat to repletion in the morning, and not eat in the afternoon, etc."

People on long fasts do not suffer from lower-leg pneuma. This is what is said. Recently, the myriad diseases of humans have all been termed "lower-leg pneuma." This is laughable—it is simply declaring the disease's name, but not knowing the cure for that disease.

The five kinds of disease above are all caused by demons of the latter age. Thus, they may all be cured by mulberry. I received a verbal explanation from Chinese doctors. Also, the mulberry plant is a plant of the buddhas and bodhisattvas: if you carry this wood, then even *devas* and *māras* will not be able to fight; how much more so for the demons who attend upon them?

Now, I have the oral transmission from Chinese doctors to cure these diseases, and in every case it is efficacious. In recent years everyone has been affected by cold pneuma, and therefore mulberry is the marvelous curative method. However, people do not know this point, and many suffer harm or early death. In recent years, many diseases of the body come from cold pneuma. Mulberry, ox-knee, Gaoliang ginger, etc.—these are beneficial drugs.

The prescriptions for mulberry prescriptions are annotated below:

Item: Method for Mulberry Decoction

A Song doctor says, "Cut a three-inch piece of a branch of mulberry the width of a finger. Crush it into three or four small pieces. Take a handful of black beans. Place all the ingredients in three *sheng* of water and boil it (cook it). When the beans are cooked, remove the mulberry and add rice. Measure the amount of rice to match the amount of the water. Boil to produce a thin gruel. In the winter start cooking from the time of cockcrow, and in the summer start from midnight. By dawn the cooking will be done. Consume it with an empty mind. Do not add any salt. Every morning, do not neglect it but eat it; then that day do not drink water, and do not get drunk. Both your body and mind will be at peace. Branches newly sprouted from a mulberry tree are especially good. If the root is big, then do not use it. Mulberry congee will cure a multitude of illnesses."

Item: Mulberry Boiled Down

Take two *fen* of mulberry branches, measured and roasted. The tips of the wood need to be dried out so they can be cut. Lay out three-*sheng* and five-*sheng* measure bags. The longer you wait, the better it is. Near the time take one *sheng* of water and half the wood, mix it up, and put it in. Boil it down and then consume it. Even if it is not completely boiled down, you may consume it without any loss. Sprouting [mulberry] wood is also appropriate.

Shindo isho says, "Mulberry: [treats] water pneuma, lung pneuma, wind pneuma, tumors and swellings; the side body, wind tumors and dryness. The four limbs are constrained and connected. Such illnesses as rising pneuma, dizziness and dazzle, coughing and dry mouth, it cures all of them. Consume it constantly, it helps digestion, is a diuretic, slims the body, brightens ear, and eye, etc."

The *Scripture of the Transcendents* (*Xian jing*) says, "Of all the transcendent drugs, if you do not have mulberry boiled down, then do not consume them."

Just drink water, and one will not be struck by wind from eating. This is the most secret method.

Item: Method for Consuming Mulberry Wood

Saw off some chips and dust. Take a pinch of it, using five fingers. Put it in fine alcohol and drink it. It is able to heal the blood pneuma of women. Of the myriad illnesses of the abdomen in the mid-body, all of them are cured by it. If one consumes it constantly, one will attain long life and no sickness. It is a transcendent technique which one must trust.

Item: Method for Chewing Mulberry Wood

Cut a piece like a tooth-wood. Chew it constantly, and the mouth, tongue, and teeth will all be free of disease. The mouth will always be fragrant and demons will not dare to approach. It is good for curing mouth ulcers. Of what is known by worldlings of the medical arts of latter times, what is as good as this? Use the root, going down three *chi* into the earth; this is the best. Above the earth, it may tend to be poisonous and level with the earth is also toxic. So therefore use the branches.

Item: Method for Mulberry Wood Pillow

Construct it like a box, and one can use it as a pillow. It will brighten the eyes and there will be no head wind. One will not experience any bad dreams. Demons will not approach. Its virtues are indeed many.

Item: Method for Ingesting Mulberry Leaves

Pick them at the beginning of the fourth month; pick and dry them in the shade. Between the ninth and tenth months, two thirds of the leaves drop. One third is left behind on the branches. Pick them and again dry them in the shade. Divide and measure the summer leaves and the winter leaves. Make it like tea and ingest it. There will be no illnesses in the abdomen. Body and mind will be light and will benefit. This is a true transcendent's technique.

Item: Ingestion of Mulberries

When they ripen, pick them and dry them in the sun. They are as big as honey pill paulownia seeds. Every day, with an empty mind consume forty-nine of them with alcohol. Consume them every day and the body will be light and free of disease. But the power of Japanese mulberries is slighter.

Item: Method for Ingesting Gaoliang Ginger

This drug comes from Gaoliang province of the Song state. In China, Khitan, and Koryŏ, it is equally prized and esteemed. It is a marvelous drug of the latter age. It cures the myriad diseases of recent times. Slice a fine bit, the size of one cash [coin], drop it in alcohol, and ingest it. Those who abstain from alcohol may use a decoction, congee, or rice to ingest it. Also, one can boil it down and ingest it. Responses to questions of amount and whether early or late depend on time. If you take it every day, pains from your loose teeth, pain in the buttocks, pain in the shoulders, and the myriad diseases of the abdomen are all cured by it. If there is pain in the legs and knees, or pain in the bones, it cures them all. If one were to dispense with the hundred drugs and just ingest tea and Gaoliang ginger, one would have no disease.

Because of the damage of cold pneuma in recent years, in curing it has been tested with no errors.

Item: Method for Drinking Tea

Use two or three square-inch spoonfuls. Suit yourself as to the amount. Use really hot water for the decoction. Just for the decoction, a small amount is good. Again, follow your inclination.

The more concentrated is the most delicious—drink it after alcohol. Drinking tea will digest food. When you drink, you should only drink tea, or drink mulberry decoction. Do not drink hot water. If you don't drink decoctions of mulberry or tea, then all kinds of illness will arise.

Item: Method for Reduction of Five Aromatics

1. *Qingmuxiang* (one *liang*)
2. Sinking fragrance (*shenxiang*) (one *fen*)
3. *Dingzi* (two *fen*)
4. *Xunlu* fragrance (one fen)
5. Musk (*shexiang*), a smidgin (*shao*)

Take the above five ingredients separately and then combine them. For each dose take an amount one cash in size, immerse in hot water, and drink. It will cure the heart viscus, and the myriad illnesses arise in the heart. The nature of these five ingredients is bitter and acrid. Therefore it is marvelous.

Once when I, Eisai, was in China I was going from Mount Tiantai to Mingzhou. It was the tenth day of the sixth month. The weather was very hot, and I was exhausted. At that time, a shopkeeper said to me, "You, O dharma master, have come far and you are sweating a lot. I fear that you will fall ill." He took one *sheng* of *dingzi* and a *sheng* and a half of water. He boiled it for a long time, making roughly two cups full, and gave it to me to ingest. Afterward, my body was refreshed and my mind became happier. Thus I knew that in the time of great heat it has the ability to cool, and in the time of great cold it can warm. These five ingredients all share this attribute.

The above methods of nourishing life in the latter age, all obtain a response to stimulus and so I have recorded them. They are all from the state of Song.

End of second fascicle of *Kissa yōjōki*.

After composing this record, I heard statements such as "people who drink tea become emaciated and are prone to illnesses." Such people do not understand and are deluded. Surely they should understand that the nature of this drug is naturally useful. Moreover, in what country, and for what people does drinking tea make one sick? If they have no proof [of their claims], then their words are like drawing wind with an empty mouth, defaming tea in vain. They are not worth half a cash.

Also they say such things as, "Gaoliang ginger is a heating foodstuff." Who are these people who witter about "producing heat?" They do not understand the nature of the drug, they do not know the signs of illness, so they should not speak about it.

8

Religion and Culture in the Tea Economy of Late Imperial China

*I*n this chapter, I examine the role of religious institutions and literati connoisseurship in the booming tea economy of late imperial China, with a focus on the Ming dynasty. Religious figures and institutions, particularly Buddhist, but also Taoist, were involved in key developments during this time—many of the most famous and coveted teas of the Ming period were grown in and around Buddhist monasteries, and Buddhist monks played prominent roles in the innovation of new teawares, especially the famous purple Yixing ware.[1] In Ming times, tea and Buddhism in particular were linked both in reality and in the imagination, as may be seen by the presence of Buddhist figures and motifs throughout the range of literati cultural productions concerned with tea—poetry, prose, paintings, objets d'art, and so on. Ming painters such as Wen Zhengming (1470–1559), Shen Zhou (1427–1509), and Xu Zhenqing (1479–1511) often incorporated tea-related themes into their works. As well as paintings, all kinds of literary genres were connected with tea—songs, plays, lyric poetry—and high levels of aesthetic attention were brought to bear on tea artifacts such as baskets, stoves, braziers, kettles, cups, and bowls.

With the Ming dynasty came a major change in the way tea was consumed, as we move into the era in which steeped tea, made from tea leaves in teapots, increasingly became the norm.[2] The early Ming writer Ye Ziqi (1327–ca. 1390) noted, "The people have stopped using powdered tea from Jiangxi; leaf tea is everywhere."[3] He was reporting on a change that had probably occurred earlier under the Mongol Yuan dynasty. By 1487, the scholar and historian Qiu Jun (1421–1495) reported that powdered tea was enjoyed only in Fujian and Guangdong and that leaf tea was drunk elsewhere throughout China and by foreigners.[4] The first Ming emperor, Taizu (Zhu Yuanzheng, r. 1368–1398), banned cake tea as tribute on the grounds that its production was too labor intensive.[5] Instead, he ordered that four types of whole-leaf tea be sent to the court as tribute.[6] Probably Zhu's tastes in tea were not particularly refined, unlike those of the Song emperors. Of peasant stock, he was said to favor the popular leaf tea from Mount Guzhu.[7] But, in addition to the influence of changing imperial tastes, the quality of loose tea had also much improved.[8] Once free of the obligation to produce cake tea, tea producers in South China concentrated on growing and selling higher quality whole-leaf tea. Consumption of cake tea still continued, of course—Ming Taizu's son, Zhu Quan, Prince of Ning (1378–1448), described his own practice of making whipped tea in his *Treatise on Tea* (*Chapu*).[9]

The practices of tasting, selection, grading, and evaluation of various varieties of tea and water, known collectively as *pin* ("connoisseurship"), reached new heights in the Ming.[10] Connoisseurs were keen to demonstrate their expertise to a wider audience and wrote about tea and associated subjects at length and in detail. The sixteenth and seventeenth centuries in particular represent a period of intense production in tea literature—as can be seen by glancing at the contents of a standard compilation of tea literature (*chashu*).[11] Ming intellectuals were intensely involved in a tea connoisseurship that was highly refined, insisting on subtle distinctions between teas produced within a few hundred meters of each other and sharing an aesthetic that often also included an idealized vision of Buddhist monastic or eremitic life.

The Ming method of making tea was quite different from the procedures we have encountered before and much closer to something that would be familiar to us as making a pot of tea. First, one boiled water in a water pot made of metal or ceramic placed atop a charcoal-fueled brazier.[12] The tea leaves were rinsed in a colander with warm boiled water. The leaves were transferred, still warm, to a stoneware teapot that was then filled with hot boiled water. Once infused, the tea was poured into small teacups. The entire pot was drained of this first infusion and the leaves allowed to remain in the teapot. Additional amounts of water were poured onto the leaves for subsequent infusions—on each round increasing the time for infusion so that the tea still retained the appropriate strength. The tea leaves were left behind in the process and only the infusion was drunk, whereas in Tang and Song methods of making tea, powdered particles of the leaves were consumed along with the hot liquid in which they were suspended.[13] As we can see, this manner of preparation was considerably less complex and required less skill than methods employed in Song times. Thus, tea in Ming times was even more readily consumable on an ad hoc basis. Tea and snacks were now a necessity at roadside halts for travelers and pilgrims, and in the great metropolises of Nanjing, Suzhou, and Yangzhou many merchants made their fortunes from selling tea. Although making tea was in many ways a much simpler process, tea connoisseurs in Ming times remained insistent that, to be appreciated, it needed to be properly prepared using the appropriate vessels and best quality raw materials.[14]

Scented teas were popular from Song times onward, but really developed in the Ming. I noted in an earlier chapter the use of expensive Borneo camphor to perfume tea leaves during the Song. In Ming times, authors described how to make teas scented with flowers such as lotus, cassia, rose, and jasmine.[15] Although some purist tea connoisseurs objected to this adulteration of the pure flavor of tea, scented teas grew in popularity in Ming and Qing times, and some teas devised then, such as jasmine tea, still remain ubiquitous today.

FAMOUS TEAS OF THE MING

The dedication of Ming tea connoisseurs allows us to have some insight into tea production at the local level and to evaluate the involvement of religious communities in tea growing and processing. Ming sources listed the existence of more than fifty famous teas by the sixteenth century. Five types of tea, identified by their places of manufacture, were generally and consistently recognized as superior in Ming tea literature: Longjing, Songluo, Luojie, Huqiu, and Wuyi. [16] Later in the chapter, I will devote some attention to each of these teas in turn and note the Buddhist affiliations of at least three of them.

Longjing (Dragon Well) tea was produced in the Fenghuang mountain range of Hangzhou fu in Zhejiang (present-day Hang County in Zhejiang).[17] The site was originally called Longhong (Dragon Pool) and was also known as Longquan (Dragon Spring). The renowned scholar Tian Yiheng (*jinshi* 1526) explains the relationship between the finest springwater and the best tea: "Of all the springs in Wulin, only Longhong is worthy of selection; as for tea also, that of Mount Longhong is the best."[18] There were many springs on the mountain range, but they all derived from the source of the old Dragon Well. Dragon Well tea was green in color, its taste was described as "sweet and delicious," and its fragrance like that of soybean flower. The expert connoisseur Tu Long (*zi*, Zhangqing, 1543–1605), a major proponent of the incorporation of Buddhist practice into literati life, insists that the true Dragon Well tea came from a site no more than ten *mu* (under two acres) in size and that anything claiming to be Dragon Well tea but produced outside that area was inferior.[19] The official and historian Xue Yingqi (*jinshi* 1535) particularly praises the rare tender buds picked in the period called "Before the Rains" (*yuqian*)—that is, the fifth day to the twentieth day of the fourth lunar month.[20]

Because Dragon Well was surrounded by other tea-producing areas, there were many counterfeit products that all used the Dragon Well brand name, and connoisseurs complained that the true product was not easy to find. The method of processing tea involved wilting the leaves by pan-firing them.[21] Although there were "tea households" whose members were skilled at this task, some mountain monks were also adept at pan-firing the precious buds of Dragon Well tea.[22] Ming connoisseurs highly esteemed this rare product, and when some became frustrated by the fake Dragon Well teas flooding the market, they made personal visits to witness firsthand this tea being picked and processed. Some recorded their visits in verse.[23] Peng Sunyi (1616–1673), for example, composed a "Song about picking tea" (Caicha ge):

> New tea from Dragon Well is deemed precious,
> In the cup, the buds stand all around;
> Do not try it unless we encounter pure guests.
> It is hard work to carry it down from the spring to Tiger's Paw.[24]

Peng's verse gives us some sense of the atmosphere in which this tea was enjoyed by some fortunate members of the elite—drunk fresh off its mountain of origin. Those who were not there to sample the new tea themselves were invited to imagine the experience through poetry. The sampling of the freshest teas at the site of their production was a recurrent theme in Ming tea poetry.

Songluo tea was produced on Mount Songluo (the name means "Pine Lichen"), which stood thirteen li north of Xiuning County, in Huizhou fu, Southern Zhili (present-day Xiuning in Anhui).[25] A Buddhist monk was responsible for the origins of this particular tea. The Huizhou region produced no tea at all until the monk Dafang (dates unknown) from Huqiu monastery in Suzhou arrived on Mount Songluo and began pan-firing the tea leaves he had picked from neighboring mountains. The tea was named "Songluo" after the mountain where he resided, rather than any place where the tea plants actually grew.[26] The color of Songluo tea was compared to pear blossom and its fragrance to bean stamens; drinking it was said to be "like munching snowflakes." The finer the tea, the whiter the color, and it was said that even if the liquid were left in the cup overnight it would leave no stain of tea. As with Dragon Well tea, production was limited by the relatively small area available for tea growing in the region; fake Songluo tea abounded and the genuine article was hard to find.[27] The techniques of production used on Mount Songluo by the monk Dafang were passed on to other sites in which tea grew more plentifully, such as Mount Hua, so that a number of neighboring counties all produced tea under the Songluo name. From as far away as Fujian, requests were made to the monks of Mount Hua for the Songluo processing methods and thus was produced the so-called Wuyi Songluo tea.[28] This self-conscious adoption of the name of a famous tea offers a telling example of the power of the brand in the market for luxury comestibles in Ming times.

Luojie tea was produced in the lush mountain valleys of Yixing County in Changzhou fu, Southern Zhili (present-day Yixing in Jiangsu). It grew in a cleft (*jie*) between two mountains, where a hermit surnamed Luo had once lived— hence the name "Luo's cleft." According to contemporary accounts, Luojie tea was cultivated at eighty-eight different sites, but there were only five that connoisseurs adjudged to be the places where the genuine product was grown.[29] Those five places were ranked in order of the quality of their tea. Tea plants growing at the rear of the old temple dedicated to a local deity produced premium-grade tea; the rear of the new temple and the site called "Chessboard Summit" (Qipan ding) produced second-grade tea. The premium sites were no larger than two or three *mu* (less than a half-acre) in size and each year produced only twenty catties (*jin,* about eleven kilograms) of tea.[30] This tea was thus exceedingly rare and keenly sought.

Works by Ming writers provide us with detailed descriptions of Luojie tea. The color of the leaf was light yellow rather than green, whereas the veins of the leaf were pale white and thick. When placed in hot water, the leaf's color softened to that of "jade dew." The taste of the tea was described as sweet and aromatic, developing as it was sipped. The fragrance of the second-grade tea was less evident, and it was white in color. The taste was nearly as refreshing and pleasant as that of the leaves grown behind the old temple, but it was thinner in flavor. The tea leaf was unique because of its large, tough veins, and the taste could be quite strong and "herbal" or "grassy," so it was necessary to steam the leaves to make the tea palatable. If picked late, the leaves and stems tended to be small and old, and pan-firing them would be insufficient to soften them. In this respect, Luojie tea was different from other famous teas of the time that were processed by pan-firing the leaves to make them wilt.[31] Since Luojie tea grew on high rocky mountains, its pneuma was thought to be refined and "empty" because of its exposure to the wind and dew. The famous painter Shen Zhou, who was a keen tea drinker, ranked Luojie tea far above the host of other teas.[32]

Huqiu tea was produced at Mount Huqiu (Tiger Hill) in Zhangzhou County, Suzhou fu in Southern Zhili (present-day Wu County in Jiangsu). This picturesque site, just a couple of miles beyond the walls of Suzhou and a popular place for excursions from the city, was dominated by a Buddhist monastery and its pagoda, which were completed in 961.[33] As with other tea-producing sites that we have discussed, most of the tea from Tiger Hill was grown on bushes planted in and around the monastery. The thin sprouts were picked before "Grain Rains" (*guyu,* the nineteenth to the twenty-first of the fourth lunar

Tiger Hill (Huqiu) reproduced from *Tianxia mingshan shenggai ji* (Ming woodblock edition).

month) and then pan-fired. The color of the tea was described as "moonlight white" and its flavor like that of bean flowers.[34] It was extolled as a particularly mild beverage. Bu Wanqi (fl. 1621) recognized Huqiu tea as the "king among teas" on account of its color, flavor, and fragrance.[35]

Because both the aroma and taste were mild, it was not to everyone's taste, but Huqiu tea's reputation by no means suffered because of this.[36] People of every class flocked to Mount Huqiu, which was the site of three famous springs: the Sword Pond (Jian chi), Lu Yu's Stone Well (Lu Yu shijin), and Tiger Running Spring (Hupao quan). Tea plants grew on the rocks and level ground west of Huqiu monastery, but later, because demand exceeded supply, tea was planted all around the monks' quarters. Because Huqiu tea was hard to store for long periods it was thought especially precious; in just a short while it would entirely lose its initial subtle flavor.[37] As a rare tea it was consumed in small Yixing teapots, which, because they were more porous, better preserved the delicate taste, color, and fragrance of the tea.[38]

True Huqiu tea was hard to obtain, and inevitably some monks were tempted to adulterate the leaves with other teas to make a "substitute tea" (*tishen cha*) that only real experts could distinguish from the genuine variety.[39] Ming regional officials often presented Huqiu tea to their superiors, but eventually the monks found the tea business too intrusive on their lives and in time many simply weeded out the excess tea plants or let the plantation go uncultivated so that the site gradually declined.[40]

Wuyi tea was produced on Mount Wuyi, located thirty *li* south of Chongan County in Jianning fu, Fujian (present-day Chongan, Fujian). The tea picked at the time of Qingming ("Pure Brightness") in early spring when the first buds were showing was rated the best, whereas that picked at "Grain Rains" was considered slightly inferior. The second and third harvests in the spring were rated of lower-middle quality. The leaves of the "Autumn Dew" harvest were white and their fragrance reminiscent of orchids, but this crop was rated no higher than teas from other areas.[41]

Wuyi tea was graded by connoisseurs depending on the various sites where it was grown. "Cliff tea" (*yancha*) came from the mountain itself, whereas "riverbank tea" (*zhoucha*) was grown along the banks of the brook. Cliff tea was esteemed over riverbank tea. Both sites were further subdivided: the north bank of the brook was rated superior, the south bank next, and the riverbank plantation lowest.[42] Experts identified no fewer than ninety-nine varieties of cliff tea, and although they were all highly regarded, connoisseurs distinguished among them according to the varying amounts of sun, rain, wind, and dew each variety received. The springs of Mount Wuyi were considered sweeter and purer than those of other mountains, and the quality of this water was said to contribute to the properties of the tea.[43] Despite the many varieties of tea at the site, the overall annual production was quite limited, as contemporary authors often noted.[44]

In contrast to Huqiu tea, for example, Wuyi tea was quite strong—it took three steepings before it became insipid, as compared with two steepings for other teas. Feng Shike (*jinshi* 1571; ca. 1547–ca. 1617) claimed that it could be steeped as many as six or seven times.[45] During the Ming Dynasty, Wuyi tea was at the height of its powers, even to the extent that it was appraised above all other teas by writers on tea such as Xu Bo (1570–1645).[46]

In addition to these five highly rated teas there were a number of significant and famous varieties rated by connoisseurs in the upper-middle category. Again, many of them were associated with Buddhist sites and institutions.

Yangxian tea was produced on Mount Yangxian in Yixing County, Changzhou fu, in Southern Zhili (present-day Yixing in Jiangsu). This tea was particularly popular with literati. Unlike most Ming teas that were wilted slowly by being fired in a hot pan, Yangxian tea leaves were steamed and then dried over a low flame. Yangxian and Guzhu teas had been famous during the Song dynasty, but were superseded in popularity by Luojie tea in the Ming. In actuality, the areas of production for Yangxian, Guzhu, and Luojie teas were not always easy to disentangle, but Ming connoisseurs insisted on distinguishing and grading them—rating Luojie tea first, Guzhu second, and Yangxian third. Poets such as Wu Kuan (1435–1504), Wen Zhengming (1470–1559), and Wang Shizhen (1526–1590) singled out Yangxian tea in their verse.[47]

The other significant teas in Ming times were from the mountain sites of Guzhu, Qingyuan, Gushan, Tianchi, Tianmu, and Jingshan.[48] There was, however, some disagreement about where the boundaries for these tea-producing areas actually lay and whether they were in fact distinct varieties. Tianchi and Huqiu teas, for example were produced quite close to each other and often mistaken for each other.[49] The realities of tea production often contrasted rather sharply with the artificiality of highly refined connoisseurship.

AESTHETICS AND THE ART OF TEA

Members of the Ming elite often already regarded matters related to tea as a kind of specialized art and needed little further convincing of the value and status of tea. In their idealized visions of rustic simplicity, Ming authors and arbiters of taste such as Xie Zhaozhe (1567–1624) and Li Rihua (1565–1635) always included tea among the daily necessities described in their works.[50] Here, for example, Li stresses the simplicity of tea in attaining tranquility of mind in a refined and elegant setting:

> A simple room with a couch and a table, burning incense and a cup of tea, empty and uncluttered with other things. Just sitting alone in contemplation, naturally a pure and numinous energy comes to my body. The foul vapors of the world are thus gradually dissipated by this pure and numinous energy.[51]

In the writings of elite Ming tastemakers we can see how the preparation and consumption of tea were highlighted as necessary elements in evoking a solitary, reflective, wistful atmosphere. In a sense, then "tea" became an idea in itself, an idea that stood for religiously inflected visions of the contemplative life. Those visions had both Buddhist and Taoist elements to them. The playwright and essayist, Tu Long, writes,

> The breeze through the bamboo makes the tea stove flutter; the scattered mists of the fourth month, setting off the semi-curve [of the moon]. The remaining snow from the window [of my study] truly causes a person's mind and bones to be completely cold. My body and pneuma yearn for transcendence.[52]

We can see that, for these influential authors, making tea was one of the quintessential scholarly activities like reading, burning incense, playing the zither, looking at paintings, and arranging flowers. They continued to insist on tea's connection with the world beyond mundane affairs. Tea evoked the hermetic, reflective life and was the natural accompaniment for a refined longing for awakening or transcendence.

The dramatist Gao Lian (1573–1620) composed a piece titled "Enjoying paintings with tea brewed from swept-off snow" (*Saoxue pengcha wanhua*) that epitomizes some of the high cultural attitudes toward tea. It extols the joys of the simple recluse's life as the poet enjoys the "pure, clean" taste of tea made with melted snow.[53] The association of tea with highly refined but simple pleasures was typical of the aesthetic approach taken by Ming connoisseurs. Writers such as Dong Qichang (1555–1636), who, like many other authors I have mentioned, was heavily invested in Buddhist ideas, extolled the rewards of tea connoisseurship as the epitome of the scholar's lifestyle.[54] In works by writers such as these we can see the highly rarefied atmosphere of tea connoisseurship and precious attitudes toward teaware and springwater that proved so tempting a target for the kind of parody in *A Dream of Red Chambers* that we read in Chapter One.

To some Ming authors, tea was not just a substance to be consumed and enjoyed; it had a moral dimension too. Zhang Dafu (1554–1630) and Tu Benjun (d. 1622), for example, offered philosophical reflections on the nature of tea as something that was uniquely both "excessive" (*yin*)—because people could easily become addicted to it—and yet also "true" (*zhen*).[55]

In short, Ming tea connoisseurs preferred to enjoy their tea in quiet, secluded, elegantly simple surroundings where they met with two or three friends and sought to be free of the restraints of their official responsibilities. They passed their time in making tea to their heart's content using mountain springwater, gazing at books and paintings, reciting poetry, meditating, and so on. In general, Ming authors emphasized the more spiritual aspects of tea drinking over an interest in the materiality or medicinal properties of tea.

A large amount of tea literature was written in the Ming—nearly fifty works were in circulation by the start of the seventeenth century. As we have seen in earlier chapters, tea connoisseurship flourished throughout the Tang and Song dynasties, with literati at every social level from minor official to powerful statesman leading developments in production and methods of consumption, but by Ming times this trend had accelerated yet further. The culture that was centered around the civil service examinations predominated, especially from the mid-Ming onward, and many men became officials via this route. Whether serving in office, retired, or un-appointed to official positions, the social status of those men who took the examinations was high. Ming literati tended to display their distinction from ordinary people by participating in associations and societies (*she*) that engaged in group activities such as writing poems about material objects, tea connoisseurship, discussions about meditation, or spending time at sites of natural beauty. As we have seen, an interest in self-cultivation and the delights of refined seclusion often led to an engagement with tea connoisseurship. On the one hand, tea drinking was a necessary daily activity in which the consumption of bland or highly flavored tea assisted with the casting off of mundane cares and worries; on the other hand, the slow and careful sampling of tea was thought conducive to developing one's insight and self-cultivation.

Xu Zhenqing's (1479–1511) poem, "Sampling tea on an autumn night" (*Qiuye shicha*), speaks of a

> Quiet courtyard, cool and fresh, with candles and flowers
> The wind sighs in the bamboo; while the moonlight effloresces.
> I idly come without companions, tending to the cloudy juice.
> Among the copper leaves, the purple shoots of tea.[56]

Tu Long writes,

> Tea, burning incense pure
> A visitor arriving at my door and I am delighted.
> A bird chirps and a blossom falls.
> There is no one and I am also carefree.[57]

In poems such as these the presence of tea epitomizes the joys of the literati lifestyle, in which tea was an essential accompaniment to both solitary reflection and intellectual companionship with selected friends.

As for interactions among literati, tea was often the medium of friendship and preferred for that purpose over alcohol.[58] As the famous and influential Yuan Hongdao (1568–1610) admits in his description of his manner of sampling famous teas in social settings, "I don't drink alcohol, but I have a craving for tea."[59] In Ming etiquette, hosts could often use an invitation to drink tea as a way of breaking the silence or dissolving conflict between guests and restoring emotional equilibrium.

In Suzhou in particular, literary culture flourished during the Ming: among the gentry the arbiter of style was Wu Kuan (1435–1504), known as "Old Man of the Gourd" (Pao weng), whereas Shen Zhou the painter was known among the populace at large. These two figures were not only intimately acquainted but they also shared the same craving for tea. Later, although Wu Kuan was appointed Minister of Rites in Beijing he was able to maintain his enthusiasm for tea drinking; in his leisure time he summoned friends to sample tea and compose verse in the rear garden of his official residence. His literary collection contains a "Love song to tea" (*Aicha ge*), which extols his companions' devotion to the beverage. At the same time, his own feelings about drinking tea stood out in sharp relief. The verse says:

> This Old Man of Decoctions loves tea as he loves alcohol,
> Thinking nothing of three *sheng* or even five *dou*
> When "Before Spring Hall" is opened, there are no surplus items,
> Just a tea stove and a tea ladle.
> In the hall, tea is brewed with nothing extra,
> To the end of the day, teacups are never far from our mouths:
> The only servants at this banquet are the tea boys;
> The only people who come in the gate are companions in tea.
> In thanks for tea there are poems and we study Lu Tong;
> Brewing tea, there are *fu*, drafted like those of Huang Number Nine.[60]
> The *Classic of Tea*'s continued chapters we don't lend to people,
> The *Tea Manual* supplements slip from our hands.
> Tea planted on ordinary days, we don't have anything to do with,
> We know the acreage of tea plantations below the mountains.
> People of the world may roam the countryside in search of tea,
> But here we have no problems.[61]

Wu Kuan's poem shows his self-conscious enjoyment in a kind of nostalgic tea connoisseurship that celebrated the verse of Lu Tong and Huang Tingjian, while reveling in the total absorption in the minutiae of expertise in the topic of tea. He himself was just such a wealthy hands-on enthusiast. He owned a tea garden, processed his own tea leaves, brewed tea, and composed tea literature that he exchanged with his fellow tea aficionados. Shen Zhou, in contrast, was poor but honest his whole life. He was quite self-sufficient and never needed to enter the city in search of diversion. His work, *A Separate Essay on Writing about Jie Tea* (*Shu Jiecha bielun*), offers a charming contrast to the "Love song to tea." Although the original book is no longer extant, we know from quotations that Shen Zhou celebrated in it a more popular and less elite attitude toward tea than did Wu Kuan.

Other celebrated tea connoisseurs of the late Ming included Zhang Dai (1597–1689), his friend the potter Min Wenshui, Zhu Rukui, Xu Maowu, and Feng Mengzhen (1546–1605).[62] Literati liked to use the character for tea in their pen names to record their personal hobby; Du Jun, for example, styled himself "Tea Village," whereas Ding Jingshen used the name "Old man who plays at tea." Even if they did not always use the character in their personal names they employed it to name gardens, residences, and so on.

Authors of tea literature sought to display their complete knowledge of all aspects of tea culture—including water, tea utensils, preparation of the brazier, and famous personalities associated with tea. Take, for example, the author of the *Commentary on Tea* (*Cha shu*), Xu Cishu (*zi* Ranming, 1549–1604), who gives a list of appropriate occasions for drinking tea:

When mind or hands are idle
When weary of declaiming verse
When one's state of mind is confused
When listening to songs and melodies
When songs and melodies end
When closing one's gate and avoiding responsibilities
When playing the zither or looking at paintings
When chatting together deep into the night
At a clear desk by a bright window
In the bridal chamber, or pavilion
When entertaining honored guests
Hosting visitors and concubines
Visiting friends who have just returned
When the weather is warm and fine
In light cloud and drizzle
On small bridges or gaily painted pleasure boats
In thick forests of trees and tall bamboo
When flowers blossom and birds sing
On hot days at lotus pavilions
Burning incense in the lesser courtyard
As drunken guests disperse
When the children have left the building
At pure and secluded temples
At famous springs and scenic rocks.[63]

Tu Long was renowned as a skilled connoisseur who was adept at distinguishing the color, fragrance, and taste of different teas from different locales. He claimed expertise in their picking, roasting, and storing and even the taste of the water used for preparing tea. Tu Long, Xu Cishu, and Feng Kaizhi were equally famous throughout South China and had all become *jinshi* in the *dingchou* year of the Wanli reign period (1577). When they were later all dismissed from office and forced to stay away from court, they traveled around the Wu-Yue region sampling tea together and engaging solely with cultural activities.

The author of *A Record of Tea Houses* (*Chaliao ji*), Lu Shusheng (1509–1605), was probably foremost among Ming tea authors in terms of his social status and longevity—he lived to the age of ninety-seven. Although he held high imperial office as the Minister for Rites, he still had the uninhibited spirit of a retired scholar. In his *Record of Loose Firewood from Nine Mountains* (*Jiushan sanqiao zhuan*) there is a passage that nicely exemplifies the confluence of an imagined Buddhist eremitic lifestyle with tea connoisseurship:

> I enter Buddhist monasteries; loitering there I forget to leave. Facing old men in the mountains, rustic elders, hermits and masters of meditation, I sit casually among the thorns, chatting of things beyond this world. We talk of cultivation in the four seasons, stories of gathering firewood and eating food. By nature I am addicted to tea, and I have written of "the seven categories of boiling tea." Here, I have carried my tea stove, gathered fallen firewood, and drawn water to brew tea. In company with my literary friends, we write poems to amuse ourselves.[64]

In the writings of Ming tea connoisseurs we can see a consistent urge to associate tea with the scholarly arts and also with Buddhist patterns of reclusion and contemplation. Again and again, elite Ming authors deliberately placed the appreciation of tea within Buddhist contexts, whether real or imagined. As we have seen from previous chapters, there was indeed a connection between tea and Buddhist institutions, but literati presented a selective image—they were not writing about the kind of formal tea ceremony described in the "pure rules" of Chan monasteries.

TEA AND THE SAṂGHA

The potential sources of revenue for the monastic economy were many, and there were sideline occupations available to monks who found donations from the laity too scarce, but the opportunities to profit from tea cultivation were particularly good and the risks involved were low. As we saw with some of the famous varieties discussed earlier, tea could be grown on otherwise unproductive land around the monastic buildings, and potentially even quite small areas under relatively minimal cultivation could produce rare and expensive teas. But growing tea also required that the monastery become involved in a system of production, and so there were monks whose designated task was to plant tea, pick tea, or process tea. Because of their daily exposure to the practicalities of producing tea for the market and their constant tasting of the product, some of these monks acquired advanced skills in the arts of tea and were recognized as experts by literati.

Many famous Ming-era teas had connections to tea-processing facilities that were attached to monasteries or run by monks. As we noted, Songluo tea was invented by the monk Dafang from Mount Huqiu in Suzhou, who went on retreat to Mount Songluo in Anhui. There, he applied the manufacturing methods that he knew from Huqiu to tea that he picked from elsewhere and thus created a renowned tea. Similarly, the famous Tianchi tea was picked and processed by monks from Tianchi monastery.

Lu Shusheng explained, "Making tea is not unrestrained; it is necessary for the quality of the person to match that of the tea. Thus, the methods are often transmitted among lofty recluses, those who have breadth of mind amidst the mist and clouds of the springs and rocks."[65] Lu's statement shows that he, like many Ming intellectuals, understood the art of tea to be a significant cultural activity that operated in an elevated realm beyond the mundane world. Also, the designation of "companions of tea" (chalu) included, according to Lu, "literati, officials, Buddhist monks, Taoist priests, old hermits, and eminent persons."[66] Although, as we have seen throughout this book, the participation of Buddhist monks and Taoist priests was a constant feature of premodern tea culture, this factor was even more noticeable in the so-called revival of Buddhism during the Ming. Many of the elite tastemakers of gentry society deliberately sought out teas produced by Buddhist monasteries. Buddhist monks grew tea, processed it, and sold it, and there were many famous springs and sources of fine water that were located on monastic land. Attempts by literati to become involved in tea connoisseurship led them inevitably to Buddhist sites, to contact with Buddhist monks, and often to a deeper interest in Buddhist ideas.

In addition to their more commercial activities around tea, monks also tended to be very hospitable to visiting literati. Wang Shizhen describes his visit to Mount Huqiu thus:

> In Jinling, there are many ancient monasteries; but this region also has many scenic landscapes, so it is often sullied by music and alcohol, which I loathe. Whenever I pass by Wuguan monastery, monks there set out only tea, supplementing wheat cakes with excellent vegetables. I am joyfully full.[67]

Although monasteries could be imagined as quiet unspoiled places, in reality, because of the number of travelers who came there, some were often bustling noisy sites full of revelers. Wang tells us how a pause for monastic tea and cake offers a welcome respite from the crowds. "Monks' huts" and "Taoist chapels" featured frequently on lists composed by literati as suitable sites for enjoying tea. Ming writers often equated the elegant and refined life with the lifestyle and customs of monks. The famous painter Shen Zhou, whom I have already quoted, offers an example of this praise for the monastic as tea master:

> Daji, a monk of Wu, lived in an old place that occupied three or four bays, so clean that no one was allowed to spit [on the ground]. He excelled at brewing tea. He had an ancient well famed for its purity and coolness. When a guest arrived, he would bring out a teacup and offer a drink: its brightness would cleanse the intestines and purify the stomach. My late father, who was close friends with him, was also addicted to tea, and always went to his place whenever he entered the city [Suzhou].[68]

The city of Suzhou was wealthy and prosperous at the time, with many talented writers, famous mountains, and temples. Shen Zhou would have had no shortage of other potential distractions, but he was addicted to tea and the arts of tea (his grandfather was also a famous connoisseur of tea), so we should take his praise of this particular monk's skills seriously.

To give another example of exchanges between monastics and secular connoisseurs, when the Zhongnan monk Mingliang arrived from Mount Tianchi he entertained Lu Shusheng with Tianchi tea and at the same time passed on the approved method of brewing it:

> First, control the level of heat, next make the water hot; this stage is known as "crab eyes" or "fish eyes." When the boiling foam sinks and rises, take this as the sign that it is ready to brew [tea]. These methods [of making tea] are all the same, but what this monk boiled and pointed was the epitome of flavor. It was pure and the milky surface was undisturbed. This was a case of "entering the *samādhi* of pure flavor."[69]

Mingliang is typical of the kind of monastic tea connoisseur who can be found throughout Ming occasional literature. Here we see an echo of the kind of language used in the Song to talk about the "*samādhi* of pointing tea." The monk excels at a seemingly routine task— making tea—but takes it to a sublime level that can only be described in terms of an advanced meditational state. To give another example of a Buddhist tea master, the "Three Teas ācārya" (*sancha heshang*) was an eccentric monk of unknown origin who was famed for his love of tea. He had no permanent home, but wandered round the slopes of Qian shan.[70] Taoists also numbered serious tea aficionados among their ranks, such as Man of the Way Xu who is described thus:

> He resided at Tianchi monastery on Mount Lu, and did not eat for nine years. He raised a black-feathered crane, and was accustomed to picking new tea in the mountains. He made the crane pick pine branches on which to brew it, and when he encountered fellow Taoists he would drink several cups with them.[71]

As we have already noted, Tianchi was a Buddhist monastery and the producer of the famous Tianchi tea. Another renowned Taoist tea master was Man of the Way Yunquan ("Cloud Spring"), who was said to have realized the "fundamental principle" of tea from his worldly sampling of different varieties. He believed that tea could be distinguished as being either "fat" (*fei*) or "lean" (*shou*). This was a concept that was not elucidated in any of the classic literature of tea.[72] Thus we can see that literati wove the contributions of religious figures into the development of new theories in tea connoisseurship.

Monasteries occupied sites where tea was grown and where pure sources of water could be found. Although there was plenty of fine tea to be found in the many monasteries of Jiangnan, the tea still needed to be matched with famous water—all the authorities agreed that only the finest waters could bring out the true taste of the tea. Among water connoisseurs the source of the water was the most significant factor, and of those sources, in Ming times the mountain spring was considered supreme. In addition, the features of the springs were thought to match those of the mountains on which they flowed.[73] Buddhist monasteries were often located on mountains that had superior geomantic characteristics, and as we have seen, tea connoisseurs who patronized their tea did not shrink from traveling long distances to obtain the desired product. Yuan Hongdao wrote a piece called "Record of Travel to Dragon Spring" (*You longjing ji*), recorded in 1597 in Hangzhou, which offers an example of the way in which his contemporaries thought about important water sources in their Buddhist contexts:[74]

> The waters of Dragon Well Spring run sweet and clear, and its rocks are elegant and shiny. The water gurgles its way up from between the rocks, making an adorable sound that can be heard for some distance. Entering the monks' cells, we found them to be high and dry, suitable for dwelling in. On one occasion, Tao Wangling, Huang Guoxin, Fang Wenzun and I drew up some springwater and brewed tea there.

Wangling raised the question of which was the better of Dragon Well tea and Heaven's Pond [Tianchi] tea. My answer was that although Dragon Well tea is excellent, too few leaves will produce a weak brew, while too many will turn out bitter. Heaven's Pond tea, however, is not like this. Generally speaking, although early season Dragon Well tea is fragrant, it still retains the flavor of leaves. Heaven's Pond has the flavor of bean, and Tiger Hill has the flavor of flowers. Only Luojie has no hint of flower or plant. It seems to taste almost metallic, and yet sometimes it will have no trace of anything at all; thus it is highly valued. Luojie leaves are quite coarse, and a catty of the real stuff can fetch more than 2,000 cash. It took me several years of searching before I finally got my hands on a few ounces! Recently a friend of mine from Huizhou sent me some Songluo Mountain tea, the flavor of which is superior to that of Dragon Well but inferior to that of Heaven's Pond. Surrounding Dragon Well are Windy Bamboo Ridge, Lion Peak, Single Cloud Rock and the Stone Sent by the Gods, each of which is worth a visit. There is a "Record of Dragon Well" written many years ago by Qin Guan. His writing is straightforward and strong, free from any pedantic style.[75]

This piece is a nice example of the way in which literati companions made on-site investigations and appraisals of tea, as well as the element of ranking (which tea is better?) that was always inherent in the practice of connoisseurship (*pin*). The descriptions of the qualities of these teas match those found in other tea literature that we already noted. Tea itself is the main topic of discussion here: monks, as is often the case, provide only part of the picturesque background to the serious business of evaluating water and tea.

But if monks sometimes played no more than a supporting role in literati tea culture, there was still a strong interest in the reputation of tea within the daily practice of Buddhist monks. The beverage was thought to be an essential component in the quiet contemplative life and in obtaining self-realization— as in these lines by Zhu Pu (1339–1381):

Washing the bowl, cultivating a vegetarian diet, brewing buds of tea.
In the mind of the way float silent dust and sand.
At leisure he does obeisance to the Buddha and makes no other
    offerings,
He draws water in a porcelain vase and soaks the wildflowers.[76]

Zhu's verse offers a typical model of a highly idealized literati view of a renunciant's practice—far from the concerns of the world, focused on making

一片雲

龍井寺

上天竺

Dragon Well monastery (upper left) reproduced from *Sancai tuhui* (Ming edition).

tea and flower arrangements with perhaps a bit of worship thrown in. Such visions of alternative ways of life were especially attractive because they stood at the opposite end of the spectrum from the pressing concerns and anxieties experienced by most Ming literati—especially those who held office and were subject to the vicious political factionalism that characterized the age. But even poems by Buddhist monks played romantic variations on the theme of the solitary renunciant brewing tea while composing poetry in natural surroundings. In his poem "On the Scriptorium" (*Ti shujing shi*), the monk Dexiang (dates unknown) writes,

> By the banks of the pond, lily magnolia blossoms newly disgorged,
> Outside the windows, plantain leaves are not yet complete.
> My true desire is to write several *gāthās*,
> The aroma of brewing tea passes west of the bamboo forest.[77]

It is hard to distinguish this poem written by a monk from those verses written by literati who imagined themselves monks. The style and content of such poems were predetermined, and tea was one of the poetic props that needed

to be included to evoke a contemplative setting. At the same time, poetry often represented the interface at which literati met with the monastic "other"
and bonded over the drinking of tea, as in this poem by Peng Sunyi:

> An old monk travels the far reaches of the world on foot,
> In his hand a scroll, he gazes out seated in the falling blossom.
> Together we speak of misty mountains 'til past noon,
> On a bamboo stove he boils tea picked "before the rains."[78]

Again, the setting and emotional content are quite conventional, the high
quality of the early picked tea offering the only clue to the old monk's sophistication and his worthiness as a poet's conversation partner. The influential critic
and connoisseur Dong Qichang, in his "Sent to the monk who brews tea" (*Zeng
jiancha seng*), depicts an even more abstract scene:

> Strange rocks and withered trees,
> Intertwine to pass their splendor down the years.
> Although stored "phoenix rounds" are good,
> He only drinks Zhaozhou tea.[79]

In Dong's verse, the monk is almost invisible, his presence only signaled
by the tea he drinks. No matter whether it was monks who wrote poetry themselves or monks' activities as described by literati, we have a strong impression
of tea as an essential attribute of the solitary awakened person. The enduring
image of the religious practitioner found in such verses was that of the monk
who dwelled beyond the world, focusing only on chanting scripture but consuming the finest teas. Tea-drinking monks in this mold were featured in verses
by authors such as Mo Shilong (1537–1587) and Hu Kui (ca. 1331–ca. 1405). In
addition to the fact that monks were thought to have ample leisure time and
that their monasteries were often involved with growing tea, their daily vegetarian diet was credited with the ability to enhance the sense of smell and
to provide them with the ability to distinguish accurately the place and type
of tea.[80]

As we have seen throughout this study, an interest in tea usually went hand
in hand with a discriminating approach to varieties of water, or to put it another way, famous teas required famous springs. From Lu Yu's chapter on water in the Tang, through specialized works on water produced in the Song and
Ming, famous tea authors wrote about springs and the utensils needed to carry
water (jars, bottles, flasks, etc.). It was unsurprising that places with famous
springs such as Huishan at Wuxi in Suzhou, or Mount Huqiu, became centers

where literati established societies such as "decoction societies" (*tangshi*), "tea societies" (*chashi*), and "reading societies" (*dushu shi*).

Connoisseurs could not discuss tea without also discoursing on water, and Ming records make plentiful references to famous springs and those who drew their water from them. On Mount Hui, for example, was located the "number two spring under heaven." When a friend of Xu Xianzhong (1493–1569) arrived after a long journey he brought as a gift a jar of water from Mount Hui. When Xu saw the water he immediately stoked up the fire to make tea in order to sample it, and he commemorated the occasion in writing his "Rhapsody on boiling Hui spring water" (*Jian Huiquan fu*). Such was the reputation of the miraculous power of the Hui spring that those who went to Mount Hui would invite their friends to come and taste tea made from the water, praising the rarity of both. Yuan Hongdao has a piece called "Recording the Hui spring," (*Ji Huiquan*) that describes how his friend Qiu Zhangru drew thirty jars of Hui springwater and ordered his servants to carry them home. The servants resented the weight, dumped the jars out into the river, replaced their contents with some water from a closer mountain spring, and fetched it home. All of Qiu's friends had gathered to sample this famous water, and they all praised it. When Qiu later discovered the true source of the water, he was truly angry. Yuan was later a magistrate in Wu County where he tasted many waters and was able to distinguish their qualities.

Although there were many who went to Mount Hui to draw water, other places like Hupao spring were also very famous. Gao Lian (1573–1620) claims,

> For springs west of the Hu, Hupao is superior and as for tea of the twin mountains, Dragon Well is best. Tea picked before "Grain Rain" at the time it is dried is lively, and when boiled with Hupao spring water its fragrance is pure and its taste is clear. To purify the poetic temper, every spring, I climb the high mountains, and I am happily absorbed in new tea for a month.[81]

Gao's brief statement epitomizes the confluence between tea, springwater, and poetry and indicates how much time the leading connoisseurs were willing to invest in their pastime.

The Ming literati elite excelled at arranging life so as to allow time and space to search for an appropriately elegant and refined way of being that emphasized the virtue of quiet (*jing*). Retired scholars enjoyed high status and had opportunities to travel through mountains and forests, enjoying the flowers and tramping over hill and dale in their search for a happiness that existed beyond their official careers. In their minds, Buddhist monasteries retained an association with seclusion and were often situated in elegant and inspiring surroundings. In addition, educated monks had the ability to understand and appreciate verse. Therefore, it was not unusual for Ming literati to befriend monks. The monks found common ground with the literati ethos and their shared cultural background, while the literati enjoyed the otherworldliness of the saṃgha and the search for awakening. The Ming Lixue scholar Xu Xiake (1587–1641) enjoyed traveling and went everywhere—to famous mountains and great rivers. In his voluminous travel records he depicted much of monks' lives.[82] He noted "brewing tea and chatting about verse" as two activities that he particularly enjoyed sharing with his religious companions.

Some members of the saṃgha were eager participants in the culture of tea connoisseurship—ranking different teas and springs alongside their literati companions. When monks came to give lectures, they might take the time to explain the arts of tea, and literati in their spare time enjoyed visiting monasteries in search of that same path. Hu Kui in his "Visiting a monk and not finding him" (*Fang seng buyu*) writes,

> In the third month the green paulownia tree is already blossoming,
> I have come wanting to taste Zhaozhou tea;
> The boy who answers the door is three feet tall,
> He tells me that the Ācārya is not at home.[83]

Even greater significance is brought to this encounter because it does not happen. Hu is frustrated by the missed opportunity to share fine tea with an eminent monk—but which does he miss more: the tea or the monk? Like their Song forebears, senior Ming monks understood the importance of etiquette toward their literati guests and tried to ensure that they had ample opportunities for enlightening discourse. Therefore, tea was served to enhance social gatherings of monks and scholars. The early Ming poet Tang Wenfeng gives a sense of how literati perceived such occasions for interaction in his "Visiting the sage Ji in the company of my companion Hu" (*Xie Hu bandu fang Ji shangren*):

> Visiting eminent monks, washing away worldly concerns,
> The fragrance of chrysanthemum in the late autumn skies.
> Lord Du's verses praise Zhi Dun,
> Master Han's words and texts show admiration for Dadian.[84]
> When you love alcohol you are permitted to expound Pengze's
>   precepts,
> Sipping tea one responds by awakening to Zhaozhou's chan.[85]
> When our reading of the *Lotus* is complete our minds are like water
> The abbot's incense floats, a cloud of smoke.[86]

We see how this verse evokes an entire history of intellectual and spiritual exchange between monks and scholars. The poem mentions the Tang poet Du Fu and the early translator Zhi Dun, as well as Han Yu's famous conversations with the Chan monk Dadian. Jiaoran's verse on drinking tea with Lu Yu and Zhaozhou's famous line "Go drink tea," along with an allusion to the poet Tao Qian's (Pengze) love of alcohol, are also woven into the fabric of the refined interplay between literati and abbot. Ming literati such as Tang were conscious that they were the inheritors of a long history of taking tea and discussing the dharma with their Buddhist counterparts. Their poems acknowledge this history, while still insisting on the significance of these meetings in their own lives.

Some members of the saṃgha were skilled not only in explaining the scriptures and in matters of tea but they also understood poetry and painting. An episode recorded by the well-known Neo-Confuciuan scholar Gao Panlong (1562–1626) offers a glimpse of the kind of aesthetic experience that might be enjoyed by both monks and their elite visitors:

> I rise early and arrive at Dragon Well spring. The spring tastes clear and cold. In the middle there is a basket of fish fully a foot in length; they appear and disappear through holes in the side. A monk of the monastery tells me that monastery has ten scenic views and leads me to each one that I may know them. . . . The monk leads me back to the retreat through curves hidden in the dark, paintings filling the walls. An open window on the mountain side, ingenious rocks curl around, with spring water he cooks up Dragon Well tea and we drink it.[87]

Gao's vignette offers a nice example of the shared culture of monks and literati and of the fantasy of the monk as the ultimate retired scholar in his mountain studio, gazing at unusual rocks. Those monks who had literary refinement were generally depicted as hastening to fetch old paintings or model calligraphy from the monastic storehouses. They would invite famous personages into their chambers, or they would bring out tea and burn incense together for mutual enjoyment. Religious discussions did not require that they neglect more mundane pleasures such as fine tea and rare artworks.

Many literati, whether in office or retirement, sought opportunities to cultivate tranquility; hence, the bamboo and wooden kiosks they had erected in their gardens and residences. Mountains and forests were secluded, but there were famous teas, renowned springs, and mountain temples in which to practice, and naturally they came to know monks there. Hu Kui and Zhu Pu wrote of their experiences spending occasional spring nights in the mountains cultivating tranquility, remaining overnight in monasteries, and drinking tea with the monks.[88]

Literati also set up thatched huts in mountain locations, echoing the practice of Lu Yu many centuries earlier; although these huts were not located within monasteries, they provided sites for meetings with monks where tea might be sampled and appreciated. The famous painter Wang Wen (1497–1576) has a poem titled "In a mountain hut I brew tea for my guests on discarded pine kernels" (*Shantang duike shi songzi jianming*) that describes this kind of meeting.[89] We may imagine that this was a common sentiment for those in search of tranquility in the mountains.

Famous mountains were sites for famous teas, so people thronged the roads while traveling to monasteries there. Tea connoisseurs sought out tea from mountain monks whose acquaintance they had long cultivated, or failing that, they paid money for the tea. As for ordinary people who drank tea, every Qingming or around the time of "Grain Rain" they would band together to go up the mountains to pick tea that they could dry themselves. Fan Yunlin (1558–1641) in his poem "Picking tea and staying overnight in a monk's cell" (*Caicha jisu sengshe*) describes the scene:

> In the drizzle I pause on the path through the pines,
> Peaceful, the wind comes from afar.
> I stay in the forest to obtain something rare,
> Hearing speech, I know that I am wandering in his footsteps.
> The wheat is flourishing like silver waves
> Fragrant smoke of tea is slender and red;
> Complete and deep, purifying conditions,
> Holding this bowl, my mind is empty.[90]

When monks came off the mountains they made gifts of tea that allowed them to make connections and networks with potential patrons among the elite. Li Rihua once wrote, for example, of an extremely rare white tea that he obtained from a monk:

> An old monk from Putuo once made a gift to me of a pouch of Lesser White Cliff tea. The leaves had white fur. When steeped they had no color. When I had drunk them up slowly this led me to feel quite discouraged. The monk said, "From that cliff, in a year come no more than five or six catties, they are the special supply of the eminent monks. Only a few people get to taste [this tea.]"[91]

In a poem on a similar theme, "A mountain monk favored me with tea" (*Shanseng hui cha*), the poet describes a gift of fine, early picked tea and the feelings it evokes in him. Again, we see a concern with the present reality of this particular tea and a remembrance of the experience of famous tea drinkers of the past—"this is like what Lu Tong drank" and what Lu Yu himself had praised:

A monk came from Tianmu monastery,
And gave me some "Before the Rains" tea.
The buds were like golden sprouts,
The spring was like white snow flowers.
I thought of Sima Xiangru's drinking,
This is what Hongjian [Lu Yu] praised.[92]
It was like what Lu Tong drank,
When he spoke of the seven cups.[93]

As we can see from these verses and prose accounts, the tea presented by mountain monks to literati was often very rare, very highly prized, and famous, so it was much appreciated by elite tea connoisseurs. The exchange no doubt benefited monastic communities too, because it transformed tea that grew relatively freely on their land into literati patronage that might otherwise have been hard to obtain.

Literati tea companions celebrated the joy of excursions to mountains and famous springs. They particularly favored mountain temples that produced famous teas, where the monks were skilled at the arts of tea. In the Jiangnan region, sites that we have mentioned frequently such as Mount Huqiu, Mount Hui, and Mount Longhong were all known for their famous landscapes and monasteries—but because they were also close to the city and one could visit just for a day trip they tended to attract a lot of visitors. The traces of the past on these mountains were often the object of poets' compositions, and as they wrote their verses, they also had to draw water and sample tea. Yuan Hongdao describes such a scene:

The monk is old and I know the monastery is also poor,
Hungry birds share his allotment of rice from the "fragrant
    gathering."[94]
Falling blossom always enough for this Man of the Way's salary.
From the characters on the stele, I know the verses about opening the
    mountain.
On the earthenware stand, the ashes are cold for the god who protects
    the dharma.
He draws three or four bowls of pure spring water.
Buds of tea, he boils and obtains a sample of the new season.

Yuan presents an exquisitely romanticized image of a poor old monk who yet enjoys access to fine teas in his decrepit surroundings. The poet is not just an impartial observer of this scene: he shows an interest in the history of the monastery—"the verses about opening the mountain"—and the current state of religious practice there—cold ashes at the altar of the protective deity of the site. It is interesting to reflect that some Ming writers definitely preferred their Buddhist sites to be in picturesque ruins than in bright, well-funded, and bustling good order.

Concerns about nourishing life and seeking health that we noted in earlier chapters remained current into Ming times. It was thought that if tea were drunk regularly but not to excess, it could clear the heart and lung system and dispel anxiety and melancholy. Zhang Qiande (1577–1643) described the medicinal efficacy of tea in terms that are familiar to us from earlier works:

> If a person drinks true tea, it can quench thirst, assist digestion and expel mucus. It reduces sleep, is diuretic, improves eyesight, benefits mental activity, prevents anxiety and removes fat.

Tea was recommended in all cases except severe illness. For minor ailments where the body required nourishment, patients were advised to drink a little liquid tea before taking any prescribed medicine. Li Shichen in his famous *Bencao gangmu* records that tea is able to treat scabies, is a diuretic, gets rid of phlegm, helps digestion, cools hot pneuma, disperses malignant pneuma, cures stroke and confusion, and cures heatstroke; when combined with vinegar it can cure diarrhea and is very efficacious.[95] There were widespread claims about tea and springwater as a panacea; for example, Mei Zhixian writes,

> In the past, immortals chiseled open this rock,
> The fountainhead then came flowing out.
> I once heard this old legend that,
> To cure illness one only need drink half a cup.[96]

Tang Shunzhi's "In sickness, I sample some new tea" (*Bingzhong shi xincha*) tells us something about the continued medicinal benefits of tea:

> For a long time I am unable to see into the orchard,
> It must have been full of fallen blossoms.
> For health there is only *materia medica*,
> For longevity there is also new tea.
> From marriage, the body has many debts,

From Poetry and Classics, the eyes have blockages.
Illness comes and all is forgotten,
Just like an old monk.[97]

Obviously, Ming intellectuals were aware that some mountain dwellers subsisted on tea and used tea when sick. Monasteries that had famous teas and famous springs to drink might tout their benefits for nourishing life, as well as their taste and rarity. Literati visiting monasteries had access to these dietetic regimes, and monasteries were seen as places of recuperation.

CONCLUSION

Tea retained strong religious affiliations in Ming times, whether in actuality or in the imagination of elite consumers. Buddhist institutions and individuals across South China were deeply invested in producing some of the most highly praised teas of the day. Ming intellectuals, especially those involved in lay Buddhist activities, stressed the spiritual aspects of the beverage and made tea connoisseurship into another aspect of refined lay Buddhist practice. They invested tea with all kinds of religious significance, but more than that they made tea an idea of its own and a repository for all their fantasies of the contemplative life.

Interactions between literati and monks naturally involved tea—whether in sampling tea, discussing the arts of tea, or using tea as a dietary supplement. The advantage in the relationship often belonged to the literati, who visited mountains to seek out monks, drew from famous springs, and paid for famous teas. We can see this in the sources that tend to privilege the literati perspective—we do not find such a wealth of detail on the Buddhist institutional side. As we can see though, by Ming times, tea was thoroughly incorporated into the texture of literati and monastic relations.

9

Conclusions

*I*n this book, we have considered tea as a religious and cultural commodity in traditional China from earliest times through to about 1800. We have looked at how the product itself and its method of preparation changed, and asked how religious ideas, institutions, and individuals affected the story of the commodity. What have we learned? First, we have discovered that commodities and beverages have a history that is just as complex as that of humans and their cultures. Second, we have seen that it is important to question normative claims about the antiquity of tea drinking and accounts of its spread that emphasize how "naturally" tea became the national drink of China. In this account, I have tried instead to represent the agency of individuals involved in constructing tea culture and the importance of the choices they made. Throughout, I have stressed the historical contingency of tea and the different ways in which the plant and the drink were understood at different times.

Many of our sources for the study of tea come from the elite strata of traditional society, some collected in the form of "tea literature" (*chashu*), some in the form of poems exchanged between literati, and some in the highly specialized genre of "tea connoisseurship" (*pincha*). Although it is important not to privilege the aesthetic judgments made by a handful of authors writing for a select audience, the construction of "taste" is a significant feature of the story of tea at all levels of society and one that ought to be represented. Issues of taste, in both senses of the word, run through the book and are intertwined with larger questions of religious and cultural values. For example, tea connoisseurship in Ming times often evoked idealized visions of contemplative lifestyles thought to be enjoyed by Buddhist monks or Taoist recluses. Tang and Song writers often equated the properties of certain types of tea or of the water they used to brew it with the geomantic or otherworldly aspects of the mountain sites where they were found. Exceptional teas were often described as elixirs, and their effects compared to attaining immortality or awakening.

Tea is and was an everyday commodity with extraordinary, otherworldly, transcendent associations. Those two aspects of its identity are in constant and creative tension throughout its history. The practical aspects of tea drinking (it relieves thirst, cheers from depression, clears the head, and nurtures the body) are mingled with religious aspirations and imagery (tea as an aid to immortality, tea makes the bones light). Because the intention behind this book has been to uncover the decisive contributions made by religious ideas, institutions, and individuals to the invention and development of tea drinking, it is worth briefly reviewing some of the ways in which each of these were significant.

IDEAS

In the realm of ideas, the rise in tea drinking in Tang China was accompanied by a Buddhist rhetoric of temperance. Not consuming alcohol was an important identifying feature of the religion for both monastics and the laity, but suitable alternatives to alcohol remained limited before the widespread availability of tea. Tea offered a viable option for consumption by monks and devout laypeople because it had properties that in some ways were comparable to those of alcohol. It seems that Buddhist ideals of the nonconsumption of alcohol were only able to have widespread influence on the population when the precept was combined with the practice of drinking tea that could be adopted as an alternative. In addition to its psychoactive and physiological effects, tea had an appeal for other reasons; like alcohol, it could serve significant ritual functions as an offering to deities, buddhas, or ancestors. Like alcohol, tea offered a means of mediating between our world and the world beyond either by changing the mental and physical state of the person drinking it or as a comestible that could be shared by humans and those beings who dwelt beyond the human realm.

Religious practitioners used tea in multiple ways to make merit for themselves or their relatives. They offered tea to buddhas and other deities as a suitably pure libation, they gave it as a funeral offering to the dead, or they donated it to quench the thirst of pilgrims. From medieval times, tea was a useful and effective ritual substitute for alcohol, which had been the standard libation since remote antiquity. Although tea was not canonically sanctioned, as it is not mentioned in Buddhist scriptural material translated from Indic sources, offerings of tea became readily accepted as a Buddhist practice in medieval China. Tea was even used in place of alcohol on ancestral altars. The idea of gaining merit by offering tea to thirsty pilgrims visiting Buddhist holy sites had important social consequences, because lay Buddhist societies formed for that express purpose but inevitably found themselves involved in other charitable and religious activities. There are also countless examples of tea being employed as a pure gift suitable for exchange between literati and monks. Tea thus offered an important conduit for the exchange of ideas and was the stimulus for the creation of important cultural statements in the form of poetry and painting.

Writers encountering tea often employed religious concepts to capture its extraordinary powers and, especially in Tang sources such as the *Classic of Tea* and poetry, emphasized the potential of tea to effect transcendence and/or transformation of the human body. Poets speak of bones becoming light, bodies sprouting wings, or of flying to Penglai, the realm of the transcendents, after drinking tea. It is difficult to say whether this is simply a poetic way of conveying the psychoactive effects of tea on the mind and body, but certainly tea became heavily and commonly invested with the meaning usually given to elixirs and other magical substances. It seems fair to say that the physiological properties of tea—heightened sensitivity, concentration of mind, prolonged states of wakefulness—were interpreted in religious terms as well as medical ones. Compilers of *materia medica* were able to describe these and other aspects of tea using plain language, so poets consciously chose to reach for a certain heightened vocabulary when writing about tea.

The mythology of tea, especially claims that it was first discovered in remote antiquity by the legendary Divine Husbandman Shennong, has proved remarkably enduring. This mythology is an artifact of the eighth-century *Classic of Tea,* which in many ways established the parameters for any intellectual discussion of tea. Despite contemporary evidence that other Tang writers knew well that tea drinking was a relatively new cultural phenomenon and did not posit any extra-human intervention in its invention, Lu Yu's determination to locate the origins of tea in antiquity effectively fixed the official story of tea for centuries to come. We have seen how tea drinking was thus essentially invented in the Tang dynasty and provided with a venerable history and mythology simultaneously with its propagation as a new beverage. It is revealing that tea does come equipped with such an august mythology: the need to provide such an illustrious backstory indicates how significant people thought this commodity was in Tang times.

In the realm of intellectual life, tea was intertwined at various times with the significant but subtle eclectic religious ideas that emerged from associates of Lu Yu in the statesman Yan Zhenqing's circle in eighth-century South China; the construction of ideals and concepts of connoisseurship in the Song; and the development of tea itself as an idea in the Ming. Poets and other writers experimented freely with the possibilities of using tea to represent a doctrine or idea. For some, tea could embody the sacred or represent an altered state of consciousness; for others a true understanding of tea was primarily an important marker of taste and social difference. Ultimately, and especially in Ming times, tea was used as an indicator or marker of the elite consumer's aspirations for a more spiritually oriented way of life. Paradoxically, a substance that was heavily commodified, often almost fetishized, in the sixteenth and seventeenth centuries was also a key signifier for an idealized spiritual and nonmaterial way of life that in the imagination of tea connoisseurs was exemplified by the image of the simple mountain monk brewing tea.

INSTITUTIONS

Throughout the book we have noted the importance of Buddhist (and, to a less visible extent, Taoist) institutions in growing, processing, and marketing tea. Within Buddhist monasteries themselves monks regularly used tea in a variety of ways: as an offering, to host important visitors and potential patrons, as an everyday beverage, and as the ritualized centerpiece of regular official monastic gatherings. Much of our information on the role of monasteries in the tea economy comes from secular sources such as gazetteers, travel records, and occasional prose pieces, rather than Buddhist sources. It is clear, however, that many famous, rare, and expensive teas (as well as many ordinary varieties, no doubt) were grown in and around monasteries on mountain sites with access to good quality springwater. The growing of tea as a cash crop by such institutions was a low-risk enterprise with the possibility of high returns; tea offered an attractive alternative source of income for foundations such as nunneries whose other prospects were limited. Tea connoisseurs in Song and Ming times often preferred to drink rare varieties of tea on site rather than risk being taken in by an adulterated or counterfeit product. Their tea-sampling pilgrimages to mountain sites sometimes stimulated their interest in Buddhist institutions that they found there.

Although we may have been able to infer the ubiquity of tea in Song-dynasty monasteries from later developments in Japanese tea culture that drew on established continental models, the extent to which tea was in competition with medicinal decoctions in the monastery remains unclear. Thanks to a closer reading of monastic regulations in their historical context, however, we can see that the ascendency of tea as a health drink was by no means assured in Song times. In the monastery and beyond, tea had to compete with a vast array of medicinal tonics in easy-to-consume powdered form. The strong demand for these popular decoctions was part of a larger enthusiasm for food as medicine in Song times. Only the fading of this fashion for dietetics left tea the undisputed champion of nonalcoholic beverages in the monastery and beyond.

Tea competed initially with alcohol for cultural space, and there was a tea "craze" in the eighth and ninth centuries during which ideas and practices around tea spread rapidly. In the eleventh and twelfth centuries there was a similar craze for health drinks, and tea had to compete against decoctions. Ultimately, the crazes passed, and tea, alcohol, and medicine came to coexist, with each occupying its own distinct cultural area.

In Song times, Buddhist monks regularly drank tea in their monasteries and also kept it on hand to entertain their literati patrons. But the most developed expression of Buddhist tea consumption was the ritualized communal consumption of tea (and decoctions) by the monastic communities of large Chan monasteries. Solemn formalized tea rituals held at regular points in the monastic calendar and derived ultimately from imperial court ritual ensured the smooth continuation of the yearly cycle, the reinforcement of group identity, and the reassertion of the hierarchy of monastic officers. Tea drinking, a practice that did not exist in Indian Buddhist monasteries, was thus made into a significant ceremonial event in Chinese Buddhist monasteries, one complete with obeisance, circumambulation, and the burning of incense.

INDIVIDUALS

Individuals with marked religious affiliations played crucial roles in the invention and dissemination of tea drinking: the Chan monk, Zang the Demon-queller; Lu Yu; his friend, the monk-poet Jiaoran; other Tang poets famous and obscure; the Japanese monk Eisai; celebrated tea masters and tea connoisseurs; and monks who possessed "the samādhi of tea" and other skills. Religious practices and worldviews strongly shaped the ways in which these people thought about the beverage they drank and promoted. It has been helpful to look closely at the lives of some important figures, such as Lu Yu, and try to understand the significance of their contributions, even while insisting on placing them in larger historical contexts that might downplay the contribution of a single extraordinary individual.

Lu Yu grew up in a Buddhist monastery and remained close to his foster father, a Buddhist monk, all his life. His most enduring relationship was his friendship with the monk Jiaoran. Whether he first started drinking tea in the monastery is unclear, but he certainly developed an early expertise in the subject of tea. His other works, aside from the *Classic of Tea,* have not survived so it is impossible to assess his entire oeuvre. To judge by the range of titles, however, it is clear that he could write with confidence on any number of topics. It is probably fortunate then that his book on tea coincided with a rapid development of interest in the topic. By default, his work became the definitive word on the topic for centuries and a blueprint that was copied by other aspiring experts on the subject.

Lu Yu's friend Jiaoran was just one of many Tang poets who wrote verses inspired by or on the subject of tea. Tea was a completely new subject for verse in the Tang, and those who took up the beverage in their poetry were able to create whole new vistas in the cultural landscape. Whether they noted tea in passing as an everyday drink or wrote hymns of praise to its divine transformative qualities, Tang poets created a language for talking about tea that would determine how writers of later generations approached the topic.

Eisai, the Japanese monk who came to China and drank tea there, showed that the power of this new drink—especially when combined with new esoteric Buddhist technologies of mudra, mantra, and maṇḍala, and with herbal medicine like mulberry—was essentially limitless. In his unique vision, only tea was capable of supplying the bitter flavor hitherto missing from the Japanese diet and thereby of eradicating the epidemics that were currently plaguing Japan. Drawing on Chinese textual materials and his own personal experience he presents a coherent vision of tea as a divine medicine for the latter days of the Buddhadharma that integrates Buddhist cosmology, Chinese *materia medica*, and the advice of contemporary Chinese doctors.

Ming tea connoisseurs continued the role played by Tang poets as cultural engineers. They promoted new types of tea and new methods for its consumption while also devising a new and finely articulated aesthetic for appreciating tea. Although many of the teas they drank were produced in Buddhist monasteries, the aesthetic they devised often owed more to their idealized vision of the simple life of the solitary Buddhist master. This was an image that owed less to reality than it did to their yearning for an alternative to their own highly regimented and stressful lives in service to the state.

The ideas that circulate about tea—that it is healthy, or spiritual, or rare and refined—were not spontaneously generated from the ether: they came from the minds of historically situated individuals who had reasons for discussing tea in certain ways. By considering the role of ideas, institutions, and individuals, it has become clear that the cultural and religious significance of tea was not a given, but was invented. By looking at a variety of materials in different genres, it has been possible to appreciate some of the textures of that process.

This book has examined a wide variety of sources: elite poetry, *materia medica,* gazetteers, monastic regulations, and the like. In some cases (like poetry, for example) there is such a wealth of material that it was necessary to devote an entire chapter to selected examples from just a single dynasty. The historical medical material appears to be mostly consistent in its discourse on tea, but even there we saw both wildly exaggerated claims for tea as a panacea and important warnings about the dangers of excessive consumption. Much more could be said about the sources included in this study, and many additional sources have been omitted.

This book shows how Buddhist and Taoist concepts, people, and places were involved in the creation of a culture of tea that was apparently well beyond the remit of those religions. It has focused on particular historical moments in the Tang, the Song, and the Ming, and that selectivity should perhaps raise important questions about how religious ideas and institutions functioned differently in those dynasties. As for future studies of the history of tea in China, virtually everything in this book could be further amplified or modified. I hope that this study will encourage scholars to consider beverages not as inert but as living organisms within an ever-changing cultural landscape. Also, I hope people will not underestimate the long-term impact of religious ideas, individuals, and institutions on the drinking habits of an empire.

Abbreviations

DZ: *Daozang* [*Zhengtong daozang* 正統道藏, 1445]. Including the *Wanli xu daozang* 萬曆續道藏, 1607. 1120 vols. Shanghai: Commercial Press, 1923–1926. Reprint. 60 vols. Taibei: Yiwen Yinshuguan, 1962.

QTS: *Quan Tang shi* 全唐詩 (*Complete Tang Poetry*), 900 *juan,* compiled by Peng Dingqiu 彭定求 (1645–1719) et al. Beijing: Zhonghua, 1960. *QTW: Quan Tang wen* 全唐文 (*Complete Prose Works of the Tang Dynasty*), 1,000 *juan,* completed in 1814 under the direction of Dong Gao 董誥 (1740–1818), et. al., Palace edition with preface dated 1814. Reprinted Shanghai guji chubanshe, 1993.

SKQS: *Siku quanshu* 四庫全書 (*Complete Books in Four Storehouses*). Taibei: Shangwu yinshuguan, 1983.

T: *Taishō Shinshū Daizōkyō* 大正新脩大藏經. Edited by Takakusu Junjirō 高楠 順次郎 et. al. Tōkyō: Taishō Issaikyō Kankōkai, 1924–1932. 100 vols.

XZJ: *Xuzang jing* 續藏經 *Continued [Buddhist] Canon*, Taipei: Xinwenfeng, 1968–1978. 150 vols. Reprint of *Dai Nihon Zokuzōkyō* 大日本續藏經. Kyōto: Zōkyō Shoin, 1905–1912.

Notes

Chapter 1: Tea as a Religious and Cultural Commodity in Traditional China

1. See, for example, Gardella 1994, Hohenegger, ed. 2009, Jamieson 2001, and Ukers 1935.
2. Following the David Hawkes translation in the Penguin edition; Hawkes 1977, vol. 2, 314–316.
3. For important studies of the effects of Buddhism on material culture in China and Japan, respectively, see Kieschnick 2003 (his discussion of tea on pp. 262–275) and Rambelli 2007.
4. The idea of China consisting of eight or nine macroregions in which trade and economic activity occur internally, rather than across the whole of China, was first suggested by William G. Skinner. See the essays in Skinner 1977.
5. *Pincha* seems to be a relatively late term, not widely used before the Ming dynasty, although it has earlier antecedents. The Tang poets Liu Yuxi (772–842) and Qiji (863–937) both wrote poems with the titles "*Changcha*" (Experiencing Tea). The tenth-century treatise *Assessing Sixteen Kinds of Boiling Water* (*Shiliu tangpin*) contains *pin* in its title and discusses some aspects of tea connoisseurship. Huang Ru (*jinshi* 1073) composed a famous work on the qualities of fine cake tea, *Essentials of Tea Connoisseurship* (*Pincha yaolu*), in 1075. For a study of a Ming-dynasty essay on tea connoisseurship, see Owyoung 2000.
6. Addison 1837, vol. 2, 135.
7. Huang 2000, 560.
8. For the history of the botanical name and the long-standing confusion about how to classify the tea plant, see Weinberg and Bealer 2001, 246–251.
9. Huang 2000, 503n. 3. This dispute, which began in the early nineteenth century, was divided along nationalist lines: British writers argued that India was the birthplace of tea, whereas Chinese scholars maintained that the honor belonged to China. See Kieschnick 2003, 262, and Chen Chuan 1984, 26–28.

10. On the tea industry in Assam see, most recently, Sharma 2011.
11. See Chen Chuan 1984, 18–20, and note in particular the chart on p. 20 that shows the linguistic relationships between the original Chinese terms and their counterparts in other languages.
12. For a recent scholarly approach to Buddhist mountain sites in China, see Robson 2009.
13. Jamieson 2001.
14. I do not have any direct proof for this suggestion. For evidence that the Tang elite had access to a wider range of sweet comestibles, see Schafer 1963.
15. Huang 2000, 563–564.
16. On *Shiliao bencao,* see Wang Shumin 2005, 303–305, and Engelhardt 2001, 184–187.
17. *Shiliao bencao yizhu,* 29–30; cf. the translation of Huang 2000, 512.
18. For a useful chart of the development of tea processing from the Warring States period to the nineteenth century, see Huang 2000, 551.
19. See descriptions of the manufacture of scented teas in ibid., 553–554.
20. *Chajing,* 6, 13; Carpenter 1974, 116.
21. Ibid.
22. Preface reproduced in Zheng Peikai and Zhu Zizhen 2007, 21. See the longer discussion and translation of Pi's preface in Chapter Five.
23. Huang 2000, 561.
24. Ibid., 519, 562.
25. Robbins 1974, 125; the text of *Pincha yaolu* may be found in Zheng Peikai and Zhu Zizhen 2007, 89–96.
26. See, for example, the discussion in Tseng 2008, 2.
27. See Simoons 1991, 459.
28. *Luoyang qielan ji,* 3, *T* 51.2092.1011b22–c1; cf. the translations of Jenner 1981, 216, and Huang 2000, 511.
29. Contained in *Guang Hongming ji* (Extended collection for propagating and clarifying [Buddhism]), 26, *T* 52.2103.287c.
30. On Chinese Buddhist attitudes toward silk, an animal product that required killing silkworms in its manufacture, see Young 2013.
31. See, for example, Knechtges 1997, 237.
32. Liu Shufen 2004, 130; on cold food powder, see Obringer 1997, 145–223. Cold food powder or "five-mineral powder" was originally a pharmaceutical prescribed for sexual dysfunction, depression, stroke, and vomiting. In the Wei dynasty (220–265) it was promoted as a panacea, and during the Jin (265–420) it was adopted by the elite for more recreational purposes. It simultaneously produced relaxation and euphoria in the user. It was called "cold food powder" because it was taken with warm wine and cold foods.
33. Liu Shufen 2007.
34. The best introduction in English to the range of practices associated with nourishing life is found in the volume edited by Kohn and Sakade 1989.

35. Huang 2000, 563.
36. Li and Thurston 1994, 99–103.
37. Huang 2000, 569.
38. For some recent academic studies of the health benefits of tea drinking, see Preedy 2012, and Zhen Yong-su et al. 2002.
39. Huang 2000, 564. I discuss this warning in more detail in Chapter Seven.
40. Quoted in *Xu chajing;* see Lin Zhengsan 1984, 209.
41. Translation from Huang 2000, 564, with modifications. *Yinshi xu zhi* is contained within the agricultural treatise *Bianmin tuzuan* (Collection of pictures for the convenience of the people), 1502, attributed to Guang Fan.
42. Clunas 1991, 171.
43. Steven Owyoung has written a helpful and informative essay on this poem: http://chadao.blogspot.ca/2008/04/lu-tung-and-song-of-tea-taoist-origins_23.html (accessed Oct 23, 2012).
44. *QTS* 388.4379. I translate and discuss the entire poem in Chapter Four. See the partial translation by Huang 2000, 554; the French translation in Cheng and Collett 2002, 5–7; and Owyoung's English rendering: http://chadao .blogspot.ca/2008/04/lu-tung-and-song-of-tea-taoist-origins_23.html.
45. See Lin Zhengsan 1984, 214.
46. Albury and Weisz 2009; Juengst 1992.
47. Liu Shufen 2004, 121.
48. On coffee in the Arab world, see Hattox 1988; on the rise of urbanity in China, see the work of Stephen H. West (e.g., West 1987, 1997).
49. Liu Shufen 2007.
50. The lack of precedent for offerings of tea in Buddhist canonical sources and in Indian Buddhist practice meant that the practice of the offering of tea to the Buddha in China was open to critique, as sometimes happened. See, for example, *"Chagong shuo"* (Statement on offerings of tea) by Qian Qianyi (1582–1664) quoted in *Xu chajing,* Zheng Peikai, and Zhu Zizhen 2007, 806–807.
51. See, for example, Chen 2006 and Chen Jinhua 2002.
52. Liao Baoxiu 1990, 2.
53. Liao Baoxiu 1990 offers a comprehensive survey of Tang teaware.
54. Pitelka 2003. See Huang 2000, 557, on Song antecedents for *Cha-no-yu.* For an erudite and critical approach to *Cha-no-yu* and its connections with China and Korea, see http://chanoyu-to-wa.tumblr.com. Surak 2013 offers an interesting account of the close connections between the tea ceremony and Japanese nationalism and state myths.
55. *Hōbōgirin* fasc. 3, 282, s.v. "Chatō."
56. *T* 45.1902.903c07.
57. See, for example, Mather 1968.
58. *T* 14.475, translated by Lamotte 1976.
59. See Ludwig 1981, 381.

60. *Fengshi wenjian ji jiaozhu,* 6.51. On *Fengshi wenjian ji,* see Luo 2012.
61. Note the remarks on this issue by Wu Zhihe 1980, 2–3.

Chapter 2: The Early History of Tea

1. "Oldest noodles unearthed in China," http://news.bbc.co.uk/2/hi/science /nature/4335160.stm; Lu Houyuan et al. 2005.
2. See, for example, Chen Chuan 1984 and the discussion of uncritical claims for the antiquity of tea drinking in Huang 2000, 506n. 5.
3. Such is the opinion of Lu Ji (261–303) given in his *Maoshi caomu niaoshou chongyu shu* (Explanation of the plants, trees, birds, beasts, insects, and fish in the Mao edition of the Classic of Poetry), part 1, p. 14. See also the following references in English-language versions of Chinese *materia medica:* Read 1977 [1936], n. 47 and n. 541; Stuart and Smith 1977, 82, 169–170, 230, 341, 344, 396, 414; Bretschneider 1882, 178–179.
4. Hucker 1985, 113, #205; *Zhouli,* 26.498.
5. *Shennong bencao jing jiaozhu,* 94. On the early Chinese *materia medica,* see Schmidt 2006.
6. Huang 2000, 510.
7. Ibid. For the *Taiping yulan* entry in question, which is headed *ming,* see *Taiping yulan yinshi bu* (Section on beverages and foodstuffs from imperial readings of the Taiping era), 732–761.
8. Examples in Huang 2000, 510–11.
9. Ibid., 508, based on an earlier translation of this passage by Derk Bodde.
10. On the *Xinxiu bencao,* see Wang Shumin 2005, 301–304.
11. Huang 2000, 512.
12. *Shiliao bencao yizhu,* 29. Huang 2000, 512.
13. Huang 2000, 512. For a recent study of *Bencao gangmu,* see Nappi 2009.
14. Knechtges 1970–1971, 90–91. Translation in Wilbur 1943, 383–392. Biography of Wang Bao at *Han shu* 64B 2821–2830.
15. See Ceresa 1993a.
16. Nunome cited in Ceresa 1993a, 209.
17. Goodrich and Wilbur 1942.
18. See Ceresa 1993a, 205, table 1.
19. Bretschneider 1882, 208.
20. Ceresa 1993a, 206.
21. *Huayang guozhi jiaobu tuzhu* (Record of the land of Huayang, critical edition, supplemented and annotated), 5, 175.
22. To avoid a taboo character in his personal name, *Sanguo zhi* gives his name as Wei Yao.
23. *Sanguo zhi,* 20.1462. Bodde 1942, 74. Huang 2000, 509.
24. *Bowuzhi jiaozheng,* 49.
25. See *Qimin yaoshu jiaoshi,* 789, 832–833.

26. For an introduction to this work, see Knechtges 1982, 1–72.
27. *Tang yunzheng*, 4.25b; cf. translation by Huang 2000, 512. Cheng Guangyu 1985, 4.
28. *Chajing*, 14–17.
29. Ibid., 13.
30. See Huang 2000, 506, for examples of this anachronistic claim from both Chinese and Western scholars.
31. Henricks 1998.
32. Ibid., 102.
33. Graham 1979, 96.
34. *Huainanzi zhuzi suoyin*, 19.1; translation from Major et al. 2010, 766–767. This passage and others from the early sources are also collected and translated by Henricks. See Henricks 1998, 106–107.
35. Henricks 1998, 107.
36. See *Bencao jing* quoted in *Taiping yulan*, 984.9b.2–5. Translation adapted from Schmidt 2006, 297.
37. *Chajing*, 14; My translation; cf. Carpenter 1974, 122.
38. *Han shu*, 30.1777. See Unschuld 1985, 113.
39. For an introduction to dietetics in medieval China, see Engelhardt 2001.
40. Unschuld 1985, 114. The history of this text is quite complex. See Schmidt 2006.
41. *Shanfu jing shoulu* (Classic of the official in charge of palace meals, manuscript edition), 524a.
42. *Rizhilu jishi* (Collected explanations on the record of daily knowledge), 7, 448–51; Zanini 2005, 1273.
43. See, for example, Nappi 2009, 24, on Lu Ji's *Maoshi caomu niaoshuo chongyu shu*.
44. The most extensive account in English of this literature is that of Campany 1996.
45. *Chajing*, 15.
46. My translation follows that of DeWoskin and Crump 1996, 190. Carpenter 1974, 126, offers an alternative translation, but it does not render the correct sense of the passage.
47. *Taiping yulan yinshi bu*, 733, #1337.
48. See Campany 1996, 377–384.
49. This collection is also known as *Soushen houji* (Further records of inquiries into spirits), written in the late Liu-Song or early Qi; see Campany 1996, 69–75.
50. Xuancheng was a Western Jin region in what is now southeast Anhui. Mount Wuchang is south of the present-day Ezhou city in Hubei.
51. *Chajing*, 15. My translation; cf. Carpenter 1974, 132–133.
52. Campany 1996, 75.
53. *Soushen houji*, 50.

54. Campany 1996, 248, and note Campany's references to anomaly accounts that feature humans with animal characteristics, n. 89.
55. Wu Hung 1987.
56. See Bokenkamp 1986; for a translation of Tao Yuanming's *Taohuayuan ji*, see that of James Hightower in Minford and Lau 2000, 515–517.
57. See *Yiyuan*, 7.4. On *A Garden of Marvels*, see Campany 1996, 78–80, and for his summary of the *Yiyuan* version of this story, see p. 380.
58. *Chajing*, 16. My translation; cf. Carpenter 1974, 133–134, and Campany 1996, 380.
59. *Chajing*, 16; the same source appears in *Taiping yulan yinshi bu*, 734, #1340. Carpenter 1974, 138.
60. *Nan Qi shu*, 3.62.
61. Guangling here presumably refers to the region of that name north of the Yangzi River in present-day Jiangsu.
62. *Chajing*, 16. Translation based on Carpenter 1974, 134–135.
63. Campany 1996, 261.
64. On this collection, see Campany 1996, 53.
65. Collected in Lu Xun 1967, 514.
66. Yuyao was a county in Zhejiang.
67. *Chajing*, 15. Carpenter 1974, 127.
68. *Yin cha ge song Zheng Rong*, QTS 821.9263.
69. *Yin cha ge qiao Cui Shi shijun*, QTS 821.9260. See Stephen Owyoung's translation of this verse: http://www.tsiosophy.com/2012/06/a-song-of-drinking-tea-to-chide-the-envoy-cui-shi-2.
70. *Chuci jiaoshi*, 303. Translation from Kroll 1996, 159.
71. *You Tiantai shan fu*. On the poem, see Chan Man Sing 1994. Sun Chuo never actually visited Tiantai shan, so he roamed the mountain solely in his imagination.
72. See Pregadio 2006, 71–72.
73. The original work *Mingyi bielu* no longer survives and is known only through quotations in *materia medica* such as *Materia Medica of the Daguan Reign Period* (*Daguan bencao*) and *Materia Medica of the Zhenghe Reign Period* (*Zhenghe bencao*). *Chajing*, 16; Carpenter 1974, 138.
74. *Chajing*, 16; cf. *Jin shu*, 95.2491–2492. The *Jin shu* biography does not mention tea.
75. Lu Xun 1967, 373–458; Wang Guoliang 1999, 155; Campany 2012, 168–171.
76. Lu Xun 1967, 415.
77. *Chajing*, 16; cf. Carpenter 1974, 135.

The *Continued Biographies of Famous Monks* says, "The Song monk Shi Fayao had the secular surname Yang, he was a native of Hedong. During the Yongjia period, he moved south of the river and met Shen Taizhen. Zhen invited him to stay at Xiaoshan monastery in Wukang (present day

Deqing, Zhejiang). Approaching seventy *sui,* he only consumed tea. During the Yongming period, the emperor ordered Wuxing to reverently escort him to the capital. He was seventy nine years old."

78. This source is no longer extant. This account is also quoted in *Taiping yulan* (see *Taiping yulan yinshi bu,* 734, #1339).
79. Liu Ziluan was the eighth son of Emperor Xiaowudi of the Liu-Song (r. 453–464).
80. Liu Zishang was Xiaowudi's second son; *zi,* Xiaoshi.
81. West of Huainan city in present-day Anhui.
82. *Chajing,* 16; Carpenter 1974, 135.
83. See the discussion in Lippiello 2001, 102–104.
84. *Laozi,* 1.32.
85. *Ruiying tuji,* 4a-b; translation from Lippiello 2001, 102.
86. Lippiello 2001, 102.
87. See, for example, Smith 2001 and McCants 2008, 176.
88. Again, see McCants 2008, 178–179.

Chapter 3: Buddhism and Tea during the Tang Dynasty

1. For a useful introduction to Buddhism and alcohol, see Michihata Ryōshū 1970.
2. Ceresa 1990, 9–15.
3. *Xin Tang shu,* 196.5612.
4. See *Fozu lidai tongzai,* 14, *T* 49.2036.611b18–c10; *Zuting shiyuan,* 4, *XZJ* 64, no. 1261, p. 366, c2–8.
5. On lay Buddhist attitudes to drinking and meat eating (albeit for a later period), see ter Haar 2001, 129–147.
6. Declercq 1998.
7. Full copies are found in the following manuscripts: Pelliot nos. 2718, 3910, 3192, 3716, 3906, and 4040; there are also partial fragments (Stein nos. 406 and 5774). On the *Chajiu lun,* see Chen 1963, Ji Yuanzhi 1991, and Lang Ji 1986.
8. Ji Yuanzhi 1991, 101–102.
9. Bon Drongpa [Bon-grong-pa] 1993, xii. The similarity of topics in the two texts is noted in passing by Stein 1972, 267.
10. A punctuated and annotated version of the Chinese transcribed from the Dunhuang manuscript may be found in Zheng Peikai and Zhu Zizhen 2007, 42–46. My translation follows Chen 1963 with some modifications.
11. *Bai shi liutie shilei ji,* 207.
12. Ceresa 1996, 19.
13. *Tang guo shi bu,* 6.
14. *Fengshi wenjian ji jiaozhu* (Record of things seen and heard by Mister Feng, collated and annotated), 6.52.

15. The reference is presumably to an episode when the King of Chu (or one of his generals) wanted to share a single goblet of wine with his troops. He threw it in the river and the soldiers drank from its waters. Thus fortified, they defeated the forces of Jin. See Chen 1963, 278n. 18.
16. The text here uses the technical term employed in Tang times for situations when the emperor permitted senior officials to offer counsel without fear of reprisal.
17. Translation adapted from Chen 1963, 278–279.
18. On the history of alcohol in early China as found in the traditional sources, see Poo 1999.
19. *Shiji* (Records of the Historian), 99.2723; Poo 1999, 15.
20. Poo 1999, 17.
21. See, for example, the *Family Rituals* of Zhu Xi (1130–1200) as translated by Patricia Ebrey 1993, 157–163.
22. See Harper 1986. Ironically, it is in the text of the *Analects* itself that we find Confucius's warning against overindulgence in alcohol.
23. For a Qing monograph on the subject of *jiuling* (rules for alcohol), see Yu Dunpei and Lou Zikuang 1975.
24. This is not to say that drinking games disappeared entirely. On drinking culture in the Ming, see Wang Chunyu 1990.
25. Translated in Edwards 1937, 191–192.
26. This work also reveals that parties in which drinking games were played were modeled on the political administration, with an "Illustrious Prefect" presiding, assisted by a "Statute Registrar" and a "Sconce-Beaker Registrar." For the topmost stratum of Tang society at least, getting drunk was indeed rather a serious business.
27. Chen 1963, 279–280.
28. *Chajiu lun*, 42–43; cf. translation of Chen 1963, 280.
29. See the later discussion on the teaware recovered from the Famen si relic crypt.
30. See Reischauer 1955, *passim*.
31. *Nittō gyūhō junreikōki*, vol. 1, 306; translation from Reischauer 1955, 220.
32. Xiangmo Zang was a disciple of the famous Northern Chan master Shenxiu (ca. 606–706). His biography (at *Song gaoseng zhuan* [Song dynasty biographies of eminent monks] 8, *T* 50.2061.760a) makes no reference to his penchant for tea. See also references at *Chuanfa zhengzong ji*, *T* 51.2078.765c; *Jingde chuandeng lu*, 4, *T* 51.2076.224a, b, c; 226a, b; and biography at 232b. See McRae 1986, 63; Faure 1991, 100; and Faure 1997, 65, 97–98, 103, 117.
33. *Fengshi wenjian ji jiaozhu*, 6.46; partially translated by Kieschnick 2003, 267.
34. Lin Zhengsan 1984, 209.
35. Ibid., 226n. 10.
36. *Chajiu lun*, 43; cf. translation of Chen 1963, 281.
37. Note the variety of orthography for Wu's name and the slightly different titles for his work found in various sources; Lin Zhengsan 1984, 226n. 11.

38. *Da Tang xinyu* (New tales of the great Tang), 11.166; *Taiping guangji* (Extensive records of the Taiping era), 143.1028.
39. Chen 1963, 281.
40. Ibid., 282.
41. *Xingxing* is the modern word for orangutan, but in medieval times referred to a kind of ape or gibbon. According to tales found in Chinese sources such as *Shu zhi* (Record of Shu), quoted in *Taiping yulan* 908.4026a, the *xingxing* has a fondness for alcohol that allowed hunters to catch it. See Schafer 1963, 209, for related lore about the *xingxing,* including accounts that credit the bibulous gibbon with the power of intelligible speech:

> *Xingxing* like alcohol and clogs, and so when people want to catch one, they set out these two things in order to entice them. When the *xingxing* first see them they are necessarily angry and say "You're tricking us!" Then they run far away. After a long while, they return. After they are urged to drink for a while, they are all drunk, and their feet all trip over the clogs. On account of this, the hunters catch them. (*Tang Guoshi bu,* 3.64)

These medieval stories are obviously ancestors of the following account given by William of Rubruck of his travels to the Mongol court in 1253–1255 (translation from Rockhill 1967, 199–200).

> One day a priest from Cathay was seated with me, and he was dressed in a red stuff of the finest hue, and I asked whence came such a color; and he told me that in the countries east of Cathay there are high rocks, among which dwell creatures who have in all respects [of] human forms, except that their knees do not bend, so that they get along by some kind of jumping motion; and they are not over a cubit in length, and all their little body is covered with hair, and they live in inaccessible caverns. And the hunters (of Cathay) go carrying with them mead, with which they can bring on great drunkenness, and they make cup-like holes in the rocks, and fill them with this mead. (For Cathay has no grape wine, though they have begun planting vines, but they make a drink of rice.) So the hunters hide themselves, and these animals come out of their caverns and taste this liquor, and cry "Chin, chin," so they have been given a name from this cry, and are called Chinchin. Then they come in great numbers, and drink this mead, and get drunk, and fall asleep. Then come the hunters, who bind the sleeper's feet and hands. After that they open a vein in their necks, and take out three or four drops of blood, and let them go free; and this blood, he told me was most precious for coloring purples.

42. See, for example, Wang Chongmin et al. 1984, 463, 470.
43. *Wen xuan,* 47.662. Liu's biography appears at *Jin shu,* 49.1375–1376.
44. Chen 1963, 283.
45. Ibid., 284.

46. For Confucius's warning against taking alcohol in excess, see Legge 1991 [1935], vol. 1, 232.

47. The best study of alcohol in literati culture in the Six Dynasties is Lu Xun 1981. See also Wang Yao 1986. For a glimpse into this hedonistic milieu, see *A New Account of Tales of the World* (*Shishuo xinyu*) in the translation of Richard B. Mather 2002, especially pp. 400–432 (chapters titled "The Free and Unrestrained" and "Rudeness and Arrogance"). On the Seven Sages of the Bamboo Grove, see Holzman 1956.

48. Translated in Giles 1964, 109–110.

49. For examples of the use of alcohol in court ritual, see *Xin Tang shu*, chapters 11–22 *passim*. An example of the use of alcohol in local ritual can be found at *Zizhi tongjian* 212.6733—a case from the middle of the eighth century when all local officials were required to lay on a formal banquet with music and drink in honor of the most worthy of the long-lived under their jurisdiction. See Schafer 1977, 134–35. Important studies of the use of alcohol in ritual include Paper 1995 and Poo 1999.

50. See, for example, Ode 209 in the Mao version of the *Classic of Poetry, Mao Shi zhengyi*. Paper 1995 explores the implications of this idea at length.

51. On Bai Juyi and Buddhism, see Ch'en 1973, 184–239. On Wang Wei as a Buddhist poet, see Wagner 1981, 119–149.

52. See, for example, his poem, "Drinking on an empty stomach with all the guests" (*Yu zhuke kongfu yin*), QTS 443.4956, translated in Harper 1986, 70. Bai's self-penned tomb inscription is titled "The Biography of a Drunken Poet" (*Zuiyin xiansheng zhuan*), on which see Shinohara 1991.

53. For the two edicts, see *Great Collection of Edicts and Statutes of the Tang* (*Tang da zhaoling ji*), 108.561–62. For a brief synopsis of the edicts, see Zheng Yayun 1984, 48–50.

54. Schafer 1965, 130–134.

55. For an example of an educated woman (in this case a Taoist nun) who did participate in Tang drinking culture, see Cahill 2000.

56. *Zuowang lun*, DZ 1036, 7a–8a; translated in Kohn 1987, 95–96.

57. See the examples in Kohn 2003, 122. Although Kohn does not remark on the fact, the problems with alcohol noted in her Taoist monastic codes are closely analogous to those found in the Buddhist materials discussed later.

58. See Pachow 2000, 151, which compares the *Sarvāstivāda vinaya* with other extant vinaya texts.

59. On the proscription of meat and alcohol in Chinese apocryphal scriptures, see Wang-Toutain 1999–2000.

60. *T* 24.1488.1048b9–16.

61. *Fayuan zhulin*, 93, *T* 53.2122.972a24–b1.

62. *T* 26.1521.56c12–17.

63. *T* 24.1488.1055a4–5.

64. On this important apocryphon, see Groner 1990; Funayama Tōru 2010.

65. *Fanwang jing*, 2, *T* 24.1484.1005b6–8.

66. *Fanwang jing*, 2, *T* 24.1484.1004c8–12.
67. See Lavoix 2002 and Kieschnick 2005.
68. *T* 85.2873.1359b–1361a.
69. *T* 85.2873.1359b–1360a; partially translated in Overmyer 1990. Wang-Toutain 1999–2000 also focuses on this scripture.
70. For a revisionist view of monastic practice at Dunhuang—using evidence that monks lived at home, were married, and drank alcohol—see Hao Chunwen 1998 and 2010. On the consumption of alcohol by Buddhists at Dunhuang, see Trombert 1999–2000.
71. See, for example, the text of the statute in Gernet 1995, 273; "[the members of the association] shall oblige her as a punishment to supply a quantity of alcohol sufficient for an entire feast."
72. Ibid., 248–277.
73. Dunhuang documents that record purchases of alcohol by Buddhist monasteries are Stein nos. 286, 372, 1398, 1519, 1600, 4373, 5039, 5050, 5786, 5830, 6186, 6452; see Giles 1957, 257; 261–265; Pelliot nos. 2032 (verso), 2040 (verso), 2042, 2049, 2271 (verso). The two complete examples are the yearly monastic budgets for Jingtu si for the years 924 and 930, found in Pelliot 2049 (verso, 1 and 2).
74. Trombert 1999–2000, 136.
75. Ibid., 164–171.
76. Liu Shufen 2006a, 375–377.
77. Ibid.
78. Ibid., 375.
79. Ibid., 380–382.
80. Ibid., 380.
81. On this painting, see Hay 1970–1971.
82. *QTW* 301.3059b–3060a; Liu Shufen 2006a, 376.
83. In English, see the early report by Han Wei 1993 and the later study by Karetzky 2000. For some issues related to the relic finds at Famen si, see the unpublished paper by Robert H. Sharf, "The Buddha's Finger Bones at Famen-si and the Art of Chinese Esoteric Buddhism."
84. See the full site report, published in two volumes with many high-quality color photographs and clear diagrams and drawings, *Shaanxi Sheng kaogu yanjiuyuan*, 2007.
85. Han Wei 1993, 45–46; Karetzky 2000, 64–65; *Shaanxi Sheng kaogu yanjiuyuan*, 2007, 130, and plates 70 and 71.
86. Han Wei 1993, 46–48; cf. *Shaanxi Sheng kaogu yanjiuyuan*, 2007, 123.
87. Han Wei 1993, 48–49; *Shaanxi Sheng kaogu yanjiuyuan*, 2007, 133, 137.
88. Han Wei 1993, 50–51; Karetzky 2000, 66; *Shaanxi Sheng kaogu yanjiuyuan*, 2007, 136–137.
89. Han Wei 1993, 52–54; Karetzky 2000, 65–66; *Shaanxi Sheng kaogu yanjiuyuan*, 2007, 131–133.
90. See Wang 2005.

91. Karetzky 2000, 63.
92. Han Wei 1993, 54.
93. See Sharf, unpublished.
94. See *Shaanxi Sheng kaogu yanjiuyuan*, 2007, plates 23–25, and 29–31.
95. *Shouyong sanshui yaoxing fa, T* 45.1902.903a7–8.
96. *Shouyong sanshui yaoxing fa, T* 45.1902.903c7. Zanini 2005, 1272; Kieschnick 2003, 267.
97. *Nanhai jigui, T* 54.2125.224c9–10; Takakusu 1896, 135; Kieschnick 2003, 268.
98. *Regulations for Instructing Novice Bhikṣus in Practicing and Maintaining the Vinaya (Jiaojie xinxue biqiu xinghu lü yi), T* 45.1897.870c23–25; Kieschnick 2003, 268.
99. Liu Shufen 2004, 2006a, 2006b, 2007.
100. *Shuyu tang* was a medicinal drink classified as *shanyao* (mountain medicine) and was the best-known decoction in Tang and Song times for nourishing life. See Liu Shufen 2004. We know this from examples in *Song Gaoseng zhuan* and other biographical materials—see sources cited by Liu Shufen 2007, 633.
101. The work is attributed to Tao Gu, but it is probably later; see Hervouet and Balazs 1978, 320.
102. See *Qingyi lu: yinshi bufen*, 124.
103. Ibid., 119:

> The Wu(-Yue) monk Wenliao was good at boiling tea. He traveled to Jingnan, where Gao Baomian's nephew (or Baomian recommended him to) Jixing (who) invited him to reside in the Ziyun chapel. Every day he tested his skills, and [Baomian's] father and son praised him as the deity of decoctions.

See also *Shiguo Chunqiu*, 103. Jingnan was a southern state. In 907 Gao Jixing was installed as military commander of Jingnan by the Later Liang; in 924 the Later Tang enfeoffed him as Prince of Nanping (modern-day Jiangling in Hubei). In 963 the state was overrun by the Song.

104. *Qingyi lu: yinshi bufen*, 119. See Cheng Guangyu 1985, 25. *Baixi* (lit. "hundred entertainments") refers to theatrical or artistic spectacles, involving acrobats or the like.
105. See, for example, http://chabaixi.baike.com.
106. See James Robson's entry on this text in Pregadio 2007, 757–758.
107. See Robson 2009, 166.
108. Gao was a powerful Tang eunuch known for his patronage of both Buddhist and Taoist institutions.
109. *Nanyue xiaolu*, DZ 453.5a–b.
110. Robson 2009, 166.
111. See *Tang huiyao*, 50; Cheng Guangyu 1985, 20.
112. See *Record of Famous Painters through the Ages (Lidai minghua ji)*, 10.
113. *Xuanzhen zi waipian*, DZ 1029, fasc. 3.4a.

114. *QTW* 162.6733. See Ip 1995.
115. See Bodde 1975, 273–288, for detailed discussion of this festival, at which drinking, followed by reciting poetry, was always an essential element.
116. Yuan Zhen (779–831), *QTS* 433.4652. Cf. Mark Edward Lewis' translation of the opening stanza, Lewis 2009, 142. In the original Chinese, this is a figure poem in the shape of a pagoda.

Chapter 4: Tea Poetry in Tang China

1. See Cheng Guangyu 1985, 16–20. The most extensive discussion of tea in Tang poetry is that of Takahashi Tadahiko 1990 on which I have drawn throughout this chapter. On the tea poetry of Tang monks, see Xiao Lihua 2009. The annotated collection of Tang tea poetry by Lü Weixin and Cai Jiade 1995 has been very helpful for this chapter.
2. On the High Tang and its verse, see Owen 1981.
3. See the translation by Steven D. Owyoung; http://www.tsiosophy.com/2012 /06/spoiled-daughter/ accessed July 7, 2012. The poem is also translated, somewhat differently, in Birrell 1982, 82–83.
4. *Chajing,* 15; Ceresa 1990, 151. The six pure liquids (*liuqing*) are mentioned in the *Rites of Zhou,* under the responsibilities of the *Shanfu.* The "nine regions" are the legendary ancient divisions of China.
5. See *QTS* 218.2288; 224.2293; 224.2399; 233.2578.
6. *QTS* 226.2433; translation in Young 2008, 230.
7. *QTS* 224.2399; Young 2008, 51.
8. *Deng Fuxian si shangfang Ran gong chanshi, QTS* 114.1158–1159. Fuxian si was the monastery founded by Empress Wu in Luoyang in memory of her mother. See Forte 2005. It is likely that the Master Ran referred to here is the Zhanran who was abbot of Fuxian monastery. See Chen 1999, 51–80.
9. See the extensive discussion in Chen 1999.
10. On Wang Wei's Buddhist ties, see Wagner 1981, especially chapter four.
11. On Wei and his verse, see Varsano 1994 and Red Pine 2009.
12. *QTS* 125.1258; Wang Wei and Zhao Diancheng 1961, 107. On the Buddhist inflections to Wang Wei's metaphors of heat and cool, see Lomova 2006.
13. *QTS* 126.1267; Wang Wei and Zhao Diancheng 1961, 118–119. The poem is translated in Barnstone, Barnstone, and Xu 1991, 61.
14. *QTS* 127.1291; Wang Wei and Zhao Diancheng 1961, 218–219.
15. *Xi yuanzhong cha sheng, QTS* 193.1994; Wei Yingwu and Tao Min 1998, 525. French translation in Cheng and Collett 2002, 27.
16. See Barrett 1991; Sharf 2007; Rambelli 2007, 14–15. See Varsano 1994 on Wei Yingwu as a "nature poet."
17. *QTS* 1818.178; Qu Tuiyuan 1980, 1127–1129.
18. Yuquan monastery, located on Mount Yuquan, in Dangyang County in modern Hubei, was one of the major monastic establishments of the Tang period. Constructed by Tiantai Zhiyi in the early 590s, it remained an

important power base for the Tiantai tradition in Tang times. See Sekiguchi Shindai 1960.

19. On this term, see Schafer 1967, 234.

20. A famous inscription by Lü Wen (772–811) for Ācārya Chengyuan of Mituo si on the Southern Marchmount, says of this monk that "in Kaiyuan 23 (735) he came to Yuquan monastery in Jinling where he studied under Huizhen, known as 'Master Zhen' (Zhen gong)." See Qu Tuiyuan 1980, 1129. For the inscription, see QTW 630.6354; discussed by James Robson 2009, 303.

21. Zhongfu's dharma name was drawn from the Hexagram number 61 of the Change Classic (Yijing).

22. Cf. the French translation in Cheng and Collett 2002, 1–2, and the English translation by Steven D. Owyoung: http://chadao.blogspot.ca/2011_04_01 _archive.html, accessed July 7, 2012.

23. Little is known about the transcendent Hongya (Master of the Edge of Vastness); see the few sources noted by Campany 2002, 273n. 513. He was either a servant in the palace of the mythical Yellow Emperor or a transcendent who was three thousand years old at the time of the sage-king Yao and still alive during the Han. "To pat Hongya on the shoulder" was a phrase meaning "to attain transcendence."

24. Wu Yan was the nickname of Zhongli Chun of the state of Qi. She was said to be "ugly beyond compare," but King Xuan of Qi (r. 319–301 BCE) was moved by her loyalty and made her his consort. Here, Li Bai compares himself to her and says that the "clear mirror" of Zhongfu's verse flatters him.

25. Xi Shi refers to legendary beauty Xi Shi or Shi Yiguang from the state of Yue in the Spring and Autumn period. She was sent to the state of Wu, along with another beauty, Zheng Dan, where she so enraptured the king that he neglected his duties, allowing Yue to defeat Wu in battle in 473 BCE.

26. I have consulted the translation of Tseng 2008, 45–46, and that of Steven D. Owyoung.

27. Stalactites were among the mineral substances commonly collected and ingested by those seeking longevity or immortality in medieval China. See, for example, Schafer 1967, 142–144, 156; Eskildsen 1998, 20, 22, 25; Unschuld 1986, 232.

28. On Li Hua, see Owen 1981, 243–246.

29. QTS 156.1588.

30. On "Cloud Mother" as mica, see Schafer 1955.

31. On this sense of "Jade Spring," see Needham and Lu 1983, 151.

32. QTS 136.1378; translation in Tseng 2008, 26. Chu is discussed by Owen 1981, 63–70. See also Schafer 1989, 63–64.

33. Schafer 1989.

34. Chajing, 15 (section 7) cites Fu Xian's (239–294) "Note to the Metropolitan commander" (Sili jiao), which says, "In the South, in Sichuan, they make a

tea congee and sell it." See Carpenter 1974, 126. *Shiliao bencao* (*Materia Medica of Curative Foodstuff*) explains how to make this congee: "boil [the tea] and reserve the water; use it to cook congee;" *Shiliao bencao yizhu*, 30.

35. *Cen Shen ji jiaozhu*, 345, 365. Cen Shen is better known as a frontier poet; see Waley 2002 (1963).

36. *QTS* 200.2086; *Cen Shen ji jiaozhu*, 270–271.

37. *QTS* 206.2153; 207.2162; 2165.

38. *QTS* 206.2153. Cf. the French translation in Cheng and Collett 2002, 28.

39. Kieschnick 2003, 222–249; see especially p. 245 for other appearances of the "corded chair" in the works of Tang literati.

40. On Liu Yuxi as poet, see Owen 2006, 42–45. On poetic exchanges between Liu Yuxi and Bai Juyi, see Yang 2003, 157–158. Bai's poem—which refers to the fragrance of tea steeping—may be found in Owen 2006, 71.

41. *QTS* 358.4036.

42. *QTS* 356.4000. Cf. French translation in Cheng and Collett 2002, 31–32.

43. *QTS* 357.432; cf. translation in Tseng 2008, 39.

44. See, for example, *QTS* 379.4247.

45. Qian Qi, *Yu Zhao Ju chayan*, *QTS* 239.2688. Translation in Tseng 2008, 31; French translation in Cheng and Collett 2002, 19.

46. *QTS* 207.2165. Cf. English translation in Tseng 2008, 34. Jiangzhou is within present-day Jiangxi Province.

47. Wei Shu (209–290 CE) was an eminent official of the Jin dynasty who was taken in as a child by his mother's family and subsequently repaid them by enjoying a prestigious career at court. See his biography in *Jin shu*, 41.947–950.

48. See McNair 1998, 99.

49. McNair 1992–1993; *QTS* 788.8882.

50. See Nielson 1973, Jia Jinhua 1992, Williams 2013. Jiaoran's criticism is collected as *Shishi jiaozhu*. There is no modern edition of his collected verse, although a single-fascicle Song collection, *Tang Jiaoran shiji*, survives in the collection *Tangren wushijia xiaoji* (A minor collection of fifty Tang poets), and there is a Ming-dynasty collection titled *Zhushan ji*, named after Mount Zhu where Jiaoran resided.

51. Faure 1997, 53; Jia 1999, 180–185; Jorgensen 2005, 621–622.

52. *QTS* 821.9260. Cf. French translation in Cheng and Collett 2002, 21; English translation by Steven Owyoung, http://www.tsiosophy.com/2012/06/a-song -of-drinking-tea-to-chide-the-envoy-cui-shi-2/ accessed July 9, 2012.

53. See the biography of Bi Zhou in *Jin shu*, 49.1380. He once tried to steal drink from a neighbor, was caught and tied to the vat of alcohol until dawn.

54. We discussed the Master of the Cinnabar Mound in an earlier chapter.

55. On the significance of sudden awakening in Chan see the essays collected in Gregory 1987.

56. *QTS* 816.9185.

57. *QTS* 818.9225.
58. *Chajing* 5, 13.
59. *QTS* 821.9266. French translation in Cheng and Collett 2002, 23–24. Pei Fangzhou (Pei Ji, fl. late eighth century) was a friend of both Jiaoran and Lu Yu.
60. The reference is to Pei Xuanren, a Western Han figure known as the True Man of Great Purity and his disciple Zhi Ziyuan. Pei was a disciple of Master Red Pine and his pronouncements are featured in the famous Shangqing work *Zhen'gao* (*Declarations of the Perfected*).
61. On the literary history of the Double Ninth festival, see Davis 1968.
62. On Tao's poetry in Tang times, see Tian 2005.
63. *QTS* 817.9211.
64. For a discussion of Lu Tong as recluse, see Cheng Guangyu 1985, 17. On this poem and its background, see Steven Owyoung: http://chadao.blogspot .ca/2008/04/lu-tung-and-song-of-tea-taoist-origins.html and http://chadao .blogspot.ca/2008/04/lu-tung-and-song-of-tea-taoist-origins_23.html.
65. Lu Tong, *Zoubi xie Meng jianyi ji xin cha*, *QTS* 388.4379. I consulted the English translations of Tseng 2008, 47–49; Hohenegger 2006, 20–21; the "semi-metric rendering" by Blofeld 1985, 11–13; and the partial French translation of Cheng and Collett 2002, 5–7.
66. *QTS* 437.4852; French translation in Cheng and Collett 2002, 33. See other examples of poets praising tea for its power over alcohol and thirst in Lin Zhengsan 1984, 214.
67. See, for example, *QTS* 449.5058 and 451.5100.
68. *QTS* 430.4750; see translation in Tseng 2008, 27–28.
69. Bai Juyi, *Zao fu yunmu san*, *QTS* 454.371; translation in Tseng 2008, 29.
70. Bai Juyi, *Shan quan jian cha you huai*, *QTS* 443.230; translation in Tseng 2008, 30.
71. That is, before the "cold food" festival when fires were prohibited.
72. "Fish eyes" is a technical term used to denote one of the stages of boiling water for tea. The size of bubbles offered a useful indicator of the heat of the water. To point tea correctly, the water should not be too hot.
73. Bai Juyi, *Xie Liliu langzhong ji xin Shu cha*, *QTS* 439.188. See translation in Tseng 2008, 1.
74. *QTS* 439.4891.
75. See, for example, "I heard in the evening that Jia the Prefect of Changzhou and Cui the Prefect of Huzhou enjoyed a gathering at Jinghui Pavilion on Tea Mountain; thinking of their joyful banquet and feeling envious, I send this poem" (*Ye wen Jia Changzhou, Cui Huzhou, chashan jinghui xiang xian huan yan yin ji ci shi*), *QTS* 447.286, translation in Tseng 2008, 37; "Mr. Qu spends the night" (*Qu sheng fangsu*), *QTS* 429.65, translation in Tseng 2008, 40; "Vice-Director Xiao sends new tea from Shu" (*Xiao Yuanwai ji xin Shu cha*), *QTS* 437.158, translation in Tseng 2008, 44.

Chapter 5: The Patron Saint of Tea

1. See Narita Shigeyuki 1998. A detailed discussion of key issues in Lu Yu's life from the surviving sources may be found in Shu Yujie 1996, 98–160.

2. *Tang guoshi bu*, 34, *Yinhua lu*, 86; *Taiping guangji*, 201.1514, *Tang caizi zhuan jiaojian*, vol. 1, 630. See also Ouyang Xiu's comments on Lu Yu's self-composed biography in *Jigu lu bawei* (Colophons to record of collecting antiquities), 9.2303. Cheng Guangyu 1985, 15.

3. *Jigu lu bawei*, 9.2303; Cheng Guangyu 1985, 15–16. See also *Tang caizi zhuan jiaojian*, vol. 1, 627.

4. For a recent overview of the Tang dynasty that includes assessments of the effects of the rebellion on economic, political, social, and cultural life, see Lewis 2009.

5. See DeBlasi 2002.

6. Sibei shi, *Tian zhi weiming fu*, QTW 433.4420; Mair 1994, 702; *Tang caizi zhuan jiaojian*, vol. 1, 626.

7. QTS 611.7053. For a study and translation of Pi Rixiu's poetry, see Nien-hauser 1979.

8. QTS 846.9569.

9. Greenbaum 2007, 165.

10. Zheng Zhong (?–83 CE), a Han-dynasty scholar.

11. From Pi's collected works: *Pizi Wensou,* 163. See the translation in Edwards 1937, vol. 1, 183–184.

12. *Wenyuan yinghua* 793, 6a–7a. The title of the piece is anachronistic—it was written in 761, but Lu Yu was not appointed Instructor to the Crown Prince until 780.

13. *Tang caizi zhuan jiaojian,* vol. 1, 622.

14. *T* 49.2036.611b18–c10.

15. *Tang caizi zhuan jiaojiaan,* vol. 1, 621–633.

16. For a discussion of the date of the collection, see Allen 2006, 105n. 1. For the account of Lu Yu, see *Guoshi bu,* p. 34.

17. *Yinhua lu,* p. 86; this account is the source for the entry in *Forest of Tang Anecdotes* (*Tang yulin*) by Wang Dang (fl. 1089), see *Tang yulin jiaozheng,* 401.

18. *Taiping guangji*, 201.1514.

19. Mair 1994; Nishiwaki Tsuneki 2000 (includes a translation into Japanese). See also Bauer 1990, 244–249, which includes a translation into German. The autobiography is found in QTW 433.4419–4421 and *Wenyuan yinghua* 793.6a–7a.

20. Mair 1994, 699.

21. For chronologies of Lu Yu's life, see Lin Zhengsan 1984, 217–225 and Narita Shigeyuki 1998, 240–250.

22. QTW 433.4420, Mair 1994, 699. Pei-yi Wu notes (Wu 1990, 18) that Lu Yu repeated the phrase "the Master's origins are unknown" verbatim from the

poet Tao Qian's (Tao Yuanming) self-penned "Biography of Master Five Willows." See also Nishiwaki Tsuneki 2000, 128.

23. See *Tang caizi zhuan jiaojian*, vol. 1, 622.

24. *Tianmen xian zhi*, 559.

25. Indeed, John Jorgensen has already pointed to some of the parallels between the two figures. Jorgensen 2005, 621–622.

26. *Tang guoshi bu*, p. 34, *Yinhua lu*, p. 86 respectively. Zhiji was also known by the honorific "Sage of Zhuqian" (Zhuqian shengren), according to Zhou Yuan's record of his visit to the site of his pagoda, which I discuss later.

27. Xita si is mentioned in a Tang poem, "The Tea Spring of Lu Yu" (*Lu Yu chaquan*) by Pei Di (716–?), a friend of the more famous Wang Wei; see *QTS* 129.1315.

28. See the biography of Yancong (557–610) in *Xu Gaoseng zhuan* (Continued biographies of eminent monks) 2, *T* 50.2060.437b7–10. On the Renshou relic-distribution campaign, see Chen 2002; see in particular pp. 85–86 for a discussion of Yancong's part in the campaign.

29. *Tianmen xianzhi*, 768.

30. *Tang caizi zhuan jiaojian*, vol. 1, 623; vol. 5, 140.

31. Mair 1994, 699.

32. Nishiwaki Tsuneki 2000, 128; see *Jigu lu bawei*, 9.2303.

33. *Tang caizi zhuan jiaojian*, vol. 1, 622.

34. *Yinhua lu*, 86; *Tang caizi zhuan jiaojian*, vol. 1, 623.

35. Johnson 1979, vol. 2, 131. Article 157.2b.

36. Certainly Lu Yu was quite familiar with the *Change Classic* throughout his life. Note, for example, the inscription of hexagrams on the tea brazier that he designed and commissioned, discussed by Owyoung 2008.

37. It is possible (but unlikely) that we know Lu Yu's dharma name. In the "Inscription for Miaoxi si on Mount Zhu in Wucheng county, Huzhou" (*Huzhou Wucheng xian Zhu shan Miaoxi si beiming*) *QTW* 339.3436, Yan Zhenqing gives the names of those who participated in his *Yunhai jingyuan* project, including both Fahai, a śramaṇa from Jinling, and Lu Yu. See McNair 1998, 98, for the passage in question. I am not convinced by the argument of Shu Yujie (1996, 102) that Fahai was Lu Yu's dharma name. The reference in the inscription is more likely to be to a known associate of Yan and Jiaoran, who was the author of a preface to *Platform Sutra of the Sixth Patriarch*; see Jorgensen 2005, 404, 633.

38. *Tang caizi zhuan jiaojian*, vol. 1, 622.

39. Translation follows Mair 1994, 700, with minor adaptations.

40. Jorgensen 2005, 621; Yampolsky 1967, 128.

41. Jorgensen 2005, 619.

42. See Knechtges 1982, 311–336.

43. The title of Lu Yu's joke book is given variously as *Xuetan* in Lu Yu's autobiography, *Huixie* in *XTS* biography, and *Tanxiao* in *Tang caizi zhuan*. Sadly, it does not survive.

44. Zhou Yuan was a native of Runan, part of present-day Henan. He is largely unknown beyond his association with Yan Zhenqing and his circle. In 816 he was appointed governor of Jingling.

45. *QTW* 620.6257.

46. For the background to his demotion, see Twitchett 1979, 723–724.

47. Lu Yu's autobiography, Mair 1994, 701; *Xin Tang shu* 192.5611; *Tang caizi zhuan jiaojian*, vol. 1, 624, which also reproduces the section of Yan Zhenqing's epitaph for Li Qiwu in which he records Li Qiwu's first meeting with Lu Yu.

48. Mair 1994, 701; *Tang caizi zhuan jiaojian*, vol. 1, 629. A native of Suzhou, Cui gained the *jinshi* degree in 726. Little is known of his early career as an official. In 744 he was appointed vice-director in the Ministry of Rites. In 752 Cui was demoted to a minor post in Jingling because of his association with a faction at court that was accused of conspiring to stage a coup.

49. *Tang caizi zhuan jiaojian*, vol. 1, 627. Jiaoran's association with Lu Yu is briefly noted in his *Song gaoseng zhuan* (Song dynasty biographies of eminent monks), biography *T* 50.2061.892a24.

50. Jorgensen 2005, 402.

51. Ibid., 407–412.

52. On Li Ye, see Cahill 2003. A famous poem addressed to Lu by Li Ye is translated in Minford and Lau 2000, 965.

53. *QTS* 249.2808 and 210.2181.

54. *QTS* 817.9210.

55. Mair 1994, 699, slightly amended, *QTW* 433.4420.

56. *QTS* 820.9243.

57. *Cong Lu Hongjian fu Yue bing xu, QTS* 250.2820.

58. *QTS* 308.3492–3493.

59. See the important discussion of this utensil and its significance by Owyoung 2008.

60. See the poem by Jiaoran recording this event, *QTS* 816.9186–9187.

61. On Yan Zhenqing as calligrapher, see McNair 1998; on his official career, see McMullen 1973 and McNair 1992–1993. Yan Zhenqing has biographies in *Jiu Tang shu* 128.3583–89 and *Xin Tang shu* 153.4847–4853. His prose works are in *QTW* 336–344, poems in *QTS* 152.1582–1584 and 788.8880–8886.

62. Zhang Zhihe, style name Zitong, was from Jinhua, southeast of Hangzhou. He served at the Hanlin Academy in Chang'an but was exiled to Nanpu, near Wanxian in the Yangzi River gorges. After he was pardoned and allowed to return, he became a recluse, calling himself Fishing Disciple Midst Mists and Waves and Obscure Reality. His poems celebrated the life of leisure, and he was also a calligrapher, percussionist, and flute player. On his relationship with Lu Yu, see Nishiwaki Tsuneki 2000, 133.

63. See McNair 1998, 97–99, and *Fengshi wenjian ji jiaozhu*, 11.

64. See *QTS* 817.9198.

65. McNair 1998, 97.

66. Ibid., 97.
67. Yan was a descendant of the sixth-century Confucian Yan Zhitui (531–591), and his clan claimed connections to the eight disciples of Confucius surnamed Yan. See McNair 1998, 33, 43. On Yan Zhenqing's important work on Tang state ritual, particularly imperial death rites, see McMullen 1999.
68. McNair 1992–1993, 83–95.
69. On Zhang's work, *Xuanzhen zi wai pian,* see Schipper and Verellen 2005, 304–305. The title was later changed to *Yuanzhen zi* because of a Qing-dynasty taboo on the character *xuan.*
70. McNair 1998, 98–99.
71. "On a spring evening, gathering at the residence of the reclusive scholar Lu to gaze at the moon" (*Chunye ji Lu chushi ju wanyue*), QTS 817.9210.
72. *Xi Yixing Quan mingfu zi Junshan zhi, ji Lu chushi Yu qiantang bieye, QTS* 817.9201.
73. Hucker 1985, #6145, #6152.
74. "On Lu Hongjian's newly opened mountain hut in Shangrao" (*Ti Lu Hongjian Shangrao xinkai shan she*), QTS 376.4220.
75. *Jiu Tang shu,* 20.352 and 112.3337.
76. *Fang Lu chushi Yu buyu, QTS* 816.9192.
77. The biography is still preserved in *QTW* 433.4421.
78. Lu Yu's biographies agree on the death date of 804, except for *Fozu lidai tongzai,* which gives 803.
79. "Seeing off Lu Cheng I returned to Huzhou, and composed this on men of the past—Lu Yu's grave at Jiaoran's stupa," QTS 379.4253.
80. See the survey of such literature in Kohn 2003, 203–225.
81. See Owyoung 2008.
82. See Liao Baoxiu 1990, 10–11.
83. See the description in *Chajing,* part 5, 12–13; Carpenter 1974.
84. The term *chashu* was first used as part of the title of a *Complete Collection of Works on Tea* (*Chashu quanji*) assembled by Yu Zheng in 1613. See Ceresa 1993b, 193.
85. Ceresa 1993b, 194–195; Zheng Peikai and Zhu Zizhen 2007, 49.
86. Ceresa 1993b, 195.
87. Zheng Peikai and Zhu Zizhen 2007, 49. Consult their reconstructed edition of the surviving text.
88. Ceresa 1993b, 196–200; biography at *Xin Tang shu,* 175.5246–5249.
89. On this period of factionalism, see Twitchett 1979, 639–654.
90. Note that *jiancha* here (although the same glyphs are used) is not connected with the Japanese term *sencha.*
91. Biography at *Jiu Tang shu,* 153; *Xin Tang shu,* 160.
92. See Zheng Peikai and Zhu Zizhen 2007, 48. The existence of a work attributed to Lu Yu titled *Shui pin* is dubious.
93. Ceresa 1993b, 198–199.

94. Biographical data at (among other places) *Xin Tang shu*, 91.3787–3788 (biography of Wen Daya 3781–3788); *QTS* 190b/5078–5079; *Tangshi jishi* (*Recorded Anecdotes of Tang Poetry*), 54.9b–10a.
95. Zheng Peikai and Zhu Zizhen 2007, 51–53.
96. Ibid., 46–47.

Chapter 6: Tea in the Song Dynasty

1. Tribute tea is discussed in Cheng Guangyu 1985, 53–55.
2. The reasons for the economic development of Fujian in the early Song are briefly outlined by Robbins 1974, 122–123.
3. See Smith 1991.
4. See examples in Cheng Guangyu 1985, 26; on the *qin* in Tang and Song poetry, see Egan 1997, 46–66.
5. Cheng Guangyu 1985, 60–61.
6. Huang 2000, 523–524, describes the processing of Song tribute tea. The term *bei* originally indicated an oven for drying tea, but in the Song came to stand for the entire tea-processing station.
7. Ibid., 524.
8. Robbins 1974, 127.
9. Ibid., 124.
10. See the illustrations of the designs used at the Northern Park in *Xuanhe Period [1119–1125] Record of Tribute Tea from the Northern Park* (*Xuanhe beiyuan gongcha lu*), Zheng Peikai and Zhu Zizhen 2007, 119–125. Note the description of tribute teas made by Zhou Mi (1232–ca. 1308) in his *Old Matters of Wulin* (*Wulin jiushi*), as translated by Owyoung 2000, 28.
11. Huang 2000, 524, table 49.
12. *Essays on Tea from the Daguan Reign Period* (*Daguan chalun*), Zheng Peikai and Zhu Zizhen 2007, 104; quoted in Huang 2000, 524.
13. *Daguan chalun,* Zheng Peikai and Zhu Zizhen 2007, 104.
14. Passages from Cai Xiang's *Cha lu* and *Daguan chalun* describe how the cakes were dried out by being carefully placed on bamboo racks above a controlled source of heat. See Zheng Peikai and Zhu Zizhen 2007, pp. 78 and 107, respectively, and the discussion in Huang 2000, 526.
15. Zheng Peikai and Zhu Zizhen 2007, 77. See Huang 2000, 553, for descriptions of how teas were scented with camphor and other substances.
16. *Xuanhe beiyuan gongcha lu,* Zheng Peikai and Zhu Zizhen 2007, 118–119.
17. Robbins 1974, 125; see the annotated critical edition of this text as reproduced in Zheng Peikai and Zhu Zizhen 2007, 89–95.
18. Zheng Peikai and Zhu Zizhen 2007, 103–111. Parts of the work are translated and discussed in Blofeld 1985, 28–38.
19. Zheng Peikai and Zhu Zizhen 2007, 104–105.
20. Ibid., 105.

21. Liao Baoxiu 1996, 25.
22. See Egan 1994, 171.
23. Zheng Peikai and Zhu Zizhen 2007, 106; Huang 2000, 557; Liao Baoxiu 1996, 28–30.
24. Owyoung 2000, 29.
25. See Clark 2001 and Needham and Ronan 1978, 121–123.
26. Huang 2000, 559.
27. Cheng Guangyu 1985, 31–32; also consider the visual evidence, such as the work attributed to Zhou Fang (active 780–810), but probably a Song copy, *Court Ladies Tuning the Lute and Drinking Tea* (handscroll, ink and color on silk, 28 × 75 cm, Nelson-Atkins Museum of Art, Kansas City).
28. Cheng Guangyu 1985, 33.
29. Yu 1980, 220–237.
30. Cheng Guangyu 1985, 21.
31. *Siming zunzhe jiaoxing lu* (Record of the teaching and practices of the Venerable of Siming), *T* 46.1937.924c; Liu Shufen 2006a, 372; Cheng Guangyu 1985, 50. See also the biography of the monk Zhihui in *Song Gaoseng zhuan*, 2, *T* 50.2061.716b24–25.
32. Cheng Guangyu 1985, 46–50.
33. Ibid., 51–53.
34. See Fang Hao 1985.
35. Robbins 1974, 130. Edict of Zhenghe 3.2.9.
36. Robbins 1974, 138.
37. Fang Hao 1985, 140.
38. *Xiangji* is the name of the Buddha who teaches in the land of fragrances described in the *Vimalakīrti nirdeśa;* in Buddhist texts it can be a polite reference to the kitchen of a monastery.
39. "Outer seven towns": in Song-dynasty Hangzhou there were nine counties, Qiantang, Renhe, Yuhang, Lin'an, Yuqian, Fuyang, Xinpo, Yanguan, and Changhua. The latter seven were called the outer seven towns.
40. *Xianchun lin'an zhi* fasc. 58 (section on local products, *Huo zhi pin*). Jing shan is in Yuhang.
41. Fang Hao 1985, 142–144.
42. *Jiatai Kuaiji zhi*, 17.
43. Fang Hao 1985, 143.
44. See Cheng Guangyu 1985, 21–24, for some examples.
45. *Wudeng huiyuan*, 4, *XZJ* 1565.93b19–21. Similar versions of this dialogue can be found throughout other Chan collections.
46. The "Master of the Jade River" refers to the Tang poet Lu Tong.
47. *Collected and Annotated Poems of [Su] Dongpo by Category* (*Jizhu fenlei Dongpo shi*); Wu Jingyi 2006, 265–266. Chinese text and French translation in Cheng and Collett 2002, 66–67.
48. A selection of his verses on tea are translated in Cheng and Collett 2002, 65–77.

49. *Jingang jing zhujie*, 2, *XZJ* 24.468.777b6–12.
50. See Zheng Jinsheng 2006 and, on dietetics during the Tang, Engelhardt 2001.
51. Hirabayashi Fumio 1978, 49–50, 67; Liu Shufen 2006a, 376–377.
52. Liu Shufen 2006a, 381.
53. Ibid., 379.
54. *Chanyuan qinggui* (Pure rules for Chan monasteries), 4, *XZJ* 63.1245.533c5–6.
55. *Chongxiu zhenghe jingshi zhenglei beiyong bencao* (Re-edited Zhenghe-period practical *materia medica* divided by category from the histories and classics) by Tang Shenwei (eleventh/twelfth centuries), 13.333 quoting *Yaoxing lun* (Treatise on the properties of drugs); translation in Zheng Jinsheng 2006, 41. *Yaoxing lun* is variously dated to the Tang or Five Dynasties; see the discussion in Zheng Jinsheng 2006, n. 8.
56. *Waitai miyao*, 31.856–857. Translation by Zheng Jinsheng 2006, 42.
57. Buswell 1992, 178.
58. *Dongjing menghua lu*, 3.117–18; Zheng Jinsheng 2006, 43.
59. *Mengliang lu*, 13.8.
60. On *fuling*, see the extensive note at Campany 2002, 310n. 73.
61. Zheng Jinsheng 2006, 44. On this government-sponsored pharmacy, see Goldschmidt 2008.
62. *Taiping Huimin hejiju fang*, 3.393–401; Zheng Jinsheng 2006, 44.
63. Schafer 1955, Campany 2002, 174n. 136. For other names of decoctions, see Liu Shufen 2006a, 364, and Liu Shufen 2004.
64. Zheng Jinsheng 2006, 45.
65. Liu Shufen 2007, 665.
66. *Mengliang lu*, 16.262 [Gernet 1962, 49]). On Song teashops known by various terms such as *chasi, chafang, chalou, chashi,* and so on, see Cheng Guangyu 1985, 57–59. Teashops featuring female entertainers were called *hua chafang* ("flower teashops").
67. *Chongxiu zhenghe jingshi zhenglei beiyong bencao,* 28.514; I have modified the translation of Zheng Jinsheng 2006, 52.
68. *Dongjing menghua lu*, 8. 202–203.
69. See, for example, the ritual use of tea in the ceremonies of the triads, ter Haar 1998, *passim*.
70. See the discussion of "Sino-Japanese *tō* (in Japanese *yu*)" in *Hōbōgirin* fasc. 3, s.v. *Chatō*.
71. Yifa 2002, 158, 186.
72. Ibid., 255n. 83; Liu Shufen 2007, 632.
73. Schlütter 2008.
74. *Chanyuan qinggui* as summarized by Liu Shufen 2007, 362.
75. Ibid., 634.
76. Ibid., 636.
77. *Zimen jingxun* (Admonishments for monastics), 6, *T* 48.2023.1070a.
78. Liu Shufen 2007, 637.
79. *Taiping guangji*, 21.143.

80. Cf. Yifa 2002, 257n. 10 :"There are two types of ceremony: *jiandian*, the tea and refreshment ceremony, and *chatang*, the tea ceremony."
81. See, for example, Yifa 2002, 294.
82. Liu Shufen 2007, 638.
83. *Chanyuan qinggui*, 5, *XZJ* 63, no. 1245, p. 536, b6–7.
84. *Chanyuan qinggui*, 4, *XZJ* 63, no. 1245, p. 534, c5. Cf. Yifa 2002, 173. She understands the terms *jiandian* and *chatang* differently, as denoting "formal tea ceremony" and "lesser tea ceremony."
85. *T* 81.2579. Image reproduced in Liu Shufen 2007, 662.
86. Reproduced in ibid., 2007, 662.
87. Ibid., 640.
88. *T* 81.2579.696a; Liu Shufen 2007, 641.
89. ter Haar 1992, pp. 27n. 31, 31n. 41, 38n. 55 and elsewhere, although he appears to understand *tang* as "hot water" rather than "decoctions."
90. *Song gaoseng zhuan*, 7, *T* 50.2061.752a14–16; Liu Shufen 2006b, 86.
91. *Yunji qiqian*, 60.1330.
92. *Chanyuan qinggui*, 3, *XZJ* 63.1245.531b16.
93. *Chanyuan qinggui*, 5, *XZJ* 63.1245.536b14–537a14. Yifa 2002, 182–185.
94. See the table in Liu Shufen 2007, 643, that shows the monastic officers lined up by rank.
95. There are some slight variations—Liu notes a different protocol in *Chanyuan qinggui* for the *jiexia* (Beginning of summer meditation retreat) node: Liu Shufen 2007, 644.
96. Illustrations of examples of these posters may be found in the Japanese annotated edition of *Chanyuan qinggui*.
97. See examples of these seating plans in Liu Shufen 2007, 664.
98. "Attending a tea ceremony," Yifa 2002, 129–131.
99. Yifa understands *shacha* to mean "the lower grade tea" because elsewhere the text refers to "higher grade tea." She writes (Yifa 2002, 294 n.24) that "[this] would seem to indicate that average, lower-grade tea was probably served on most occasions." Cf. Liu's interpretation (Liu Shufen 2007, 648) of *shacha* as tea powder. She points out that the tea ceremony in question was a grand ritual, not an ordinary occasion at which one might serve inferior tea.
100. On the "holy monk," whose identity remains unspecified in *Chanyuan qinggui*, see Yifa 2002, 70–72.
101. Ibid., 183.
102. *Dajian chanshi xiao qinggui*, *T* 81.2577.622c17–24.
103. Liu Shufen 2007, 651; Yifa 2002, 181.
104. Liu Shufen 2007, 652.
105. Yifa 2002, 130.
106. Liu Shufen 2007, 653; Liu Shufen 2006a, 365; Hirabayashi Fumio 1978, 140.
107. *Beiji qianjin yaofang* (Supplementary essential prescriptions worth a thousand in gold), 161–162.
108. Yifa 2002, 163.

109. Note the serving of tea and decoction at court ceremonies as early as the late Tang; see Cheng Guangyu 1985, 20.
110. Liu Shufen 2007, 655.
111. Cui Yuanhan (729–795) has described some of the rules for banquets in his *Ban Cao shitang biji*, QTW 523.5321.
112. Li Ao (d. 780) also noted that the rules for the dining hall written on yellow silk were hung on the north wall of the hall and re-inscribed every year. See his *Quan Henan Yin fugu shi shu*, *Li Wengong ji*, 8.6b–8b.
113. Liu Shufen 2007, 656.
114. There were indeed contemporary complaints that monks were not versed in the "ritual and music of the three dynasties;" Liu Shufen 2007, 658.
115. *Zimen jingxun*, 7, *T* 48.2023.1074c11–12.
116. *Chanyuan qinggui*, 4, *XZJ* 63.1245.533a2–4. Yifa 2002, 163.
117. Yifa 2002, 146.
118. Ibid., 148.
119. Ibid., 149.

Chapter 7: Tea Comes to Japan

1. For the text of *Kissa yōjōki* and a useful discussion of its contents and background, see Furuta Shōkin 2000. In English, the best introduction is that of Sen 1998, 57–74. There is a French study and translation by Girard 2011.
2. See Welter 2006, 104n. 34.
3. Takahashi Tadahiko 1994, 331.
4. Goble 2011, 9.
5. Takahashi Tadahiko 1994, 332. See *Taiping yulan yinshi bu*, 732–761.
6. On Jīvaka, see Zysk 1991, 52–61 and Salguero 2009. For a version of the Buddhist story of Jīvaka, see, for example, *Sifen lü* (*Dharmagupta vinaya*), *T* 22.1438.850c–855a.
7. On the five viscera in Chinese medicine, see Sivin 1987, 213–236, 349–378.
8. *Kissa yōjōki* (Furuta Shōkin 2000), 78.
9. Ibid., 81.
10. Chen 2009, 241–243.
11. The argument is a complex one, not easily summarized here. See Chen 2009.
12. See the extensive correlation between *Taishō* 905 and Zhiyi's *Mohe zhiguan* as explained by Chen 2009, 226–227.
13. Ibid., 241–243.
14. On this topic, see Hayashi Yoshirō 2004.
15. Hurst 1979, 104.
16. On "lower-leg pneuma" (*jiaoqi*) disease, see Smith 2008.
17. Furth 1999, 82.
18. Smith 2008, 287.
19. On these diseases, see Hanson 2011.

20. On Lin Hong and his work, see Sabban 1997.
21. *Shanjia qinggong,* 109. My thanks to Robban Toleno for sharing his translation of this passage. Cf. the partial translation by Huang 2000, 564. I believe that Huang has missed the thrust of some of Lin Hong's arguments.
22. I follow a modern critical edition of the text as found in Furuta Shōkin 2000. For the sake of consistency with the remainder of the book I have provided the Chinese readings rather than the Japanese for most of the terminology in Eisai's text.
23. *Sida* (Sanskrit *mahābhūta*) are the four "gross" elements of which all matter is composed. The elements are earth, water, fire, and wind. *Wuzang* are the five viscera.
24. It is possible that *tō/tang* could refer to hot baths here, but later references are to decoctions.
25. There are discrepancies in the various manuscripts about which syllable is related to which Buddha. See Drott 2010, 265.
26. The later examples are taken from *Taiping yulan.* Another source Eisai used, in addition to *Taiping yulan,* is *Zhenglei bencao* by Tang Shenwei. Mori Shikazō 1999 (342–531) has made the closest study of Eisai's use of this source.
27. *Mao* is probably an error for *chuan.*
28. This quotation is taken from *Taiping yulan,* which uses the character *cha* in place of the earlier *tu. Taiping yulan yinshi bu,* 732. See Chapter Two for a discussion of this lexical change and for various entries perhaps referring to tea from *Erya,* an early lexicon for the Chinese classics.
29. The parenthetical explanations are likely by Eisai himself.
30. "Tangdu" refers here to the Southern Song capital of Lin'an or Hangzhou.
31. See Chen Zugui and Zhu Zizhen 1981, 205 #17.
32. The states are located in the Kunlun mountains of what is now Vietnam.
33. See Chen Zugui and Zhu Zizhen 1981, 206, #21. *Nanyue zhi* was compiled by Shen Huaiyuan (557?–589?).
34. *Chajing,* 8; Carpenter 1974, 59.
35. This is from Guo Pu's commentary on *Erya,* which we discussed in Chapter Two. See Ceresa 1990, 155.
36. The complete title of this work is *The Record of the Lord of Paulownia's Selection of Drugs (Tongjun caiyao lu,* also known as *Tongjun yao lu).* Tao Hongjing cites this work, so it must have been composed before his day. This source is also quoted in *Chajing,* 16; Ceresa 1990, 167; Carpenter 1974, 138–139.
37. *Chajing,* 8; Carpenter 1974, 59.
38. *Wuxing ji* was compiled by a former governor of the region, Shan Qianzhi (d. 454 or 455). *Chajing,* 7; Ceresa 1990, 169.
39. See *Chajing,* 16; Ceresa 1990, 163; Carpenter 1974, 136; *Taiping yulan,* 867. I discuss this passage in Chapter Two.
40. *Guangya* is a glossary dictionary compiled by Zhang Yi (third century) as an expansion of *Erya.* See *Chajing,* 14; Carpenter 1974, 123; Ceresa 1990, 141.

41. Greatrex 1987, 84.
42. See *Chajing,* 14; Ceresa 1990, 141; Carpenter 1974, 122. I discuss this "Food Canon" in Chapter Two.
43. The quotation is from *Shennong bencao jing (Materia Medica Classic of the Divine Husbandman),* which I discuss in Chapter Two. See *Chajing,* 17; Ceresa 1990, 171; Carpenter 1974, 141.
44. See *Chajing,* 15; Carpenter 1974, 131; Ceresa 1990, 155.
45. Retired Scholar Hu and his text remain unidentified. See *Chajing,* 15; Carpenter 1974, 132; Ceresa 1990, 155.
46. *New Record* is an alternative name for Tao's *Miscellaneous Records (Za lu).* Cf. *Chajing,* 16, which gives a different quotation from this text. Ceresa 1990, 165–166; Carpenter 1974, 138.
47. *Chajing,* 16; Carpenter 1974, 139.
48. *Taiping yulan,* 867. Du You was a Western Jin poet.
49. See *Chajing,* 7; Ceresa 1990, 151.
50. I discuss this poem in Chapter Four.
51. Six *indriya;* sometimes *liuqing.* The term "six cognitive faculties" is a Buddhist interpretation of the phrase "six purities." As we noted in Chapter Four, however, Zhang's reference is in fact to the six pure liquids mentioned in the *Rites of Zhou.*
52. *Bencao shiyi* was compiled by the Tang author Chen Cangqi.
53. This quotation does not appear in the extant *Tiantai shan ji.*
54. *Bai shi liutie shilei ji* (Mister Bai's categorized collection in six tablets), usually known by its abbreviated title, is a famous encyclopedic collection composed by Bai Juyi.
55. This section contains three examples copied from *Taiping yulan* followed by Eisai's personal notes.
56. This date falls around February 5–18.
57. No text of this name is known. There are four scriptures in the canon containing dhāraṇīs associated with the wisdom king Āṭavika, also known as Daigensui (the Great Commander), and the Indic protector god revered as master of all demons. Numbered 1237 to 1240 in the *Taishō* canon, these four scriptures are known collectively as the "Techniques of Daigensui" (*Daigensui hō*). The ritual to Daigensui was the major Shingon rite for state protection. See Duquenne 1983.
58. "Great yellow" is the name of a drug.
59. Ox-knee, Blume (*Achyranthes bidentata*).

Chapter 8: Religion and Culture in the Tea Economy of Late Imperial China

1. Bartholomew 1990, 42, 44.
2. Wu Zhihe 1980, 1.
3. Owyoung 2009, 49. Chen Zugui and Zhu Zizhen 1981, 287.

4. Owyoung 2009, 49, Chen Zugui and Zhu Zizhen 1981, 542.
5. Brook 1998, 126–127.
6. Owyoung 2009, 49.
7. Chen Zugui and Zhu Zizhen 1981, 296.
8. Huang 2000, 529.
9. Owyoung 2009, 49. Zheng Peikai and Zhu Zizhen 2007, 173–177.
10. On the meanings of *pin,* see Owyoung 2000, 43n. 1. On the larger culture of Ming connoisseurship and its relation to commerce and transport systems, see Brook 1998.
11. Zheng Peikai and Zhu Zizhen 2007.
12. See Owyoung 2000.
13. Ibid., 31.
14. Ibid.
15. Huang 2000, 553–554.
16. Wu Zhihe 1980, 22–26.
17. See Owyoung 2000, 35. On the famous Dragon Well as described in the writings of Qin Guan (1049–1100), see Strassberg 1994, 199–203.
18. See his *Minor Grading of Springs for Simmering* (*Zhuquan xiaopin*); Zheng Peikai and Zhu Zizhen 2007, 197.
19. *Desultory Remarks on Furnishing the Abode of the Retired Scholar* (*Kaopan yushi*), first published in 1606, 3.8. On Tu Long's commitment to Buddhism, see Brook 1993, 67. On *Desultory Remarks*, see Clunas 1991.
20. *Zhejiang tongzhi* (Comprehensive gazetteer of Zhejiang), 101.17.
21. Huang 2000, 533.
22. See Tu Long's entry on Dragon Well tea, citation above, n. 19.
23. See Wu Zhihe 1980, 22, for examples.
24. *Mingzhai ji* (Tea-fast collection), 17.167.
25. See Owyoung 2000, 34.
26. See *Cha lu* (Records of tea) by Feng Shike (*jinshi* 1571); Zheng Peikai and Zhu Zizhen 2007, 336.
27. See *Ming shuo* (Sayings about tea) by Wu Congxian (Wanli era); Zheng Peikai and Zhu Zizhen 2007, 610.
28. Wu Zhihe 1980, 9.
29. *Luojie chaji* (Record of Luojie tea) by Xiong Mingyu (1579–1649); Zheng Peikai and Zhu Zizhen 2007, 338–339.
30. *Cha shu* (Commentary on tea), Zheng Peikai and Zhu Zizhen 2007, 269.
31. *Cha shu,* Zheng Peikai and Zhu Zizhen 2007, 270.
32. *Xu chajing,* 763, citing Shen Shitian's [Shen Zhou], *Shu Jiecha bielun hou* (Postface to the separate discussion of Jie tea).
33. See Strassberg 1994, 305–307.
34. Owyoung 2000, 31–32.
35. *Huqiu shan zhi* (Gazetteer of Mount Huqiu), 10.16.
36. *Xu chajing,* 763.

37. Ibid.
38. Owyoung 2000, 48n. 130.
39. *Xu chajing,* 763. Owyoung 2000, 32.
40. *Xu chajing,* 764.
41. *Xu chajing,* 816, citing Wang Zi's (date unknown). *Chashuo.*
42. *Fujian tong ji* (Comprehensive record of Fujian), 4.7.
43. Ibid.
44. *Xu chajing,* 816.
45. *Fujian tongzhi* (Comprehensive gazetteer of Fujian), 60.10.
46. See his *Cha kao* (Investigation of tea); Zheng Peikai and Zhu Zizhen 2007, 609.
47. Wu Zhihe 1980, 26.
48. Most of these teas are touched upon in Owyoung 2000.
49. Owyoung 2000, 32.
50. Wu Zhihe 1980, 2. On Xie Zhaozhe, see *Dictionary of Ming Biography,* 546–550.
51. *Liuyanzhai sanbi* (Notes from Liuyan studio, book 3), 4.6.
52. *Shaluo guan qingyan* (Pure speech from the Sala Hall), 1.
53. *Sishi youshang lu* (A record of the joys of seclusion through the four seasons), 18.
54. See his "Inscription on the Director of Tea" (*Chadong tici*), Zheng Peikai and Zhu Zizhen 2007, 371.
55. See *Wan-Ming ershi jia xiaopin* (Minor works by twenty late-Ming writers), 221, and Tu Benjun's *Mingji* (Tea shoots), 315.
56. *Gujin tushu jicheng* (Synthesis of illustrations and books past and present), vol. 87, p. 197.
57. *Shaluo guan qingyan,* 3a.
58. Wu Zhihe 1980, 10.
59. *Gujin tushu jicheng,* vol. 15, p. 917.
60. "Huang Nine" is a nickname of the Song poet and statesman Huang Tingjian.
61. *Paoweng jiazang ji* (Family storehouse collection of the Old Man of the Gourd), 4.53–54.
62. See Zhang Dai, "Old Man Min's Tea | China Heritage Quarterly," n.d. http://www.chinaheritagequarterly.org/features.php?searchterm=029_zhang.inc&issue=029. Also Spence 2007, 36–39, and Ye 1999, 88–90.
63. *Cha shu,* Zheng Peikai and Zhu Zizhen 2007, 274.
64. Du Lianzhe 1977, 255–256.
65. *Chaliao ji,* Zheng Peikai and Zhu Zizhen 2007, 223. Cf. English translation in Peltier 2011, 130.
66. *Chaliao ji,* 223.
67. *Yanzhou shanren xu gao* (Continued declarations of a mountain recluse from Yanzhou), 160.27.

68. Quoted in *Xu chajing*, 805.
69. *Chaliao ji*, 223.
70. Zheng Zhongkui, *Lengshang*, 6.1–2.
71. *Xu chajing*, 809.
72. *Xu chajing*, 766.
73. See, for example, *Zhuquan xiaopin*, 2.
74. For a brief introduction to Yuan and a selection of his travel writing, see Strassberg 1994, 303–312; see also Campbell 2002, 2003.
75. *Yuan Zhonglan quanji* (Complete works of Yuan Zhonglan), *youji*, 14. Translation by McDowall 2010 with modifications.
76. Zhu Pu, *Xicun shi ji, buyi*, 2.
77. *Gujin tushu jicheng*, 87.198.
78. *Mingzhai ji*, 10.127.
79. *Rongtai ji*, 2.38.
80. Wu Zhihe 1980, 8.
81. *Sishi youshang lu*, 1.
82. On Xu's travel writing, see Ward 2000.
83. *Dounan laoren ji*, 5.75b.
84. The references are to the Tang poets Du Fu and Han Yu and to Buddhist monks they praised in their writings. On Han Yu and Dadian, see Hartman 1986, 93–104.
85. The references are to the poet Tao Qian, one-time magistrate of Pengze, who loved alcohol, and the Chan master Zhaozhou, who commanded his student to "go drink tea!"
86. *Wutong ji*, 3.30b.
87. *Wulin youji* (Record of travels around Wulin), 5.
88. See Hu Kui's poem, "On a spring night caught in the rain I spend the night at the old monastery in Changzhou" (*Chunye yuyu su Changzhou gusi*), *Dounan laoren ji*, 5.42. Zhu Pu wrote, "On a spring night I passed by Ninghai monastery" (*Chunye guo Ninghai si*), *Lanjian ji*, 5.2.
89. *Wang Zhongshan xiansheng jixuan* (Selected poetry of Master Wang Zhongshan), 7.44.
90. *Shuliao guan ji*, 99.
91. *Xu chajing*, 813.
92. Sima Xiangru (179–127 BCE) was sometimes credited with listing tea as a product of his native Shu.
93. *Yimen guangdu*, 31.31.
94. *Xiangji* refers to the monastery kitchen.
95. *Bencao gangmu*, 1069.
96. *Chongyang an ji*, 17.33.
97. *Jingchuan xiansheng wenji*, 2.39.

Glossary

a 玖
Aicha ge 愛茶歌
An Lushan 安祿山

Bagong shan 八公山
baguan shiliuzi 八關十六子
Bai Juyi 白居易
Bai shi liutie shilei ji 白氏六帖事類集
Bai shi liutie 白氏六帖
Bai shi shouxia shi 白士首夏詩
Bai shi wenji 白士文集
baitang 白湯
baitu lou 白兔樓
baixi 百戲
Baiyun 白雲
Ban Cao shitang biji 判曹食堂壁記
Baolin zhuan 寶林傳
baoxing 寶形
Baoyan 寶嚴
Baoyun 寶雲
baye 八葉
bei 焙
Beiji qianjin yaofang 備急千金要方
Beiyuan 北苑
bencao 本草
Bencao gangmu 本草綱目
Bencao shiyi 本草拾遺
bian 辨
Biancai 辯才

Bianjing 汴京
Bianmin tuzuan 便民圖纂
Bingzhong shi xincha 病中試新茶
binlangzi 檳榔子
biqiu 比丘
bohe tang 薄荷湯
Boluo 博羅
bore tang 般若湯
Bowu zhi 博物志
Boxing 博興
boyeti 波夜提
Bu Wanqi 卜萬祺

Caicha ge 采茶歌
Caicha jisu sengshe 採茶寄宿僧舍
Caicha lu 採茶錄
Cai Xiang 蔡襄
Cai Xiji 蔡希寂
caoyao 草藥
Cen Shen 岑參
cha 茶
cha 搽 (entry in *Qimin yaoshu*)
chabang 茶榜
cha baixi 茶百戲
chabian 茶遍
chaci 茶詞
chadao 茶道
Chadong tici 茶董題詞
chafang 茶坊

237

Chagong shuo 茶共說
chaguo 茶果
chahu 茶戶
Chajing 茶經
Chajiu lun 茶酒論
Cha kao 茶考
chali 茶禮
chaliao 茶寮
Chaliao ji 茶寮記
chalou 茶樓
chalu 茶侶
Cha lu 茶祿
chalu 茶侶
chaming 茶茗
changcha 嘗茶
Changhua 昌化
Changlu 常魯
Changming 昌明
Changsheng 長城
Changxing 長興
Changzhou 常州
chanlin 禪林
cha no e 茶の会
cha no yoriai 茶の寄合
Cha-no-yu 茶の湯
Chanyuan qinggui 禪苑清規
Chapu 茶譜
chashen 茶神
chashi 茶室 (tea room)
chashi 茶社 (tea society)
chashitsu 茶室
Cha shu 茶疏 (Commentary on Tea)
Cha shu 茶述
Chashu quanji 茶書全集
chashu 茶書 (tea books)
Chashu quanji 茶書全集
Chashuo 茶說
chasi 茶肆
chatang 茶堂 (tea hall)
chatang 茶湯 (tea and decoction)
chatō 茶湯
chatuo 茶托
chaxian 茶筅

chayao 茶藥
cha yaowan 茶藥丸
Cha zhong zayong 茶中雜詠
chazhuang 茶狀
chen 塵
Chen Cangqi 陳藏器
Chengyuan 承遠
Chen Jiru 陳繼儒
Chen Wu 陳務
Chenyuan 貞元
cheqiancao 車前草
chi 尺
chicha 喫茶
chicha qu 喫茶去
chi cong xuefa 恥從削髮
Chifeng 赤峰
chijian 赤箭
Chi mingzhou zuo 喫茗粥作
Chongan 崇安
chongbing 虫病
Chongguo He shi wu shou 重過
    何氏
Chongxiu zhenghe jingshi zhenglei
    beiyong bencao 重修政和經史證類備
    用本草
Chongyang an ji 重陽庵集
Chou Letian xianwo jianji 酬樂天閑臥
    見寄
Chouyan shaoyin Xu sheren jianguo
    buyu 酬嚴少尹徐捨人見過不遇
Chu 楚
chuan 荈
Chuanfa yuan 傳法院
Chuanfa zhengzong ji 傳法正宗記
Chuan fu 荈賦
chuanming men 荈茗門
Chuci 楚辭
Chu Guangxi 儲光羲
Chuiyun 垂雲
Chunxi 淳熙
Chunye guo Ninghai si 春夜過寧海寺
Chunye ji Lu chushi ju wanyue 春夜集
    陸處士居玩月

Chunye yuyu su Changzhou gusi 春夜遇雨宿長州古寺

chuoming fan zhenji 啜茗翻真偈

Ciguang yuan 慈光院

cishi 刺史

Cishou chanshi shizong zhengui 慈受禪師示眾箴規

Congbi xie Meng jianyi ji xin cha 走筆謝孟諫議寄新茶

Cong Lu Hongjian fu Yue bing xu 送陸鴻漸赴越並序

Cui Guofu 崔國輔

Cui Yuanhan 崔元翰

dade 大德

Dafang 大方

Dafangguang huayan shi-e pin jing 大方廣華嚴十惡品經

Daguan bencao 大觀本草

Daguan chalun 大觀茶論

daguo 大國

Dahe 大和

Dahui Zonggao 大慧宗杲

Daicha xin yin fang 代茶新飲方

Daigensui daishō giki misshō 大元帥大將儀軌祕鈔

Daigensui hō 大元帥法

Dai Shulun 戴叔倫

Dai yincha xu 代飲茶序

Dajian chanshi xiao qinggui 大鑑禪師小清規

Dali 大歷

Daming shui ji 大明水記

Dangyan shan 當陽山

Danqiuzi 丹丘子

daoren 道人

Daoxuan 道宣

Da Tang xinyu 大唐新語

Da Tang zhuanzai 大唐傳載

Dazhidu lun 大智度論

Deng Chengdu lou shi 登成都樓詩

Deng Fuxian si shangfang Ran gong chanshi 登福先寺上方然公禪室

denglu 燈錄

Dexiang 德祥

Dezong 德宗

diancha 點茶

diancha sanmei 點茶三昧

diantang 點湯

dianxin 點心

ding 疔

dingchou 丁丑

Ding Jingshen 丁敬身

Dingzi 丁子

Dongjing menghua lu 東京夢華錄

Dongling 東陵

Dong Qichang 董其昌

Dongting 洞庭

dongzhi 冬至

doukou tang 豆蔻湯

Dounan laoren ji 斗南老人集

Duan Beizhi 段碨之

Duan jiu-ruo wen 斷酒肉文

Du Fu 杜甫

dugu 獨鈷

Dui Lu Xun yin Tianmu shan cha yin ji Yuan zhushi Sheng 對陸迅飲天目山茶因寄元居士晟

Du Jun 杜濬

Dunhuang 敦煌

dushu shi 讀書社

Du You 杜育

Eisai 栄西

Ennin 圓仁

erchen tang 二陳湯

Erya 爾雅

Fahai 法海

Famen si 法門寺

fan 煩

fangcan tang 放參湯

Fangle si 方樂寺

Fang Lu chushi Yu buyu 訪陸處士羽不遇

Fang seng buyu 訪僧不遇

Fang Xuanling 房玄齡
fannao 煩惱
Fanwang jing 梵網經
Fan Yunlin 范允臨
Fayao 法瑤
Fayuan zhulin 法苑珠林
fazuo 法座
fei 肥
Fei Wen 斐汶
Fenghuang 鳳凰
Feng Kaizhi 馮開之
Feng Mengzhen 馮夢禎
Feng Shike 馮時可
Fengshi wenjian ji 封氏聞見記
fengyao 風藥
Fozu lidai tongzai 佛祖歷代通載
Fucha shan shui ji 浮茶山水記
Fucheng 府城
Fu de yeyu kongdi jie song Lu Yu gui Long shan 賦得夜雨空滴階送陸羽歸龍山
Fujian tong ji 福建通紀
Fujin 福金
Fuling 涪陵
fuling 伏苓
fuling 茯苓 (poria cocos)
fuqi jueli 服氣絕粒
Fuquan 福全
Furong 芙蓉
Fu Xi 伏羲
Fuxian si 福先寺
Fuyang 富陽,

gancao 甘草
Ganhe 乾和
ganlu 甘露
gao 膏
Gao Jixing 高季興
Gao Lian 高濂
Gao Lishi 高力士
gaolu 皋盧
Gao Panlong 高攀龍
Gaoseng zhuan 高僧傳

Gaoyang 高陽
Gaozu 高祖
goko 五鈷
gong'an 公案
gongcha 貢茶
Gonggong 共工
Gounu 苟奴
Gozō mandara giki shō 五藏曼荼羅儀軌抄
guada 掛搭
guanbei 官焙
Guang Fan 鄺璠
Guang Hongming ji 廣弘明集
Guangling qilao zhuan 廣陵耆老傳
Guangya 廣雅
Guangzhi 廣智
Guangzhou ji 廣州記
Guan xiao wen 觀孝文
Guanyin 觀音
gui 鬼
guichou 癸丑
guihai 癸亥
guihua tang 桂花湯
guimao 癸卯
Guo Lu Hongjian jiuju 過陸鴻漸舊居
Guoluo cha 過羅茶
Guo Pu 郭璞
Guoqing si 國清寺
Guoshi bu 國史補
Guoyu 國語
Gushan 鼓山
gushi 穀食
Gu Yanwu 顧炎武
guyu 穀雨
Guzhou 顧州
Guzhu shan 顧渚山
Guzhu shan ji 顧渚山記

Handi 漢地
Hang 杭
Hangzhou fu 杭州府
Hanjia 漢家
Han shu 漢書

Hedong 河東

Hei shan 墨山

Henan Yan yin di jian su pilu fang bieren fu shiyun 河南嚴尹弟見宿弊廬訪別人賦十韻

He Yanzhi 何延之

heye tang 荷葉湯

hōgyō 寶形

Hōin dai kashō-i 法印大和尚位

Honglou meng 紅樓夢

Hongming ji 弘明集

houpo tang 厚朴湯

Hu (river) 湖

hua chafang 花茶坊

Huainan 淮南

Huainanzi 淮南子

Huaisu 懷素

Huamu zhi 華木志

Huang Ru 黃儒

Huang Tingjian 黃庭堅

Huangfu Ran 皇甫冉

Huangfu Song 皇甫松

Huangfu Zeng 皇甫曾

huangqi 黃耆

Hua shan 華山

Hua Tuo shilun 華陀食論

Huayang guozhi 華陽國志

Huazhou 滑州 (present-day Hua County in Henan)

Huazhou 華州

Huihong 惠洪

Huineng 慧能

Huishan 惠山

Huishan si ji 惠山寺記

huishi 會食

huixiang tang 茴香湯

Huixie 詼諧

Huizhen 慧真

Huizhou fu 徽州

Huizong 徽宗

Hu jushi shizhi 壺居士食志

Hu Kui 胡奎

hun 魂

Huo zhi pin 貨之品

Hupao quan 虎跑泉

Huqiu 虎丘

Huqiu 虎邱 (name of tea)

Huqiu shan zhi 虎丘山志

Huqiu si 虎邱寺

huzhang 虎杖

Huzhou 湖州

Huzhou cishi ji 湖州刺史記

Huzhou Wucheng xian Zhu shan Miaoxi si beiming 湖州烏程縣杼山妙喜寺碑銘

Ji 疾 (personal name)

Ji 積

jia 櫃

Jia Baoyu 賈寶玉

jiachi 加持

Jia Ming 賈銘

jian 盞

Jian'an 建安

jiancha 煎茶

Jiancha shui ji 煎茶水記

Jian chi 劍池

jiandian 煎點

Jianfu si 薦福寺

Jiangling 江陸

Jiangning 江寧縣

jiangyan cha 姜鹽茶

Jian Huiquan fu 煮惠泉賦

Jianning fu 建寧府

Jiantang 錢唐

Jianxi 建溪

jianyu 漸愉

Jianzhou 建州

Jiaojie xinxue biqiu xinghu lü yi 教誡新學比丘行護律儀

Jiaonü shi 嬌女詩

jiaoqi 脚氣

Jiaoran 皎然

Jiatai Kuaiji zhi 嘉泰會稽志

Jici 季疵

jie 岕 (cleft)

jie 節 (node)

jiegeng 桔梗

Jietan si 戒壇寺

jiexia 結夏 （beginning of summer）

jiexia 解夏 (end of summer)

Jigu lu bawei 集古錄跋尾

Ji Huiquan 記惠泉

jin 斤

Jin 晉

jing 精

jing 靜 (quiet)

Jingang jing zhujie 金剛經註解

Jingchuan xiansheng wenji 荊川先生
    文集

Jingde chuandeng lu 景德傳燈錄

Jingling 竟陵

Jing shan 徑山

Jingtu si 淨土寺

Jingzhou 荊州

Jingzhou tudi ji 荊州土地記

Jinhua 金華

jinjie cha 金桔茶

Jin shu 晉書

Jin ting 進艇

Jin Wudi 晉武帝

Jinxiang 金鄉

Jin Xiaowu 晉孝武

Jin Yuandi 晉元帝

jiu 酒 (alcohol)

jiu 韭 (Chinese chives)

jiu 久 (long-lasting)

jiu 九 (nine)

Jiu de song 酒德頌

jiuling 酒令

jiuqu 九區

Jiushan sanqiao zhuan 九山散樵傳

Jiuyun 九醞

Jiuzhen guan 九真觀

jiuzhou 九州

Jizhu fenlei Dongpo shi 集注分類東
    坡詩

Jōjin 成尋

juewei 蕨薇

Juhua 菊花

Jun shan 君山

junzi 君子

jupi tang 橘皮湯

Kai 楷

Kaiyuan 開元

Kaiyuan shijiao lu 開元釋教錄

Kannon 觀音

Kaopan yushi 考槃余事

Kenpo 建保

Kissa yōjōki 喫茶養生記

kōjutsu 甲戌

Kou Zongshi 寇宗奭

ku 苦

Kuaiji dong xiaoshan 會稽東小山

kucai 苦菜

ku cha 苦茶

Kunlun 崑崙

kuping 苦平

kusi 庫司

kutu 苦荼

lacha 蠟茶

Lanjian ji 藍澗集

Lanting ji xu 蘭亭集序

Lanting shimo ji 蘭亭始末記

lao 酪

laojiang 酪漿

Lengshang 冷賞

leng yinzi 冷飲子

li 禮

liang 涼

Liang Wudi 梁武帝

Li Ao 李翱

Li Bai 李白

Li Chongzhao 李沖昭

lichun 立春

Lidai minghua ji 歷代名畫記

Li Dechui 李德垂

Li Fengji 李逢吉

Li Fu 李復

Li Hua 李華

Li Jiayou 李嘉祐
Li Jilan 李季蘭
Li Jiqing 李季卿
Lin Daiyu 林黛玉
ling 靈
Lingche 靈徹
Lingyan si 靈嚴寺
Lin Hong 林洪
Li Qiwu 李齊物
Li Rihua 李日華
Li Shichen 李時珍
Liu Bochu 劉伯芻
liugen 六根
liuhua 流華
Liu Jingshu 劉敬叔
Liu Ling 劉伶
liuqing 六情 (six feelings)
liuqing 六清 (six liquids)
Liuyanzhai sanbi 六研齋三筆
Liu Yuxi 劉禹錫
Liu Zhongyong 柳中庸
Liu Ziluan 劉子鸞
Li Ye 李冶
Li Zhao 李肇
Longgai si 龍蓋寺
Longhong 龍泓
Longjing 龍井
Longquan 龍泉
Longshan 龍山
Longxing si 龍興寺
Lu 陸
lücha 綠茶
Lu Ji 陸璣
Lunyu 論語
Lunyu yuzhu 論語玉柱
Luo 羅
Luojie 羅岕
Luojie chaji 羅岕茶記
Luoyang qielan ji 洛陽伽藍記
Lu San 陸三
Lüshi chunqiu 呂氏春秋
Lu Shusheng 陸樹聲
Lu Tingcan 陸廷燦

Lu Tong 盧仝
Lü Wen 呂溫
Lu Wenxue zizhuan 陸文學自傳
Lu Yu 陆羽
Lu Yu chaquan 陸羽茶泉
Lu Yu shijin 陸羽石井

mao 凨
Mao shan 茅山
Maoshi 毛詩
*Maoshi cao mu niao shou chong yu
   shu* 毛詩草木鳥獸蟲魚疏
mei 美 (delicious)
mei 魅 (goblin)
meilie 昧劣
Mei Zhixian 梅志暹
Mengcai 孟載
Meng Jiao 孟郊
mian 麵
Miaoxi si 妙喜寺
Miaoyu 妙玉
Min 閩
ming 命 (destiny)
ming 茗
Mingcao 茗草
Mingji 茗苡
Mingliang 明亮
mingmi 茗糜
Ming shuo 茗說
Mingxiang ji 冥祥記
Mingyi bielu 名醫別錄
mingyin 茗飲
Mingzhai ji 茗齋集
mingzhi 茗汁
Mingzhou 明州
Min Wenshui 閔汶水
Mituo si 彌陀寺
Mohe zhiguan 摩訶止観
moshi 末世
Mo Shilong 莫是龍
Mozi 墨子
mu 畝
Mujaku Dōchū 無著道忠

*Muqiu hui Yan jingzhao houting
   zhuzhai* 暮秋會嚴京兆後廳竹齋
*Mushou Jingling yin you sita zhu san
   huoshuo* 牧守竟陵因遊西塔著三感說
muxiang tang 木香湯
Myōan Eisai 明菴栄西

Nancheng fu 南城賦
nanmu 南木
Nan Qi shu 南齊書
nanren 南人
Nanyang 南陽
Nanyue xiaolu 南嶽小錄
Nanyue zhi 南越志
Nei 內
Nianchang 念常
niansong tang 念誦湯
Ning 寧
niuxi gen 牛膝根
nongjia 農家
Nüwa 女媧

Oolong 烏龍
ou 甌
Ouyang Xiu 歐陽修

Pao weng 鮑翁
Paoweng jiazang ji 鮑翁家藏集
Pei Di 裴迪
Pei Fangzhou 裴方舟
Pei Ji 裴濟
peike 陪客
Pei Wen 裴汶
Pei Xuanren 裴玄仁
pengcha 烹茶
Penglai 蓬萊
Pengshan 彭山
Peng Sunyi 彭孫貽
pengtu 烹茶
piancha 片茶
pincha 品茶
Pincha yaolu 品茶要錄
ping 瓶

Pi Rixiu 皮日休
po 魄
poqi tang 破氣湯
pu 酺
Puguang 溥光
Puji 普濟
Putao 蒲桃

qi 氣
Qi 齊
Qian 謙
Qian Chu 錢俶
qiangwei 薔薇
Qianjin yifang 千金翼方
Qian Qi 錢起
Qian Qianyi 錢謙益
Qian shan 鉛山
Qian Shuoyou 潛說友
Qiantang 錢塘
Qiao Cui Shi shijun 誚崔石使君
Qiji 齊己
Qimen 蘄門
Qimin yaoshu 齊民要術
qin 琴
qingcha 青茶
qinggui 清規
Qingming 清明
qingmuxiang 青木香
qingtan 清談
Qingtang 青塘
Qin Guan 秦觀
Qingyi lu 清異錄
Qingyuan 清源
Qingzhuo Zhengcheng 清拙
   正澄
Qin Jing 秦精
Qiongjiang 瓊漿
Qipan ding 棋盤頂
Qipo 耆婆
Qiu Jun 丘濬
*Qiuri guo Hongju fashi siyuan, bian
   song gui Jiangling* 秋日過鴻舉法師寺
   院，便送歸江陵

Qiuxiao Zhaoyin si dongfeng chayan song neidi Yan Bojun gui Jiangzhou 秋曉招隱寺東峰茶宴送內弟閻伯均歸江州

Qiuye shicha 秋夜試茶

Qiu Zhangru 丘長孺

Qixia shan 棲霞山

Quan Deyu 權德輿

Quan Henan Yin fugu shi shu 勸河南尹復故事書

Quan Tang shi 全唐詩

Qu sheng fangsu 麴生訪宿

ren 仁

Renhe 仁和,

Renshou 仁壽

Rizhi lu 日知祿

Rizhu 日鑄

Rongtai ji 容臺集

Rongzhou 容州

Ruiying tuji 瑞應圖記

Runan 汝南

Runzhou 潤州

sancha 散茶

sancha heshang 三茶和尚

san gui 三桂 (three types of cassia)

San gui 三葵

Sanguo zhi 三國志

sangzhou 桑粥

sanhuang 三皇

Sanshu shitchi hajigoku tengosshō shutsusangai himitsu darani kō 三種悉地破地獄轉業障出三界秘密陀羅尼法

San Tendai Godaisan ki 參天台五臺山記

Saoxue pengcha wanhua 掃雪烹茶玩畫

sarei 茶禮

sengtang nei jiandian 僧堂內煎點

shacha 煞茶

Shaluo guan qingyan 娑羅館清言

Shamini jie jing 沙彌尼戒經

Shan Daokai 單道開

Shandong 山東

Shanfu 膳夫

Shanfu jing shoulu 膳夫經手錄

Shangqing 上清

Shangrao 上饒

shangsi 上巳

Shanhai jing 山海經

Shanjia qinggong 山家清供

Shan Qianzhi 山謙之

Shan quan jian cha you huai 山泉煎茶有懷

Shanseng hui cha 山僧惠茶

Shantang duike shi songzi jianming 山堂對客拾松子煮茗

Shanwuwei 善無畏

shanyao 山藥

shao 少

Shaoxing 紹興

she 蔎

shelun 設論

shen 神

shengjiang tang 生薑湯

Shenglian shi 勝蓮社

shengsheng 生生

Shen Huaiyuan 沈懷遠

Shennong 神農

Shennong bencao jing 神農本草經

Shennong Huangdi shijin 神農黃帝食禁

Shennong jing 神農經

Shennong qiuyu shu 神農求雨書

Shennong shi jing 神農食經

Shen Shitian 沈石田

Shen Taizhen 沈台真

shenxiang 沈香

Shenyi ji 神異記

Shen Zhou 沈周

Shen Zuobin 沈作賓

shexiang 麝香

shi 事 (records)

shi 嗜 ("have a passion for something")

shi 詩 (poetry)

Shiguo Chunqiu 十國春秋

Shi hou 食後

Shiji 史記

shiji 食忌

Shijing 詩經

Shiliao bencao 食療本草

Shiliu tang pin 十六湯品

Shimen 石門

Shimen wenzi Chan 石門文字禪

Shindo isho 新度醫書

Shishuo xinyu 世說新語

Shi Su 施宿

shitang 食堂

Shi Yiguang 施夷光

Shizhu piposha lun 十住毘婆沙論

Shizu Wu 世祖武

Shōsōrin ryaku shingi 小叢林略清規

shou 瘦

shouming 守命

Shouyong sanshui yaoxing fa 受用三水
    要行法

Shouzhou 壽州

Shu 蜀

shuangjing 雙井

Shui jing 水經

Shui pin 水品

Shu Jiecha bielun 書芥茶別論

Shu Jiecha bielun hou 書芥茶別論後

Shuliao guan ji 輸寮館集

Shuofu 說郛

shuowang zuntang cha 朔望巡堂茶

shuyu tang 薯蕷湯

Shu zhi 蜀志

Shuzhou 舒州

Shu zhucha quan pin 述煮茶全品

Sibei shi 四悲詩

sida 四大

Sifen lü 四分律

Sili jiao 司隸教

sima 司馬

Sima Chengzhen 司馬承貞

Siming zunzhe jiaoxing lu 四明尊者教
    行錄

siseng yuanhu 寺僧園戶

Sishi youshang lu 四時幽賞錄

sōjō 僧正

Song gaoseng zhuan 宋高僧傳

Song Huizong 宋徽宗

Song lu 宋錄

Song Lu Hongjian Qixia si cai cha 送陸
    鴻漸棲霞寺采茶

Song Lu Hongjian shanren cai cha hui
    送陸鴻漸山人採茶回

Songluo 松蘿

Song shan 嵩山

Song Xiaowudi 宋孝武帝

Sonshō darani hajigoku hō misshō
    尊勝陀羅尼破地獄法秘鈔

sōtō 桑湯

Soushen houji 搜神後記

Soushen ji 搜神記

sui 歲

Suiren 燧人

Sui Yangdi 隋煬帝

Su Jing 蘇敬

Sun Chuo 孫綽

Sun Hao 孫皓

Sun Rouzhi 孫柔之

Sun Simiao 孫思邈

sushi 宿食

Su Shi 蘇軾

Su Yi 蘇廙

Su Yu 蘇虞

Suzhou 蘇州

Suzong 肅宗

Taichang si taizhu 太常寺太祝

Taiping guangji 太平廣記

Taiping huimin heji jufang 太平惠民和
    劑局方

Taiping xingguo si 太平興國寺

Taiping yulan 太平御覽

Taiping yulan yinshi bu 太平御覽飲食部

Taishan 泰山

Taiyi 太一

Taiyuan 太原

Taizi wenxue 太子文學

Taizong 太宗

Taizu 太祖

tang 湯

tangbang 湯榜
tangbian 湯遍
Tang caizi zhuan 唐才子傳
Tang da zhaoling ji 唐大詔令集
Tangdu 唐都
Tanggong shan 唐貢山
Tang huiyao 唐會要
tangjian 湯盞
Tang Jiaoran shiji 唐皎然詩集
tangli 湯禮
tangmo 湯末
Tang pin 湯品
Tangren wushijia xiaoji 唐人五十家小集
Tang Shenwei 唐慎微
tangshi 湯社
Tang shi 唐史
Tang shiliu fa 湯十六法
Tang Shun 唐順
tangtou 堂頭
tangtou shizhe 堂頭侍者
Tangtu 唐土
Tang Wenfeng 唐文鳳
tangyao 湯藥
Tang yulin 唐語林
Tang yunzheng 唐韻正
Tanxiao 談笑
Tao Gu 陶穀
Tao Hongjing 陶弘景
Taohua yuan shi 桃花源詩
Tao Yuanming 陶淵明
Tao Zongyi 陶宗儀
Tianbao 天寶
Tianchi 天池
Tianmen 天門
Tianmen xianzhi 天門縣誌
Tianmu 天目
Tianning si 天寧寺
Tiantai ji 天台記
Tiantai Zhiyi 天臺智顗
Tian Yiheng 田藝蘅
Tian zhi weiming fu 天之未明賦
Tianzhu 天竺

Tiaoxi 苕溪
Ti Lu Hongjian Shangrao xinkai shan she 題陸鴻漸上饒新開山舍
tishen cha 替身茶
Ti shujing shi 題書經室
Tongjun caiyao lu 桐君採藥錄
Tongjun lu 桐君錄
Tongjun yao lu 桐君採藥錄
Tong yue 僮約
tu 茶
Tu Benjun 屠本畯
Tu Long 屠隆
Tu Zhangqing 屠長卿

Waitai miyao 外臺秘要
Wang 王
Wang Anshi 王安石
Wang Bao 王褒
Wang Dan 王讜
Wang Danyang cun Lu chushi buyu 往丹陽尋陸處士不遇
Wang Fu 王敷 (author of *Chajiu lun*)
Wang Fu 王浮
Wang Ji 王績
wangliang 魍魎
Wang Rixiu 王日休
Wang Shizhen 王世貞
Wang Su 王肅
Wang Tao 王燾
Wang Wei 王維
Wang Wen 王問
Wang Xianqiao 王仙喬
Wang Xizhi 王羲之
Wang Yan 王琰
Wang Yanzhou 王弇州 (aka Wang Shizhen 王世貞)
Wang Yi 王逸
Wang Zhongshan xiansheng jixuan 王仲山先生詩選
Wang Zi 王梓
Wanli 萬曆
Wan-Ming ershi jia xiaopin 晚明二十家小品

Wei 魏
Wei Huacun 魏華存
Wei Shu 魏舒
Weiyang 維揚
Wei Yao 韋曜
Wei Yingwu 韋應物
Wei Zhao 韋昭
Wen 溫
Wenliao 文了
Wen Tingyun 溫廷筠
Wen xuan 文選
wenxun 問訊
wenyibing 溫疫病
Wenyuan yinghua 文苑英華
Wen Yun 溫雲
Wen Zhengming 文徵明
Wu 吳
wucan shangtang cha 五參上堂茶
Wuchang shan 武昌山
Wucheng 烏程
Wu Congxian 吳從先
Wudeng huiyuan 五燈會元
Wudu 武都
Wuen 晤恩
wugu 五鈷
Wu huangdi 武皇帝
Wu Jiong 毋煚
Wukang 武康
Wu Kuan 吳寬
Wulin jiushi 武林舊事
Wulin youji 武林遊記
wunei 五內
Wu Sheng 吳生
Wutai shan 五臺山
Wutong ji 梧岡集
Wuwei 武威
wuwei tang 五味湯
Wuxi 無錫
wuxing 五行
Wuxing 吳興
Wuxing ji 吳興記
Wuxing liguan ji 吳興歷官記
Wuxue diancha 無學點茶

Wuyan yueye chuocha lianju 五言月夜
  啜茶聯句
Wuyang 武陽
Wuyi 武夷
Wuyi Songluo 武夷松蘿
wuzang 五藏
Wu Zetian 武則天

Xiahou Kai 夏侯愷
Xian jing 仙經
xiancha houtang 先茶後湯
Xianchun lin'an zhi 咸淳臨安志
xiang 想
xiang'an 香案
xianggong jinshi 鄉貢進士
xiangji 香積
Xianglin 香林
xianglu 香爐
Xianglu feng xia xinzhi caotang 香爐峰
  下新置草堂
Xiangmo 降魔
Xiangmo Zang 降魔藏
xianren 仙人
xianrenchang cha 仙人掌茶
Xianya zhuan 仙芽傳
Xiaoshan si 小山寺
Xiaoshi 孝師
Xiao Tong 蕭統
Xiao Yi 蕭翼
Xiao yuanwai ji xin Shu cha 蕭員外寄
  新蜀茶
Xicun shi ji 西村詩集
Xie Hu bandu fang Ji shangren 偕胡伴
  讀訪繼上人
Xie Li liu langzhong ji xin Shu cha
  謝李六郎中寄新蜀茶
Xie Zhaozhe 謝肇浙
Xie Zhaozhe 謝肇淛 (alternative
  characters for personal name)
Xiji 義寂
Xin'an wang 新安王
xing 性
xingcha 行茶

Xingsheng wanshou si 興聖萬壽禪寺

xingshuang tang 杏霜湯

xingtang 行湯

xingxiang 行香

xingxing 猩猩

Xin lu 新錄

xinnian 新年

Xinpo 新坡,

Xin Tang shu 新唐書

Xin Wenfang 辛文房

Xinxiu bencao 新修本草

Xinzhou 信州

Xiong Mingyu 熊明遇

Xi shan lanruo shicha ge 西山蘭若試茶歌

Xi Shi 西施

Xi ta 西塔

Xiuning 休寧

Xiuwu 脩務

Xi Yixing Quan mingfu zi Junshan zhi, ji Lu chushi Yu qiantang bieye 喜義興權明府自君山至, 集陸處士羽青塘別業

Xi yuanzhong cha sheng 喜園中茶生

Xi yue yuntai ge song Danqiuzi 西岳雲台歌送丹丘子

Xu Bo 徐勃[火+勃]

Xu chajing 續茶經

Xu Cishu 許次紓 (*zi* Ranming 然明)

Xu daoren 徐道人

Xu Gaoseng zhuan 續高僧傳

Xu Jingzong 許敬宗

Xu Maowu 徐茂吳

Xu mingseng zhuan 續名僧傳

Xu soushen ji 續搜神記

Xu Xiake 徐霞客

Xu Xianzhong 徐獻忠

Xu Yanzu 許延族

Xu Zhenqing 徐禎卿

Xuan宣 (King)

Xuancheng 宣城

Xuanhe beiyuan gongcha lu 宣和北苑貢茶錄

Xuanji 懸濟

Xuanjian 玄鑒

Xuanshi shan 玄石山

Xuanzhen zi waipian 玄真子外篇

Xuanzhen zi 玄真子

Xuanzong 玄宗

Xue Baochai 薛寶釵

Xuetan 謔談

Xue Yingqi 薛應旂

xunlu 薰爐

xunlu 薰陸 (fragrance)

xuntang chicha 巡堂喫茶

yaming 牙茗

Yan 剡 (county)

Yan Bojun 閻伯均

yancha 巖茶

Yancong 彥琮

Yandi 炎帝

Yang 楊 (surname)

Yang Ye 楊曄

yangsheng yinliao 養生飲料

yangu tang 鹽鼓湯

Yanguan 鹽官,

yanshou tangzhu 延壽堂主

Yangxian 陽羨

Yangzhou 揚州

Yan Liben 閻立本

Yan Zhenqing 顏真卿

Yan Zhitui 顏之推

Yanzhou shanren xu gao 弇州山人續稿

Yanzhu 顏渚

Yaoxing lun 藥性論

Ye Qingchen 葉清臣

Ye wen Jia Changzhou, Cui Huzhou, chashan jinghui xiang xian huan yan yin ji ci shi 夜聞賈常州、崔湖州茶山境會想羨歡宴因寄此詩

yi 易 (change)

yi 義

Yijing 易經 (Change Classic)

Yijing 義淨 (monk)

Yimen guangdu 夷門廣牘
yin 飲 (drink)
yin 淫 (excessive)
Yin cha ge song Zheng Rong 飲茶歌送
鄭容
Yingtian 應天
Yinhua lu 因話錄
Yinshi xu zhi 飲食須知
yinyi zhuan 隱逸傳
yinzi 飲子
Yishu zhuan 藝術傳
Yiwen leiju 藝文類聚
yiwen zhi 藝文志
Yixing (county) 義興
Yixing 宜興
Yiyuan 異苑
yizhi tang 益智湯
yong 癰
Yonghu 邕湖
Yongjia 永嘉
Yongming 永明
Youche 油車
You longjing ji 遊龍井記
Youpose jie jing 優婆塞戒經
youpose wujie 優婆塞五戒
You Tiantai shan fu 遊天台山賦
yu (region) 域
Yu 玉
Yuan Danqiu 元丹丘
Yuan Zhen 元稹
Yuan Zhonglan quanji 袁中郎全集
Yuan Zhonglang 袁中郎 (*zi* Hongdao
宏道)
Yuanming 元明
Yuanyou 遠遊
Yuanzhen zi 元真子
yucha 浴茶
Yuezhou 越州
Yuhang 餘杭
Yu Hong 虞洪
Yunhai jingyuan 韻海鏡源
Yunji qiqian 雲笈七籤
yunmu 雲母

Yunmuquan si 雲母泉寺
Yunquan daoren 雲泉道人
Yuqian 於潛
yuqian 雨前 (before the rains)
Yuquan si 玉泉寺
Yuyao 餘姚
Yuzhang 豫章
Yu Zhao Ju chayan 與趙莒茶讌
Yu Zheng 喻政
Yu zhuke kongfu yin 與諸客空腹飲
yuzhu 浴主

Za lu 雜錄
zaochun 早春
Zao fu yunmu san 早服雲母散
zao tang 棗湯
Zeng 鄭
Zeng jiancha seng 贈煎茶僧
Zeng Wu guan 贈吳官
Zenrin shōkisen 禪林象器箋
Zhang Dafu 張大復
Zhang Dai 張岱
Zhang Heng 張衡
Zhang Hua 張華
Zhang Ji 張籍
Zhang Mengyang 張孟陽
Zhang Qiande 張謙德
zhangre 瘴熱
zhangtu 掌荼
Zhangxing zhou 長興州
Zhang Yi 張揖
Zhang Youxin 張又新
Zhang Zhihe 張志和
Zhangzhou 長洲
Zhanran 湛然
Zhao 趙
Zhao Ju 趙莒
Zhao Lin 趙璘
Zhaoyin si 招隱寺
Zhaozhou Congshen 趙州從諗
Zhejiang 浙江
Zhejiang tongzhi 浙江通志
zhen 貞

Zhen'gao 真誥
Zheng Dan 鄭旦
Zhenghe 政和
Zhenghe bencao 政和本草
Zhenglei bencao 証類本草
Zhen gong 真公
Zhengtang dushu ji 鄭堂讀書記
Zheng Zhong 鄭众
Zheng Zhongkui 鄭仲夔
Zhenjiang 鎮江
zhi 致 (send)
zhi 志 (will)
zhi 智 (wisdom)
Zhide 至德
Zhi Dun 支遁
zhiguai 志怪
Zhihui 智慧
Zhiji 智積
Zhili 直隸
zhishi cha 執事茶
zhizi 梔子
Zhi Ziyuan 支子元
Zhongfu 中孚
Zhong Lichun 鐘離春
Zhongnan 終南
Zhou 酎
zhoucha 洲茶
Zhou Fang 周昉
Zhouli 周禮
Zhou Mi 周密
Zhou shu 周書
Zhou Yuan 周願
Zhou Zhongfu 周中孚
Zhuangzi 莊子

Zhucha ji 煮茶記
Zhu Ci 朱泚
Zhulin si 竹林寺
Zhu Pu 朱樸
Zhuqian shengren 竺乾聖人
Zhu Quan 朱權
Zhuquan xiaopin 煮泉小品
Zhurong 祝融
Zhu Rukui 朱汝奎
Zhushan ji 杼山集
Zhu Xi 朱熹
Zhuye 竹葉
Zhu Yuanzheng 朱元璋
Ziluan 子鸞
Zimen jingxun 緇門警訓
Zishang 子尚
Zishou 資壽
zisu tang 紫蘇湯
Zitong 子同
Ziyuan 子元
Zizhi tongjian 資治通鑑
Zoubi xie Meng jianyi ji xin cha 走筆謝
　孟諫議寄新茶
Zou Runfu 鄒潤甫
Zou Zhen 鄒湛
zui lou 醉樓
Zuixiang ji 醉鄉記
Zuixiang riyue 醉鄉日月
Zuiyin xiansheng zhuan 醉飲先
　生傳
Zuo Si 左思
Zuowang lun 坐忘論
Zuozhuan 左傳
Zuting shiyuan 祖庭事苑

Bibliography

PRIMARY SOURCES

Baishi liutie shilei ji 白氏六帖事類集 (Categorized collection of Mr. Bai's six categories), reprint of Song edition, 2 vols. Taipei: Xinxing, 1961.

Beiji qianjin yaofang 備急千金要方 (Revised essential prescriptions worth a thousand in gold) by Sun Simiao 孫思邈, (581–682). Taibei: Zhongguo yiyao yanjiusuo, 1990.

Bencao gangmu 本草綱目 (Guidelines and details of *materia medica*) by Li Shizhen 李時珍 (1518–93). Beijing: Renmin weisheng chubanshe, 1982.

Bianmin tuzuan 便民圖纂 (Collection of pictures for the convenience of the people), attr. Guang Fan 鄺璠. Beijing: Nongye chubanshe, 1982.

Bowuzhi jiaozheng 博物志校證 (Annotated critical edition of a vast record of things), comp. Zhang Hua 張華 third century, edited by Fan Ning 范寧. Beijing: Zhonghua shuju, 1980.

Cen Shen ji jiaozhu 岑參集校注 (Critical annotated edition of collected works of Cen Shen) by Cen Shen 岑參 (8th cent.), edited by Chen Tiemin 陳鐵民. Shanghai: Shanghai guji chubanshe, 1981.

Chajing 茶經 (Classic of Tea) by Lu Yu 陆羽 (733–804). In Zheng Peikai and Zhu Zizhen 2007.

Cha kao 茶考 (Investigation of tea) by Xu Bo 徐勃[火+勃] (1570–1645). In Zheng Peikai 鄭培凱 and Zhu Zizhen 朱自振, *Zhongguo lidai chashu huibian jiaozhu ben* 中國歷代茶書匯編校注本 (Collected annotated edition of works on tea from Chinese history). Hong Kong: Shangwu yinshu guan, 2007.

Cha lu 茶錄 (Records of tea) by Feng Shike 馮時可 (*jinshi* 1571). In Zheng Peikai and Zhu Zizhen 2007.

Cha shu 茶疏 (Commentary on Tea). In Zheng Peikai and Zhu Zizhen 2007.

Chongxiu zhenghe jingshi zhenglei beiyong bencao 重修政和經史證類備用本草 (Re-edited Zhenghe period practical *materia medica* divided by category from the histories and classics) by Tang Shenwei 唐慎微 (11th/12th century). Beijing: Renmin weisheng chubanshe, 1957.

Chongyang an ji 重陽庵集 (Collection of double-yang chapel). Shanghai: Shanghai shudian, 1994.

Chuci jiaoshi 楚辭校釋 (Songs of Chu, annotated) by Wang Siyuan 王泗原. Beijing: Xinhua shudian, 1990.

Congshu jicheng 叢書集成 (Complete collection of books from [various] collectanea). Shanghai: Commercial Press, 1935–1937.

Da Tang xinyu 大唐新語 (New tales of the great Tang), 13 *juan,* compiled by Liu Su 劉肅 (fl. ca. 820). Beijing: Zhonghua shuju, 1984.

Dongjing menghua lu 東京夢華錄 (Dream of the splendors of the eastern capital) by Meng Yuanlao 孟元老. *SKQS* edn.

Dounan laoren ji 斗南老人集 (Collection of the old man south of the dipper) by Hu Kui 胡奎 (ca. 1331–ca. 1405). Taibei: Taiwan shangwu yinshuguan, 1974.

Fengshi wenjian ji jiaozhu 封氏聞見記校注 (Record of things seen and heard by Mister Feng, collated and annotated), 10 *juan,* by Feng Yan 封演, *jinshi* 756. Collated and annotated by Zhao Zhenxin 趙貞信. Beijing: Zhonghua shuju, 1958.

Fujian tong ji 福建通紀 (Comprehensive record of Fujian). Taibei: Datong shuju, 1968.

Fujian tongzhi 福建通志 (Comprehensive gazetteer of Fujian). Taibei: Huawen shuju, 1968.

Gujin tushu jicheng 古今圖書集成 (Synthesis of illustrations and books past and present), 10,000 *juan,* compiled by Chen Menglei 陳夢雷, Jiang Tingxi 蔣廷錫, et al., presented to the emperor in 1725, Palace edition of 1726. Reprinted Chengdu, Zhonghua shuju and Bashu shushe, 1985, 82 vols.

Han shu 漢書 (Book of the [former] Han), covering the period of the Former Han (206 BCE–8 CE) and of Wang Mang's Xin dynasty (9–23); 120 *juan,* compiled 58–76 by Ban Gu 班固 (32–92). Beijing: Zhonghua shuju, 1962.

Huainanzi zhuzi suoyin 淮南子 逐字 索引 (*A Concordance to the Huainanzi*) by D. C. Lau et al. Hong Kong: Commercial Press, 1982.

Huayang guozhi jiaobu tuzhu 華陽國志校補圖注 (Record of the land of Huayang, critical edition, supplemented and annotated) by Chang Qu 常璩, collated and annotated by Ren Naijiang 任乃強. Beijing: Zhonghua shuju, 1987.

Huqiu shan zhi 虎丘山志 (Gazetteer of Huqiu shan). Haikou: Hainan chubanshe, 2001.

Jiatai Kuaiji zhi 嘉泰會稽志 (Kuaiji gazetteer of the Jiatai reign period [1201–1204]), completed in 1201 by Shen Zuobin 沈作賓 and Shi Su 施宿. *SKQS* edn.

Jigu lu bawei 集古錄跋尾 (Colophons to record of collecting antiquities) by Ouyang Xiu in *Ouyang Xiu quanji* 歐陽修全集 (Collected works of Ouyang Xiu). Beijing: Zhonghua shuju, 2001.

Jingchuan xiansheng wenji 荊川先生文集 (Collection of the Master of Jingchuan). Taibei: Taiwan shangwu yinshuguan, 1967.

Jin shu 晉書 (Book of Jin, 265–419), 130 *juan*, decreed 644, compiled 646–648 by Fang Xuanling 房玄齡 (578–648) et al. Beijing: Zhonghua, 1974.

Jizhu fenlei Dongpo shi 集注分類東坡詩 (Collected and annotated poems of [Su] Dongpo, arranged by category) by Wang Shipeng 王十朋 (1112–1171). Shanghai: Shangwu yinshu guan, 1922.

Kaopan yushi 考槃余事 (Desultory remarks on furnishing the abode of the retired scholar) by Tu Long 屠隆 (*zi*, Zhangqing 長卿, 1543–1605). Beijing: Zhonghua shuju, 1985.

Lanjian ji 藍澗集 (Orchid gully collection) by Zhu Pu 朱樸 (1339–1381). *SKQS* edn.

Lidai minghua ji 歷代名畫記 (Record of famous painters through the ages) by Zhang Yanyuan 張彥遠 (9th cent.), Beijing: Renmin meishu chubanshe, 1963.

Liuyanzhai sanbi 六研齋三筆 (Notes from Liuyan studio, book 3) by Li Rihua 李日華 (1565–1635). *SKQS* edn.

Li Wengong ji 李文公集 (Collected works of Li Ao李翱 [d. 780]). *Sibu congkan* 四部叢刊 edn.

Luojie chaji 羅岕茶記 (Record of Luojie tea) by Xiong Mingyu 熊明遇 (1579–1649). In Zheng Peikai and Zhu Zizhen 2007.

Maoshi caomu niaoshou chongyu shu 毛詩草木鳥獸蟲魚疏 (Explanation of the plants, trees, birds, beasts, insects, and fish in the Mao edition of the Classic of Poetry) by Lu Ji 陸璣 (261–303). *Congshu jicheng* edn.

Mao Shi zhengyi 毛詩正義 (True meaning of the Mao version of the Classic of Poetry) in *Shisanjing zhushu* 十三經注疏 (The Thirteen Classics with commentaries and subcommentaries), 1815, Ruan Yuan 阮元 (1764–1849), ed. Beijing: Beijing daxue chubanshe, 2000.

Mengliang lu 夢梁錄 (Dream of Hangzhou) by Wu Zimu 吳自牧, 1274. *SKQS* edn.

Mingji 茗芨 (Tea shoots) by Tu Benjun 屠本畯 (d. 1622). Taibei: Dongfang wenhua, 1975.

*Ming shuo*茗說 (Sayings about tea) by Wu Congxian 吳從先 (Wanli era), in Zheng Peikai and Zhu Zizhen 2007.

Mingzhai ji 茗齋集 (Tea fast collection) by Peng Sunyi 彭孫貽 (1616–1673). Shanghai: Shanghai guji chubanshe, 2009.

*Nan Qi shu*南齊書 (Book of the Southern Qi, 479–501), 59 *juan*, compiled privately by Xiao Zixian 蕭子顯 (489–537). Beijing: Zhonghua shuju, 1972.

Nittō gyūhō junreikōki 入唐求法巡禮行記 (Record of a pilgrimage to China in search of the dharma) by Ennin 圓仁 (794–864). Tokyo: Heibonsha, 1970.

Paoweng jiazang ji 匏翁家藏集 (Family storehouse collection of the old man of the gourd) by Wu Kuan 吳寬 (1435–1504). *Sibu congkan* edn.

Pincha yaolu 品茶要錄 (Essentials of tea connoisseurship). In Zheng Peikai and Zhu Zizhen 2007.

*Pizi wensou*皮子文藪 (Master Pi's literary marsh) by Pi Rixiu 皮日休, ca. 834–ca. 883, edited by Zheng Qingdu 鄭慶篤, Xiao Difei 蕭滌非. Shanghai: Shanghai guji chubanshe, 1981.

*Qimin yaoshu jiaoshi*齊民要術校釋 (Essential arts to save the people, collated and annotated) by Miao Qiyu繆啓愉, Jia Sixie 賈思勰 (6th cent.). Beijing: Nongye chubanshe, 1998.

*Qingyi lu. Yin shi bu fen*清异录. 饮食部分 (A record of things pure and strange: Section on foodstuffs and drinks). Beijing: Zhongguo shangye chubanshe, 1985.

Quan Tang shi 全唐詩 (Complete Tang poetry), 900 *juan*, compiled by Peng Dingqiu 彭定求 (1645–1719) et al. Beijing: Zhonghua shuju, 1960.

Quan Tang wen 全唐文 (Complete prose works of the Tang dynasty), 1,000 *juan*, completed in 1814 under the direction of Dong Gao 董誥 (1740–1818), et al. Palace edition with preface dated 1814. Reprinted Shanghai: Shanghai guji chubanshe, 1993.

Rizhi lu jishi 日知錄集釋 (Collected explanations on the record of daily knowledge) by Gu Yanwu 顧炎武, 1613–1682; commentary by Huang Rucheng 黃汝成, 1799–1837; Luan Baoqun 欒保羣, 1799–1837, et al. Shanghai: Shanghai guji chubanshe, 2006.

*Rongtai ji*容臺集 (Collection of the Terrace of Etiquette) by Dong Qichang董其昌 (1555–1636). Taibei: Guoli zhongyuang tushuguan, 1968.

Ruiying tuji 瑞應圖記 (Illustrations of auspicious omens) by Sun Rouzhi孫柔之 (6th cent.). Shanghai: Shanghai shudian, 1994.

Sanguo zhi 三國志 (Monograph on the Three Kingdoms), 65 *juan*, by Chen Shou 陳壽 (233–297). Beijing: Zhonghua shuju, 1971.

Shaluo guan qingyan 娑羅館清言 (Pure speech from the Sala hall) by Tu Long 屠隆 (1543–1605). *SKQS* edn.

Shanfu jing shoulu 膳夫經手錄 (Classic of the official in charge of palace meals, manuscript edition) by Yang Ye 楊曄 (9th cent.), *Xuxiu siku quanshu* edn.

*Shanjia qinggong*山家清供 (Pure offerings for mountain recluses) by Lin Hong 林洪. Beijing: Zhongguo shangye chubanshe, 1985.

Shennong bencao jing jiaozhu 神農本草經校註 (Annotated critical edition of the *materia medica* classic of the Divine Husbandman). Beijing: Xueyuan chubanshe, 2008.

Shiguo Chunqiu 十國春秋 (Springs and autumns of the Ten Kingdoms) by Wu Renchen 吳任臣 (1628?–1689?). Beijing: Zhonghua shuju, 1983.

Shiji 史記 (Records of the Historian, to 99 BCE), 130 *juan*, by Sima Qian 司馬遷 (145–86 BCE) and his father Sima Tan 司馬談, completed ca. 90 BCE. Beijing: Zhonghua shuju, 1959.

Shiliao bencao yizhu 食療本草譯注 (*Materia medica* of curative foodstuff, annotated). Shanghai: Shanghai guji chubanshe, 1992.

Shiliu tangpin 十六湯品 (Assessing sixteen kinds of boiling water). In Zheng Peikai and Zhu Zizhen 2007.

Shishi jiaozhu 詩式校注 (Critical annotated edition of poetic evaluations) by Jiaoran 皎然 (8th cent.). Beijing: Renmin wenxue chubanshe, 2003.

Shuliao guan ji 輸寥館集 (Collection of lost and lonesome studio). Taibei: Guoli zhongyang tushuguan, 1971.

Shuoku 說庫 (Storehouse of sayings) compiled by Wang Wenru 王文濡, first printed 1915. Reprinted Taibei: Xinxing shuju, 1963.

Siku quanshu 四庫全書 (Complete books in four storehouses). Taibei: Shangwu yinshuguan, 1983.

Sishi youshang lu 四時幽賞錄 (A record of the joys of seclusion through the four seasons). *Congshu jicheng* edn.

Soushen houji 搜神後記 (Further records of inquiries into spirits). Beijing: Zhonghua shuju, 1981.

Taiping guangji 太平廣記 (Extensive records of the Taiping era), 500 *juan*, compiled by Li Fang 李昉 and others 977–978. Beijing: Zhonghua shuju, 1961.

Taiping huimin hejiju fang 太平惠民和劑局方 (Prescriptions of the Taiping era pharmacy for the welfare of the people). 1107. Beijing: Renmin weisheng chubanshe, 1962.

Taiping yulan 太平御覽 (Imperial readings compiled in the Taiping era) by Li Fang 李昉 [983], edited by Wang Yunwu 王雲五. Beijing: Zhonghua shuju reprint of *Sibu congkan,* third series, 1960; 5th reprint, 1995.

Taiping yulan yinshi bu 太平禦覽飲食部 (Section on beverages and foodstuffs from imperial readings of the Taiping era). Beijing: Zhongguo shangye chubanshe, 1993.

Tang caizi zhuan jiaojian 唐才子傳校箋 (Traditions of talented men of the Tang, annotated critical edition), 5 vols. Beijing: Zhonghua shuju, 1987.

Tang da zhaoling ji 唐大詔令集 (Great collection of edicts and statutes of the Tang), 130 *juan,* edited by Song Minqiu 宋敏求 (1019–1079), completed 1070. Shanghai: Shangwu yinshuguan, 1959.

Tang guoshi bu; Yinhua lu 唐國史補; 因話錄 (Tang supplement to the state history; Records of hearsay) by Li Zhao 李肇, Zhao Lin 趙璘. Shanghai: Shanghai guji chubanshe, 1957.

Tang huiyao 唐會要 (Essential regulations of the Tang), 100 *juan*, by Wang Pu 王溥 (922–982), completed in 961. Wang Pu's work is a continuation of Su Mian's 蘇冕 *Huiyao* 會要 in 40 *juan* (completed 804) and of the *Xu huiyao* 續會要 by Yang Shaofu 楊紹復 et al. in 40 *juan* (completed 853). *Guoxue jiben congshu* 國學基本叢書, Shanghai: Shangwu yinshuguan, 1935. Repr. Beijing: Zhonghua shuju, 1955.

Tangren wushijia xiaoji 唐人五十家小集 (A minor collection of fifty Tang poets) by Jiang Biao 江標 (1860–1899). Suzhou: Lingjiange, 1895.

Tangshi jishi 唐詩紀事 (Recorded anecdotes of Tang poetry) by Ji Yougong 計有功 (fl. 1121–1161). Beijing: Zhonghua shuju, 1965.

Tang yulin jiaozheng 唐語林校證 (A forest of Tang anecdotes, collated and corrected) by Wang Dang 王讜 (fl. 1089) et al. Beijing: Zhonghua shuju, 1987.

Tang yunzheng 唐韻正 (Tang rhymes corrected) by Gu Yanwu 顧炎武 (1613–1682), 1667. SKQS edn.

Tianmen xianzhi 天門縣誌 (County gazetteer for Tianmen). Wuhan: Hubei renmin chubanshe, 1989.

Waitai miyao 外台秘要 (Secret essentials from the imperial library) by Wang Tao王燾 (8th cent.). Beijing: Renmin weisheng chubanshe, 1955.

Wang Zhongshan xiansheng jixuan 王仲山先生詩選 (Selected poetry of Master Wang Zhongshan). Taipei: Taiwan xuesheng shuju, 1971.

Wan-Ming ershi jia xiaopin 晚明二十家小品 (Minor works by twenty late Ming writers) by Xu Wei 徐渭 (1521–1593). Shanghai: Shanghai shudian, 1984.

Wen xuan 文選 (Selections of literature), 60 *juan,* edited by Xiao Tong蕭統 (501–531); 1809 edition by Hu Kejia 胡克家 (1757–1816) based on a text of the Chunxi 淳熙 era (1174–1189); this edition includes the commentary of Li Shan 李善 (d. 689); reprint includes Hu Kejia's *Wen xuan kaoyi* 文選考異. Taipei: Yiwen yinshuguan, 1979.

Wenyuan yinghua 文苑英華 (Beautiful flowers from the garden of literature), 1,000 juan, compiled by Li Fang 李昉 et al. between 982–987. Beijing: Zhonghua shuju, 1966.

Wulin youji 武林遊記 (Record of travels around Wulin). Shanghai: Shanghai shudian, 1994.

Wutong ji 梧岡集 (Paulownia collection). *SKQS* edn.

Xianchun lin'an zhi 咸淳臨安志 (Gazetteer of Lin'an from the Xianchun reign [1265–1274]) by Qian Shuoyou 潛說友. *SKQS* edn.

Xicun shi ji 西村詩集 (West village collection of verse) by Zhu Pu 朱樸. *SKQS* edn.

Xin Tang shu 新唐書 (New book of the Tang, 618–907), 225 *juan,* by Ouyang Xiu 歐陽修 (1007–1072), Song Qi 宋祁 (998–1061) et al. 1043–1060. Beijing: Zhonghua shuju, 1974.

Xu chajing 續茶經 (Continuation of the *Classic of Tea*) by Lu Tingcan 陸廷燦 (18th cent.) in Zheng Peikai and Zhu Zizhen 2007.

Xuxiu siku quanshu 續修四庫全書 (Continued complete books in four storehouses). Shanghai: Shanghai guji chubanshe, 2002.

Xuzang jing 續藏經 (Continued [Buddhist] Canon). Taipei: Xinwenfeng, 1968–1978. 150 vols. Reprint of *Dai Nihon Zokuzōkyō*大日本續藏經. Kyoto: Zōkyō shoin, 1905–1912.

Yanzhou shanren xu gao 弇州山人續稿 (Continued declarations of a mountain recluse from Yanzhou). Taipei: Wenhai chuban she, 1970.

Yimen guangdu 夷門廣牘 (Extensive archives from Yimen). Taibei: Taiwan shangwu yinshu guan, 1969.

Yinhua lu 因話錄, see *Tang guoshi bu; Yinhua lu.*

Yiyuan 異苑 (A garden of marvels) by Liu Jingshu 劉敬叔 (fl. early 5th cent.). *Shuoku* edn.

Yuan Zhonglan quanji 袁中郎全集 (Complete works of Yuan Zhonglan). Taipei: Shijie chubanshe, 1956.

Yunji qiqian 雲笈七籤 (Seven slips from a cloudy satchel), comp. ca. 1028–1029 by Zhang Junfang 張君房 (fl. 1008–1029). Beijing: Zhonghua shuju, 2003.

Zhejiang tongzhi 浙江通志 (Comprehensive gazetteer of Zhejiang). Taibei: Huawen shuju, 1967.

Zhouli 周禮 (Rites of Zhou), in *Shisanjing zhushu* 十三經注疏 (The Thirteen Classics with commentaries and subcommentaries), 1815, Ruan Yuan 阮元 (1764–1849), ed. Beijing: Beijing daxue chubanshe, 2000.

Zhuquan xiaopin 煮泉小品 (Minor grading of springs for simmering) by Tian Yiheng 田藝蘅 (*jinshi* 1526). Taipei: Yiwen yinshu, 1956.

Zizhi tongjian 資治通鑑 (Comprehensive mirror for the aid of government), 294 *juan,* compiled by Sima Guang 司馬光 (1019–1086). Beijing: Zhonghua shuju, 1963.

SECONDARY SOURCES

Addison, Joseph. 1837. *The Works of Joseph Addison.* 3 vols. New York: Harper & Co.

Albury, W. R., and G. M. Weisz. 2009. "Depicting the Bread of the Last Supper: Religious Representation in Italian Renaissance Society." *Journal of Religion & Society* 11: 1–17.

Allen, Sarah M. 2006. "Tales Retold: Narrative Variation in a Tang Story." *Harvard Journal of Asiatic Studies* 66, no. 1:105–143.

Barnstone, Tony, Willis Barnstone, and Haixin Xu. 1991. *Laughing Lost in the Mountains: Poems of Wang Wei.* Hanover, N.H.: University Press of New England.

Barrett, T. H. 1991. "Devil's Valley to Omega Point: Reflections on the Origins of a Theme from the Nō." In *The Buddhist Forum, II,* edited by Tadeusz Skorupski, 1–12. London: School of Oriental and African Studies.

Bartholomew, Terese Tse. 1990. "A Concise History of Yixing Ware." In *Art of the Yixing Potter: The K. S. Lo Collection, Flagstaff House Museum of Tea Ware,* edited by Kueihsiang Lo, 42–57. Hong Kong: Urban Council.

Bauer, Wolfgang. 1990. *Das Antlitz Chinas: die autobiographische Selbstdarstellung in der chinesischen Literatur von ihren Anfängen bis heute.* München: C. Hanser.

Birrell, Anne. 1982. *New Songs from a Jade Terrace: An Anthology of Early Chinese Love Poetry.* London: Allen & Unwin.

Blofeld, John. 1985. *The Chinese Art of Tea.* Boston: Shambhala.

Bodde, Derk. 1942. "Early References to Tea Drinking in China." *Journal of the American Oriental Society* 62, no. 1:74–76.

———. 1975. *Festivals in Classical China: New Year and Other Annual Observances During the Han Dynasty, 206 B.C.–A.D. 220.* Princeton, N.J.: Princeton University Press.

Bokenkamp, Stephen R. 1986. "The Peach Flower Font and the Grotto Passage." *Journal of the American Oriental Society* 106, no. 1:65–78.

Bon Drongpa [Bon-grong-pa]. 1993. *The Dispute Between Tea and Chang (Ja-chang Iha-mo'i bstan-bcos).* Translated by Alexander Fedotov and Sangye Tandar Naga. Dharamsala: Library of Tibetan Works and Archives.

Bretschneider, Emil. 1882. *Botanicon Sinicum. Notes on Chinese Botany from Native and Western Sources.* London: Trübner.

Brook, Timothy. 1993. *Praying for Power: Buddhism and the Formation of Gentry Society in Late-Ming China.* Cambridge, Mass.: Harvard University Press.

———. 1998. *The Confusions of Pleasure: Commerce and Culture in Ming China.* Berkeley: University of California Press.

Buswell, Robert E. 1992. *The Zen Monastic Experience: Buddhist Practice in Contemporary Korea.* Princeton, N.J.: Princeton University Press.

Cahill, Suzanne. 2000. "Pien Tung-hsüan: A Taoist Holy Woman of the T'ang Dynasty (618–907)." In *Women Saints in World Religions,* edited by Arvind Shama, 205–220. Albany: State University of New York Press.

———. 2003. "Resenting the Silk Robes That Hide Their Poems: Female Voices in the Poems of Tang Dynasty Daoist Nuns." In *Tang Song nuxing yu shehui (Women and society during the Tang and Song dynasties),* edited by Zheng Xiaotong, Gao Shilun, and Rong Xinjiang, 519–566. Shanghai: Zishu.

Campany, Robert Ford. 1996. *Strange Writing: Anomaly Accounts in Early Medieval China.* Albany: State University of New York Press.

———. 2002. *To Live as Long as Heaven and Earth: A Translation and Study of Ge Hong's Traditions of Divine Transcendents.* Berkeley: University of California Press.

———. 2012. *Signs from the Unseen Realm.* Honolulu: University of Hawai'i Press.

Campbell, Duncan. 2002. "The Epistolary World of a Reluctant 17th Century Chinese Magistrate: Yuan Hongdao in Suzhou." *New Zealand Journal of Asian Studies* 4, no. 1:159–193.

———. 2003. "Yuan Hongdao's 'A History of the Vase,'" *New Zealand Journal of Asian Studies* 5, no. 3:77–93.

Carpenter, Francis Ross 1974. *The Classic of Tea*. Boston: Little, Brown.

Ceresa, Marco. 1990. *Il Canone del tè*. Milano: Leonardo.

———. 1993a. "Discussing an Early Reference to Tea-Drinking in China: Wang Bao's *Tongyue*." *Annali di Ca' Foscari Serie Orientale* 25 XXXI, no. 3:203–211.

———. 1993b. "Oltre il *Chajing*: Trattati sul tè di epoca Tang." *Annali dell'Istituto Universitario Orientale di Napoli* 53, no. 2:193–210.

———. 1995. "Herbe amère et douce rosée. Notes sur l'histoire de la terminologie du goût du thé en Chine." In *Savourer, Goûter*, edited by F. Blanchon, 269–284. Paris: Presses de l'Université de Paris-Sorbonne.

———. 1996. "Diffusion of Tea-Drinking Habit in Pre-Tang and Early Tang Period." *Asiatica Venetiana* 1:19–25.

Chan, Hok-Lam. 1979. "Tea Production and Tea Trade Under the Jurchen-Dynasty," In *Studia Sino-Mongolica: Festschr. fur Herbert Franke*, edited by Wolfgang Bauer, 109–125. Wiesbaden: Steiner.

Chan Man Sing 陳萬成. 1994. "Sun Chuo's Rhapsody on Mount Tiantai and its Daoist Background 孫綽<遊天台山賦>與道教." *New Asia Bulletin*《新亞學報》 13:255–262.

Chen Chuan 陳椽. 1984. *Chaye tongshi* 茶葉通史 (A comprehensive history of tea). Beijing: Nongye chubanshe.

———. 1993. *Lun cha yu wenhua* 論茶與文化 (A discussion of tea and culture). Beijing: Nongye chubanshe.

Chen Jinhua. 2002. "Śarīra and Scepter: Empress Wu's Political Use of Buddhist Relics." *Journal of the International Association of Buddhist Studies* 25, nos. 1–2:33–150.

Chen, Jinhua. 1999. "One Name, Three Monks: Two Northern Chan Masters Emerge from the Shadow of the Contemporary, the Tiantai Master Zhanran 湛然 (711–782)." *Journal of the International Association of Buddhist Studies* 22, no. 1:1–91.

———. 2002. *Monks and Monarchs, Kinship and Kingship: Tanqian in Sui Buddhism and Politics*. Kyoto: Italian School of East Asian Studies.

———. 2006. "*Pañcavārṣika* Assemblies in Liang Wudi's (r. 502–549) Buddhist Palace Chapel." *Harvard Journal of Asiatic Studies* 66, no. 1:43–103.

———. 2009. *Legend and Legitimation: The Formation of Tendai Esoteric Buddhism in Japan*. Louvain: Peeters.

Chen, Tsu-lung. 1963. "Note on Wang Fu's *Ch'a Chiu Lun*." *Sinologica* 6:271–287.

Chen Zugui 陳祖槼 and Zhu Zizhen 朱自振. 1981. *Zhongguo chaye lishi ziliao xuanji* 中國茶葉歷史資料選輯 (Selected historical materials on tea in China). Beijing: Nongye chubanshe.

Ch'en, Kenneth. 1973. *The Chinese Transformation of Buddhism*. Princeton, N.J.: Princeton University Press.

Cheng Guangyu 程光裕. 1985. "Cha yu Tang-Song sixiang jie ji zhengzhi shehui guanxi" 茶與唐宋思想界及政治社會關係 (The relationship between tea and Tang-Song intellectual life, government, and society)." In *Zhongguo chayi luncong* 中國茶藝論叢 (Collected essays on the tea arts of China), 1–61. Taipei: Dali chubanshe.

Cheng, Wing fun, and Hervé Collett. 2002. *L'extase du thé: poèmes traduits du chinois*. Millemont: Moundarren.

Clark, Hugh R. 2001. "An Inquiry into the *Xianyou Cai*: Cai Xiang, Cai Que, Cai Jing, and the Politics of Kinship." *Journal of Song-Yuan Studies* 31:67–101.

Clunas, Craig. 1991. *Superfluous Things: Material Culture and Social Status in Early Modern China*. Cambridge: Polity Press.

———. 1998. "Wine Foaming in Gold, Tea Brewing in Jade: Drinking Culture in Ming Dynasty China." *Oriental Art* 44, no. 2: 8–10.

Davis, A. R. 1968. "The Double Ninth Festival in Chinese Poetry: A Study of Variations upon a Theme." In *Wen-lin: Studies in the Chinese Humanities*, edited by Chow Tsê-tsung, 45–64. Madison: University of Wisconsin Press for the Dept. of East Asian Languages and Literature of the University of Wisconsin.

DeBlasi, Anthony. 2002. *Reform in the Balance: The Defense of Literary Culture in Mid-Tang China*. Albany: State University of New York Press.

Declercq, Dominik. 1998. *Writing Against the State: Political Rhetorics in Third and Fourth Century China*. Leiden: Brill.

DeWoskin, Kenneth J., and J. I. Crump. 1996. *In Search of the Supernatural: The Written Record*. Stanford, Calif.: Stanford University Press.

Dictionary of Ming Biography. 1976. Edited by L. Carrington Goodrich and Fang Zhaoying. New York: Columbia University Press.

Drott, Edward R. 2010. "Gods, Buddhas, and Organs: Buddhist Physicians and Theories of Longevity in Early Medieval Japan." *Japanese Journal of Religious Studies* 37, no. 2:247–273.

Du Lianzhe 杜聯喆. 1977. *Mingren zizhuan wenchao* 明人自傳文鈔 (Autobiographical writings of Ming men). Taipei: Yiwen yinshu.

Duquenne, Robert. 1983. "Daigensui." In *Hōbōgirin* fasc. 6.

Ebrey, Patricia Buckley. 1993. *Chinese Civilization: A Sourcebook*. New York: Free Press.

Edwards, E. D. 1937. *Chinese Prose Literature of the T'ang Period*. 2 vols. London: Arthur Probstain and Co.

Egan, Ronald C. 1994. *Word, Image, and Deed in the Life of Su Shi*. Cambridge, Mass.: Harvard Council on East Asian Studies.

———. 1997. "The Controversy over Music and 'Sadness' and Changing Conceptions of the Qin in Middle Period China." *Harvard Journal of Asiatic Studies* 57, no. 1:5–66.

Engelhardt, Ute. 2001. "Dietetics in Tang China and the First Extant Works of Materia Dietetica." In *Innovation in Chinese Medicine,* edited by Elisabeth Hsu, 173–192. Cambridge: Cambridge University Press.

Eskildsen, Stephen. 1998. *Asceticism in Early Taoist Religion.* Albany: State University of New York Press.

Fang Hao 方豪. 1985. "Songdai senglu duiyu zaicha zhi gongxian 宋代僧侶對於栽茶之貢獻 (The Song dynasty saṃgha in relation to the labour of tea planting)." In *Zhongguo chayi lunzong*中國茶藝論叢 (Collection of essays on the tea arts of China), edited by Wu Zhihe 吳智和, 137–148. Taipei: Dali chubanshe.

Faure, Bernard. 1991. *The Rhetoric of Immediacy: A Cultural Critique of Chan/Zen Buddhism.* Princeton, N.J.: Princeton University Press.

———. 1997. *The Will to Orthodoxy: A Critical Genealogy of Northern Chan Buddhism.* Stanford, Calif.: Stanford University Press.

Forte, Antonino. 2005. "The Origins of Luoyang's Great Fuxian Monastery." Unpublished manuscript.

Fukuda Sōi 福田宗位. 1974. *Chūgoku no chasho* 中国の茶書 (Tea books of China). Tokyo: Tokyodo Shuppan.

Funayama Tōru 船山徹. 2010. "Bonmōkyō gekan senkō setsu no saikentō 梵網経下巻先行説の再検討 [Re-examining the precedence of the second fascicle of the Scripture of Brahma's Net (Fanwang jing 梵網経)." In *Sangyō kōshō ronsō zokuhen* 三教交渉論叢続編 [Interactions between the three teachings II], edited by Mugitani Kunio 麥谷邦夫, 127–156. Kyoto: Kyōto daigaku Jinbun kagaku kenkyūsho 京都大学人文科学研究所 [Institute for Research in Humanitites, Kyoto University].

Furth, Charlotte. 1999. *A Flourishing Yin: Gender in China's Medical History, 960–1665.* Berkeley: University of California Press.

Furuta Shōkin 古田紹欽. 2000. *Eisai Kissa yōjōki* 栄西 喫茶養生記. Tokyo: Kōdansha.

Fu Shuqin 傅樹勤 1984. *Chashen Lu Yu* 茶神陸羽 (Lu Yu, god of tea). Beijing: Nongye chubanshe.

Gardella, Robert Paul. 1994. *Harvesting Mountains: Fujian and the China Tea Trade, 1757–1937.* Berkeley: University of California Press.

Gernet, Jacques. 1962. *Daily Life in China on the Eve of the Mongol Invasion, 1250–1276.* New York: Macmillan.

———. 1995. *Buddhism in Chinese Society: An Economic History from the Fifth to the Tenth Centuries.* New York: Columbia University Press.

Giles, Herbert A. 1964. *Gems of Chinese Literature: Prose.* Taipei: Literature House.

Giles, Lionel. 1957. *Descriptive Catalogue of the Chinese Manuscripts from Tunhuang in the British Museum.* London: Trustees of the British Museum.

Gineste, Muriel. 1997. "Tea Origins and Practices in Vietnam," *Vietnamese Studies* (Hanoi) no. 56 (126):29–46.

Girard, Frédéric. 2011. "Yōsai, premier théoricien du thé au Japon, et son *Traité pour nourrir le principe vital par la consommation du thé.*" In *Manabe Shunshō hakase kiko kinen ronshū* 真鍋俊照博士古稀記念論集, 1–41. Kyoto: Hōzōkan.

Goble, Andrew Edmund. 2011. *Confluences of Medicine in Medieval Japan: Buddhist Healing, Chinese Knowledge, Islamic Formulas, and Wounds of War.* Honolulu: University of Hawai'i Press.

Goldschmidt, Asaf. 2008. "Commercializing Medicine or Benefiting the People? The First Public Pharmacy in China." *Science in Context* 21, no. 3:311–350.

Goodman, Jordan. 1993. *Tobacco in History: The Cultures of Dependence.* London: Routledge.

Goodrich, L. Carrington, and C. Martin Wilbur. 1942. "Additional Notes on Tea." *Journal of the American Oriental Society* 62, no. 3:195–197.

Graham, A. C. 1979. "The Nung-chia 農家 'School of the Tillers' and the Origins of Peasant Utopianism in China." *Bulletin of the School of Oriental & African Studies* 42, no. 1:66–100.

Greatrex, Roger. 1987. "The *Bowu zhi:* An Annotated Translation." Ph.D. diss., Föreningen för Orientaliska Studier, Stockholm.

Greenbaum, Jamie. 2007. *Chen Jiru (1558–1639): The Background to, Development and Subsequent Uses of Literary Personae.* Leiden: Brill.

Gregory, Peter N., ed. 1987. *Sudden and Gradual: Approaches to Enlightenment in Chinese Thought.* Honolulu: University of Hawai'i Press.

Groner, Paul. 1990. "The Fan-wang ching and Monastic Discipline in Japanese Tendai: A Study of Annen's *Futsū jubosatsukai kōshaku.*" In *Chinese Buddhist Apocrypha,* edited by Robert E. Buswell Jr., 251–290. Honolulu: University of Hawai'i Press.

Hanson, Marta E. 2011. *Speaking of Epidemics in Chinese Medicine: Disease and the Geographic Imagination in Late Imperial China.* Abingdon, Oxon: Routledge.

Han Wei. 1993. "Tang Dynasty Tea Utensils and Tea Culture: Recent Discoveries at Famen Temple." *Chanoyu Quarterly* 74:38–58.

Hao Chunwen 郝春文. 1998. *Tang houqi Wudai Song chu Dunhuang sengni de shehui shenghuo* 唐后期五代宋初敦煌僧尼的社会生活 (The social life of monks and nuns in the late Tang, Five Dynasties and early Song). Beijing: Zhongguo shehui kexue chubanshe.

———. 2010. "The Social Life of Buddhist Monks and Nuns in Dunhuang During the Late Tang, Five Dynasties, and Early Song." *Asia Major* 23, no. 2:77–95.

Harper, Donald John. 1986. "The Analects Jade Candle: A Classic of T'ang Drinking Custom." *T'ang Studies* 4:69–90.

Hartman, Charles. 1986. *Han Yü and the T'ang Search for Unity*. Princeton, N.J.: Princeton University Press.

Hattox, Ralph S. 1985. *Coffee and Coffeehouses: The Origins of a Social Beverage in the Medieval Near East*. Seattle: University of Washington Press.

Hawkes, David [trans]. 1977. *The Story of the Stone: A Chinese Novel in Five Volumes*. Harmondsworth: Penguin.

Hay, Jonathan (Han Chuang). 1970–1971. "Hsiao I Gets the Lan-t'ing Manuscript by a Confidence Trick." *National Palace Museum Bulletin, Gugong tongxun* 5, no. 3: 1–13; 6, no. 3:1–17.

Hayashi Yoshiro 林美朗. 2004. "*Kissa yōjōki* no kinnen goshu no yamaishō 喫茶養生記』の近年五種の病相. (Five types of contemporary disease in *Kissa yōjōki*)." *Bulletin of Tokai Women's College* 23:193–197.

Henricks, Robert G. 1998. "Fire and Rain: A Look at Shen Nung 神農 (The Divine Farmer) and His Ties with Yen Ti 炎帝 (The 'Flaming Emperor' or 'Flaming God')." *Bulletin of the School of Oriental and African Studies* 61, no. 1:102–124.

Hervouet, Yves, and Etienne Balazs. 1978. *A Sung Bibliography. Bibliographie des Song*. Hong Kong: Chinese University Press.

Hirabayashi Fumio 平林文雄. 1978. *San Tendai Godaisan ki: kōhon narabi ni kenkyū* 《参天台五台山記: 校本並びに研究》(Travels to Mounts Tiantai and Wutai: critical edition and study). Tokyo: Kazama Shobō.

Hōbōgirin 法寶義林 *Dictionnaire encyclopédique du Bouddhisme d'après les sources chinoises et japonaises:* fascicules 1 (1929), 2 (1930), 3 (1937), 4 (1967), 5 (1979), 6 (1983), 7 (1994), 8 (2003).

Hohenegger, Beatrice. 2006. *Liquid Jade: The Story of Tea from East to West*. New York: St. Martin's Press.

———. ed. 2009. *Steeped in History: The Art of Tea*. Los Angeles: Fowler Museum at UCLA.

Holzman, Donald. 1956. "Les Sept Sages de la Forêt des Bambous et la société de leur temps." *T'oung Pao* 44:317–346.

Huang, H. T. 2000. *Science and Civilisation in China, Volume 6: Biology and Biological Technology. Part V: Fermentations and Food Science*. Edited by Joseph Needham. Cambridge: Cambridge University Press.

Hucker, Charles O. 1985. *A Dictionary of Official Titles in Imperial China*. Stanford, Calif.: Stanford University Press.

Hurst, G. Cameron III. 1979. "Michinaga's Maladies. A Medical Report on Fujiwara no Michinaga." *Monumenta Nipponica* 34, no. 1:101–112.

Ip, Po-chung Danny 葉寶忠. 1995. "The Life and Thought of Lü Wen (772–811) 呂溫的生平與思想研究." Ph.D. diss., University of Hong Kong.

Jamieson, Ross W. 2001. "The Essence of Commodification: Caffeine Dependencies in the Early Modern World." *Journal of Social History* 35, no. 2:269–294.

Jenner, W. J. F. 1981. *Memories of Loyang: Yang Hsüan-Chih and the Lost Capital (493–534)*. Oxford: Oxford University Press.

Jia Jinhua 贾晋华. 1992. *Jiaoran nianpu* 皎然年谱 (Chronological biography of Jiaoran). Xiamen: Xiamen daxue chubanshe.

Jia, Jinhua. 1999. "The Hongzhou School of Chan Buddhism and the Tang Literati." Ph.D. diss., University of Colorado.

Ji Yuanzhi 暨远志. 1991. "Tangdai cha wenhua de jijiexing—Dunhuang xieben 'Chajiu lun' yanjiu zhi er 唐代茶文化的阶段性—-敦煌写本《茶酒论》研究之二" (The development of Tang tea culture—research on the Dunhuang manuscript "Chajiu lun" part 2). *Dunhuang yanjiu* 2:99–107.

Johnson, Wallace Stephen. 1979. *The T'ang Code*. Princeton, N.J.: Princeton University Press.

Jorgensen, John J. 2005. *Inventing Hui-neng, The Sixth Patriarch: Hagiography and Biography in Early Ch'an*. Leiden: Brill.

Juengst, Sara. 1992. *Breaking Bread: The Spiritual Significance of Food*. Louisville, Ky.: Westminster John Knox Press.

Karetzky, Patricia. 2000. "Imperial Splendor in the Service of the Sacred: The Famen Tea Treasures." *T'ang Studies*, nos. 18–19: 61–85.

Kieschnick, John. 2003. *The Impact of Buddhism on Chinese Material Culture*. Princeton, N.J.: Princeton University Press.

———. 2005. "Buddhist Vegetarianism in China." In *Of Tripod and Palate: Food, Politics, and Religion in Traditional China*, edited by Roel Sterckx, 186–212. New York: Palgrave MacMillan.

Knechtges, David R. 1970–1971. "Wit, Humor, and Satire in Early Chinese Literature (to A.D. 220)." *Monumenta Serica* 29:79–98.

———. 1982. *Wen xuan, or, Selections of Refined Literature. Volume One: Rhapsodies on Metropolises and Capitals*. Princeton, N.J.: Princeton University Press.

———. 1997. "Gradually Entering the Realm of Delight: Food and Drink in Early Medieval China." *Journal of the American Oriental Society* 117, no. 2:229–239.

Kohn, Livia. 1987. *Seven Steps to the Tao: Sima Chengzhen's Zuowanglun*. Nettetal: Steyler Verlag.

———. 2003. *Monastic Life in Medieval Daoism: A Cross-Cultural Perspective*. Honolulu: University of Hawai'i Press.

Kohn, Livia, and Yoshinobu Sakade. 1989. *Taoist Meditation and Longevity Techniques*. Ann Arbor: Center for Chinese Studies, University of Michigan.

Kou Dan 寇丹 2002. *Lu Yu yu Chajing yanjiu* 陆羽与《茶经》研究 (Research on Lu Yu and the *Classic of Tea*). Hong Kong: Tianyu yuanshu.

Kroll, Paul W. 1996. "An Early Poem of Mystical Excursion." In *Religions of China in Practice*, edited by Donald S. Lopez Jr., 156–165. Princeton, N.J.: Princeton University Press.

Lamotte, Etienne. 1976. *The Teaching of Vimalakīrti (Vimalakīrtinirdeśa): From the French Translation with Introduction and Notes (L'enseignement de Vimalakīrti)*. London: Pali Text Society.

Lang Ji 朗吉. 1986. "Dunhuang hanwen juanzi 'Chajiu lun' yu zangwen 'Chajiu xiannü' de bijiao yanjiu 敦煌漢文卷子《茶酒論》與藏文《茶酒仙女》 的比較研究 (Research on the Chinese *Discussion between Tea and Alcohol* and the Tibetan *Immortal Maid of Tea and Alcohol*)." *Dunhuang xue jikan* 1:64–68.

Lavoix, Valérie. 2002. "La contribution des laïcs au végétarisme: croisades et polémiques en Chine du Sud autour de l'an 500." In *Bouddhisme et lettrés dans la Chine médiéval*, edited by Catherine Despeux, 103–143. Louvain: Peeters.

Legge, James. 1991 (1935). *The Chinese Classics: With a Translation, Critical and Exegetical Notes, Prolegomena, and Copious Indexes, I & II Confucian Analects, The Great Learning, The Doctrine of the Mean, The Works of Mencius*. 5 vols. Vol. 1–2. Taipei: SMC Publishing.

Lewis, Mark Edward. 2009. *China's Cosmopolitan Empire: The Tang Dynasty*. Cambridge, Mass.: Belknap Press of Harvard University Press.

Li, Zhisui, and Anne F. Thurston. 1994. *The Private Life of Chairman Mao: The Memoirs of Mao's Personal Physician*. New York: Random House.

Liao Baoxiu 廖寶秀. 1990. "Cong kaogu chutu yinqi lun Tangdai de yincha wenhua 從考古出土飲器論唐代飲茶文化 (A discussion of Tang dynasty tea-drinking culture on the basis of excavated drinking vessels)." *Gugong xueshu jikan* 8, no. 3:1–58.

———. 1996. *Songdai chichafa yu chachi zhi yanjiu* 宋代吃茶法與茶器之研究 (Research on Song Dynasty methods of drinking tea and teaware). Taipei: Guoli Gugong bowu yuan.

Lin Zhengsan 林正三. 1984. "Tangdai yincha fengqi tantao 唐代飲茶風氣探討 (On the fashion for drinking tea during the Tang)." *Guoli bianyiguan guankan* 13, no. 2:208–228.

Lippiello, Tiziana. 2001. *Auspicious Omens and Miracles in Ancient China: Han, Three Kingdoms and Six Dynasties*. Sankt Augustin: Monumenta Serica Institute.

Liu, Hsin-ju. 1996. *Silk and Religion: An Exploration of Material Life and the Thought of People, AD 600–1200*. Delhi: Oxford University Press.

Liu Shufen 劉淑芬. 2004. "'Ke zhi ze she cha, yuan qu ze she tang'–Tang, Song shiqi shisu shehui shenghuo zhong de cha yu tang 「客至則設茶，欲去則設湯」——唐、宋時期世俗社會生活中的茶與湯 ('When a guest arrives tea is served, on his departure decoctions are served'—tea and decoctions in Tang and Song period secular social life)." *Yanjing xuebao (New Series)* 16:117–155.

———. 2006a. "Jielü yu yangsheng zhi jian—Tang-Song siyuan zhong de wanyao, ruyao he yaojiu 戒律與養生之間—唐宋寺院中的丸藥、乳藥和藥酒 (Between self-cultivation and the monastic code: Tea and medicinal soup in Tang and Song monastic life)." *Zhongyang yanjiuyuan lishi yuyan yanjiusuo jikan (Bulletin of the Institute of History and Philology, Academia Sinica)* 77:357–400.

———. 2006b. "Tang, Song siyuan zhong de cha yu tangyao 唐、宋寺院中的茶與湯藥 (Tea and medicinal decoctions in Tang and Song monasteries)." *Yanjing xuebao (New Series)* 19:67–97.

———. 2007. "Chanyuan qinggui zhong suojian de chali yu tangli 《禪苑清規》中所見的茶禮與湯禮 (Tea and medicinal soup ceremonies as seen in the *Chanyuan qinggui*)." *Zhongyang yanjiuyuan lishi yuyan yanjiusuo jikan (Bulletin of the Institute of History and Philology, Academia Sinica)* 78:629–670.

Lomova, Olga. 2006. "From Suffering the Heat to Enjoying the Cool: Remarks on Wang Wei as a Buddhist Poet." In *Studies in Chinese Language and Culture—Festschrift in Honour of Christoph Harbsmeier on the Occasion of His 60th Birthday*, edited by Christoph Anderl and Halvor Eifring, 417–425. Oslo: Hermes Academic Publishing.

Lu Houyuan, Xiaoyan Yang, Maolin Ye, Kam-Biu Liu, Zhengkai Xia, Xiaoyan Ren, Linhai Cai, Naiqin Wu, and Tung-Sheng Liu. 2005. "Culinary Archaeology: Millet Noodles in Late Neolithic China." *Nature* 437, no. 7061:967–968.

Lu, Weijing. 2004. "Beyond the Paradigm—Tea-Picking Women in Imperial China." *Journal of Women's History* 15, no. 4:19–46.

Lü Weixin 呂維新, and Cai Jiade 蔡嘉德, eds. 1995. *Cong Tangshi kan Tangren chado shenghuo* 從唐詩看唐人茶道生活 (The Tang way of tea from the perspective of Tang poetry). Taipei: Lu Yu chayi.

Lu Xun 魯迅, ed. 1967. *Gu xiaoshuo gouchen* 古小說鈎沈 (Ancient tales rescued from oblivion). Beijing: Renmin wenxue chubanshe.

———. 1981. "Wei-Jin fengdu ji wenzhang yao ji jiu zhi guanxi 魏晉風度及文章藥及酒之關係 (The relationship between alcohol and medicine in Wei-Jin customs and literature)." In *Lu Xun quanji* 魯迅全集 (Complete works of Lu Xun), 523–553. Beijing: Zhonghua shuju.

Ludwig, Theodore M. 1981. "Before Rikyu: Religious and Aesthetic Influences in the Early History of the Tea Ceremony." *Monumenta Nipponica* 36, no. 4:367–390.

Luo, Manling. 2012. "What One Has Heard and Seen: Intellectual Discourse in a Late Eighth-Century Miscellany." *Tang Studies* 30:23–44.

MacFarlane, Alan, and Iris MacFarlane. 2003. *Green Gold: The Empire of Tea.* London: Ebrey Press.

Mair, Victor H. 1994. "The Autobiography of Instructor Lu." In *The Columbia Anthology of Traditional Chinese Literature,* edited by Victor H. Mair, 699–702. New York: Columbia University Press.

Major, John S., Sarah A. Queen, Andrew Seth Meyer, and Harold D. Roth. 2010. *The Huainanzi: A Guide to the Theory and Practice of Government in Early Han China.* New York: Columbia University Press.

Mather, Richard B. 1968. "Vimalakīrti and Gentry Buddhism." *History of Religions* 8, no. 1:60–73.

———. 2002. *A New Account of Tales of the World: Shih-shuo Hsin-yü.* second edn. Ann Arbor: Center for Chinese Studies, University of Michigan.

McCants, Anne E. C. 2008. "Poor Consumers as Global Consumers: The Diffusion of Tea and Coffee Drinking in the Eighteenth Century." *Economic History Review* 61, no. 1:172–200.

McDowall, Stephen (trans.). 2010. *Four Months of Idle Roaming: The West Lake Records of Yuan Hongdao.* Asian Studies Institute Translation Papers. Wellington, NZ: Victoria University of Wellington.

McMullen, David. 1973. "Historical and Literary Theory in the Mid-Eighth Century." In *Perspectives on the T'ang,* edited by Arthur F. Wright and Denis Twitchett, 301–342. New Haven, Conn.: Yale University Press.

———. 1999. "The Death Rites of Tang Daizong." In *State and Court Ritual in China,* edited by Joseph P. McDermott, 150–196. Cambridge: Cambridge University Press.

McNair, Amy. 1992–1993. "Draft Entry for a T'ang Biographical Dictionary: Yen Chen-ch'ing." *T'ang Studies* 10–11:123–147.

———. 1998. *The Upright Brush: Yan Zhenqing's Calligraphy and Song Literati Politics.* Honolulu: University of Hawai'i Press.

McRae, John R. 1986. *The Northern School and the Formation of Early Ch'an Buddhism.* Honolulu: University of Hawai'i Press.

Michihata Ryōshū 道端良秀. 1970. "Bukkyō to shu—dokushu to yakushu 仏教と酒—毒酒と薬酒 (Buddhism and alcohol: toxic alcohol and medicinal alcohol)." In *Chūgoku Bukkyō shi no kenkyū: Bukkyō to shakai rinri* 中国仏教史の研究：仏教と社会倫理, 214–348. Kyoto: Hōzōkan.

Minford, John , and Joseph S. M. Lau, eds. 2000. *Classical Chinese Literature: An Anthology of Translations.* Hong Kong: Chinese University Press.

Mintz, Sidney W. 1986. *Sweetness and Power: The Place of Sugar in Modern History.* New York: Penguin Books.

Mori Shikazō 森鹿三. 1999. *Honzōgaku kenkyū* 本草学研究 (Studies in *materia medica*). Osaka: Kyōu Shorin.

Nappi, Carla Suzan. 2009. *The Monkey and the Inkpot: Natural History and Its Transformations in Early Modern China.* Cambridge, Mass.: Harvard University Press.

Narita Shigeyuki 成田重行. 1998. *Chasei Riku U: Chakyō o arawashita ijin no shōgai* 茶聖陸羽 : 茶経を著した偉人の生涯 (The sage of tea, Lu Yu: The life of the author of the *Classic of Tea*). Kyoto: Tankōsha.

Needham, Joseph, and Lu Gwei-Djen, eds. 1983. *Science and Civilisation in China, Vol. V. Chemistry and Chemical Technology, Part. 5. Spagyrical Discovery and Invention: Physiological Alchemy.* Cambridge: Cambridge University Press.

Needham, Joseph, and Colin A. Ronan. 1978. *The Shorter Science and Civilisation in China: An Abridgement of Joseph Needham's Original Text.* Cambridge: Cambridge University Press.

Nielson, Thomas P. 1973. *The T'ang Poet Chiao-jan.* Tempe: Center for Asian Studies, Arizona State University.

Nienhauser, William H. 1979. *P'i Jih-hsiu.* Boston: Twayne Publishers.

Nishiwaki Tsuneki 西脇常記. 2000. "'Roku Bungaku jiden kō' 『陸文學自傳』考 (A study of the autobiography of Instructor Lu)." In *Tōdai no shisō to bunka* 唐代の思想と文化, edited by Nishiwaki Tsuneki, 113–140. Tokyo: Sōbunsha.

Nunome Chōfū 布目潮渢. 1995. *Chūgoku kissa bunka shi* 中国喫茶文化史 (History of Chinese tea-drinking culture). Tokyo: Iwanami Shoten.

Nunome Chōfū and Nakamura Takashi 中村喬 1976. *Chūgoku no chasho* 中国の茶書 (Tea literature of China). Tokyo: Heibonsha.

Obringer, Frederic. 1997. *L'aconit et l'orpiment: drogues et poisons en Chine ancienne et médiévale.* Paris: Fayard.

Overmyer, Daniel L. 1990. "Buddhism in the Trenches: Attitudes Toward Popular Religion in Chinese Scriptures Found at Tun-Huang." *Harvard Journal of Asiatic Studies* 50, no. 1:197–222.

Owen, Stephen. 1981. *The Great Age of Chinese Poetry: The High T'ang.* New Haven, Conn.: Yale University Press.

———. 2006. *The Late Tang: Chinese Poetry of the Mid-Ninth Century (827–860).* Cambridge, Mass.: Harvard University Asia Center.

Owyoung, Steven D. 2000. "The Connoisseurship of Tea: A Translation and Commentary on the 'P'in-ch'a' Section of the *Record of Superlative Things* by Wen Chen-heng (1585–1645)." *Kaikodo Journal*, Spring: 25–50.

———. 2008. "'Lu Yü's Brazier' Taoist Elements in the T'ang Book of Tea." *Kaikodo Journal*, Spring: 232–252.

———. 2009. "Tea in China: From its Mythological Origins to the Qing Dynasty." In *Steeped in History: The Art of Tea*, edited by Beatrice Hohenegger, 30–53. Los Angeles: Fowler Museum at UCLA.

Pachow, W. 2000. *A Comparative Study of the Prātimokṣa: On the Basis of Its Chinese, Tibetan, Sanskrit, and Pali Versions*. Delhi: Motilal Banarsidass Publishers.

Paper, Jordan D. 1995. *The Spirits Are Drunk: Comparative Approaches to Chinese Religion*. Albany: State University of New York Press.

Peltier, Warren V. 2011. *The Ancient Art of Tea: Discover Happiness and Contentment in a Perfect Cup of Tea*. Tokyo: Tuttle Pub.

Pitelka, Morgan, ed. 2003. *Japanese Tea Culture: Art, History, and Practice*. New York: RoutledgeCurzon.

Poo, Mu-chou. 1999. "The Use and Abuse of Wine in Ancient China." *Journal of the Economic and Social History of the Orient* 42, no. 2:1–29.

Preedy, Victor R. ed. 2012. *Tea in Health and Disease Prevention*. London: Academic Press.

Pregadio, Fabrizio. 2006. *Great Clarity: Daoism and Alchemy in Early Medieval China*. Stanford, Calif.: Stanford University Press.

———. 2007., ed. *The Encyclopedia of Taoism*. 2 vols. London: Routledge.

Qu Tuiyuan 瞿蛻園. 1980. *Li Bai ji jiaozhu* 李白集校注 (Collated and edited collected works of Li Bai). Shanghai: Shanghai guji chubanshe.

Rambelli, Fabio. 2007. *Buddhist Materiality: A Cultural History of Objects in Japanese Buddhism*. Stanford, Calif.: Stanford University Press.

Read, Bernard. 1977 [1936]. *Chinese Medicinal Plants from the Pen Ts'ao Kang Mu A. D. 1596*. Taibei: Southern Materials Center.

Red Pine. 2009. *In Such Hard Times: The Poetry of Wei Ying-wu*. Port Townsend, Wa.: Copper Canyon Press.

Reischauer, Edwin O. 1955. *Ennin's Diary: The Record of a Pilgrimage to China in Search of the Law*. New York: Ronald Press Co.

Robbins, Michael. 1974. "The Inland Fukien Tea Industry: Five Dynasties to the Opium War." *Transactions of the International Conference of Orientalists in Japan* 19:121–142.

Robson, James. 2009. *Power of Place: The Religious Landscape of the Southern Sacred Peak (Nanyue) in Medieval China*. Cambridge, Mass.: Harvard University Asia Center.

Rockhill, William Woodville (trans.). 1967. *The Journey of William of Rubruck to the Eastern Parts of the World, 1253–1255*. Nendeln, Liechtenstein: Kraus Reprint.

Sabban, Françoise. 1997. "La diète parfaite d'un lettré retiré sous les Song du Sud." *Études chinoises* 16, no. 1:7–57.

Salguero, C. Pierce. 2009. "The Buddhist Medicine King in Literary Context: Reconsidering an Early Medieval Example of Indian Influence on Chinese Medicine and Surgery." *History of Religions* 48, no. 3:183–210.

Schafer, Edward H. 1955. "Notes on Mica in Medieval China." *T'oung Pao* 43:265–285.

———. 1963. *The Golden Peaches of Samarkand: A Study of T'ang Exotics.* Berkeley: University of California Press.

———. 1965. "Notes on T'ang Culture II." *Monumenta Serica* 24:130–154.

———. 1967. *The Vermilion Bird: T'ang Images of the South.* Berkeley: University of California Press.

———. 1977. "T'ang." In *Food in Chinese Culture: Anthropological and Historical Perspectives,* edited by K. C. Chang, 85–140. New Haven, Conn.: Yale University Press.

———. 1989. *Mao Shan in T'ang times.* 2nd rev. ed, *Monograph (Society for the Study of Chinese Religions) no. 1.* Boulder, Co.: Society for the Study of Chinese Religions.

Schipper, Kristofer, and Franciscus Verellen, eds. 2005. *The Taoist Canon: A Historical Companion to the Daozang.* 3 vols. Chicago: University of Chicago Press.

Schivelbusch, Wolfgang. 1992. *Tastes of Paradise: A Social History of Spices, Stimulants, and Intoxicants.* New York: Pantheon Books.

Schlütter, Morten. 2008. *How Zen Became Zen: The Dispute over Enlightenment and the Formation of Chan Buddhism in Song-Dynasty China.* Honolulu: University of Hawai'i Press.

Schmidt, F. R. A. 2006. "The Textual History of the *Materia Medica* in the Han Period: A System-Theoretical Reconsideration." *T'oung Pao* 92, nos. 4–5:293–324.

Sekiguchi Shindai 関口真大. 1960. "Gyokusen Tendai ni tsuite, 玉泉天台について (On the Tiantai of Yuquan)." *Tendai gakuhō* 天台学報 1:10–17.

Sen, Soshitsu. 1998. *The Japanese Way of Tea: From its Origins in China to Sen Rikyu.* Honolulu: University of Hawai'i Press.

Shaanxi Sheng kaogu yanjiuyuan 陝西省考古研究院. 2007. *Famen si kaogu fajue baogao* 法门寺考古发掘报告 (Report of archaeological excavation at Famen Temple). Beijing: Wenwu chubanshe.

Sharf, Robert H. 2007. "How to Think with Chan Gongans." In *Thinking with Cases: Specialized Knowledge in Chinese Cultural History,* edited by Charlotte Furth, Judith Zeitlin, and Hsiung Ping-chen, 205–243. Honolulu: University of Hawai'i Press.

———. Unpublished. "The Buddha's Finger Bones at Famen-si and the Art of Chinese Esoteric Buddhism."

Sharma, Jayeeta. 2011. *Empire's Garden: Assam and the Making of India, Radical Perspectives.* Durham, N.C.: Duke University Press.

Shinohara, Koichi. 1991. "Structure and Communitas in Po Chü-i's Tomb Inscription." *Chung-hwa Buddhist Journal* 4:379–450.

Shu Yujie 舒玉杰. 1996. *Zhongguo cha wenhua jingu daguan* 中国茶文化今古大观 (A compendium of Chinese tea culture, ancient and modern). Beijing: Beijing chubanshe.

Simoons, Frederick J. 1991. *Food in China: A Cultural and Historical Inquiry.* Boca Raton, Fla.: CRC Press.

Sivin, Nathan. 1987. *Traditional Medicine in Contemporary China: A Partial Translation of Revised Outline of Chinese Medicine (1972): With an Introductory Study on Change in Present Day and Early Medicine.* Ann Arbor: Center for Chinese Studies, University of Michigan.

Skinner, G. William, ed. 1977. *The City in Late Imperial China.* Stanford, Calif.: Stanford University Press.

Smith, Hilary A. 2008. "Understanding the *jiaoqi* Experience: The Medical Approach to Illness in Seventh-century China." *Asia Major* 21, no. 1:273–292.

Smith, Paul J. 1991. *Taxing Heaven's Storehouse: Horses, Bureaucrats, and the Destruction of the Sichuan Tea Industry, 1074–1224.* Cambridge, Mass.: Council on East Asian Studies, distributed by Harvard University Press.

Smith, S. D. 2001. "The Early Diffusion of Coffee Drinking in England." In *Le commerce du café avant l'ère des plantations coloniales,* edited by M. Tuchscherer, 245–268. Cairo: Institut français d'archéologie orientale.

Song Zhaolin 宋兆麟. 1991. "Cha shen—Lu Yu 茶神—陸羽 (Lu Yu: God of Tea)." *Nongye kaogu* 22, 148–149.

Spence, Jonathan D. 2007. *Return to Dragon Mountain: Memories of a Late Ming Man.* New York: Viking.

Stein, Rolf Alfred. 1972. *Tibetan Civilization.* Translated by J. E. Stapleton Driver. London: Faber.

Strassberg, Richard E. 1994. *Inscribed Landscapes: Travel Writing from Imperial China.* Berkeley: University of California Press.

Stuart, G. A., and F. Porter Smith. 1977. *Chinese Materia Medica: Vegetable Kingdom.* New York: Gordon Press.

Surak, Kristin. 2013. *Making Tea, Making Japan: Cultural Nationalism in Practice.* Stanford, Calif.: Stanford University Press.

Takahashi Tadahiko 高橋忠彦. 1990. "Tōshi ni mieru Tōdai cha to Bukkyō 唐詩にみえる唐代の茶と仏教 (Tea and Buddhism in the Tang dynasty from the perspective of Tang poetry)." *Tōyō bunka* 70:145–178.

———. 1994. "Chūgoku chashi ni okeru "Kissa yōjōki" no igi 中国茶史における『喫茶養生記』の意義 (The significance of *Kissa yōjōki* for the history of tea in China)." *Tokyo gakuhei daigaku kiyō, dai 2 bumon, jinbun kagaku* 東京学芸大学紀要. 第2部門, 人文科学, 45: 331–339.

Takakusu, Junjiro. 1896. *Record of the Buddhist Religion as Practised in India and the Malay Archipelago (A.D. 671–695) by I-tsing.* London: Clarendon Press.

ter Haar, Barend J. 1992. *The White Lotus Teachings in Chinese Religious History.* Leiden: Brill.

———. 1998. *The Ritual and Mythology of the Chinese Triads: Creating an Identity.* Leiden: Brill.

———. 2001. "Buddhist-Inspired Options: Aspects of Lay Religious Life in the Lower Yangzi from 1100 until 1340." *T'oung Pao* 87, nos. 1–3: 92–152.

Tian, Xiaofei. 2005. *Tao Yuanming and Manuscript Culture.* Seattle: University of Washington Press.

Trombert, Eric. 1999–2000. "Bière et bouddhisme: la consommation de boissons alcoolisées dans les monastères de Dunhuang aux VIIIe-Xe siècles." *Cahiers d'Extrême-Asie* 11:129–181.

Tseng, Chin-yin. 2008. "Tea Discourse in the Tang Dynasty (618–907 CE): Conceptions of Social Engagements." M.A. thesis, Committee on Regional Studies–East Asia, Harvard University.

Twitchett, Denis Crispin, ed. 1979. *The Cambridge History of China, Vol. 3: Sui and T'ang China, 589–906, Part 1.* Cambridge: Cambridge University Press.

Ukers, William H. 1935. *All About Tea.* New York: Tea and Coffee Trade Journal Company.

Unschuld, Paul U. 1985. *Medicine in China: A History of Ideas.* Berkeley: University of California Press.

———. 1986. *Medicine in China: A History of Pharmaceutics.* Berkeley: University of California Press.

Varsano, Paula M. 1994. "The Invisible Landscape of Wei Yingwu (737–792)." *Harvard Journal of Asiatic Studies* 54, no. 2:407–435.

Wagner, Marsha L. 1981. *Wang Wei.* Boston: Twayne Publishers.

Waley, Arthur. 2002 (1963). "A Chinese Poet in Central Asia." In *The Secret History of the Mongols and Other Pieces,* 21–38. Thirsk: House of Stratus.

Wang Chongmin 王重民 , and et al., eds. 1984. *Dunhuang Bianwen ji* 敦煌變文集 (Collection of Dunhuang transformation texts). Beijing: Renmin wenxue.

Wang Chunyu 王春瑜. 1990. *Mingchao jiu wenhua* 明朝酒文化 (Ming dynasty alcohol culture). Taipei: Dongda.

Wang, Eugene Yuejin. 2005. "Of the True Body: The Buddha's Relics and Corporeal Transformation in Sui-Tang China." In *Body and Face in Chinese Visual Culture,* edited by Wu Hung, and Katherine Mino, 79–118. Cambridge, Mass.: Harvard University Press.

Wang Guoliang 王國良. 1999. *Mingxiangji yanjiu* 冥祥記研究 (Research on *Signs from the unseen realm*). Taipei: Wenshi zhexue chubanshe.

Wang Shumin. 2005. "The Dunhuang Manuscripts and Pharmacology in Medieval China." In *Medieval Chinese Medicine: The Dunhuang Medical Manuscripts,* edited by Christopher Cullen and Vivienne Lo, 295–305. London: Routledge.

Wang Wei 王維 (701–761) and Zhao Diancheng 趙殿成 (1685–1756) annot. 1961. *Wang Youcheng ji jian zhu* 王右丞集箋注 (Annotated collected works of Wang Youcheng). Beijing: Zhonghua shuju.

Wang Yao 王瑤. 1986. "Wenren yu jiu 文人與酒" (Literati and alcohol)." In *Zhonggu wenxueshi lun* 中古文學史論, 44–76. Beijing: Beijing daxue chubanshe.

Wang-Toutain, Françoise. 1999–2000. "Pas de boissons alcoolisées, pas de viande: une particularité du bouddhisme chinois vue à travers les manuscrits de Dunhuang." *Cahiers d'Extrême-Asie* 11:91–128.

Ward, Julian. 2000. *Xu Xiake (1587–1641): The Art of Travel Writing.* London: Curzon.

Weinberg, Bennett Alan, and Bonnie K. Bealer. 2001. *The World of Caffeine: The Science and Culture of the World's Most Popular Drug.* New York: Routledge.

Wei Yingwu 韋應物 and Tao Min 陶敏. 1998. Wei Yingwu ji jiaozhu 韋應物集校注 (Critical annotated edition of Wei Yingwu's collected works). Shanghai: Shanghai guji chubanshe.

Welter, Albert. 2006. "Zen Buddhism as the Ideology of the Japanese State: Eisai and the *Kōzen gokokuron.*" In *Zen Classics: Formative Texts in the History of Zen Buddhism,* edited by Steven Heine and Dale S. Wright, 65–112. Oxford: Oxford University Press.

West, Stephen H. 1987. "Cilia, Scale and Bristle—The Consumption of Fish and Shellfish in the Eastern Capital of the Northern Song." *Harvard Journal of Asiatic Studies* 47, no. 2:595–634.

———. 1997. "Playing with Food: Performance, Food, and the Aesthetics of Artificiality in the Sung and the Yuan." *Harvard Journal of Asiatic Studies* 57, no. 1:67–106.

Wilbur, C. Martin. 1943. *Slavery in China During the Former Han Dynasty, 206 B.C.–A.D. 25.* Chicago: Field Museum of Natural History.

Williams, Nicholas Morrow. 2013. "The Taste of the Ocean: Jiaoran's Theory of Poetry." *Tang Studies* 31, no. 1:1–27.

Wu, Pei-yi. 1990. *The Confucian's Progress: Autobiographical Writings in Traditional China.* Princeton, N.J.: Princeton University Press.

Wu Hung. 1987. "The Earliest Pictorial Representations of Ape Tales: An Interdisciplinary Study of Early Chinese Narrative Art and Literature." *T'oung Pao* 73, nos. 1–3:86–112.

Wu Jingyi 吳靜宜. 2006. "Tiantai zong yu chachan de guanxi 天臺宗與茶禪的關係. (Connections between the Tiantai School and the Chan of Tea)." *Taibei daxue zhongwen xuebao* 台北大學中文學報 1:259–289.

Wu Juenong 吳覺農 ed. 1990. *Zhongguo difangzhi chaye lishi ziliao xuanji* 中国地方志茶叶历史资料选辑 (Selected historical materials on tea drinking from Chinese gazetteers). Beijing: Nongye chubanshe。

Wu Zhihe 吳智和. 1980. "Mingdai sengjia, wenren dui cha tuiguang zhi gong-xian 明代僧家、文人對茶推廣之貢獻 (Contributions of Ming dynasty monks and literati to the expansion of tea)." *Mingshi yanjiu zhuankan* 明史研究專刊 3:1–74.

Xiao Lihua 蕭麗華. 2009. "Tangdai sengren yincha shi yanjiu 唐代僧人飲茶詩研究 (Research on poems about drinking tea by Tang monks)." *Taida wenshi zhexue bao* 臺大文史哲學報 71:209–230.

Xue Qiao 薛翹 and Liu Jinfeng 劉勁峰. 1991. "Zhong-Ri chanseng de jiaowang yu Riben chadao de yuanyuan 中日禪僧的交往与日本茶道的淵源 (Exchanges between Chinese and Japanese Chan monks and the origins of the Japanese Way of Tea)." *Nongye kaogu* 22:139–147.

Yampolsky, Philip B. 1967. *The Platform Sutra of the Sixth Patriarch*. New York: Columbia University Press.

Yang, Xiaoshan. 2003. *Metamorphosis of the Private Sphere: Gardens and Objects in Tang-Song Poetry*. Cambridge, Mass.: Harvard University Asia Center.

Yao Guokun 姚國坤, Jiang Yufa 姜堉發, and Chen Peizhen 陳佩珍. 2004. *Zhongguo chawenhua yiji* 中國茶文化遺跡 (Traces of Chinese tea culture). Shanghai: Shanghai wenhua chubanshe.

Ye, Yang. 1999. *Vignettes from the Late Ming: A Hsiao-p'in Anthology*. Seattle: University of Washington Press.

Yifa. 2002. *The Origins of Buddhist Monastic Codes in China: An Annotated Translation and Study of the Chanyuan qinggui*. Honolulu: University of Hawai'i Press.

Young, David. 2008. *Du Fu: A Life in Poetry*. New York: Alfred A. Knopf.

Young, Stuart H. 2013. "For a Compassionate Killing: Chinese Buddhism, Sericulture, and the Silkworm God Aśvaghoṣa." *Journal of Chinese Religions* 41, no. 1:25–58.

Yu, Anthony C. (trans. and ed.). 1980. *The Journey to the West, Volume Three*. Chicago: University of Chicago Press.

Yu Dunpei 俞敦培, and Lou Zikuang 樓子匡. 1975. *Jiuling congchao* 酒令叢鈔 (Compendium of rules for alcohol). Taipei: Dongfang wenhua shuju.

Zanini, Livio. 2005. "Una bevanda cinese per il Buddha." In *Caro Maestro . . . Scritte in onore di Lionello Lanciotti per l'ottantesimo compleanno*, edited by M. Scarpari and T. Lippiello, 1271–1283. Venezia: Cafoscarina.

Zhen Yong-su et al., eds. 2002. *Tea: Bioactivity and Therapeutic Potential*. London: Taylor and Francis.

Zheng Jinsheng. 2006. "The Vogue for 'Medicine as Food' in the Song Period (960–1279 CE)." *Asian Medicine* 2, no. 1:38–58.

Zheng Peikai 鄭培凱 and Zhu Zizhen朱自振. 2007. *Zhongguo lidai chashu huibian jiaozhu ben* 中國歷代茶書匯編校注本 (Collected annotated edition of works on tea from Chinese history). Hong Kong: Shangwu yinshu guan.

Zheng Yayun 鄭雅芸. 1984. *Gujin lun jiu* 古今論酒 (Discussions on alcohol, past and present). Taipei: Xidai shuban gong.

Zhu Chongsheng 朱重聖. 1980. "Woguo yincha chengfeng zhi yuanyin ji qi dui Tang Song shehui yu guanfa zhi yingxiang 我國飲茶成風之原因及其對唐宋社會與官府之影響 (The origins of tea drinking in China against the background of society and government)." *Shixue huikan* 史學會刊 10:93–150.

Zhu Jifa 竺濟法. 1994. *Mingren chashi* 名人茶事 (Anecdotes about tea and famous people). Taipei: Linyu wenhua.

Zysk, Kenneth G. 1991. *Asceticism and Healing in Ancient India: Medicine in the Buddhist Monastery*. New York: Oxford University Press.

Index

Page numbers in boldface refer to illustrations.

About the Author

James A. Benn is professor of Buddhism and East Asian religions at McMaster University. He is a historian of medieval Chinese religions and has published on topics such as self-immolation, spontaneous human combustion, and Chinese Buddhist apocrypha. He is the author of *Burning for the Buddha: Self-Immolation in Chinese Buddhism* (University of Hawai'i Press, 2007).

Production Notes for Benn / *Tea in China*
Cover design by Mardee Melton
Composition by Westchester Publishing Services
    with display type in Warnock Pro and text type in Minion Pro
Printing and binding by Sheridan Books, Inc.
Printed on 60 lb. House White, 444 ppi.